German for Travelers

Fodor's LIVING LANGUAGE®

German
for
Travelers

Fodor's Travel Publications   New York, Toronto, London, Sydney, Auckland

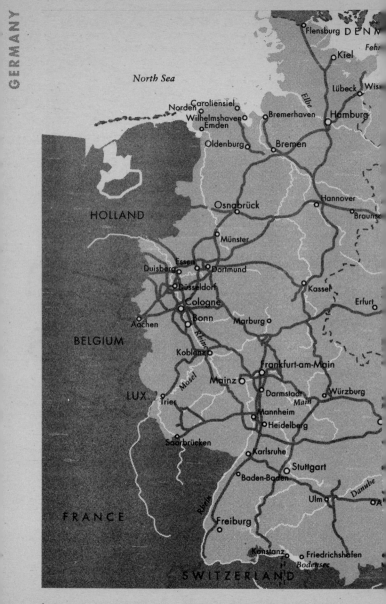

FORMER LOCATION OF BERLIN WALL

Fennstr. str. Chaussee
Seiler Str.
Brunnen str.
sitzowstr.

Rathenower Str.
Fritz-Schloss-park

Invalidenstr.
Garten str.

MITTE
Torstr.

Turmstr.
Alt - Moabit
Paulstr.
Luisenstr.

Pergamon Museum
Nationalgalerie
Fernsehturm

Moltkestr.
Zeughaus (Arsenal)
Schloss pl.

Schloss Bellevue
Reichstag
Unter den Linden
Deutsche Staatsoper

sser Spreeweg
str. des 17 Juni
Brandenburger Tor
Wilhelmstr.

iegesäule
Tiergarten
Entlastungsstr.

Tiergarten str.
Leipzigerstr.

Bauhaus Museum
Nationalgalerie
Potsdamer Platz

FORMER LOCATION OF BERLIN WALL
Oranienstr.

Potsdamerstr.
Schönebergerstr.
Friedrichstr.
Lindenstr.

Kurfürsten str.
Wilhelmstr.
KREUZBERG

otzstr.
Prinzen str.

EBERG
enstr.
Urban - str.

Potsdamerstr.
Yorckstr.
Yorckstr.
0   1/2 mile
0   3/4 km
N

runewaldstr.
Kreuzergstr.

Monumentenstr.
Viktoria Park

Hauptstr.
Westangenle
Kolonnenstr.
Dudenstr.
Mehringdamm
Volkspark Hasenheide

Tempelhof Airport

FODOR'S GERMAN FOR TRAVELERS

EDITORS: Emmanuelle Morgen, Christopher Warnasch

Contributors: Jennifer Abramsohn, Helga Schier

Editorial Production: Marina Padakis

Maps: David Lindroth, *cartographer;* Rebecca Baer and Robert P. Blake, *map editors*

Design: Guido Caroti, *cover and interior designer;* Jolie Novak, Melanie Marin, *photo editors;* Kayley LeFaiver, *graphics*

Cover Photo: Ernest Haas/Stone

Production/Manufacturing: Pat Ehresmann

COPYRIGHT

ISBN 0-676-90480-7

ISSN 1538-6074

SPECIAL SALES

Fodor's Travel Publications are available at special discounts for bulk purchases for sales promotions or premiums. Special editions, including personalized covers, excerpts of existing guides, and corporate imprints, can be created in large quantities for special needs. For more information, contact your local bookseller or write to Special Markets, Fodor's Travel Publications, 280 Park Avenue, New York, NY 10017. Inquiries from Canada should be directed to your local Canadian bookseller or sent to Random House of Canada, Ltd., Marketing Department, 2775 Matheson Boulevard East, Mississauga, Ontario L4W 4P7. Inquiries from the United Kingdom should be sent to Fodor's Travel Publications, 20 Vauxhall Bridge Road, London SW1V 2SA, England.

PRINTED IN THE UNITED STATES OF AMERICA

10 9 8 7 6 5 4 3 2 1

CONTENTS

PREFACE

You don't need to know German to get along in the German-speaking world. The hundreds of German phrases in this guide will see you through almost every situation you encounter as a tourist, from asking for directions at the start of your trip to conversing in a bar at the end. To make yourself understood, all you have to do is read the phonetics that appear after each expression, just as you would any English sentence. You'll come closer to approximating German sounds if you study the pronunciation guide at the beginning of the book, and you can really polish your speech with *Fodor's German for Travelers* cassettes or CDs, on which native speakers pronounce the guide's key German dialogues. The words and phrases that appear in boldface in the book are those that are recorded in the audio supplement.

If you want to understand the structure of the language and begin to learn it on your own, check out the grammar chapter, Chapter 16. Additionally, a two-way 1,600-word dictionary at the end references all the key words in the book.

To help you get the most out of your trip, read the travel tips and cultural information about Germany interspersed throughout the chapters. You'll find, among other things, traditional German menu items, bank and store hours, metric conversion tables, and federal holidays, all gathered by Fodor's expert resident-writers.

Before you start chatting away, be sure to familiarize yourself with the table of contents on the previous pages, so that you know where to quickly find phrases and information when you need them.

Gute Reise! [GOO-the RYE-zeh] Have a good trip!

THE GERMAN STATE OF MIND

Germany as we know it developed from of a number of tribes, including the Franks, Saxons, Swabians, and Bavarians. These ethnic groups long ago lost their original character, but their traditions and dialects live on. Since time immemorial, different characteristics have been ascribed to each region—the Saxons are said to be hardworking, Swabians thrifty, Rhinelanders happy-go-lucky, and Mecklenburgers reserved. Whether these types hold true is still jokingly debated among Germans today. What is true, however, is that each region has its own food and drink specialties (the famed sausage and beer, of course, but fine wine and fish dishes as well), making the country a culinary extravaganza for the adventurous tourist.

Today's 16 states, or Länder, evolved from, and loosely correspond to, the ethnic regions. They are ruled by a democratically elected federal government, with two houses of representatives. Each state has its own local government, which rules on matters such as education and local transport.

The lingua franca of Germany is High German, *Hochdeutsch,* first established by Martin Luther when he translated the Bible into German in 1522. It is the language taught in schools (and in this book), spoken by TV announcers, and used in commerce. Yet within each state, Germany's varied dialects are very much alive. If a native of Mecklenburg, a Bavarian, and a Rhinelander were to converse in their respective pure dialects, they would find it all but impossible to understand one another.

Some other generalizations to keep in mind about Germany and the Germans: The northern states are more likely to be Lutheran, the southern Catholic. The north is politically liberal, the south is a conservative stronghold. People from the north are said to be cooler and more reserved; southerners warmer and more open. The former Eastern states don't fit so neatly into these categories. Under Communist rule from 1945 to 1990, the east is less populous, poorer, and has weaker infrastructure than the west.

The German landscape cannot be summed up neatly, except to say that it offers a little bit of everything. In the North, the dry, sandy lowlands are dotted with heaths and moors, lakes and deciduous forests. The North Sea and Baltic coasts draw summer vacationers who prefer its windblown dunes to the heat of the Mediterranean. In Bavaria and the south, the Alps and their foothills provide a playground of ski resorts and lakes for sports enthusiasts. The terraced hills and vineyards of Rhine and Mosel rivers, and the central mountain ranges, whose evergreen forests (the Black and Bavarian, for example) have had such an impact on German imagination and folklore, provide the country's psychological and physical North–South divide. And all of this is found within 375,000 square km, a land mass approximately the size of Montana.

Despite plenty of damp, gray weather, Germans tend to be outdoorsy and hearty, if not downright athletic. Germans are brought up with the idea that a daily dose of fresh air is the key to good health. A key expression of this idea is the Sunday afternoon walk. Go to any German forest or park on Sunday after the midday meal, and you will see families out for their regular stroll—before they stop at a café to take part in another obligatory German ritual, *Kaffee und Kuchen*.

Germans not only walk a lot, they ride bicycles a lot as well. From the briefcase-toting commuter to the parent carting the kids to daycare, bicycles are used as an alternative to more expensive, and less healthful, cars or public transportation. That most cities and towns have well-marked, and well respected, bicycle lanes, also helps make this possible. On a similar note, visitors to Germany—both drivers and pedestrians—are urged to know and obey the traffic rules.

Germans work about 35–48 hours a week, and most have six weeks of vacation per year. A highly evolved spa culture, borrowed from Nordic neighbors, thrives amid the search for ever more inventive methods of relaxation. To try one out, look for the word *Bad* or *Thermalbad* on brochures and signs. (Note that nudity is common, even in intergender spas.) German swimming pools and water parks are spotless, modern facilities.

In today's Germany, health-food stores and vegetarian restaurants are common, and topics like the genetic manipulation of foods and environmental health hazards regularly grab headlines. Jogging, gym workouts, or participating in team sports are a part of the daily routine for many Germans. But despite this widespread health-consciousness, smoking is very common. Even the most serious organic food-buying vegetarian joggers here tend to light up, and bars, cafés, and restaurants are usually thick with a haze of blue smoke. Non-smoking sections in restaurants are almost unheard of. Trains, however, do have marked non-smoking compartments.

The lack of smoking regulations may stand out as an oddity, since so many other activities here—even those occurring on private property—are indeed heavily regulated. If you don't like to follow rules, or if the idea of putting the good of the group before the welfare of the individual bothers you, then Germany may not be the best place for a prolonged stay.

Service in a German restaurant may be considered painfully slow compared to that in some other countries. On the other hand, you will never be rushed out of your seat. In fact, you will need to call for the bill in order to get it, the idea being that the table is yours for the evening, and you should be allowed to linger as long as you want. Something else that may seem jarring at first: People can and do join other parties at a table in a restaurant if seating is tight. Waiters and shopkeepers may seem downright grumpy to someone used to "service with a smile," but they simply have a more businesslike approach, to give you what you want without much fuss. As in a restaurant, you are unlikely to be offered help in a shop or department store unless you ask for it. The presumption is that you would prefer to be left alone unless you indicate otherwise.

Mark Twain, in his 1880 essay "The Awful German Language," was frustrated by the fact that German grammar has so many rules. Even worse, he wrote, as soon as you learned a point of grammar, you would find "more exceptions to the rule than instances of it." Twain was referring to the language, but he could just as easily have been talking about the people. Every generalization one can make about Germans begets a whole array of exceptions.

As with any activity that has a big payoff, learning German will take time. Many Germans speak English quite well, but if you make the effort to communicate in the native language, you will get to know firsthand this interesting, complex country and its people, and you will sooner gain access to the "real" Germany—whatever that turns out to be.

PRONUNCIATION GUIDE

This guide follows standard High-German pronunciation, the accepted pronunciation among educated German speakers throughout Germany, Austria, Switzerland, and Luxembourg. There are a number of different variant dialects spoken in these countries, which may be difficult for you to understand at first, but you will be understood if you use the pronunciation given here. However, there are some German sounds that simply do not exist in English, so the transcriptions offered here are only an approximate guide. To improve your pronunciation use the audiocassette or CD supplement. It follows this text closely and gives you the opportunity to listen to and imitate native speakers of German. Try also to imitate the native speakers you encounter during your travels, and don't be afraid to practice your German with them. Some may want to practice their English, but most will be flattered by your attempts to learn their language and will gladly help you.

PRONUNCIATION CHART

The chart below is your guide to the transcriptions used in this book. Study it to see how German sounds are properly pronounced. With practice you will be able to follow the transcriptions without having to consult this chart. Keep in mind these basic guidelines for correct German pronunciation:

1) German spelling is more consistent than English; once you learn the sounds, it will be easy to pronounce a word correctly just by reading it.

2) In general, German is spoken vigorously and crisply; words are not run together as often as they are in English.

3) Pay special attention to the vowels; they determine the overall pronunciation of a word and are crucial to making yourself understood.

4) There are no gliding vowel sounds in German, as in the English word *main*; German vowels are pronounced as single pure sounds, without moving the lips or tongue.

5) German vowels are generally long when doubled or followed by *h* or by a single consonant, and short when followed by two or more consonants.

6) The vowels *ö* and *ü* (modified with an umlaut), as well as the consonants *r* and *ch*, have no real sound equivalents in English and should be paid special attention (see explanations marked with * in charts below).

7) German words are generally stressed on the first syllable or, if they begin with an unaccented prefix, on the root syllable; stressed syllables are indicated in this text's transcriptions by capital letters as follows: *sagen* [ZAA-gen].

8) German sentence intonation, the variation of rising and falling voice pitch, is similar to English.

Vowels

German Spelling	Approximate Sound in English	Phonetic Symbol	Example (Phonetic Transcription)
a (long)	f<u>a</u>ther	[aa]	Vater [F<u>AA</u>-te(r)]
a (short)	c<u>a</u>t (between c<u>a</u>t and c<u>u</u>t)	[ah]	kann [kahn]
e (long)	d<u>ay</u>	[ay]	geben [G<u>AY</u>-ben]
e (short)	b<u>e</u>st	[eh]	fest [f<u>eh</u>st]
e (unstressed)	th<u>e</u> (between <u>eh</u> and <u>uh</u>)	[eh]	bitte [BIT-t<u>eh</u>]
-er (last syllable)	fath<u>er</u> (but barely pro- nounce the <u>r</u>)	[e(r)]	Vater [FAA-t<u>e(r)</u>]
-en, -el, -et	(similar to English)	—	leben [LAY-b<u>en</u>]
i (long)	f<u>ee</u>t	[ee]	ihm [<u>ee</u>m]
i (short)	b<u>i</u>t	[i]	bitte [B<u>I</u>T-teh]
o (long)	n<u>o</u>te	[oh]	oder [<u>OH</u>-de(r)]
o (short)	l<u>o</u>st (between l<u>o</u>st and l<u>u</u>st)	[o]	Post [p<u>o</u>st]
u (long)	m<u>oo</u>n, s<u>ui</u>t	[oo]	gut [g<u>oo</u>t]
u (short)	p<u>u</u>t	[u]	Mutter [M<u>U</u>T-te(r)]
y	like German <u>ü</u>, see below	[ew]	typisch [T<u>EW</u>-pish]

Vowels Modified with an Umlaut

German Spelling	Approximate Sound in English	Phonetic Symbol	Example (Phonetic Transcription)
ä (long)	day, like German long e	[ay]	spät [shpayt]
ä (short)	let, like German short e	[eh]	hätte [HEHT-teh]
ö (long or short)	*fur, but r is barely pronounced	[u(r)]	schön [shu(r)n]
ü (long or short)	*few, or as in French rue	[ew]	Tür [tewr]

Vowel Combinations (Diphthongs)

ai, ay, ei, ey	bite, ice, eye, rye	[i . . . e] or [eye] or [-ye]	sein [zine] eitel [EYE-tel] drei [drye]
au	now	[ow]	braun [brown]
eu, au	boy	[oy]	Leute [LOY-teh]
ie	feet	[ee]	Dienst [deenst]

Consonants

f, k, l, m, n, p, t, x	pronounced in most cases as in English	same English letters used as phonetic symbols	
b (at end of word or between vowel and consonant)	up, tap	[p]	gelb [gehlp] Obst [opst]
b (elsewhere)	like English b, bad	[b]	Buch [bookh]
c (before ä, e, i, ö)	fits (rarely occurs in words of German origin)	[ts]	circa [TSEER-kah]
c (elsewhere)	cat	[k]	Café [kah-FAY]
ch (after a, o, u, au)	*hard ch, as in ugh, or Scottish loch, produced in back of mouth like clearing throat.	[kh]	Loch [lokh]

7

German Spelling	Approximate Sound in English	Phonetic Symbol	Example (Phonetic Transcription)
ch (after e, i, umlauts, consonants)	*soft <u>ch</u>, as exaggerated <u>h</u> in <u>H</u>ubert, produced in front of mouth	[kh]	Licht [li<u>kh</u>t]
chs	ba<u>cks</u>	[ks]	sechs [zeh<u>ks</u>]
d (at end of syllable or word)	ba<u>t</u>	[t]	Bad [baa<u>t</u>]
d (elsewhere)	like English <u>d</u>, <u>d</u>oes	[d]	dunkel [<u>D</u>UN-kel]
g (at end of word)	pi<u>ck</u>	[k]	weg [veh<u>k</u>]
ig (at end of word)	soft <u>ch</u>, as exaggerated <u>h</u> in <u>H</u>ubert	[kh]	billig [BIL-li<u>kh</u>]
g (elsewhere)	hard <u>g</u> (<u>g</u>o)	[g]	gehen [<u>G</u>AY-en]
h (after a vowel)	silent, as in <u>h</u>onor	[ ]	sehen [ZAY-en]
h (elsewhere)	<u>h</u>old	[h]	Haus [<u>h</u>ows]
j	<u>y</u>es	[y]	jawohl [<u>y</u>aa-VOHL]
qu	<u>k</u> + <u>v</u>, <u>k</u>it + <u>v</u>at	[kv]	Quelle [<u>KV</u>EHL-eh]
r	*<u>r</u>id, always rolled when stressed, may be either trilled with tongue tip or gargled; when unstressed, like the <u>r</u> in weste<u>r</u>n	[r]	Radio [<u>R</u>AA-dee-oh] gestern [GEHS-tern]
s (before or between vowels)	<u>z</u>oo	[z]	sind [<u>z</u>int]
s (elsewhere)	<u>s</u>ee, be<u>st</u>	[s]	was [vah<u>s</u>]
sch	<u>sh</u>ine	[sh]	schon [<u>sh</u>ohn]
sp, st (at start of syllable)	<u>sh</u>ine, <u>sh</u> + p/t	[sh]	Stein [<u>sh</u>tine] spät [<u>sh</u>payt]
		[s]	weiß [<u>v</u>ice]

German Spelling	Approximate Sound in English	Phonetic Symbol	Example (Phonetic Transcription)
th	<u>t</u>in, <u>h</u> is silent	[t]	Thema [<u>T</u>AY-mah]
tsch	<u>ch</u>ur<u>ch</u>	[ch]	deutsch [doy<u>ch</u>]
tz	ca<u>ts</u>	[ts]	Platz [plahts]
v	<u>f</u>our (in words of German origin)	[f]	vier [<u>f</u>eer]
v	<u>v</u>isa (in words of foreign origin)	[v]	Visum [<u>V</u>EE-zoom]
w	<u>v</u>est	[v]	Wert [<u>v</u>ehrt]
z	ca<u>ts</u>	[ts]	Zoo [<u>ts</u>oh]

Pronouncing the German Alphabet

The German alphabet looks the same as the English one, except for the umlauted vowels, *ä, ö,* and *ü* and the letter *ß*, or *esset*, the name of which combines the two letters s + z [EHS-tseht], but it is pronounced just like the double s [s]. The letters of the German alphabet are pronounced differently from their English counterparts, and there are also some differences in the way the German language is written, the main one being that all nouns are capitalized. The following table gives the correct pronunciation of the alphabet, using the phonetic symbols introduced above, as well as corresponding proper German names, which are often used to clarify the spelling of a word over the telephone. Germans would say, for instance: *A wie Anton* [ah vee AHN-tohn] to specify the letter A as in the name Anton.

A [ah]	as in	Anton [AHN-tohn]
Ä [ay]		Ärger [EHR-ge(r)]
B [bay]		Berta [BEHR-tah]
C [tsay]		Caesar [TSAY-zahr]
CH [sh]		Charlotte [shahr-LOT-teh]
D [day]		Dora [DOH-rah]
E [ay]		Emil [AY-meel]
F [ehf]		Friedrich [FREET-rikh]
G [gay]		Gerda [GEHR-dah]
H [haa]		Heinrich [HINE-rikh]

I [ee]	Ida [EE-dah]
J [yot]	Jutta [YOOT-tah]
K [kah]	Konrad [KON-raat]
L [ehl]	Ludwig [LOOD-vikh]
M [ehm]	Martin [MAAR-tin]
N [ehn]	Nordpol [NORT-pohl]
O [oh]	Otto [OT-toh]
Ö [u(r)]	Ökonom [u(r)-ko-NOHM]
P [pay]	Paula [POW-lah]
Q [koo]	Quelle [KVEHL-leh]
R [ehr]	Richard [RIKH-ahrt]
S [ehs]	Siegfried [ZEEK-freet]
T [TAY]	Theodor [TAY-o-dohr]
U [oo]	Ulrich [OOL-rikh]
Ü [ew]	Übel [EW-bel]
V [fow]	Viktor [VIK-tohr]
W [vay]	Wilhelm [VIL-hehlm]
X [eeks]	Xanten [KSAHN-ten]
Y [EWP-see-lawn]	Ypsilon [EWP-see-lawn]
Z [tseht]	Zeppelin [TSEH-peh-leen]

APPROACHING PEOPLE

COURTESY

Please.	Bitte.	BIT-teh.
Thank you.	Danke.	DAHN-keh.
You're welcome.	Bitte.	BIT-teh.
	(or) Gern geschehen.	gehrn geh-SHAY-en.
Excuse me/Sorry.	Entschuldigung.	ehnt-SHOOL-di-gung.
	(or) Verzeihung.	fehr-TSYE-ung.
It doesn't matter.	Das macht nichts.	dahs mahkht nikhts.

GREETINGS

Good morning.	Guten Morgen.	GOO-ten MOR-gen.
Good day/afternoon.	Guten Tag.	GOO-ten taak.
Good evening.	Guten Abend.	GOO-ten AA-behnt.
Good night.	Gute Nacht.	GOO-teh nahkht.
Hello. (telephone only)*	Hallo.	HAH-loh.
Good-bye.	Auf Wiedersehen.	owf VEE-de(r)-zay-en.
Good-bye. (telephone)	Auf Wiederhören.	owf VEE-de(r)-hu(r)-ren.
See you soon.	Bis bald.	bis bahlt.
See you later.	Bis später.	bis SHPAY-te(r).
See you tomorrow.	Bis morgen.	bis MOR-gen.
This is Mr./Mrs./Ms./Miss	Das ist Herr/Frau/Fräulein . . .**	dahs ist hehr/frow/FROY-line . . .
How do you do?/Pleased to meet you.	Sehr erfreut.	zehr ehr-FROYT.

*There is no German equivalent for the informal conversational "hello"; informally the shortened form of *Guten Tag—Tag—*is used, otherwise one of the other above greetings is used, depending on the time of day.

**Fräulein* is used nowadays only to address waitresses and telephone operators. Unmarried women are addressed as *Frau.* There is no German equivalent for Ms.

How are you?	Wie geht es ihnen?	vee gayt ehs EE-nen?
Very well, thank you.	Sehr gut, danke.	zehr goot DAHN-keh.
And you?	Und ihnen?	unt EE-nen?
Also well, thank you.	Auch gut, danke.	owkh goot DAHN-keh.

QUESTION WORDS

Who?	Wer?	vehr?
Whom?	Wem?/Wen?*	vaym/vayn?
What?	Was?	vahs?
Why?	Warum?	vah-ROOM?
When?	Wann?	vahn?
Where?	Wo?	voh?
Where to?	Wohin?	voh-HIN?
Where from?	Woher?	voh-HAYR?
Which?	Welcher/Welche/Welches?	VEHL-khe(r)/VEHL-kheh/VEHL-khes?
How?	Wie?	vee?
How far?	Wie weit?	vee vite?
How many?	Wie viele?	vee FEE-leh?
How much does it cost?	Wieviel kostet das?	VEE-feel KOS-tet dahs?

ASKING FOR HELP

| Excuse me. | Entschuldigung.** | ehnt-SHOOL-di-gung. |
| Could you help me? | Könnten Sie mir helfen? | KU(R)N-ten zee meer HEHL-fen? |

---

*German has four different grammatical cases (see Grammar in Brief); these forms for whom [*wem* (dative/indirect object) or *wen* (accusative/direct object)] depend on the function in the sentence.

**There is no generally used German equivalent for "madam" or "sir." If you don't know the person's name, no form of address is used.

Do you speak English?	Sprechen Sie Englisch?	SHPREKH-en zee EHN-glish?
Do you understand English?	Verstehen Sie Englisch?	fehr-SHTAY-en zee EHN-glish?
Yes./No.	Ja./Nein.	jaa/nine.
I'm sorry.	Es tut mir leid.	ehs toot meer lite.
I don't speak any/much German.	Ich spreche kein/kaum Deutsch.	ikh SHPREKH-eh kine/kowm doych.
What's your name?	Wie heißen Sie?	vee HICE-en zee?
My name is . . .	Ich heiße . . .	ikh HICE-eh . . .
I'm American/ English.	Ich bin Amerikaner(-in)/ Engländer(-in).*	ikh bin ah-meh-ri-KAH-ne(r){-rin}/EHN-glehn-de(r){-rin}.
I'm a tourist.	Ich bin Tourist(in).	ikh bin too-RIST-(in).
I don't understand.	Ich verstehe nicht.	ikh fehr-STAY-eh nikht.
I understand a little.	Ich verstehe ein wenig.	ikh fehr-STAY-eh ine VEH-nikh.
Repeat, please.	Wiederholen Sie, bitte.	vee-de(r)-HOH-len zee BIT-teh.
Please speak more slowly.	Bitte, sprechen Sie langsamer.	BIT-teh SHPREKH-en zee LAHNG-zaam-me(r).
What do you call this/that in German?	Wie heißt dies/das auf Deutsch?	vee heyst dees/dahs owf doych?
Could you write that down, please?	Könnten Sie das bitte aufschreiben?	KU(R)N-ten zee dahs BIT-teh OWF-SHRYE-ben?
Spell it, please.	Buchstabieren Sie es, bitte.	Bookh-shtah-BEE-ren zee ehs, BIT-teh.
Could you translate this for me/us?	Könnten Sie mir/uns das übersetzen?	KU(R)N-ten zee meer/uns dahs ew-be(r)-ZEHT-sen?

*The "in" ending indicates a female person (*Amerikanerin*). With nationalities and professions, no indefinite article is used, for instance: I am a student
= *Ich bin Student*.

What does that mean?	Was bedeutet das?	vahs beh-DOY-tet dahs?
Okay./Agreed.	In Ordnung.	in ORT-nung.
Of course./That's right.	Sicher./Das stimmt.	ZIKH-e(r)/dahs shtimt.
Thank you very much.	Vielen Dank.	FEE-len dahnk.

EMERGENCIES

Watch out!	Pass auf!	pahs owf!
Be careful!	Vorsicht!	FOR-zikht!
Fire!	Feuer!	FOY-e(r)!
Help!/Get help!	Hilfe!/Holen Sie Hilfe!	HIL-feh/HOH-len zee HIL-feh!
Hurry!	Schnell!	shnehl!
I'm lost.	Ich habe mich verirrt.	ikh HAA-beh mikh fehr-EERT.
I'm sick.	Ich bin krank.	ikh bin krahnk.
Call a doctor/the police/the fire department!	Rufen Sie einen Arzt/die Polizei/die Feuerwehr!	ROO-fen zee INE-en-ahrtst/dee po-lee-TSYE/dee FOY-e(r)-vehr!
It's an emergency.	Es ist ein Notfall.	ehs ist ine NOHT-fahl.
Stop!	Halt!	hahlt!
Stop that thief/man/woman!	Haltet den Dieb/Mann/die Frau (auf)!	HAHL-tet dehn deep/mahn/dee frow owf!
Leave me alone!	Lassen Sie mich in Ruhe!	LAHS-en zee mikh in ROO-eh!
. . . was stolen!	. . . wurde gestohlen!	. . . VUR-deh geh-SHTOH-len!
_My camera	_Meine Kamera	_MINE-eh KAH-meh-raa
_My wallet	_Meine Brieftasche	_MINE-eh BREEF-tahsh-eh
Who speaks English here?	Wer spricht hier Englisch?	vehr sprikht heer EHNG-lish?

14

Emergency Telephone Numbers

Police	Polizei [po-lee-TSYE]	110 (Germany) 117 (Switzerland) 133 (Austria)
Fire	Feuerwehr [FOY-e(r)-vehr]	112 (Germany) 118 (Switzerland) 122 (Austria)
Ambulance	Krankenwagen [KRAHN-ken-vaa-gen]	112 (Germany) 144 (Austria and Switzerland)

2 THE BASICS

COLORS

red	rot	ROHT
yellow	gelb	GEHLP
green	grün	GREWN
blue	blau	BLAU
brown	braun	BRAUN
orange	orange	oh-RAHN-zhuh
purple	purpurn	POOR-poorn
black	schwarz	SHVARTZ
gold	gold	GOHLT
silver	silber	ZIHL-ber
white	weiß	VAIS

NUMBERS* AND QUANTITIES

Take time to learn how to count in German. You'll find that knowing the numbers will make everything easier during your trip.

Cardinal Numbers

zero	null	nul
one	eins	ines
two	zwei	tsvye
three	drei	drye
four	vier	feer
five	fünf	fewnf
six	sechs	zehks
seven	sieben	ZEE-ben
eight	acht	ahkht

*In Germany, as elsewhere in Europe, numerical punctuation is different than in English. The use of commas and decimal points is reversed, so that 1,000 English style becomes 1.000, and 6.5 is written 6,5 (*sechs Komma fünf*) in German and pronounced [ze(k)hs KOH-mah fewnf].

nine	neun	noyn
ten	zehn	tsayn
eleven	elf	ehlf
twelve	zwölf	tsvu(r)lf
thirteen	dreizehn	DRYE-tsayn
fourteen	vierzehn	FEER-tsayn
fifteen	fünfzehn	FEWNF-tsayn
sixteen	sechzehn	ZEHKH-tsayn
seventeen	siebzehn	ZEEP-tsayn
eighteen	achtzehn	AHKH-tsayn
nineteen	neunzehn	NOYN-tsayn
twenty	zwanzig	TSVAHN-tsikh
twenty-one	einundzwanzig	INE-unt-tsvahn-tsikh
twenty-two	zweiundzwanzig	TSVYE-unt-tsvahn-tsikh
twenty-three	dreiundzwanzig	DRYE-unt-tsvahn-tsikh
thirty	dreißig	DRYE-sikh
forty	vierzig	FEER-tsikh
fifty	fünfzig	FEWNF-tsikh
sixty	sechzig	ZEHKH-tsikh
seventy	siebzig	ZEEP-tsikh
eighty	achtzig	AHKHT-tsikh
ninety	neunzig	NOYN-tsikh
one hundred	(ein) hundert	(ine) HUN-dert
one hundred one	hunderteins	hun-dert-INES
one hundred two	hundertzwei	hun-dert-TSVYE
one hundred ten	hundertzehn	hun-dert-TSAYN
one hundred twenty	hundertzwanzig	hun-dert-TSVAHN-tsikh
two hundred	zweihundert	TSVYE-hun-dert
three hundred	dreihundert	DRYE-hun-dert
one thousand	(ein) tausend	(ine) TOW-zehnt
one thousand two hundred	tausendzweihundert	TOW-zehnt-tsvye-hun-dert
two thousand	zweitausend	TSVYE-tow-zehnt

17

| one million | eine Million | INE-eh mil-YOHN |
| one billion | eine Milliarde | INE-eh mil-YAAR-deh |

Ordinal Numbers*

first	erste	EHR-steh
second	zweite	TSVYE-teh
third	dritte	DRIT-teh
fourth	vierte	FEER-teh
fifth	fünfte	FEWNF-teh
sixth	sechste	ZEHKS-teh
seventh	siebte	ZEEP-teh
eighth	achte	AHKH-teh
ninth	neunte	NOYN-teh
tenth	zehnte	TSAYN-teh

Quantities

half	halb	haalp
half a pound	ein halbes Pfund	ine HAAL-behs pfunt
half an hour	eine halbe Stunde	INE-eh HAAL-beh SHTUN-deh
half of	die Hälfte von	dee HEHLF-teh fon
a quarter	ein Viertel	ine FEER-tel
a third	ein Drittel	ine DRIT-tel
a dozen	ein Dutzend	ine DU-tsehnt
ten percent	zehn Prozent	tsayn pro-TSEHNT
5.6%	5,6 Prozent	fewnf KO-mah zehks pro-TSEHNT
once	einmal	INE-maal
twice	zweimal	TSVAY-maal
the last time	das letzte Mal	das LET-steh maal

*Ordinal numbers are treated like adjectives in German, agreeing in gender
and number, and receive the appropriate adjective endings; for instance, "my
first game" = *mein erstes Spiel* [mine EHR-stes shpeel].

a lot of, many	viele	FEE-leh
few, a few	wenig, ein paar	VEH-nikh, ine paar
some	einige	INE-ni-geh
enough	genug	geh-NOOKH
a pair of	ein Paar	ine paar

DAYS, MONTHS, AND SEASONS
Days of the Week (*Tage der Woche*)

(on) Monday	(am) Montag	[ahm] MOHN-taak
Tuesday	Dienstag	DEENS-taak
Wednesday	Mittwoch	MIT-vokh
Thursday	Donnerstag	DON-nehrs-taak
Friday	Freitag	FRYE-taak
Saturday	Samstag/Sonnabend	ZAHMS-taak/ZON-aa-behnt
Sunday	Sonntag	ZON-taak

Months of the Year (*Monate des Jahres*)

January	Januar/Jänner (Austrian)	YAH-noo-aar/YEH-ne(r)
February	Februar	FAY-broo-aar
March	März	mehrts
April	April	ah-PRIL
May	Mai	mye
June	Juni	YOO-nee
July	Juli	YOO-lee
August	August	ow-GUST
September	September	zehp-TEHM-be(r)
October	Oktober	ok-TOH-be(r)
November	November	no-VEHM-be(r)
December	Dezember	deh-TSEHM-be(r)

The Four Seasons (*Die vier Jahreszeiten*)

(in the) winter	(im) Winter/der Winter	[im] VIN-te(r)/dehr VIN-te(r)
spring	der Frühling	dehr FREW-ling
summer	der Sommer	dehr ZOM-me(r)
autumn	der Herbst	dehr hehrpst

THE DATE

What is today's date?	Der wievielte ist heute?	dehr vee-FEEL-teh ist HOY-teh?
What day is it today?	Welchen Tag haben wir heute?	VEHL-khen taak HAA-ben veer HOY-teh?
Today is Friday, April 13.	Heute ist Freitag, der dreizehnte (13te) April.	HOY-teh ist FRYE-taak, dehr DRYE-tsayn-teh ah-PRIL.
It's Wednesday, July 11, 2003.	Es ist Mittwoch, der elfte Juli, zweitausend drei.	ehs ist MIT-vokh, dehr EHLF-teh YOO-lee, TSVAI TAU-zent DRAI.

HOLIDAYS

January 1	New Year's Day	Neujahr*
January 6	Epiphany	Dreikönigstag (Austria and parts of Germany)
March–April	Good Friday Easter Easter Monday	Karfreitag (not Austria) Ostern Ostermontag
May 1	May Day (Labor Day)	Tag der Arbeit (not Switzerland)
May–June	Ascension Day Pentecost (Whitmonday) Corpus Christi	Christi Himmelfahrt Pfingstmontag Fronleichnam (Austria only)
August 1	National Day	Nationalfeiertag (Switzerland only)

*As elsewhere, most of the celebrating is done on New Year's Eve, *Sylvesterabend*.

August 15	Assumption	Mariä Himmelfahrt (Austria only)
October 3	German Unity Day	Tag der deutschen Einheit (Germany only)
October 26	National Day	Nationalfeiertag (Austria only)
November 1	All Saints' Day	Allerheiligen (Austria only)
December 8	Immaculate Conception	Mariä Empfängnis (Austria only)
December 25	Christmas Day	Weihnachten
December 26	St. Stephen's Day	Weihnachtstag
Merry Christmas!	Fröhliche Weihnachten!	FRU(R)-likh-eh VYE-nahkh-ten
Happy New Year!	Glückliches Neues Jahr!	GLEWK-likh-ehs NOY-ehs yaar!
Happy Easter!	Frohe Ostern!	FROH-eh OHS-tern!
Happy Holidays!	Frohe Feiertage!	FROH-eh FYE-e(r)-taa-geh!
Happy Birthday!	Alles Gute zum Geburtstag!	AH-lehs GOO-teh tsoom geh-BOORTS-taak!
Congratulations!	Herzlichen Glückwunsch!	HEHRTS-likh-en GLEWK-voonsh!

AGE

How old are you?	**Wie alt sind Sie?**	**vee ahlt zint zee?**
I'm forty years old.	**Ich bin vierzig Jahre alt.**	**ikh bin VEER-tsikh YAA-reh ahlt.**
How old is he/she?	Wie alt ist er/sie?	vee ahlt ist ehr/zee?
He/she is thirty.	Er/Sie ist dreißig.	ehr/zee ist DRYE-sikh.
I'm older/younger than she is.	Ich bin älter/jünger als sie.	ich bin EHL-te(r)/YEWN-ge(r) ahls zee.
I was born in 1950.	Ich bin neunzehn-hundertfünfzig geboren.	ikh bin NOYN-tsayn-hun-dert-FEWNF-tsikh geh-BOH-ren.

| When's her birthday? | Wann hat sie Geburtstag? | vahn haht zee geh-BURTS-taak? |
| Her birthday is March 15. | Ihr Geburtstag ist am fünfzehnten März. | eer geh-BURTS-taak ist ahm FEWNF-tsayn-ten mehrts. |

TELLING TIME AND EXPRESSIONS OF TIME

What time is it?/How late is it?	Wieviel Uhr ist es?/Wie spät ist es?	VEE-feel oor ist ehs?/vee shpayt ist ehs?
At what time?	Um wieviel Uhr?	oom VEE-feel oor?
It's . . .	Es ist . . .	ehs ist . . .
_two o'clock.	_zwei Uhr.	_tsvye oor.
_2:10.	_zwei Uhr zehn.	_tsvye oor tsayn.
_ten past two.	_zehn nach zwei.	_tsayn nahkh tsvye.
_3:40.	_drei Uhr vierzig.	_drye oor FEER-tsikh.
_twenty to four.	_zwanzig vor vier.	_TSVAHN-tsikh for feer.
_4:30.	_vier Uhr dreißig.	_feer oor DRYE-sikh.
_half past four.*	_halb fünf.*	_haalp fewnf.
_6:15.	_sechs Uhr fünfzehn.	_zehks oor FEWNF-tsayn.
_quarter past six.*	_viertel nach sechs/viertel sieben.*	_VEER-tel nahkh zehks/VEER-tel ZEE-ben.
_twelve o'clock midnight/noon.	_zwölf Uhr Mitternacht/Mittag.	_tsvu(r)lf oor MIT-te(r)-nahkht/MIT-taak.
_one in the afternoon.	_ein Uhr nachmittags.	_ine oor NAHKH-mit-taaks.

*It will be easier for you to tell time by simply stating the hour and minutes, as in the above examples, 2:10, 3:40, 4:30. When expressing quarter and especially half-hour intervals, however, German speakers usually stress the upcoming hour, so half past four becomes literally "halfway toward five," and 4:45 becomes *dreiviertel fünf,* "three quarters toward five," but you will also hear *viertel vor fünf,* "quarter to five," as one would say in English.

_eleven at night.	_elf Uhr nachts.	_ehlf oor nahkhts.
five minutes ago.	vor fünf Minuten.	for fewnf mi-NOO-ten.
in half an/quarter of an hour.	in einer halben Stunde/ Viertelstunde.	in INE-e(r) haal-ben SHTUN-deh/VEER-tel-SHTOON-deh.
since 10:30 A.M.	seit halb elf morgens.	zite haalp ehlf MOR-gens.
after 8:00 P.M.	nach acht Uhr abends.	nahkh ahkht oor AA-behnts.
before 6:00 A.M.	vor sechs Uhr morgens.	for zehks oor MOR-gens.
more than 10 minutes	mehr als zehn Minuten.	mehr ahls tsayn mi-NOO-ten.
less than 30 seconds	weniger als dreißig Sekunden.	VAY-ni-ge(r) ahls DRYE-sikh zeh-KOON-den.
She came . . .	Sie kam . . .	zee kahm . . .
_on time.	_rechtzeitig.	_REHKHT-tsye-tikh.
_late.	_spät.	_shpayt.
_early.	_frühzeitig.	_FREW-tsye-tikh.
My watch is	Meine Uhr geht	MINE-eh oor gayt
fast/slow.	vor/nach.	for/nahkh.

The 24-Hour Clock

In normal conversation, Europeans generally express time the way we do, but for official listings, like transportation schedules, business hours, and theater times, the 24-hour system, our "military time," is used. After 12 noon, just keep counting. 1:00 P.M. becomes 12 plus 1 = 13.00, or *dreizehn Uhr;* 12 midnight becomes 24.00, or *vierundzwanzig Uhr.* Once you pass 12 noon, you can convert official time back to the 12-hour system by subtracting 12. A typical evening show time, 7:30 P.M. would be 19.30, *neunzehn Uhr dreißig.* Note that in place of the colon, a decimal point is used. Use this chart for quick reference:

Official Time Chart

1 A.M.	01.00	ein Uhr	ine oor
2 A.M.	02.00	zwei Uhr	tsvye oor
3 A.M.	03.00	drei Uhr	drye oor
4 A.M.	04.00	vier Uhr	veer oor
5 A.M.	05.00	fünf Uhr	fewnf oor
6 A.M.	06.00	sechs Uhr	zehks oor
7 A.M.	07.00	sieben Uhr	ZEE-ben oor
8 A.M.	08.00	acht Uhr	ahkht oor
9 A.M.	09.00	neun Uhr	noyn oor
10 A.M.	10.00	zehn Uhr	tsayn oor
11 A.M.	11.00	elf Uhr	ehlf oor
12 noon	12.00	zwölf Uhr	tsvu(r)lf oor
1 P.M.	13.00	dreizehn Uhr	DRYE-tsayn oor
2 P.M.	14.00	vierzehn Uhr	FEER-tsayn oor
3 P.M.	15.00	fünfzehn Uhr	FEWNF-tsayn oor
4 P.M.	16.00	sechzehn Uhr	ZEHKH-tsayn oor
5 P.M.	17.00	siebzehn Uhr	ZEEP-tsayn oor
6 P.M.	18.00	achtzehn Uhr	AHKH-tsayn oor
7 P.M.	19.00	neunzehn Uhr	NOYN-tsayn oor
8 P.M.	20.00	zwanzig Uhr	TSVAHN-tsikh oor
9 P.M.	21.00	einundzwanzig Uhr	INE-unt-tsvahn-tsikh oor
10 P.M.	22.00	zweiundzwanzig Uhr	TSVYE-unt-tsvahn-tsikh oor
11 P.M.	23.00	dreiundzwanzig Uhr	DRYE-unt-tsvahn-tsikh oor
12 midnight	24.00	vierundzwanzig Uhr	FEER-unt-tsvahn-tsikh oor

Expressions of Time

now	jetzt	yehtst
earlier	früher	FREW-e(r)
later	später	SHPAY-te(r)
before	vor/vorher	for/FOR-hehr
after/afterward	nach/nachher	nahkh/NAHKH-hehr
soon	bald	bahlt
once	einmal	INE-maal
in the morning	morgens	MOR-gens

at noon	um Mittag	oom MIT-taag
in the afternoon	nachmittags	NAHKH-mit-taags
in the evening	abends	AA-behnts
at night	nachts	nahkhts
at midnight	um Mitternacht	oom MIT-te(r)-nahkht
tomorrow	morgen*	MOR-gen
yesterday	**gestern**	**GEHS-tern**
the day after tomorrow	übermorgen	EW-be(r)-mor-gen
the day before yesterday	vorgestern	FOR-gehs-tern
this week	diese Woche	DEE-zeh VOKH-eh
next week	nächste Woche	NAYKH-steh VOKH-eh
last week	vorige Woche	FOR-i-geh VOKH-eh
every day	jeden Tag	YAY-den taak
in three days	in drei Tagen	in drye TAA-gen
two days ago	vor zwei Tagen	for tsvye TAA-gen
on Saturdays	samstags/sonnabends	ZAHMS-taags/ZON-aa-behnts
on weekends	an den Wochenenden	ahn dehn VOKH-en-ehn-den
on weekdays	wochentags	VOKH-en-taags
during the week	während der Woche	VAY-rehnt dehr VOKH-eh
a working day	ein Arbeitstag	ine AHR-bites-taak
a day off	ein freier Tag	ine FRYE-e(r) taak
in January	im Januar	im YAH-noo-aar
last January	im vorigen Januar	im FOR-i-gen YAH-noo-aar
next January	im nächsten Januar	im NAYKH-sten YAH-noo-aar

*When capitalized, *Morgen* means morning, as in *Guten Morgen* (good morning).

since July	seit Juli	zite YOO-lee
before/after June	vor/nach Juni	for/nahkh YOO-nee
during May	während des Monats Mai	VAY-rehnt dehs MOH-naats mye
(not) until March	(nicht) bis März	(nikht) bis mehrts
the beginning of August	Anfang August	AHN-fahng OW-gust
the middle of November	Mitte November	MIT-teh no-VEHM-be(r)
the end of December	Ende Dezember	EHN-deh deh-TSEHM-be(r)
each/every month	jeden Monat	YAY-den MOH-naat
this month	in diesem Monat	in DEE-zem MOH-naat
next month	im nächsten Monat	im NAYKH-sten MOH-naat
last month	im letzten Monat	im LEHT-sten MOH-naat
this year	dieses Jahr	DEE-zehs yaar
next year	nächstes Jahr	NAYKH-stehs yaar
last year	letztes Jahr	LEHT-stehs yaar
every year	jedes Jahr	YAY-dehs yaar
in what year	in welchem Jahr	in VEHL-khem yaar
in the 19th century	im neunzehnten Jahrhundert	im NOYN-tsayn-ten yaar-HUN-dert
in the forties	in den vierziger Jahren	in dehn VEER-tsikh-e(r) YAA-ren
in 1980	(im Jahre) 1980*	[im YAA-reh] NOYN-tsayn-hun-dert-AHKH-tsikh

*_im Jahre_ (in the year) is optional; just the date 1980 by itself already means "in 1980."

TEMPERATURE CONVERSIONS

In Germany, Switzerland, and Austria, temperature is measured in degrees Celsius, or centigrade. To convert degrees Celsius into degrees Fahrenheit, use this formula:

To convert centigrade to Fahrenheit

$$\left(\frac{9}{5}\right)C° + 32 = F°$$

1. Divide by 5
2. Multiply by 9
3. Add 32

To convert Fahrenheit to centigrade

$$(F° - 32)\frac{5}{9} = C°$$

1. Subtract 32
2. Divide by 9
3. Multiply by 5

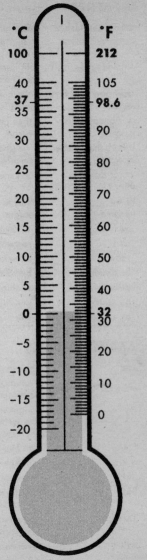

WEATHER

What wonderful/terrible weather!	Was für ein schönes/furchtbares Wetter!	vahs fewr ine SHU(R)-nehs/FOORKHT-baa-rehs VEH-te(r)!
A lovely day, isn't it?	Ein herrlicher Tag, nicht wahr?	ine HEHR-likh-e(r) taak, nikht waar?
How hot/cold it is today!	Wie heiß/kalt es heute ist!	vee hice/kahlt ehs HOY-teh ist!
Is it always this warm?	Ist es immer so warm?	ist ehs IM-me(r) zoh vahrm?
What's the weather forecast?	**Wie ist die Wettervorhersage?**	**vee ist dee VEHT-te(r)-for-hehr-zaa-geh?**
What do you think?	Was meinen Sie?	vahs MINE-en zee?
Will it ____ tomorrow?	**Wird es morgen . . .**	**virt ehs MOR-gen . . .**
_be nice	_schön sein?	_shu(r)n zine?
_rain	_regnen?	_REHG-nen?
_snow	_schneien?	_SHNYE-en?
_be cloudy	**_bewölkt sein?**	**_beh-WU(R)LKT zine?**
_be sunny	_sonnig sein?	_ZON-nikh zine?
_be windy	_windig sein?	_VIN-dikh zine?
_be stormy	_stürmisch sein?	_SHTEWR-mish zine?

ABBREVIATIONS

Abt.	Abteilung	compartment
ACS	Automobil-Club der Schweiz	Automobile Association of Switzerland
ADAC	Allgemeiner Deutscher Automobil-Club	General Automobile Association of Germany
a.M.	am Main	on the Main River
a.Rh.	am Rhein	on the Rhine River
Bhf.	Bahnhof	railway station
BRD	Bundesrepublik Deutschland	Federal Republic of Germany
BMW	Bayerische Motorenwerke	Bavarian Motor Works
bzw.	beziehungsweise	or/respectively
CDU	Christlich-Demokratische Union	Christian Democratic Union Party

DB	Deutsche Bundesbahn	Federal German Railways
DBP	Deutsche Bundespost	Federal German Postal Service
d.h.	das heißt	i.e. (that is)
DIN	Deutsche Industrie-Norm	German Industrial Standard
e.V.	eingetragener Verein	registered association
FKK	Freikörperkultur	Free Body Culture (nudism)
Frl.	Fräulein	Miss
Fr.	Frau	Mrs.
GmbH	Gesellschaft mit beschränkter Haftung	limited company
Hbf.	Hauptbahnhof	main railway station
Hr.	Herr	Mr.
JH	Jugendherberge	youth hostel
LKW	Lastkraftwagen	truck
MEZ	Mitteleuropäische Zeit	Central European Time
Mio.	Million	million
Mrd.	Milliarde	billion
Mwst.	Mehrwertsteuer	value-added tax
n. Chr.	nach Christus	A.D.
ÖAMTC	Österreichischer Automobil-Motorrad- und Touring-Club	Austrian Automobile, Motorcycle, and Touring Association
ÖBB	Österreichische Bundesbahn	Austrian Federal Railways
PKW	Personenkraftwagen	passenger car
Pl.	Platz	square
PS	Pferdestärke	horsepower
PTT	Post, Telephon, Telegraph	Post, Telephone, and Telegraph Office
SBB	Schweizerische Bundesbahn	Swiss Federal Railways
SPD	Sozialdemokratische Partei Deutschlands	Social Democratic Party of Germany
St.	Stock	floor
Str.	Straße	street
TCS	Touring-Club der Schweiz	Touring Association of Switzerland
usw.	und so weiter	etc.
v.	von	of, from
v.Chr.	vor Christus	B.C.
z.B.	zum Beispiel	e.g. (for example)
z.Z.	zur Zeit	at present

3 AT THE AIRPORT

As a tourist, you should proceed through Customs as smoothly and rapidly as airport security and the number of arriving passengers will allow. After your passport has been checked and you have collected your luggage, you will notice that customs clearance is divided into two sections, one marked by a green arrow: ANMELDEFREIE WAREN (Nothing to Declare); the other marked by a red arrow: ANMELDEPFLICHTIGE WAREN (Goods to Declare). Goods obtained within the European Union are not subject to taxation when you travel between EU countries. Personal belongings and most other goods you bring into Europe from outside the Union are also duty-free, except gifts worth more than €50, and tobacco products and alcohol above certain quantities. Visitors age 17 and older are allowed 200 cigarettes or 100 cigarillos or 50 cigars or 250 grams of tobacco (twice that if you live outside of Europe); 2 liters of still table wine; 1 liter of spirits over 22% volume or 2 liters of spirits under 22% volume (such as sparkling wines) or 2 more liters of table wine; 60 milliliters of perfume and 250 milliliters of toilet water.

When leaving Europe, you may bring up to $400 worth of souvenirs duty-free back to the United States. Residents of the United Kingdom don't pass through Customs when returning from a trip spent wholly in the European Union. Canadian residents who have been out of Canada for more than a week may return with C$500 worth of goods duty-free; if they've been away less than a week but more than 48 hours, they may return with C$200 worth of goods. Australian residents 18 and older may bring home A$400 worth of souvenirs duty-free, and New Zealanders 17 and older may bring home NZ$700 worth of souvenirs.

Customs officials at major airports generally have a working knowledge of English, but you may find the following dialogue and phrases helpful.

DIALOGUE
Customs and Immigration (Passkontrolle)

Zollbeamtin:	Guten Tag. Darf ich bitte Ihren Pass sehen?	GOO-ten taak. dahrf ikh BIT-teh EE-ren pahs ZAY-en?
Reisender:	Ja bitte, hier ist er.	yaa BIT-teh, heer ist ehr.
Zollbeamtin:	Sind Sie Amerikaner?	zint zee ah-meh-ri-KAH-ne(r)?
Reisender:	Ja, bin ich.	yaa, bin ikh.
Zollbeamtin:	Wie lange bleiben Sie im Lande?	vee LAHNG-eh BLYE-ben zee im LAHN-deh?
Reisender:	Ich werde zwei Wochen hier sein.	ikh VEHR-deh tsvye VOKH-en heer zine.
Customs Official:	Hello. May I please see your passport?	
Traveler:	Yes, please. Here it is.	
Customs Official:	Are you an American?	
Traveler:	Yes, I am.	
Customs Official:	How long will you be staying in the country?	
Traveler:	I'll be here for two weeks.	

CLEARING CUSTOMS (ZOLLABFERTIGUNG)

What nationality are you?	Welche Staatsangehörigkeit haben Sie?	VEHL-kheh SHTAHTS-ahn-geh-HU(R)-rikh-kite HAA-ben zee?
I'm	Ich bin . . .	ikh bin . . .
_American.	_Amerikaner(in).	_ah-meh-ri-KAH-ne(r) {-rin}.
_Canadian.	_Kanadier(in).	_kah-NAH-deer {-rin}.
_English.	_Engländer(in).	_EHN-glehn-de(r) {-rin}.
What's your name?	Wie heißen Sie?	vee HICE-en zee
My name is . . .	Ich heiße . . .	ikh HICE-eh . . .

Where will you be staying?	Wo werden Sie absteigen?	voh vayr-den zee op-SHTYE-gen?
I'm staying at the ____ Hotel.	Ich bleibe im Hotel ____ ab.	ikh BLYE-beh im ho-TEL ____ ahb.
Is this a vacation trip?	Machen Sie eine Urlaubsreise?	MAHKH-en zee INE-eh OOR-lowps-rye-zeh?
I'm just passing through.	Ich bin auf der Durchreise.	ikh bin owf dehr DURKH-RYE-zeh.
I'm here on a business trip.	Ich bin auf Geschäftsreise.	ikh bin owf geh-SHEHFTS-RYE-zeh.
I'll be here for . . .	Ich werde hier für ____ sein.	ikh VEHR-deh heer fewr ____ zine.
_a few days.	_ein paar Tage	_ine paar TAA-geh
_a week.	**_eine Woche**	**_INE-eh VOKH-eh**
_several weeks.	_einige Wochen	_INE-i-geh VOKH-en
_a month.	_einen Monat	_INE-en MOH-naat
Your passport, please.	Ihren Pass, bitte.	EE-ren pahs, BIT-teh.
Do you have anything to declare?	Haben Sie etwas zu verzollen?	HAA-ben zee EHT-vahs tzoo vehr-TSO-len?
No, I have nothing to declare.	**Nein, ich habe nichts zu verzollen.**	**nine, ikh HAA-beh nikhts tzoo vehr-TSOL-len.**
Please open this bag.	Bitte, öffnen Sie diese Tasche.	BIT-teh, U(R)F-nen zee DEE-zeh TAHSH-eh.
On these items you'll have to pay duty.	Auf diese Artikel müssen Sie Zoll zahlen.	owf DEE-zeh ahr-TEE-kel MEWS-sen zee tsol TSAA-len.
But they're . . .	Aber sie sind . . .	AH-be(r) zee zint . . .
_for personal use.	_zum persönlichen Gebrauch.	_tsoom pehr-ZU(R)N-likh-en geh-BROWKH.
_gifts.	_Geschenke.	_geh-SHEHN-keh.
Have a pleasant stay!	Angenehmer Aufenthalt!	AHN-geh-neh-meh(r) OW-fehnt-HAHLT!

LUGGAGE AND PORTERS

Larger airports and train stations usually have porters, but they are becoming scarce these days, so you may prefer to use a luggage cart, available at most airports in the baggage claim area and usually free of charge.

I need . . .	Ich brauche . . .	ikh BROW-kheh . . .
_a porter.	_einen Gepäckträger.	_INE-en geh-PEHK-tray-ge(r).
_a luggage cart.	_einen Kofferkuli. koo-lee.	_INE-en KOF-fe(r)-koo-lee.
Here's my luggage.	Hier ist mein Gepäck.	heer ist mine geh-PEHK.
Please take my bags . . .	Bitte, bringen Sie mein Gepäck . . .	BIT-teh, BRING-en zee mine geh-PEHK . . .
_to the taxi stand.	_zum Taxistand.	_tsoom TAHK-see-shtahnt.
_to the bus stop.	_zur Bushaltestelle.	_tsoor BUS-hahl-teh-shtehl-leh.
_to the metro/train.	_zur U-Bahn/ S-Bahn.	_tsoor OO-baan/ EHS-baan.
_to the luggage lockers.	_zu den Schließfächern.	_tsoo dehn SHLEES-feh-khe(r)n.
Please be careful with this suitcase.	Vorsicht bitte mit diesem Koffer.	FOR-zikht BIT-teh mit DEE-zem KOF-fe(r).
How much do I owe you?	Wieviel macht das?	VEE-feel mahkht dahs?

AIRPORT TRANSPORTATION AND SERVICES

Where is/are . . .	Wo ist/sind . . .	voh ist/zint . . .
_the car rental agencies?	_die Agenturen zur Autovermietung?	_dee ah-gehn-TOO-ren tsoor OW-toh-fehr-mee-tung?
_taxis?	_Taxis?	_TAHK-sees?
_buses/trains to the city?	_Busse/Züge in die Stadt?	_BUS-eh/ TSEW-geh in dee shtaht?

33

_the information booth?	_die Auskunft?	_dee OWS-koonft?
_the ticket counter?	_der Fahrkarten-schalter?	_dehr FAAR-kahr-ten-shahl-te(r)?
_the luggage claim area?	_die Gepäckausgabe?	_dee geh-PEHK-ows-gaa-beh?
_the lost and found?	_das Fundbüro?	_dahs FUNT-bew-roh?
_a currency exchange office?	_eine Wechselstube?	_INE-eh VEHK-sel-SHTOO-beh?
_the newsstand?	_der Zeitungsstand?	_dehr TSYE-tungs-shtahnt?
_the post office?	_die Post?	_dee post?
_the restroom?	_die Toilette?	_dee toy-LEHT-teh?
_the exit?	_der Ausgang?	_dehr OWS-gahng?
_a telephone?	_ein Telefon?	_ine tay-lay-FOHN?

FLIGHT ARRANGEMENTS

Is there a direct flight to Zurich?	Gibt es einen Direktflug nach Zürich?	gipt ehs INE-en dee-REHKT-flook nahhk TSEW-rikh?
Or do I have to change planes?	Oder muss ich um-steigen?	OH-de(r) mus ikh OOM-shtye-gen?
How many stops are there?	Wieviele Zwischen-landungen gibt es?	vee-FEEL-eh TSVISH-en-lahn-doon-gen gipt ehs?
Can I make a connection to Stuttgart?	Habe ich Anschluss nach Stuttgart?	HAA-beh ikh AHN-shlus nahhk SHTUT-gahrt?
When does it leave?	Wann fliegt es ab?	vahn fleegt ehs ahp?
What is the arrival time?	Was ist die Ankunftszeit?	vahs ist dee AHN-koonfts-tsite?
Please give me . . .	Geben Sie mir bitte . . .	GAY-ben zee meer BIT-teh.
_a one-way ticket.	_eine Hinflugkarte.	_INE-eh HIN-floog-kahr-teh.

34

_a round-trip ticket.	_eine Hin- und Rückflugkarte.	_INE-eh HIN unt REWK-floog-kahr-teh.
_a seat in first class.	_einen Platz in der ersten Klasse.	_INE-en plahts in dehr EHR-sten KLAHS-seh.
_a seat in tourist/coach class.	_einen Platz in der zweiten/ Touristen- klasse.	_INE-en plahts in dehr TSVYE-ten/too- RIS-ten KLAHS-eh.
_a seat for nonsmokers.	_einen Platz für Nichtraucher.	_INE-en plahts fewr NIKHT-rowkh-e(r).
_a window seat.	_einen Fensterplatz.	_INE-en FEHN-ste(r)- plahts.
_an aisle seat.	_einen Platz zum Gang.	_INE-en plahts tsoom gahng.
What's my seat number?	Welche Platznummer habe ich?	VEHL-kheh PLAHTS- num-me(r) HAA-beh ikh?
And the flight number?	Und die Flugnummer?	unt dee FLOOK-num- me(r)?
What gate does it leave from?	Von welchem Flugsteig ist der Abflug?	von VEHL-khem FLOOK-shtike ist dehr AHP-flook?
When do I have to check in?	Wann muss ich mich zum Flug melden?	vahn mus ikh mikh tsoom flook MEHL- den?
I have only hand luggage.	Ich habe nur Handgepäck.	ikh HAA-beh noor HAANT-geh-pehk.
I'd like to check these suitcases.	Ich möchte diese Koffer abgeben.	ikh MU(R)KH-teh DEE- zeh KOF-fe(r) AHP- gay-ben.
I'd like to ____ my reservation.	Ich möchte meine Reservier- ung . . .	ikh MU(R)KH-teh MINE- seh reh-zehr-VEE- rung . . .
_confirm	_bestätigen.	_beh-SHTAY-ti-gen.
_change	_umändern.	_OOM-ehn-de(r)n.
_cancel	_stornieren	_shtor-NEE-ren.

COMMON AIRPORT TERMS AND SIGNS

Ankunft	AHN-koonft	Arrival
Abflug	AHP-flook	Departure
Inlandflüge	IN-lahnd-flew-geh	Domestic Flights
Auslandflüge	OWS-lahnd-flew-geh	International Flights
Zollabfertigung	TSOL-ahp-fehr-ti-gung	Customs Clearance
Anmeldefreie Waren	AHN-mehl-deh-frye-eh WAH-ren	Nothing to Declare
Anmeldepflichtige Waren	AHN-mehl-deh-pflikh-ti-geh WAH-ren	Goods to Declare
Gepäckannahme	geh-PEHK-ahn-naa-meh	Baggage Check
Gepäckausgabe	geh-PEHK-ows-gaa-beh	Baggage Claim
Gepäckschein	geh-PEHK-shine	Baggage Tag
Auskunft	OWS-koonft	Information
Autovermietung/ Autoverleih	OW-toh-fehr-mee-tung/ OW-toh-fehr-lye	Car Rental

ABOUT THE CURRENCY

In Germany and Austria, the monetary unit is the *euro* (OY-roh), which replaced the *Deutsche Mark* and the *Schilling* in January 2002. The euro is divided into 100 cents, and its symbol is €.

Coins: 1, 2, 5, 10, 20, and 50 cents; 1 and 2 euros.

Banknotes: 5, 10, 20, 50, 100, 200, and 500 euros

Exchange rates fluctuate, but the euro is often nearly equivalent to the United States dollar or half a British pound.

In Switzerland, which is not a member of the European Monetary Union, the unit of currency is the *Franken* (FRAHN-ken), or Swiss franc, abbreviated *Fr.* It is divided into 100 *Rappen* (RAHP-pen), abbreviated *Rp.* Despite increased competition across Europe, Switzerland remains one of the most expensive countries on the continent. A cup of coffee or a beer costs about 2.50 SF in a simple restaurant, sometimes double that in city hotels and fine restaurants. A lunch special averages 14–18 SF, and a short cab ride might cost 15 SF.

Coins: 5, 10, 20, and 50 rappen; 1, 2, and 5 francs.

Banknotes: 10, 20, 50, 100, 500, and 1,000 francs.

Banks in Germany are generally open weekdays from 8:30 to 4, and on Thursday until 6 or 8 PM. Some close for an hour around lunchtime. On Saturday, most banks open at 9 and close at 1 PM. Banks in airports and major train stations open as early as 6:30 and close as late as 10:30. Swiss and Austrian banking hours may differ somewhat. Currency-exchange offices, called *Wechselstuben* [VEHK-sel-shtoo-behn] or *Geldwechsel* [GEHLT-vehks-el] (money exchange), are often open outside the regular banking hours.

Rates are usually best at banks and at ATMs in the Cirrus and Plus networks. At banks, you will probably need your passport to change money. At ATMs, you can use only four-digit PIN numbers; note that transaction fees may be higher than at home. Make sure your credit cards have been programmed for use at ATMs if you want to use them to get cash advances. Three different rates are usually posted:

1) **Ankauf** [AHN-kowf]—the rate for buying a particular currency. This is the rate you will receive when you sell dollars, for instance, to obtain euros.

2) **Verkauf** [fehr-KOWF]—the rate for selling a particular currency. This is always lower than the *Ankauf* rate, so wait until you return home to exchange euros or Swiss francs.

3) **Reiseschecks** [RYE-zeh-shehks]—traveler's check rates, which are slightly lower than cash rates.

Although Germans prefer to use cash for most transactions, major credit cards and Eurocheques are now accepted at most hotels and department stores. Many restaurants and small shops, however, accept only cash.

DIALOGUE   At the Bank (Auf Der Bank)

Kundin:	Könnten Sie mir bitte hundert Dollar wechseln?	KU(R)N-ten zee meer BIT-teh HUN-dert DOL-lahr VEHK-seln?
Kassierer:	Sicher. Der Wechselkurs heute ist ein Euro fünfzehn pro Dollar. Das wären also einhundertfünfzehn Euro.	ZIKH-e(r). dehr VEHK-sel-koors HOY-teh ist ine OY-roh FEWNF-tsayhn pro DOL-lahr. dahs VAY-ren AHL-zoh ine HUN-dert FEWNF-tsayhn OY-roh
Kundin:	Schön. Hier haben Sie meine Reiseschecks.	shu(r)n. heer HAA-ben zee MINE-eh RYE-zeh-shehks.
Kassierer:	Würden Sie bitte die Schecks unterschreiben? Und ich brauche auch Ihren Reisepass, bitte.	VEWR-den zee BIT-teh dee shehks UN-te(r)-SHRYE-ben? unt ikh BROW-kheh owkh EE-ren RYE-zeh-pahs, BIT-teh.
Kundin:	Natürlich. Hier ist er.	nah-TEWR-likh. heer ist ehr.
Customer:	Could you please change $100 for me?	
Teller:	Certainly. The exchange rate today is one euro fifteen to the dollar. So that would be 115 euros.	

Customer:	Fine. Here are my traveler's checks.
Teller:	Would you please sign the checks? And I need your passport, too.
Customer:	Of course. Here it is.

CHANGING MONEY

Where's the nearest bank?	Wo ist die nächste Bank?	Vo ist dee NAYKH-steh bahnk?
Is there a currency exchange office nearby?	Gibt es in der Nähe eine Wechselstube?	Gipt ehs in dehr NAY-eh INE-eh VEHK-sel SHTOO-beh?
I'd like to change . . .	Ich möchte ____ wechseln.	Ikh MU(R)KH-teh ____ VEHK-seln.
_dollars.	_Dollar	_DOL-lahr
_this check.	_diesen Scheck	_DEE-zen shehk
_some traveler's checks.	_einige Reiseschecks	_INE-ni-geh RYE-zeh-shehks
Do you accept personal checks?	Lösen Sie Barschecks ein?	LU(R)-zen zee BAAR shehks ine?
Will you accept . . .	Nehmen Sie ____ an?	NAY-men zee ____ ahn?
_my credit card?	_meine Kreditkarte	_MINE-eh kray-DEET KAHR-teh
_a bank draft/cashier's check?	_eine Bankanweisung	_INE-eh BAHNK-ahn-vye-zung
_a money order?	_eine Zahlungs-anweisung	_INE-eh TSAA-lungs-ahn-vye-zung
Do you need . . .	Brauchen Sie . . .	BROW-khen zee . . .
_my passport?	_den Reisepass?	_dehn RYE-zeh pahs?
_identification?	_den Personal-ausweis?	_dehn pehr-zoh-NAAL-OWS-vice?
_a letter of credit?	_einen Kreditbrief?	_INE-en kray-DEET-breef?
What's the exchange rate for . . . ?	Wie ist der Wechselkurs für . . . ?	Vee ist dehr VEHK-sel-koors fewr . . . ?

What commission do you charge?	Welche Gebühr erheben Sie?	VEHL-kheh geh-BEWR ehr-HAY-ben zee?
Where do I sign?	Wo unterschreibe ich?	Voh oon-te(r)-SHRYE-beh ikh?
I'd like to buy . . .	Ich möchte ____ kaufen.	Ikh MU(R)KH-teh ____ KOW-fen.
_Euros	_Euro	_OY-roh
_Swiss francs	_Schweizer Franken	_SHVYE-tse(r) FRAHN-ken
Please give me . . .	Geben Sie mir bitte . . .	GAY-ben zee meer BIT-teh. . . .
_small bills	_kleine Scheine.	_KLINE-eh SHINE-eh.
_large bills.	_große Scheine.	_GROHS-seh SHINE-eh.
_the rest in change.	_den Rest in Kleingeld.	_dehn rehst in KLINE-gehlt.

PAYING THE BILL

The bill, please.	Die Rechnung, bitte.	dee REHKH-nung, BIT-teh.
We'd like separate checks.	Wir möchten getrennt bezahlen.	veer MU(R)KH-ten geh-TREHNT beh-TSAA-len.
What is this charge for?	Wofür ist dieser Betrag?	vo-FEWR ist DEE-ze(r) beh-TRAHK?
Is service included?	Ist die Bedienung inbegriffen?	ist dee beh-DEE-nung IN-beh-grif-fen?
Can I pay with my credit card?	Kann ich mit meiner Kreditkarte bezahlen?	kahn ikh mit MINE-e(r) kray-DEET-KAHR-teh beh-TSAA-len?
That is for you.	Das ist für Sie.	dahs ist fewr zee.

TIPPING

Most restaurants include a service charge of about 15% on the check, indicated at the bottom of a menu with the words *Bedienung inbegiffen* (service included). Additionally, it is customary to round out the check and give the extra small change (about 5%) directly to the waiter when paying for the meal. Leaving money on the table is considered rude.

Tip bartenders and servers about €.50 for each round of drinks. Tip rest room and checkroom attendants €.25–€.50 or about 0.50 SF.

Give hotel porters, doormen, and bellhops €2.50–€5 or 5 SF, depending on how often services are performed. Leave room-cleaning staff no more than €1, or 2 SF, per day, and tip €1 for room service, too.

Railway and airport porters usually charge a fixed rate, but you may tip an additional €.50–€1, or 1 SF–2 SF. Tip taxi drivers by rounding up your fare €1, or 50 rappen, or more if you have a lot of luggage.

Tip barbers and hairdressers €1–€3, or 2 SF–5 SF, depending on the service you receive.

5 GETTING AROUND

EXPLORING ON FOOT

In general you will find European cities easy to get around in on foot. Most have maintained an old central core or *Altstadt*, which was designed more or less expressly for foot traffic. Naturally the automobile has made considerable inroads in these cities, but urban planning, even in the newer districts and suburbs, is still relatively *fußgängerfreundlich* (friendly to pedestrians). Wide sidewalks, pedestrian bridges and tunnels, and *Grünanlagen* (green areas, or parks) abound, and nearly all the larger German, Swiss, and Austrian cities now boast impressive new *Fußgängerzonen* (pedestrian zones), centrally located areas in which streets have been closed to vehicles and transformed into attractive shopping centers. *Radwege* (cycling paths) are also quite prevalent, and cycling in general is a much safer means of urban transport here than in U.S. cities.

If you are staying in a city for any length of time, it will be worth your while to purchase a *Stadtplan* (city map), which can be obtained at bookstores, newsstands, or street kiosks. One of the best-known German publishers of such city map-guides is *Falk-Verlag*.

Directions

When providing street directions, Europeans do not indicate distance by the number of city blocks, but rather by the number of streets (*Straßen*), intersections (*Kreuzungen*), and traffic lights (*Ampeln*), or simply in meters or kilometers. They are also likely to refer to specific landmarks, monuments, and pieces of architecture.

Do you have a map of the city?	Haben Sie einen Stadtplan?	HAA-ben zee INE-en SHTAHT-plaan?
Could you show me this on the map, please?	Könnten Sie mir dies bitte auf dem Plan zeigen?	KU(R)N-ten zee meer dees BIT-teh owf dehm plaan TSYE-gen?
Can I get there on foot?	Kann ich zu Fuß dahin?	kahn ikh tsoo foos dah-HIN?

How far is it?	Wie weit ist es?	vee vite ist ehs?
I think I'm lost.	Ich glaube ich habe mich verlaufen.	ikh GLOW-beh ikh HAA-beh mikh fehr-LOW-fen.
How do I get to this address?	Wie komme ich zu dieser Adresse?	vee KOM-meh ikh tsoo DEE-ze(r) ah-DREHS-seh?
How long will it take on foot?	Wie lange dauert es zu Fuß?	vee LAHNG-eh DOW-ehrt ehs tsoo foos?
Where is . . .	Wo ist . . .	voh ist . . .
_the Hotel Kaiser Hof?	_das Hotel Kaiser Hof?	_dahs ho-TEL KYE-ze(r) hohf?
_ . . . Street?	_die ____ Straße?	_dee ____ SHTRAAS-eh?
_ . . . Square?	_der ____ Platz?	_dehr ____ plahts?
How can I get to . . .	Wie komme ich . . .	vee KOM-meh ikh . . .
_the center of town?	_zum Stadtzentrum?	_tsoom SHTAHT-tsehn-trum?
_the main train station?	_zum Hauptbahnhof?	_tsoom HOWPT-baan-hohf?
_the nearest subway station?	_zur nächsten U-Bahn-Station?	_tsoor NAYKH-sten OO-baan staht-SYON?
_the nearest bus stop?	_zur nächsten Bushaltestelle?	_tsoor NAYKH-sten BUS-hahl-teh-shtehl-eh?

Responses You'll Hear to Your Requests for Directions:

geradeaus	geh-RAA-deh-ows	straight ahead
links/nach links	links/nahkh links	left, to the left
rechts/nach rechts	rehkhts/nahkh rechts	right, to the right
an der Ecke	ahn dehr EH-keh	on the corner
auf dem Platz	owf dehm plats	on the square
zwei Straßen weiter	tsvye SHTRAAS-sen VITE-e(r)	two blocks further

43

nach der Ampel	nahkh dehr AHM-pel	after the traffic light
vor der Kreuzung	for dehr KROY-tsung	before the intersection
neben der Bank	NAY-ben dehr bahnk	next to the bank
bei der Post	bye dehr post	near/next to the post office
hinter der Kirche	HIN-te(r) dehr KIR-kheh	behind the church
vor dem Dom	for dehm dohm	in front of the cathedral
in der Nähe des Flusses	in dehr NAY-eh dehs FLUS-ehs	near the river
über die Brücke	EW-be(r) dee BREW-keh	over the bridge
unter dem Turm	UN-te(r) dehm toorm	under the tower
Es ist zu weit zu Fuß.	ehs ist tsoo vite tsoo foos.	It's too far to walk.
Es ist gerade um die Ecke.	ehs ist geh-RAA-deh oom dee EH-keh.	It's right around the corner.

DIALOGUE   On the Street (Auf Der Straße)

Touristin:	Verzeihung, wie komme ich zum Schloss Charlottenburg?	fehr-TSYE-ung, vee KOM-meh ikh tsoom shlos shahr-LOT-ten-boork?
Berliner:	Ganz einfach. Gehen Sie diese Straße geradeaus bis zum Ende. Dann sehen Sie links schon das Schloss.	gahnts INE-fahkh. GAY-en zee DEE-zeh SHTRAAHS-eh geh-RAA-deh-ows bis tsoom EHN-deh. dahn ZAY-en zee links shohn dahs shlos.
Touristin:	Kann ich zu Fuß dahin?	kahn ikh tsoo foos dah-HIN?
Berliner:	Sicher. Versäumen Sie auch nicht den schönen Park hinter dem Schloss.	ZIKH-e(r). fehr-ZOY-men zee owkh nikht dehn SHU(R)-nen pahrk HIN-te(r) dehm shlos.
Touristin:	Bestimmt nicht. Danke für den Hinweis.	beh-SHTIMT nikht. DAHN-keh fewr dehn HIN-vice.
Berliner:	Viel Spaß noch in Berlin!	feel shpahs nohkh in behr-LEEN!

....

Tourist:	Excuse me, how do I get to the Charlottenburg castle?
Berliner:	It's quite simple. Go straight down this street to the end. Then you'll see the castle on your left.
Tourist:	Can I walk there?
Berliner:	Sure. And don't miss the nice park behind the castle.
Tourist:	I'll be sure not to. Thanks for the tip.
Berliner:	Enjoy yourself in Berlin!

PUBLIC TRANSPORTATION

You can go just about anywhere in Europe by public transportation, and the system of trains, buses, and urban mass transit in Germany, Austria, and Switzerland is one of the most efficient in the world. Many of the large German cities (Berlin, Bonn, Cologne, Düsseldorf, Frankfurt, Hamburg, and Munich), as well as Vienna, have modern subway or *U-Bahn* (*Untergrundbahn* = underground train) systems, which can be used in combination with the commuter trains or *S-Bahn* (*Stadtbahn* = city train) to reach the outlying suburbs. *Busse* (buses) are in use everywhere, and some cities still have a tram or *Straßenbahn* (streetcar) system.

In most cities tickets can be used interchangeably on these various systems and usually must be purchased in advance from automats or ticket stands in the stations. Instructions in English for buying and using tickets, as well as overview maps and timetables for these transport systems can also be found in the individual stations. Fares vary according to distance. Most of the *U-Bahn, S-Bahn,* and *Straßenbahn* networks operate on the "honor system," that is, you can board the trains without a ticket. If you are caught, however, there is a stiff fine for *schwarz fahren* (riding without a ticket). Many cities offer discounted prices for blocks of tickets or special unlimited travel passes, which may be worth your while if you travel frequently within a city. The *U-Bahn* and *S-Bahn* usually stop running from 1 to 5 AM.

Riding the Subway, Commuter Trains, Streetcars, and Buses

Where is the nearest . . .	Wo ist die nächste. . . .	voh ist dee NAYKH-steh
_subway station?	_U-Bahn-Station?	_OO-baan-staht-SYON?
_commuter train station?	_S-Bahn-Station?	_EHS-bann-staht-SYON?
_streetcar stop?	_Straßenbahn-haltestelle?	_shtraahs-sen-baan-HAHL-teh-shtehl-eh?
_bus stop?	_Bushaltestelle?	BUS-hahl-teh-shtehl-leh?
Where can I buy a ticket?	Wo kann ich eine Fahrkarte kaufen?	voh kahn ikh INE-eh FAAR-kahr-teh KOW-fen?
How much is the fare?	Wieviel kostet eine Fahrt?	VEE-feel KOS-tet INE-eh faart?
Is this ticket still valid?	Ist diese Fahrkarte noch gültig?	ist DEE-zeh FAAR-kahr-teh nohkh GEWL-tikh?
How much is a one-week tourist pass?	Wieviel kostet eine Touristen-Woch-enkarte?	VEE-feel KOS-tet INE-eh too-RIS-ten-VOKH-en-kahr-teh?
Which train/bus/**line** goes to ____?	Welcher Zug/Bus/**Welche Linie fährt nach ____?**	VEHL-khe(r) tsook/bus/ **VEHL-kheh LEEN-yeh fehrt nahkh ____?**
Where does this train go?	Wohin fährt dieser Zug?	VOH-hin fehrt DEE-ze(r) tsook?
How long does the trip take?	Wie lange dauert die Fahrt?	vee LAHNG-eh DOW-ehrt dee faart?
What's the next stop?	Was ist die nächste Haltestelle?	vahs ist dee NAYKH-steh HAHL-teh-shtehl-eh?
Where do I have to change trains/buses?	Wo muss ich um-steigen?	voh mus ikh OOM-shtye-gen?
Which line do I take then?	Welche Linie nehme ich dann?	VEHL-kheh LEEN-yeh NAY-meh ikh dahn?
Please tell me when to get off.	**Sagen Sie mir bitte, wann ich aussteigen muss.**	ZAA-gen zee meer BIT-teh, vahn ikh OWS-shtye-gen mus.

TAKING A TAXI

Taxis can be hailed in the street, but they won't always stop. You can phone a local taxi company or go to a *Taxistand* (taxi stand), strategically located throughout most city centers. Rates are clearly posted and will also indicate extra charges for luggage and other additional services.

Is there a taxi stand nearby?	Gibt es einen Taxistand in der Nähe?	gipt ehs INE-en TAHK-see-shtahnt in dehr NAY-eh?
Please call me a taxi.	Rufen Sie mir bitte ein Taxi.	ROO-fen zee meer BIT-teh ine TAHK-see.
What is the fare to/from the airport?	Wieviel kostet die Fahrt zum/vom Flughafen?	VEE-feel KOS-tet dee faart tsoom/fom FLOOK-haa-fen?
I'm in a hurry.	Ich habe es eilig.	ikh HAA-beh ehs EYE-likh
How long will the trip take?	Wie lange dauert die Fahrt?	vee LAHNG-eh DOW-ehrt dee faart?
And during rush hour?	Und bei starkem Verkehr?	unt bye SHTAR-kem fehr-KEHR?
Take me to this address please.	Fahren Sie mich bitte zu dieser Adresse.	FAA-ren zee mikh BIT-teh tsoo DEE-ze(r) ah-DREHS-seh.
Please put my bags in the trunk.	Legen Sie bitte mein Gepäck in den Kofferraum.	LAY-gen zee BIT-teh mine geh-PEHK in dehn KO-fe(r)-rowm.
Please slow down!	Fahren Sie langsamer bitte!	FAA-ren zee LAHNG-sah-me(r) BIT-teh!
Stop at the next corner.	Halten Sie an der nächsten Ecke.	HAHL-ten zee ahn dehr NAYKH-sten EH-keh.
Let me off here please.	Lassen Sie mich bitte hier aussteigen.	LAHS-sen zee mikh BIT-teh heer OWS-shtye-gen.
How much do I owe you?	Wieviel macht das?	VEE-feel mahkht dahs?
Keep the change.	Das stimmt so.	dahs shtimt zoh.

47

GOING BY TRAIN

Germany, Austria, and Switzerland all have extensive, well-run national rail systems. Rail travel is the preferred mode of economical transportation for most Europeans. The trains are fast, reliable, and comfortable.

Most long-distance trains have first- and second-class compartments, and a *Speisewagen* (dining car), serving full-course meals or snacks at relatively high prices. Overnight trains offer *Schlafwagen* (sleeping cars) in first class or *Liegewagen* (couchette or bunk-style sleeping cars) in second class. Both must be reserved in advance. Certain express trains charge a *Zuschlag* (extra fee, see list below). To reserve a second-class seat on some trains, it may be necessary to purchase a *Platzreservierung* (seat ticket) in addition to the ticket itself. Tickets are usually inspected and punched on the train, not at the gate. In Germany, Austria, and Switzerland, children under age 6 ride free, and kids 6–15 years old ride for half-price. Look for posted timetables or computerized ticket-vending machines. ABFAHRT in yellow is for departures. ANKUNFT in white is for arrivals.

Types of Trains

EC, or Euro City, trains connect major European cities (a *Zuschlag,* or surcharge, is required.) *IC,* or Inter City, trains connect major cities within one country—Germany, Austria, and Switzerland each operate IC lines. *ICE,* or Inter City Express, trains are super-fast IC trains. They connect major cities on a national basis. You pay a surcharge depending on how far you travel. The *ICN,* or Inter City-Neigezug, is the Swiss version of the ICE. *IR,* or Inter-Regio, trains provide fast service between large and medium-size cities. *RE,* or Regional Express, trains provide rapid service between small towns and a city center within a particular region. *RB,* or Regionalbahn, trains provide basic local service between all stations in a given region. In Austria and Switzerland, these trains are sometimes called *Regionalzug.*

At the Station

Where is/are . . .	Wo ist/sind . . .	voh ist/zint . . .
_the train station?	_der Bahnhof?	_dehr BAAN-hohf?

_the ticket window?	_der Fahrkarten-schalter?	_dehr FAAR-kahr-ten-shahl-te(r)?
_the booking/ reservations office?	_die Platzreser-vierung?	_dee PLAHTS-reh-zehr-vee-rung?
_the baggage check?	_die Gepäckauf-bewahrung?	_dee geh-PEHK-owf-beh-vaa-rung?
_the baggage lockers?	_die Schließfächer?	_dee SHLEES-feh-khe(r)?
_the baggage carts?	_die Kofferkulis?	_dee KOF-fe(r)-koo-lees?
_the lost and found?	_das Fundbüro?	_dahs FUNT-bew-roh?
_the restroom?	_die Toilette?	_dee toy-LEH-teh?
_the waiting room?	_der Wartesaal?	_dehr VAHR-teh-zaal?
_the exit?	_der Ausgang?	_dehr OWS-gahng?
_a telephone?	_ein Telefon?	_ine tay-lay-FOHN?
_platform 2?	_Bahnsteig zwei?	_BAAN-shtike tzvye?
_track 5?	_Gleis fünf?	_glice fewnf?

Tickets, Reservations, and Inquiries

I'd like a ____ ticket to Bonn.	Ich möchte eine Fahrkarte nach Bonn . . .	ikh MU(R)KH-teh INE-eh FAAR-kahr-teh nakh bohn.
_first-class.	_erste Klasse.	_EHR-steh KLAHS-seh.
_second-class.	_zweite Klasse.	_TSVYE-teh KLAHS-seh.
_half-price.	_zum halben Preis.	_tsoom HAAL-ben price.
_one-way.	_einfach.	_INE-fahkh.

49

English	German	Pronunciation
_round-trip.	_hin und zurück.	_hin unt tsoo-REWK.
_for the next train.	_für den nächsten Zug.	_fewr dehn NAYKH-sten tsook.
How much is the ticket?	**Was kostet die Fahrkarte?**	**vahs KOS-tet dee FAAR-kahr-teh?**
I'd like to reserve . . .	Ich möchte ____ reservieren lassen.	ikh MU(R)KH-teh ____ reh-zehr-VEE-ren LAHS-sen.
_a (window) seat.	_einen (Fenster) platz	_INE-en (FEHN-ste(r)) plahts
_two nonsmoking seats.	_zwei Plätze im Nichtraucherabteil	_tsvye PLEH-tseh im NIKHT-row-khe(r)-AHP-tile.
_two berths in the sleeping car.	_zwei Plätze im Schlafwagen	tsvye PLEH-tseh im SHLAHF-vah-gen
_a couchette/bunk.	_einen Platz im Liegewagen	_INE-en plahts im LEE-geh-vah-gen
Where is/are . . .	Wo ist/sind . . .	voh ist/zint . . .
_the train station?	_der Bahnhof?	_dehr BAAN-hohf?
_the ticket window?	_der Fahrkartenschalter?	_dehr FAAR-kahr-ten-shahl-te(r)?
_the booking/reservations office?	_die Platzreservierung?	_dee PLAHTS-reh-zehr-vee-rung?
_the baggage check?	_die Gepäckaufbewahrung?	_dee geh-PEHK-owf-beh-vaa-rung?
I'd like to check these bags.	**Ich möchte dieses Gepäck aufgeben.**	**ikh MU(R)KH-teh DEE-zehs geh-PEHK OWF-GAY-ben.**
When does the next train for Salzburg leave?	**Wann fährt der nächste Zug nach Salzburg?**	**vahn fehrt dehr NAYKH-steh tsook nahkh ZAHLTS-boork?**
Is it a through train?	Ist es ein durchgehender Zug?	ist ehs ine DURKH-gay-ehn-de(r) tsook?

Will it stop in Munich?	Hält der Zug in München?	hehlt dehr tsook in MEWN-khen?
Is there a connection to Graz?	Gibt es einen Anschluss nach Graz?	gipt ehs INE-en AHN-shlus nahkh grahts?
Do I have to change trains?	**Muß ich umsteigen?**	mus ikh OOM-shtye-gen?
When does it arrive in Linz?	Wann kommt er in Linz an?	vahn komt ehr in lints ahn?
Is there _____ on the train?	Hat der Zug . . .	haht dehr tsook . . .
_a dining car	_einen Speisewagen?	_INE-en SHPYE-zeh-vah-gen?
_a sleeping car	_einen Schlafwagen?	_INE-en SHLAHF-vah-gen?
_a through coach to Vienna	_einen Kurswagen nach Wien?	_INE-en KOORS-vaa-gen nahkh veen?
From which platform does the train to Ulm leave?	Auf welchem Bahnsteig fährt der Zug nach Ulm ab?	owf VEHL-khem BAAN-shtike fehrt dehr tsook nahkh oolm ahp?
At which track does the train from Nurenberg arrive?	**Auf welchem Gleis kommt der Zug aus Nürnberg an?**	owf VEHL-khem glice komt dehr tsook ows NU(R)RN-behrk ahn?
Do you have a timetable?	**Haben Sie einen Fahrplan?**	HAA-ben zee INE-en FAAR-plaan?

On Board

All aboard.	Einsteigen bitte.	INE-shtye-gen BIT-teh.
Excuse me. May I get by?	Entschuldigung. Darf ich vorbei?	ehnt-SHOOL-di-gung. dahrf ikh for-BYE?
Is this seat free?	Ist dieser Platz besetzt?	ist DEE-ze(r) plahts beh-ZEHTST?
I think you're sitting in my seat.	Ich glaube, Sie sitzen auf meinem Platz.	ikh GLOW-beh zee ZIT-tsen owf MINE-em plahts.

Could you help me please with my suitcase?	Könnten Sie mir bitte mit dem Koffer helfen?	KU(R)N-ten zee meer BIT-teh mit dehm KOF-fe(r) HEHL-fen?
How long will the train stop here?	Wie lange hält der Zug hier?	vee LAHNG-eh hehlt dehr tsook heer?
What town is this?	Wie heißt dieser Ort?	vee heyst DEE-ze(r) ort?
Where should I change trains/get off?	Wo soll ich umsteigen/aussteigen?	voh zol ikh OOM-shtye-gen/OWS-shtye-gen?

TRAVELING BY BOAT

When does the ship/ferry for Bremerhaven leave?	Wann fährt das Schiff/die Fähre nach Bremerhaven?	vahn fehrt dahs shif/dee FEH-reh nahkh breh-me(r)-HAA-fen?
Will it also stop in Hamburg?	Legt es auch in Hamburg an?	laykt ehs owkh in HAAM-boork ahn?
How much does a tour of the harbor cost?	Wieviel kostet eine Hafen-rundfahrt?	VEE-feel KOS-tet INE-eh HAA-fen-runt-faart?
Where is the point of embarkation?	Wo ist der Anlegeplatz?	voh ist dehr AHN-lay-geh-plahts?

COMMON PUBLIC SIGNS

Achtung	Attention/Caution
Angebot	Sale (of a specific item)
Aufzug	Elevator/Lift
Ausfahrt	Highway Exit
Ausgang	Pedestrian Exit
Auskunft	Information
Außer Betrieb	Out of Order
Ausverkauf	Clearance Sale
Ausverkauft	Sold Out
Belegt	No Vacancies/Full
Besetzt	Occupied

Betreten des Rasens verboten	Keep Off the Grass
Bitte klingeln	Please Ring
Bitte nicht stören	Please Do Not Disturb
Damen	Ladies
Drücken	Push/Press
Einfahrt	Highway Entrance
Eingang	Pedestrian Entrance
Eintreten ohne zu klopfen	Enter Without Knocking
Eintritt frei	No Admission Charge
Frei	Vacant/Free
Frisch gestrichen	Wet Paint
Für Unbefugte verboten	No Trespassing
Gefahr	Danger
Geöffnet von ____ bis ____	Open from ____ to ____
Geschlossen	Closed
Geschlossene Gesellschaft	Private Party
Heiß	Hot
Kalt	Cold
Herren	Men
Kasse	Cashier
Kein Zutritt	No Entry
Lebensgefahr	Mortal Danger
Lift	Elevator/Lift
Nicht berühren	Do Not Touch
Nichtraucher	No Smoking Section
Notausgang	Emergency Exit
Notruf	Emergency Telephone
Nur für Anlieger	Residents Only
Privatstrand	Private Beach
Privatweg	Private Road
Radweg	Cycling Path
Rauchen verboten	No Smoking

Raucher	Smoking Section/Compartment
Reserviert	Reserved
Schlussverkauf	Clearance Sale
Unbefugtes Betreten verboten	No Trespassing
. . . verboten	. . . Prohibited
Vorsicht	Caution
Vorsicht, bissiger Hund	Beware of Dog
Ziehen	Pull
Zimmer frei	Vacancies/Room(s) to Let
Zu verkaufen	For Sale
Zu vermieten	For Rent/To Let

If you are planning to stay in any of the major tourist centers during the high season (summer or specific holidays), you will need to book lodgings well in advance. At other times you can rely on the referral services of the local *Fremdenverkehrsbüro** (tourist information office), usually located near the main train station in most cities and towns. Ask to see their *Hotel- verzeichnis* (hotel guide). Hotels and inns in Germany, Austria, and Switzerland are officially rated based on a five-star system similar to the one used in France. The number of stars refers to the number of amenities and facilities in a hotel, and to room sizes, but not to the character or style of a property.

The terms *Pension* and *Fremdenheim* indicate a boarding- house offering either *Vollpension* (full board) or *Halbpension* (half board, meaning breakfast and one other meal). *Hotel Garni* means bed and breakfast only. The sign *Zimmer frei* in- dicates a room or rooms to rent, often in private homes. *Gasthaus* or *Gasthof* usually refer to a country inn, while *Rasthof* means a motel or wayside lodge with restaurant, off the *Autobahn* or main highway. The accommodations of many *Jugendherbergen* (youth hostels) are no longer as spartan as they used to be and are often open to people who are long past their student days. In resort areas, you may want to investigate renting a *Ferienwohnung* (furnished apartment).

DIALOGUE   At the Front Desk (An Der Rezeption)

Reisender:	Haben Sie ein Doppelzimmer für eine Nacht?	HAA-ben zee ine DOP-pehl-tsim-me(r) fewr INE-eh nahkht?
Empfangsdame:	Moment mal. Ja, wir haben eins mit Doppelbett im dritten Stock zum Hof.	mo-MEHNT mahl. yaa, veer HAA-ben ines mit DOP-pehl-beht im DRIT-ten shtok tsoom hohf.
Reisender:	Schön. Ist es ein Zimmer mit Bad?	shu(r)n. ist ehs ine TSIM-me(r) mit baat?

*Referred to also as: *Verkehrsverein, Verkehrsamt, Verkehrsverband,* or (in spas) as *Kurkommission.*

Empfangsdame:	**Nein, aber es gibt eine Toilette und Dusche.**	nine, AH-be(r) ehs gipt INE-eh toy-LEHT-teh unt DOO-sheh.
Reisender:	**In Ordnung. Darf ich es sehen?**	in ORT-nung. dahrf ikh ehs ZAY-en?
Empfangsdame:	**Selbstverständlich. Folgen Sie mir, bitte.**	zehlpst-fehr-STEHNT-likh. FOHL-gen zee meer, BIT-teh.

Traveler:	Do you have a double room for one night?
Receptionist:	One moment. Yes, we have one with a double bed on the third floor* facing the courtyard.
Traveler:	Fine. Does the room have a bath?
Receptionist:	No, but it has a toilet and shower.
Traveler:	That's all right. May I see it?
Receptionist:	Of course. Follow me, please.

*Our first floor is referred to in Germany as the *Erdgeschoss*; our second floor becomes their first, and so forth.

HOTEL ARRANGEMENTS AND SERVICES

Most larger hotels will have staff who speak English, but in smaller ones these phrases may be useful.

I have a reservation in the name of Brown.	**Ich habe auf den Namen Brown ein Zimmer reservieren lassen.**	ikh HAA-beh owf dehn NAA-men Brown ine TSIM-me(r) reh-zehr-VEE-ren LAHS-en.
Here's the confirmation.	Hier ist die Bestätigung.	heer ist dee beh-SHTEH-ti-gung.
Do you have any vacancies?	**Haben Sie noch Zimmer frei?**	HAA-ben zee nohkh TSIM-me(r) frye?
Could you recommend another hotel that might not be booked up?	Können Sie mir ein anderes Hotel empfehlen, das vielleicht nicht ausgebucht ist?	KU(R)-nen zee meer ine AHN-dehr-ehs ho-TEL ehm-PFAY-len, dahs fee-LYEKHT nikht OWS-geh-bookht ist?

I'd like . . .	Ich hätte gern . . .	ikh HEHT-teh gehrn . . .
_a room for two nights.	_ein Zimmer für zwei Nächte.	_ine TSIM-me(r) fewr tsvye NEHKH-teh.
_a single room.	_ein Einzelzimmer.	_ine INE-tsehl-tsim-me(r).
_a double room.	_ein Doppelzimmer.	_ine DOP-pehl-tsim-me(r).
_a room on the ground/top floor.	_ein Zimmer im Erdgeschoss/ obersten Ge- schoss.	_ine TSIM-me(r) im EHRT-geh-shos/OH- behr-sten geh- SHOS.
. . . a room with . . .	. . . ein Zimmer mit . . .	. . . ine TSIM-me(r) mit . . .
_a double bed.	_einem Doppelbett.	_INE-em DOP-pehl- beht.
_twin beds.	_zwei Einzelbetten.	_tsvye INE-tsehl-beht- ten.
_a private bath.	_Privatbad.	_pri-VAAT-baat.
_a shower and toilet.	_Dusche und WC.	_DOO-sheh unt VAY- tsay.
_a balcony.	_Balkon.	_bahl-KOHN.
_a nice view.	_schönem Ausblick.	_SHU(R)-nem OWS- blik.
_a radio and TV.	_Radio und Fernseher.	_RAA-dee-oh unt FEHRN-zay-e(r).
_air-conditioning.	_Klimaanlage.	_KLEE-mah-ahn-laa-geh.
We need a quiet room . . .	Wir brauchen ein ruhiges Zimmer . . .	veer BROW-khen ine ROO-i-gehs TSIM- me(r) . . .
_toward the back.	_zum Hof.	_tsoom hohf.
_(not) facing the street.	_(nicht) zur Straße.	_(nikht) tsoor SHTRAAS-eh.
How much is it . . .	Wieviel kostet es . . .	VEE-feel KOS-tet ehs . . .
_per night?	_pro Nacht?	_pro nahkht?
_per week?	_pro Woche?	_pro VOKH-eh?
_for bed and breakfast?	_für Übernachtung mit Frühstück?	_fewr ew-behr- NAHKH-tung mit FREW-shtewk?

_for full board?	_für Vollpension?	_fewr FOL-pehn-ziohn?
_for half board?	_für Halbpension?	_fewr HAALP-pehn-ziohn?
_without meals?	_ohne Mahlzeiten?	_OH-neh MAAL-tsite-en?
Does that include breakfast/tax?	Ist Frühstück/Mehrwertsteuer im Preis inbegriffen?	ist FREW-shtewk/MEHR-vehrt-shtoy-e(r) im price IN-beh-grif-en?
Can you show me the room?	**Können Sie mir das Zimmer zeigen?**	KU(R)-nen zee meer dahs TSIM-me(r) TSYE-gen?
It's fine. I'll take it.	Gut. Ich nehme es.	goot. ikh NAY-meh ehs.
No, I don't like it.	Nein, es gefällt mir nicht.	nine, ehs geh-FEHLT meer nikht.
Do you have anything . . .	Haben Sie etwas . . .	HAA-ben zee EHT-vahs . . .
_larger/better?	_Größeres/Besseres?	_GRU(R)S-eh-rehs/BEHS-eh-rehs
_less expensive/quieter?	_Preiswerteres/Ruhigeres?	_PRICE-vehr-teh-rehs/ROO-i-geh-rehs?
What is my room number?	Welche Zimmernummer habe ich?	VEHL-kheh TSIM-me(r)-num-me(r) HAA-beh ikh?
May I leave the key at the front desk?	Kann ich den Schlüssel bei der Rezeption lassen?	kahn ikh dehn SHLEWS-el bye dehr reh-tsehp-TSYOHN LAHS-en?
May I leave this in your safe?	Darf ich dies in Ihrem Tresor aufbewahren?	dahrf ikh dees in EE-rem treh-ZOHR OWF-beh-vaa-ren?
Please have my luggage brought to my room.	**Lassen Sie bitte mein Gepäck ins Zimmer bringen.**	LAHS-en zee BIT-teh mine geh-PEHK ins TSIM-me(r) BRING-gen.
Are there any messages/letters for me?	Gibt es für mich Nachrichten/Post?	gipt ehs fewr mikh NAKH-rikh-ten/post?

Would you please wake me at seven?	Würden Sie mich bitte um sieben Uhr wecken?	VEWR-den zee mikh BIT-teh oom ZEE-ben oor VEH-ken?
I wish not to be disturbed.	Ich will nicht gestört werden.	ikh vil nikht geh-SHTU(R)T VEHR-den.
May I/we have . . .	Kann ich/können wir ____ haben?	kahn ikh/KU(R)-nen veer ____ HAA-ben?
_an extra bed?	_ein zusätzliches Bett	_ine TSOO-zehts-likh-ehs beht
_an extra pillow?	_ein extra Kopfkissen	_ine EHK-straa KOPF-kis-sen
_a blanket?	_eine Decke	_INE-eh DEH-keh
_bath towels?	_Badetücher	_BAA-deh-tew-khe(r)
_some soap?	_etwas Seife	_EHT-vahs ZYE-feh
_a roll of toilet paper?	_eine Rolle Toilettenpapier	_INE-eh RO-leh toy-LEHT-ten-paa-peer
_a hair dryer?	_einen Haartrockner	_INE-en HAAR-trohkh-ne(r)
_extra hangers?	_extra Kleiderbügel	_EHK-straa KLYE-dehr-bew-gehl
_some ice cubes?	_Eiswürfel	_ICE-vewr-fel
_an ashtray?	_einen Aschenbecher	_INE-en AH-shehn-beh-khe(r)
Where is . . .	Wo ist . . .	voh ist . . .
_the chambermaid?	_das Zimmer-mädchen?	_dahs TSIM-me(r)-mayt-khen?
_the bellhop?	_der Hotelpage?	_dehr ho-TEL-paa-zheh?
_the receptionist?	_die Empfangsdame/ der Empfangschef?	_dee ehm-PFAHNGS-dah-meh/dehr ehm-PFAHNGS-shehf?
_the switchboard operator?	_die Telefonistin?	_dee tay-lay-foh-NIS-tin?
_the manager?	_der Direktor?	_dehr dee-REHK-tor?
_the elevator?	_der Aufzug/ Fahrstuhl?	_dehr OWF-tsook/FAAR-shtool?

59

_the dining room?	_der Speisesaal?	_dehr SHPYE-zeh-zaal?
_the checkroom?	_die Garderobe?	_dee gahr-deh-ROH-beh?
Could you please mail this for me?	Können Sie das bitte für mich aufgeben?	KU(R)-nen zee dahs BIT-teh fewr mikh OWF-gay-ben?
Could you get me . . .	Können Sie mir ____ besorgen?	KU(R)-nen zee meer ____ beh-ZOR-gen?
_an iron?	_ein Bügeleisen	_ine BEW-gehl-eye-zen
_a typewriter?	_eine Schreibmaschine	_INE-eh SHRIPE-mah-shee-neh
_a baby-sitter?	_einen Babysitter	_INE-en "Babysitter"
What's the voltage here?	Welche Stromspannung gibt es hier?	VEHL-kheh SHTROHM-shpah-nung gipt ehs heer?
May we have breakfast in our room?	Können wir im Zimmer frühstücken?	KU(R)-nen veer im TSIM-me(r) FREW-shtew-ken?

PROBLEMS

My room hasn't been made up.	Mein Zimmer ist nicht gemacht.	mine TSIM-me(r) ist nikht geh-makht.
The ____ doesn't work.	. . . ist defekt.	. . . ist deh-FEHKT.
_door lock	_Das Türschloss	_dahs TEWR-shlos
_light switch	_Der Lichtschalter	_dehr LIKHT-shahl-te(r)
_lamp	_Die Lampe	_dee LAHM-peh
_plug	_Der Stecker	_dehr SHTEH-ke(r)
_heating	_Die Heizung	_dee HYE-tsung
_air-conditioning	_Die Klimaanlage	_dee KLEE-mah-ahn-laa-geh
_fan	_Der Ventilator	_dehr vehn-tee-LAA-tor
_faucet	_Der Wasserhahn	_dehr VAHS-se(r)-haan

The _____ is clogged.	. . . ist verstopft.	. . . ist fehr-SHTOPFT.
_toilet	_Die Toilette	_dee toy-LEHT-teh
_bathtub	_Die Badewanne	_die BAA-deh-vahn-neh
_washbasin	_Das Waschbecken	_dahs VAHSH-beh-ken
There's no hot water.	Es gibt kein warmes Wasser.	ehs gipt kine VAHR-mehs VAHS-se(r).
Can we switch rooms?	Können wir die Zimmer wechseln?	KU(R)-nen veer dee TSIM-me(r) VEHK-seln?

CHECKING OUT

We're leaving early tomorrow.	Wir reisen morgen früh ab.	veer RYE-zen MOR-gen frew ahp.
Please have our bill ready.	**Bereiten Sie bitte die Rechnung vor.**	**beh-RYE-ten zee BIT-teh dee REHKH-nung for.**
May I pay with a credit card?	Kann ich mit Kreditkarte bezahlen?	kahn ikh mit kray-DEET-kahr-teh beh-TSAA-len?
I think you've made a mistake on my bill.	Ich glaube, Sie haben sich verrechnet.	ikh GLOW-beh, zee HAA-ben zikh fehr-REHKH-neht.
Would you please have our luggage brought down?	**Würden Sie bitte unser Gepäck herunterbringen lassen?**	**VEWR-den zee BIT-teh UN-ze(r) geh-PEHK heh-RUN-te(r)-bring-en LAHS-en?**
Could you order us a taxi?	Können Sie uns ein Taxi bestellen?	KU(R)-nen zee uns ine TAHK-see beh-SHTEHL-len?
It's been a very enjoyable stay.	Der Aufenthalt war sehr angenehm.	dehr OW-fehnt-hahlt vahr zehr AHN-geh-nehm.

CAMPING

In German-speaking countries, *zelten* (camping) has become a very popular and sophisticated activity, and there are many excellent, well-equipped campgrounds. Authorized sites are indicated on many maps, and local tourist offices as well as camping guides can help you to locate them. Many youth hostels provide camping facilities. Should you decide to camp elsewhere, always ask for permission from the landowner first.

Is there a campsite anywhere near here?	Gibt es hier in der Nähe einen Campingplatz?	gipt ehs heer in dehr NAY-eh INE-en KEHM-ping-plahts?
Do you mind if we camp on your property?	Haben Sie etwas dagegen, wenn wir auf Ihrem Grundstück zelten?	HAA-ben zee EHT-vahs dah-GAY-gen, vehn veer owf EE-rem GRUNT-shtewk TSEHL-ten?
Does this youth hostel have a campsite?	Hat diese Jugendherberge einen Zeltplatz?	haht DEE-ze(r) YOO-gehnt-hehr-behr-geh INE-en TSEHLT-plats?
Is there/Are there . . .	Gibt es . . .	gipt ehs . . .
_electricity?	_Stromanschluss?	_SHTROHM-ahn-shlus?
_drinking water?	_Trinkwasser?	_TRINK-vahs-se(r)?
_showering facilities?	_eine Duschmöglichkeit?	_INE-eh DOOSH-mu(r)-glikh-kite?
What are the fees . . .	Wie hoch sind die Gebühren . . .	vee hohkh zint dee geh-BEW-ren . . .
_per day?	_pro Tag?	_pro taak?
_per week?	_pro Woche?	_pro VOKH-eh?
_for a tent?	_für ein Zelt?	_fewr ine tsehlt?
_for a trailer?	_für einen Wohnwagen?	_fewr INE-en VOHN-vaa-gen?
Where are the toilets and washroom?	Wo sind die Toiletten und der Waschraum?	voh zint dee toy-LEHT-ten unt dehr VAHSH-rowm?
Where can we wash our dishes/clothes?	Wo können wir Geschirr spülen/Wäsche waschen?	voh KU(R)-nen veer geh-SHIR SHPEW-len/VEH-sheh VAHSH-en?

| Can we buy butane gas here? | Können wir hier Butangas kaufen? | KU(R)-nen veer heer bu-TAAN-gahs KOW-fen? |
| Where can we go shopping? | Wo können wir einkaufen? | voh KU(R)-nen veer INE-kow-fen? |

7 DINING OUT

Most of the larger cities in the German-speaking countries now offer an impressive array of enticing exotic cuisines, ranging from those of other Western European countries (especially France, Italy, Greece, and Spain) to those of the Balkans, the Slavic countries, the Middle East, the Far East, and Latin America. In some cities, you may even have to search for a traditional restaurant featuring *die deutsche Küche* (German cuisine), but in most places they still abound, and the better ones are well worth a visit and are usually quite reasonably priced.

Traditional German cooking tends to be rich and hearty, with generous portions of beef, pork, and potatoes. But even in Germany, the trend toward low-fat, healthy fare is prevalent. As elsewhere in Europe, every region has its own specialties, and most towns boast their own *Brauerei* (breweries) or *Kellerei* (wine cellars). German beer, bread, and sausage are arguably the best in the world, and the variety of these as well as other traditional staples like smoked and pickled meats and fish is quite remarkable. For lovers of venison and other game dishes, Germany will be a special treat. In traditional places—a *Gaststätte, Gasthaus,* or *Kneipe*—strangers will often share tables. The polite thing to do is to wish the others *Guten Appetit** when they start to eat and *Auf Wiedersehen* when they leave.

*In Austria and Bavaria, the greeting *Mahlzeit* is exchanged both before and after the meal.

DIALOGUE   At the Restaurant (Im Restaurant)

Kellnerin:	Möchten Sie jetzt bestellen?	MU(R)KH-ten zee yehtzt beh-SHTEHL-len?
Gast:	Ja, gibt es eine hiesige Spezialität?	yaa, gipt ehs INE-eh HEE-zi-geh shpeh-tsyah-li-TAYT?
Kellnerin:	Ich empfehle Ihnen den Hasenpfeffer.	ikh ehm-PFAY-leh EE-nen dehn HAA-zen-pfehf-fe(r).
Gast:	Schön. Das nehme ich.	shu(r)n. dahs NAY-meh ikh.
Kellnerin:	Etwas zu trinken?	EHT-vahs tsoo TRIN-ken?

Gast:	**Ja, bringen Sie mir bitte ein Glas Mineralwasser.**	yaa, BRIN-gen zee meer BIT-teh ine glaas mi-neh-RAAL-vahs-e(r).

Waitress:	Would you like to order now?
Guest:	Yes, is there a local speciality?
Waitress:	I recommend the spicy rabbit stew.
Guest:	Fine, I'll take that.
Waitress:	Something to drink?
Guest:	Yes, please bring me a glass of mineral water.

TYPES OF EATING AND DRINKING PLACES

Bierhalle [BEER-hahl-eh]	Beer hall serving *Bier vom Fass* (beer from the barrel), hot meals, cold cuts, sausages, and salads. The most famous are in Munich, home of the world's largest annual beer festival, the *Oktoberfest*, beginning in late September.
Bierstube [BEER-shtoo-beh]	Similar to an American tavern or an English pub, featuring local beers, other alcoholic beverages, and a limited menu of hot and cold dishes.
Café [kah-FAY]	Coffee shop serving coffee and tea in addition to pastries, ice cream, snacks, and drinks. The Swiss version is called *tearoom*, the Austrian, *Kaffeehaus* (KAH-fay-hows). Vienna is famous for its long, rich tradition of *Kaffeehauskultur* (coffee house culture).
Gasthaus/Gasthof [GAHST-hows/GAHST-hohf]	Rustic inn, usually in the country, featuring local specialties, and home-style cooking. Lodging is sometimes also offered. The Austrian equivalent is referred to as a *Beisel* (BYE-zel).

65

Kneipe [KNYE-peh]	A pub, similar to a *Bierstube*, common in cities and towns throughout Germany. Those frequented by students are called *Studentenkneipen*. Berlin has a very famous *Kneipenkultur*.
Konditorei [kon-dee-toh-RYE]	Pastry and sweet shop, usually attached to a salon serving coffee and tea with the pastries. A variation called the *Milchbar* (MILKH-baar) or, in Austria, *Milkstübl* (MILKH-shtew-bil), serves flavored milk drinks and yogurt dishes with pastries.
Raststätte/Rasthof [RAHST-shteht-teh/RAHST-hohf]	Wayside restaurant with lodge, located off the *Autobahn* or main highway.
Ratskeller [RAHTS-kehl-le(r)]	Cellar restaurant in the *Rathaus* (town hall), usually an old, carefully restored building. Often the best place to sample local specialities.
Restaurant [rehs-to-RAHNT]	Urban eating place, usually featuring an extensive menu including both local and foreign specialties. Also called *Gaststätte*.
Schnellrestaurant [SHNEL-rehs-tow-RAHNT]	Snack bar, often with counter service as in McDonald's—which, along with other fast food establishments, is making considerable inroads all over Europe.
Schnellimbiss [SHNEHL-im-bis]	Snack bar, also called *Würstelstand* (sausage stand) or even "*Snack Bar*," located outside, serving beer, *Pommes frites* (french fries), sausages, and other meat snacks.

Weinstube [VINE-shtoo-beh] Similar to the *Bierstube,* but featuring local wines instead of beer. The Austrian version, *Heuriger* (literally: of this year), serves new, rather potent wine and is identified by a wreath of vines over the door. The Viennese suburb of Grinzing is famous for its colorful and cozy *Heurige.*

Wirtshaus [VIRTS-hows] Another name for *Gasthaus.* The proprietor is referred to as *der Wirt.*

MEALS AND MEALTIMES

Frühstück [FREW-shtewk] Breakfast is served from 7–10 AM and is usually included in the price of a hotel room. It can range from the simple "continental" style (bread, butter, jam, and coffee or tea) to more elaborate buffets that may include fresh fruit, eggs, and cold cuts.

Mittagessen [MIT-taak-ehs-sen] Lunch is served from 12–2 PM and tends to be the main meal of the day. It usually includes soup, meat or fish, and vegetables.

Kaffee [KAH-fay] This afternoon snack from 4–5 PM is a weekend tradition, especially Sundays, and usually consists of coffee or tea and cake or pastries, but can also be more substantial, including bread, cheese, and cold cuts. It also goes by the names *Vesperbrot, Jause* (in Austria), and *Zvieri* (in Switzerland).

Abendessen [AA-behnt-ehs-sen] Dinner is served from 6–9 PM and is often a light meal of bread, cold cuts, salad, and cheese. Restaurants, however, will still serve full-course meals in the evening.

GOING TO A RESTAURANT

English	German	Pronunciation
I'm hungry/thirsty.	Ich habe Hunger/Durst.	ikh HAA-beh HUN-ge(r)/durst.
Can you recommend a good restaurant?	Können Sie mir ein gutes Restaurant empfehlen?	KU(R)-nen zee meer ine GOO-tes rehs-to-RAHNT ehm-PFAY-len?
I'm looking for a(n) ____ restaurant.	Ich suche ein ____ Restaurant.	ikh ZOO-kheh ine ____ rehs-to-RAHNT.
_inexpensive	_preiswertes	_PRICE-vehr-tes
_first-class	_erstklassiges	_EHRST-klahs-ig-ehs
What's the name of the restaurant?	Wie heißt das Restaurant?	vee heyst dahs rehs-to-RAHNT?
How do you get there?	Wie kommt man dahin?	vee komt mahn dah-HIN?
Do I need reservations?	Braucht man eine Vorbestellung?	browkht mahn INE-eh FOR-beh-shteh-lung?
I would like to reserve a table . . .	Ich möchte einen Tisch ____ bestellen.	ikh MU(R)KH-teh INE-en tish ____ beh-SHTEHL-en.
_for four people.	_für vier Personen.	_fewr feer pehr-ZOH-nen
_for this evening.	_für heute Abend	_fewr HOY-teh AA-behnt
_for 8 P.M.	_für acht Uhr.	_fewr ahkht oor
_near the window.	_am Fenster.	_ahm FEHN-ste(r)
_outside.	_im Freien.	_im FRYE-en
_on the terrace.	_auf der Terrasse.	_owf dehr teh-RAAS-seh
_in the nonsmoking section.*	_in der Nicht-raucherecke.	_in dehr NIKHT-rowkh-e(r)-eh-keh.
Waiter/Waitress!	Herr Ober/Fräulein, bitte!	hehr OH-be(r)/FROY-line, BIT-teh!

---

*In Europe, restaurants with nonsmoking sections are less common than in the United States.

The menu, please.	Die Speisekarte, bitte.	dee SHPYE-zeh-kahr-teh, BIT-teh.
What would you recommend?	Was würden Sie uns empfehlen?	vahs VEWR-den zee uns ehm-PFAY-len?
Do you have . . .	Haben Sie . . .	HAA-ben zee . . .
_local dishes?	_hiesige Gerichte?	_HEE-zi-geh geh-RIKH-teh?
_a speciality of the day?	_ein Tagesgericht?	_ine TAA-gehs-geh-rikht?
_a set menu of the day?	_ein Tagesgedeck?	_ine TAA-gehs-geh-dehk?
We're ready to order.	Wir möchten bestellen.	veer MU(R)KH-ten beh-SHTEHL-len.
We need more time.	Wir brauchen mehr Zeit.	veer BROW-khen mehr tsite.
We'd like something to drink/eat.	Wir hätten gern etwas zu trinken/essen.	veer HEH-ten gehrn EHT-vahs tsoo TRIN-ken/EHS-sen.
To begin with I'd like . . .	Als erstes möchte ich . . .	ahls EHR-stehs MU(R)KH-teh ikh . . .
Next . . .	Als nächstes . . .	ahls NAYKH-stehs . . .
And finally . . .	Und zum Schluss . . .	unt tsoom shlus . . .
That's all.	Das wäre alles.	dahs VAY-reh AH-lehs.
Will it take long?	Wird es lange dauern?	virt ehs LAHNG-eh DOW-ern?
We're in a hurry.	Wir haben es eilig.	veer HAA-ben ehs EYE-likh.
Where can I wash my hands?	Wo kann ich mir die Hände waschen?	voh kahn ikh meer dee HEHN-deh VAHSH-en?
Where are the restrooms?	Wo sind die Toiletten?	woh zint dee toy-LEHT-ten?

RESTAURANT ITEMS

| We need another . . . | Wir brauchen noch . . . | veer BROW-khen nohkh . . . |
| _glass. | _ein Glas. | _ine glaas. |

English	German	Pronunciation
_cup.	_eine Tasse.	_INE-eh TAHS-seh.
_plate.	_einen Teller.	_INE-en TEHL-le(r).
_knife.	_ein Messer.	_ine MEHS-se(r).
_fork.	_eine Gabel.	_INE-eh GAA-bel.
_spoon.	_einen Löffel.	_INE-en LU(R)f-fel.
_set of silverware.	_ein Besteck.	_ine beh-SHTEHK.
_napkin.	_eine Serviette.	_INE-eh sehr-VYEH-teh.
_ashtray.	_einen Aschenbecher.	_INE-en AH-shen-behkh-e(r).
Could you bring me/us some . . .	**_Könnten Sie mir/uns etwas ____ bringen?**	**_KU(R)N-ten zee meer/uns EHT-vahs ____ BRIN-gen?**
_tap water?*	_Leitungswasser	_LYE-tungs-vahs-se(r)
_bread?	_Brot	_broht
_butter?	_Butter	_BUT-te(r)
_salt?	_Salz	_zahlts
_pepper?	_Pfeffer	_PFEHF-fe(r)
_seasoning?	_Gewürz	_geh-VEWRTS
_mustard?	_Senf	_zehnf
_oil and vinegar?	_Essig und Öl	_EHS-sikh unt u(r)l
_sugar?	_Zucker	_TSU-ke(r)
_saccharin?	_Sacharin	_zah-kah-REEN
_lemon?	_Zitrone	_tsi-TROH-neh
_horseradish?	_Meerrettich	_MEHR-reht-tikh
_ketchup?	_Tomatenketchup	_to-MAA-ten-keh-chup

SPECIAL DIETS

English	German	Pronunciation
I'm on a diet.	Ich mache eine Diät.	ikh MAH-kheh INE-eh dee-AYT.
Do you have vegetarian dishes?	**Haben Sie vegetarische Gerichte?**	**HAA-ben zee veh-geh-TAH-rish-eh geh-RIKH-teh?**

*Water is not generally supplied in European restaurants, and if you order a glass of water, you'll be charged for mineral water. Always ask if the tap water is drinkable: *Kann man das Leitungswasser trinken?*

Are there dishes for diabetics?	Gibt es Gerichte für Diabetiker?	gipt ehs geh-RIKH-teh fewr dee-ah-BAY-ti-ke(r)?
I don't eat pork.	Ich esse kein Schweinefleisch.	ikh EHS-eh kine SHVINE-eh-flyshe.
I can't eat anything spicy.	Ich darf nichts Scharfes essen.	ikh dahrf nikhts SHAHR-fes EHS-en.
I shouldn't eat anything containing . . .	Ich soll nichts essen, was ____ enthält.	ich zol nikhts EHS-sen, vahs ____ ehnt-HEHLT.
_salt/sugar.	_Salz/Zucker	_zahlts/TSU-ke(r)
_fat/flour.	_Fett/Mehl	_feht/mayl
_milk/alcohol.	_Milch/Alkohol	_milkh/AHL-koh-hol

PHRASES YOU'LL HEAR

Haben Sie schon einen Tisch bestellt?	HAA-ben zee shohn INE-en tish beh-SHTEHLT?	Did you make reservations?
Wieviele Personen?	vee-FEEL-eh pehr-ZOH-nen?	How many people?
Möchten Sie hier sitzen?	MU(R)KH-ten zee heer ZIT-tsen?	Would you like to sit here?
Brauchen Sie einen Kinderstuhl?	BROW-khen zee INE-en KIN-de(r)-shtool?	Do you need a high chair?
Haben Sie schon gewählt?	HAA-ben zee shohn geh-VAYLT?	Are you ready to order?
Was wünschen Sie?	vahs VEWN-shen zee?	What would you like?
Möchten Sie Getränke bestellen?	MU(R)KH-ten zee geh-TREHN-keh beh-SHTEHL-en?	Would you like to order drinks?
Heute ist ____ zu empfehlen.	HOY-teh ist____tsoo ehm-PFAY-len.	Today I recommend . . .
Was hätten Sie gern dazu?	vahs HEHT-ten zee gehrn dah-TSOO?	What would you like with it?
Und anschließend?	unt AHN-shlee-sehnt?	And to follow?

Ihr Essen kommt gleich.	eer EHS-en komt glyekh.	Your meal is coming right away.
Was kann ich Ihnen noch bringen?	vahs kahn ikh EE-nen nohkh BRIN-gen?	What else can I bring you?
Hätten Sie gern eine Nachspeise?	HEH-ten zee gehrn INE-eh NAHKH-shpye-zeh?	Would you like to have a dessert?
Ist alles in Ordnung?	ist AH-lehs in ORT-nung?	Is everything all right?
Hat's geschmeckt?	hahts geh-SHMEHKT?	Did you enjoy your meal?
Möchten Sie zusammen bezahlen?	MU(R)KH-ten zee tsoo-ZAHM-men beh-TSAA-len?	Would you like a single bill?
Ist hier noch frei?*	ist heer nohkh frye?	Is this seat free?

COMPLAINTS (*REKLAMATIONEN*)

Something is missing.	Es fehlt etwas.	ehs faylt EHT-vahs.
Please bring us another glass/set of silverware.	Bringen Sie uns bitte noch ein Glas/Besteck.	BRIN-gen zee uns BIT-teh nohkh ine glaas/beh-SHTEHK.
The tablecloth isn't clean/is dirty.	Das Tischtuch ist nicht sauber/ist schmutzig.	dahs TISH-tookh ist nikht ZOW-be(r)/ist SHMUT-tsikh.
Did you forget the soup/drinks?	Haben Sie die Suppe/Getränke vergessen?	HAA-ben zee dee ZOOP-peh/geh-TREHN-keh fehr-GEHS-sen?
There must be a mistake.	Es muss ein Irrtum sein.	ehs mus ine IR-toom zine.
I didn't order this.	Das habe ich nicht bestellt.	dahs HAA-be ikh nikht beh-SHTEHLT.
Could you bring me something else?	Können Sie mir dafür etwas anderes bringen?	KU(R)-nen zee meer daa-FEWR EHT-vahs AHN-deh-rehs BRIN-gen?

*In crowded *Kneipen* and *Cafés*, strangers may ask to share your table with this question.

The soup/food is cold.	Die Suppe/das Essen ist kalt.	dee ZOOP-peh/dahs EHS-sen ist kahlt.
The butter/milk isn't fresh.	Die Milch/Butter ist nicht frisch.	dee milkh/BUT-te(r) ist nikht frish.

THE BILL (*DIE RECHNUNG*)

The bill, please.	Die Rechnung, bitte.	dee REHKH-nung, BIT-teh.
May I pay?	Darf ich zahlen?	dahrf ikh TSAA-len?
We'd like separate checks.	Wir möchten getrennt bezahlen.	veer MU(R)KH-ten geh-TREHNT beh-TSAA-len.
Is service included?	Ist die Bedienung inbegriffen?	ist dee beh-DEE-nung IN-beh-grif-en?
Do you accept credit cards/traveler's checks?	Nehmen Sie Kreditkarten/ Reiseschecks?	NAY-men zee kray-DEET-kahr-ten/RYE-zeh-shehks?
That is for you.	Das ist für Sie.	dahs ist fewr zee.
The meal was delicious.	Das Essen war vorzüglich.	dahs EHS-sen vahr for-TSEWG-likh.
And the service was excellent.	Und die Bedienung war ausgezeichnet.	unt dee beh-DEE-nung wahr OWS-geh-tsyekh-neht.

A service charge of 15% is usually included in the bill, indicated at the bottom of the check or menu with the words *Bedienung inbegiffen* (service included.) However, diners will tip about 5% extra, giving the change directly to the waiter when paying for the meal.

READING THE MENU

Most restaurants and other eating places post their *Speisekarte* (menu) outside, so guests can orient themselves before entering. In addition to the usual à la carte entries, many restaurants offer one or more set meals, *Tagesgedeck* or *Tagesmenü*. These meals change daily, include several courses, often feature local dishes, and are usually favorably priced. Restaurants offering traditional fare may announce this with phrases such as *gut bürgerliche Küche* (good, plain cooking—often quite refined and elegant) or *gepflegte Küche* (elegant, well-prepared cuisine). The following is a list of common menu terms and phrases with their English equivalents.

Tageskarte	TAA-gehs-kahr-teh	Daily menu
Tagesmenü/ -gedeck	TAA-gehs-meh-new/ -geh-dehk	Set meal of the day
Tagesgericht	TAA-gehs-geh-rikht	Dish of the day
Tagessuppe	TAA-gehs-zoop-peh	Soup of the day
Spezialität des Hauses	shpeh-tsyah-li-TAYT dehs HOW-zehs	Speciality of the house
Heute zu empfehlen	HOY-teh tsoo ehm-PFAY-len	Recommended dishes
Der Küchenchef empfiehlt . . .	dehr KEW-khen-shehf ehm-PFEELT . . .	Our chef recommends . . .
Hausgemacht	HOWS-geh-mahkht	Homemade
Nach ____ Art	nahkh ____ ahrt	In the ____ style
Nach Wahl	nahkh vaal	For your selection
Fertige Speisen	FEHR-ti-geh SHPYE-zen	Prepared meals (not to order)
Nur auf Bestel- lung	noor owf beh-SHTEHL- lung	Made to order
. . . Minuten Wartezeit	. . . mi-NOO-ten VAHR-teh-tsite	Preparation time
Extraaufschlag	EHK-strah-owf-shlahk	Additional charge
. . . im Preis inbegriffen	. . . im price IN-beh- grif-fen	Included in the price
Alle Preise sind inklusive Bedienung und Mehrwertsteuer (Mwst).	AH-leh PRYE-zeh zint IN-kloo-see-veh beh- DEE-nung unt MEHR- vehrt-shtoy-e(r).	All prices include service and value- added tax (VAT).

Typical Menu Categories

These are the usual headings in the order you'll find them in most menus.

Vorspeisen und kalte Platten	FOR-shpye-zen unt KAHL-teh PLAHT-ten	Appetizers and Cold Cuts

Suppen und Eintopfgerichte	ZOOP-pen unt INE-topf-geh-rikh-teh	Soups and Stews
Hauptgerichte	HOWPT-geh-rikh-teh	Main Dishes
Fleischgerichte	FLYSHE-geh-rikh-teh	Meat Dishes
Fisch und Meeresfrüchte/ Vom Meer	fish unt MAY-rehs-frewkh-teh/fom mayr	Fish and Seafood/ From the Sea
Wild und Geflügel	vilt unt geh-FLEW-gel	Game and Poultry
Beilagen, Neben- und Kleingerichte	BYE-laa-gen, NAY-ben-unt KLINE-geh-rikh-teh	Accompaniments, Side and Small Dishes
Salate	zah-LAA-teh	Salads
Gemüsegerichte	geh-MEW-zeh-geh-rikh-teh	Vegetable Dishes
Reis- und Kartoffelgerichte	rice- unt kahr-TOF-el-geh-rikh-teh	Rice and Potato Dishes
Teigwaren und Nudelgerichte	TIKE-vaa-ren unt NOO-del-geh-rikh-teh	Pasta and Noodle Dishes
Eierspeisen	EYE-e(r)-shpye-zen	Egg Dishes
Wurst und Käse	voorst unt KAY-zeh	Sausages and Cheese
Nachtisch/Süß-speisen	NAHKH-tish/ZEWS-shpye-zen	Desserts
Gebäck	geh-BEHK	Pastries
Eis/Glacé	ice/GLAH-say	Ice Cream
Obst und Nüsse	opst unt NEWS-seh	Fruit and Nuts
Getränke	geh-TREHN-keh	Beverages/Drinks
Wein und Bier	vine unt beer	Wine and Beer
Andere alkoholische Getränke	AHN-deh-reh ahl-koh-HOH-lish-eh geh-TREHN-keh	Other Alcoholic Drinks
Alkoholfreie Getränke	ahl-koh-hol-FRYE-eh geh-TREHN-keh	Nonalcoholic Drinks
Warme Getränke	VAAR-meh geh-TREHN-keh	Hot Beverages

METHODS OF COOKING AND PREPARATION

For meat:

gebacken	geh-BAH-ken	**baked**
geröstet	geh-RU(R)S-tet	**roasted**
geschmort	geh-SHMOHRT	braised or stewed
gekocht	geh-KOKHT	boiled
in der Pfanne gebraten	in dehr PFAH-neh geh-BRAA-ten	panfried
im Ofen gebraten	im OH-fen geh-BRAA-ten	oven roasted
gegrillt	**geh-GRILT**	**grilled, broiled**
vom Spieß	fom shpees	from the spit
gedämpft	geh-DEHMPFT	steamed, stewed
gefüllt	geh-FEWLT	stuffed
blutig	**BLOO-tikh**	**rare, underdone**
mittel	**MIT-tel**	**medium**
gut durchbraten	**goot durkh-BRAA-ten**	**well-done**

For fish:

blau	blow	**boiled in bouillon**
in Butter geschwenkt	in BUT-te(r) geh-SHVEHNKT	sautéed in butter
im schwimmenden Fett	im SHVIM-en-den feht	deep-fried
gebacken	geh-BAH-ken	**baked**
paniert	**pah-NEERT**	**breaded**
mariniert	**mah-ri-NEERT**	**marinated**
geräuchert	**geh-ROY-khert**	**smoked**

TYPICAL DISHES

The following is a representative listing of well-known dishes served in Germany, Austria, and Switzerland.

Aal in Gelee [aal in zheh-LAY] — Eel in aspic

Aalsuppe [AAL-zoop-peh] — Eel soup

Ausgebackene Spätzli [OWS-geh-bah-keh-neh SHPEHTST-lee] — Fried dumplings with egg sauce (Swiss)

Bauernfrühstück [BOW-ern-frew-shtwek] — Scrambled eggs with bacon, tomatoes, onions, potatoes

Bauernschmaus [BOW-ern-shmows] — Bacon, pork, sausage, dumplings, with sauerkraut and potatoes (Austrian)

Bauernsuppe [BOW-ern-zoop-peh] — Cabbage and sausage soup

Bayerisches Kraut [BYE-rish-es krowt] — Fresh cabbage cooked with apples, sugar, and wine

Berliner Bouletten/Frikadellen [behr-LEEN-e(r) boo-LEHT-ten/fri-kah-DEHL-len] — Fried meat ball patties/Croquettes (Berlin specialty)

Bismarckheringe [BIS-mahrk-hay-rin-geh] — Marinated herrings with onions

Bohnensuppe [BOH-nen-zoop-peh] — Thick bean soup with bacon

Bouillon/Fleisch-/Hühner-brühe [BOO-yohn/flyshe-/HEW-ne(r)-brew-eh] — Clear soup/beef-chicken broth

Brathähnchen/-hendl [BRAAT-hehn-khen/-hehn-del] — Roast chicken

Bratheringe [BRAAT-hay-rin-geh] — Fried sour herring

Bratkartoffeln [BRAAT-kahr-tof-eln] — Fried potatoes

Bratwurst [BRAAT-voorst] — Fried pork sausage

Bündnerfleisch [BEWND-ne(r)-flyshe] — Thinly sliced, air-dried beef (Swiss)

Dampfnudeln [DAHMPF-noo-deln] — Steamed noodles

Eisbein [ICE-bine] — Pickled pig's knuckle

Emmentaler Schnitzel [EHM-men-taa-le(r) SHNIT-tsel]	Veal cutlets fried between slices of Emmentaler cheese
Entenbraten [EHN-ten-braa-ten]	Roast duck
Erdäpfelknödel [EHR-dehp-fel-knu(r)-del]	Potato and semolina-dumplings (Austrian)
Falscher Hase/Hackbraten [FAHL-she(r) HAA-zeh/HAHK-braa-ten]	Meatloaf
Faschiertes [fah-SHEER-tes]	Minced meat (Austrian)
Fischsuppe [FISH-zoop-peh]	Fish soup
Fondue [fon-DEW]	Melted cheese with white wine, kirsch, and garlic; diners dip bits of bread (or meat) into the pot of cheese
Forelle blau [fo-REHL-leh blow]	Trout boiled in bouillon
Forelle Steiermark [fo-REHL-leh SHTYE-e(r)-mahrk]	Trout fillet with white sauce and bacon strips (Austrian)
Gänsebraten [GEHN-zeh-braa-ten]	Roast goose
Gefülltes Kraut [geh-FEWL-teskrowt]	Cabbage leaves stuffed with ground meat, eggs, rice, and bread crumbs; called *Kohlroulade* in Austria
Gemischter Salat [geh-MISH-te(r) zah-LAAT]	Mixed salad
Gemüseplatte [geh-MEW-zeh-plaht-teh]	Mixed vegetables
Geschnetzeltes [geh-SHNEHT-tsehl-tes]	Braised chipped veal in thick white wine sauce (Swiss)
Geselchtes [geh-ZEHLKH-tes]	Smoked, salted pork
Grießnockerlnsuppe [GREES-nok-ehrln-zoop-peh]	Semolina-dumpling soup (Austrian)
Grüner Salat [GREW-ne(r) zah-LAAT]	Fresh lettuce salad with oil and vinegar
Gulasch/Gulaschsuppe [GOO-lahsh/ -zoop-peh]	Beef stew in spicy paprika gravy/Soup version of dish
Gurkensalat [GOOR-ken-zah-laat]	Cucumber salad

Hammelbraten [HAHM-el-braa-ten]	Roast mutton
Hasenpfeffer [HAA-zen-pfehf-fe(r)]	Spicy rabbit stew
Hirschbraten [HEERSH-braa-ten]	Roast venison
Hühnerbraten [HEW-ne(r)-braa-ten]	Roast chicken
Jungfernbraten [YUNG-fehrn-braa-ten]	Roast suckling pig
Kaiserfleisch [KYE-ze(r)-flyshe]	Boiled, smoked pork (Austrian)
Kalbsbraten/-brust [KAHLPS-braaten/-broost]	Roast veal/Breast of veal
Karpfen in Bier [KAHRP-fen inbeer]	Carp poached in beer and red wine with onions and peppercorns
Kartoffelklöße/-knödel [kahr-TOF-fel-klews-eh/-knu(r)-del]	Potato dumplings; *Knödel* is the Austrian word for dumpling
Kartoffelpitte [kahr-TOF-fel-pit-teh]	Baked potatoes with pears, milk, and bacon (Swiss)
Kasseler Rippenspeer [KAHS-eh-le(r) RIP-pen-shpayr]	Pickled, smoked pork chops
Krautsalat [KROWT-zah-laat]	Cabbage salad with caraway seeds
Krenfleisch [KRAYN-flyshe]	Pork (headcheese) with horseradish and shredded vegetables (Austrian)
Labskaus [LAAPS-kows]	Thick meat stew with mashed potatoes and vegetables; sailors' version includes herring and onions
Leberkäs [LAY-be(r)-kays]	Meatloaf made of pork liver
Leberknödelsuppe [LAY-be(r)-knu(r)-del-zoop-peh]	Beef broth with liver dumplings (Austria)
Leipziger Allerlei [LIPE-tsig-e(r) AH-lehr-lye]	Vegetable stew with peas, carrots, cauliflower, asparagus, and cabbage
Matjeshering/-filet [MAH-tyehs-hay-ring/-fi-lay]	Salted, young herring in thick sauce with new potatoes

Maultasche [MOWL-tahsh-eh]	Bite-sized pasta sacks filled with veal pork and spinach (Swabian speciality)
Ochsenschwanzsuppe [OKS-en-shvahnts-zoop-peh]	Oxtail soup
Pfannkuchen [PFAHN-koo-khen]	Pancakes
Pickelsteiner Eintopf [PIK-el-shtine-e(r) INE-topf]	Meat (usually beef) and vegetable stew
Pommes frites [pom frit]	French fries
Pökelfleisch [PU(R)-kehl-flyshe]	Marinated pork or beef
Räucheraal/-hering/-lacks [ROY-khe(r)-aal/-hay-ring/-lahks]	Smoked eel, herring, and salmon
Rehrücken [RAY-rew-ken]	Roast saddle of venison
Reibekuchen [RYE-beh-koo-khen]	Potato pancakes
Rinderbraten [RIN-de(r)-braa-ten]	Roast beef
Rippchen mit Sauerkraut [RIP-khen mit SOW-e(r)-krowt]	Pickled pork ribs with sauerkraut
Rollmops [ROL-mops]	Marinated herring filled with diced onions, gherkins, and white peppercorns
Rösti [RU(R)SH-tee]	Hash brown potatoes (Swiss)
Rühreier [REWR-eye-e(r)]	Scrambled eggs
Sauerbraten [ZOW-e(r)-braa-ten]	Marinated pot roast in spicy gravy
Schinken [SHIN-ken]	Ham
Schinkenröllchen mit Spargel [SHIN-ken-ru(r)l-khen mit SHPAHR-gel]	Ham slices with asparagus filling
Schlachtplatte [SHLAHKHT-plah-teh]	Mixed cold meats and sausages
Schweinebraten/-kotelett [SHVINE-eh-braa-ten/-kot-let]	Roast pork/Pork chops
Semmelsuppe [ZEHM-mehl-zoop-peh]	Dumpling soup (Austrian)

Serbische Bohnensuppe [ZEHR-bish-eh BOH-nen-zoop-peh]	Spicy bean soup
Spanferkel [SHPAAN-fehr-kel]	Roast suckling pig
Spätzle [SHPEHTS-leh]	Thick noodles served with browned butter and bread-crumbs (Swabian speciality)
Spiegeleier [SHPEE-gel-eye-e(r)]	Fried eggs
Strammer Max [SHTRAHM-me(r) mahks]	Spiced, minced pork with fried eggs, onions, and rye bread
Topfenknödel [TOP-fen-knu(r)-del]	Cheese dumplings with fried breadcrumbs (Austria)
Wiener Backhendl [VEE-ne(r) BAHK-hehn-del]	Fried chicken (Viennese speciality)
Wiener Schnitzel [VEE-ne(r) SHNIT-tsel]	Breaded veal cutlet
Wildbraten [VILT-braa-ten]	Roast venison
Wildgulasch [VILT-goo-lahsh]	Spicy game stew
Wildschweinrücken [VILT-shvine-rew-ken]	Roast wild boar saddle
Zigeuner Schnitzel [tsi-GOY-ne(r) SHNIT-tsel]	Pork or veal cutlet in hot, spicy sauce
Zwiebelsuppe [TSVEE-bel-zoop-peh]	Onion soup

SAUSAGES

Wurst (sausage) is perhaps the most typical German food. Many dishes, both warm and cold, include *Wurst* in some form, and most restaurants offer a *Wurstplatte* [VOORST-plah-teh] (sausage platter). Many sausages bear the names of the cities or regions they come from, like *Nürnberger Bratwurst*. The best place to sample sausage is a *Metzgerei* [MEHTST-geh-rye] or *Fleischerei* [FLYSHE-eh-rye] (butcher), where you may ask for a *Kostprobe* [KOST-proh-beh] (tasting sample).

Bierwurst [BEER-voorst]	Beer sausage (smoked pork and beef)
Blutwurst [BLOOT-voorst]	Blood sausage
Bockwurst [BOK-voorst]	Large frankfurter sausage

Currywurst [KUH-ree-voorst]	Pork sausage with curry
Jagdwurst [YAAGT-voorst]	Smoked pork with mustard and garlic
Leberwurst [LAY-be(r)-voorst]	Soft liver sausage
Mettwurst [MEHT-voorst]	Spicy, soft sausage spread
Nürnberger Bratwurst [NEWRN-behr-ge(r) BRAAT-voorst]	Fried pork-and-veal sausage
Regensburger [RAY-gens-boor-ge(r)]	Smoked, highly spiced pork sausage
Weißwurst [VICE-voorst]	White, spiced pork-and-veal sausage (Munich speciality)
Wienerli or Wienerwurst [VEE-nehr-lee] [VEE-nehr-voorst]	Thin, Vienna-style frankfurter

CHEESES

An assortment of cheeses is usually not a separate course of a meal, as in France, but most German, Swiss, and Austrian restaurants offer a *Käseteller* [KAY-zeh-tehl-le(r)] (cheese platter), including three or four different cheeses. For a much wider selection, visit a *Käsegeschäft* (cheese shop) or the *Feinschmecker* (gourmet) section of a supermarket or department store.

Allgäuer Bergkäse [AHL-goy-e(r) BEHRK-kay-zeh]	Hard, mild cheese with holes, like our Swiss cheese
Altenburger [AHL-ten-boor-ge(r)]	Soft, mild goat's cheese
Bierkäse [BEER-kay-zeh]	Soft, sharp cheese spread
Edamer [AY-dah-me(r)]	Hard, mild cheese, like Dutch original
Edelpilzkäse [AY-del-pilts-kay zeh]	Sharp, soft blue cheese (Austrian)
Frischkäse [FRISH-kay-zeh]	Curd cheese or cream cheese (many kinds)
Emmentaler [EHM-men-taa-le(r)]	Hard, mild cheese with holes (Swiss)
Greyerzer [GRAY-yehr-tse(r)]	Similar to Emmentaler, but without the holes; Swiss version of French Gruyère

Kümmelkäse [KEWM-mehl-kay-zeh]	Hard, mild cheese flavored with caraway
Limburger [LIM-boor-ge(r)]	Strong, soft cheese with herbs
Liptauer [LIP-tow-e(r)]	Cream cheese flavored with paprika and herbs (Austrian)
Münster [MEWN-ste(r)]	Strong, hard cheese flavored with caraway
Quark [kvahrk]	Smooth curd cheese spread
Räucherkäse [ROY-khe(r)-kay-zeh]	Smoked cheese, hard and mild
Tilsiter [TIL-zit-e(r)]	Semihard, mild, slightly sour cheese
Topfen [TOP-fen]	Curd cheese (Austrian)

DESSERTS

If you have a sweet tooth, you'll have plenty of opportunity to indulge it and also be amazed by the array of delicious and delicate pastries and sweets throughout the German-speaking world. Menus will list desserts under various headings: *Nachtisch, Nachspeise,* or *Süßspeise. Gebäck* or *Mehlspeise* (pastries) and *Eis* or *Glacé* (ice cream) may be listed separately. In Vienna, you will inevitably hear the question *"Mit Schlag?"* ("With whipped cream?")* One of the most frequently served pastries is the *Obsttorte,* a sponge cake shell filled with custard and a type of fruit, such as apple (in the *Apfeltorte*) or strawberry (in the *Erdbeertorte*). Other popular choices are flavored puddings and cream-filled cakes, such as the *Mokkatorte* (coffee layer cake).

-auflauf [-owf-lowf]	soufflé
-creme [-kraym]	pudding
-eis/-glacé [-ice/-glah-se(h)]	ice cream
-gebäck [geh-behk]	pastry

*Austrians also use the word *Schlagobers,* while the Germans prefer *Schlagsahne* and the Swiss, *Schlagrahm.* They all mean the same and can give a perfect dessert the deliciously fattening, final touch.

-kompott [-kom-pot]	compote
-kuchen [-koo-khen]	cake
-pudding [-pu-ding]	pudding
-strudel [-shtroo-del]	delicate, thin, flaky pastry
-torte [-tor-teh]	tart or layer cake

Some notable, traditional desserts you'll be tempted by:

Apfelrösti [AHP-fel-ru(r)sh-tee]	Apple and bread slices fried in butter (Swiss)
Apfelstrudel [AHP-fel-shtroo-del]	Strudel filled with sliced apples, raisins, nuts, and jam
Berliner [behr-LEE-ne(r)]	Doughnut filled with raspberry
Bienenstich [BEE-nen-shtikh]	Almond-honey cake
Cremeschnitte [KRAYM-schnit-teh]	Napoleon
Götterspeise [GU(R)-te(r)-shpye-zeh]	Fruit gelatin
Gugelhupf [GOO-gel-hupf]	Pound cake with raisins and almonds (Austrian, Bavarian)
Hefekranz [HAY-feh-krahnts]	Circular coffee cake with almonds and fruit
Kaiserschmarren [KYE-ze(r)-shmahrn]	Shredded pancakes with raisins, sugar, cinnamon, and/or syrup (Austrian)
Käsekuchen [KAY-sehk-koo-kehn]	Cheesecake, a little lighter than the American version
Linzertorte [LIN-tse(r)-tor-teh]	Crushed almond cake with raspberry (Austrian)
Mohnkuchen [MOHN-koo-khen]	Poppy seed cake
Mohrenkopf [MOHR-en-kopf]	Chocolate, whipped-cream-filled meringue
Palatschinken [pah-lah-TSHIN-ken]	Crêpes filled with different jams, cheeses, or (as a main course) meats (Austrian)
Rote Grütze [ROH-teh GREW-tseh]	Fresh raspberry and currant pudding topped with cream (North German)

Sachertorte [ZAHKH-e(r)-tor-teh]	Chocolate layer cake with apricot jam and chocolate icing (famous Viennese specialty)
Salzburger Nockerl [ZAHLTS-boor-ge(r) NOK-erl]	Light, sweet soufflé (Austrian)
Schillerlocken [SHIL-le(r)-lok-en]	Pastry filled with vanilla cream sometimes served with fruit
Schwarzwälder Kirschtorte [SHVAHRTS-vehl-de(r) KEERSH-tor-teh]	Creamy, chocolate layer cake with cherries and cherry brandy (famous Black Forest speciality)
Topfenstrudel [TOP-fen-shtroo-del]	Strudel filled with creamy, vanilla-flavored curd cheese (Austrian)
Windbeutel [VINT-boy-tel]	Cream puff (literally: "wind bag")
Zitronenrolle [TSIT-troh-nehn-roh-leh]	Sponge cake roll with lemon-cream filling
Zwetschgenknödel [TSVEHTSH-ken-knu(r)-del]	Plum dumplings, boiled and fried in bread crumbs, served warm (Austrian)

WINES

Germany produces mostly white wines, the best known coming from the Rhine and Mosel River valleys. Along the Danube, the Wachau region in Austria is also famous for its white wines, while the Burgenland vineyards near the Hungarian border and those in German-speaking Switzerland produce mostly red wine. The system for categorizing wine in these countries is based primarily on the percentage of natural grape sugar in the wine: the more sugar, the higher the quality. The better German wines are classified as *Qualitätswein* or *Qualitätswein mit Pradikat* for the best. These wines are enjoyed by themselves, with dinner, or as dessert wines. Sometimes sugar is added to sweeten a wine, which is then labled euphemistically *verbessert* (improved); otherwise the terms *Naturwein* or *naturrein* (naturally pure) indicate normal production methods. *Kabinett* wines are typically dry and accompany meals. German wines are always produced from just one sort of grape, unless they are labeled *Deutsche*

Tafelwein (German table wine), which is usually a blend. These wines are enjoyed by themselves or as dessert wines.

Germans are fond of sparkling wine, called *Schaumwein* or *Sekt,* and produce some of the best anywhere. They also enjoy new, still fermenting wines, referred to variously, depending on the region, as *Neuer Wein, Most, Sauser, Federweißer,* or, in Austria, as *Heuriger.** German wines are named after the region or vineyard where the grapes are produced, but usually the type of grape is indicated as well. The most common white wine grapes are *Müller-Thurgau, Sylvaner,* and *Riesling.* You will also encounter the following terms, which denote in ascending order the relative quality and degree of sweetness according to the time of harvest and condition of the grapes.

Spätlese [SHPAYT-lay-zeh]	Dry wines from grapes harvested later than those used for the normal vintage
Auslese [OWS-lay-zeh]	Semidry wines from selected, very ripe grapes
Beerenauslese [BAY-ren-ows-lay-zeh]	Slightly sweet wines from a special harvest of overripe grapes
Trockenbeerenauslese [TRO-ken-bay-ren-ows-lay-zeh]	Sweet dessert wines from selected dried, raisinlike grapes; similar to French sauternes
Eiswein [ICE-vine]	Very rare honey-sweet, thick, liqueurlike wines from grapes harvested in midwinter; thus, the name "ice wine."

Ordering Wines

May I see the wine list, please?	Die Weinkarte, bitte.	dee VINE-kahr-teh, BIT-teh.
Can you recommend a good local wine?	Können Sie mir einen guten Wein aus dieser Gegend empfehlen?	KU(R)-nen zee meer INE-en GOO-ten vine ows DEE-ze(r) GAY-gehnt ehm-PFAY-len?

*This Austrian wine name is also applied to the establishment where it is served and consumed. See page 65, Types of Eating and Drinking Places.

Where is this wine from?	Woher kommt dieser Wein?	voh-HEHR komt DEE-ze(r) vine?
Is this a good vintage?	Ist das ein guter Jahrgang?	ist dahs ine GOO-te(r) YAAR-gahng?
Is this wine . . .	Ist dieser Wein . . .	ist DEE-ze(r) vine . . .
_(very) dry?	_(sehr) trocken?	_(zehr) TRO-ken?
_(a little) sweet?	_(etwas) süß?	_(EHT-vahs) zews?
_light/heavy?	_leicht/schwer?	_lyekht/shvehr?
_full-bodied?	_vollmundig?	_VOL-mun-dikh?
I'd like a glass/bottle/ carafe of . . .	**Ich möchte ein Glas/eine Flasche/eine Karaffe . . .**	**ikh MU(R)KH-teh ine glaas/INE-eh FLAHSH-eh-INE-eh kah-RAH-feh . . .**
_house wine.	_Hauswein.	_HOWS-vine.
_white wine.	_Weißwein.	_VICE-vine.
_red wine.	_Rotwein.	_ROHT-vine.
_rosé.	_Rosé/Schiller-wein.	_roh-ZAY/SHIL-le(r)-vine.
_sparkling wine.	_Sekt.	_zehkt.
Please bring me another . . .	Bringen Sie mir bitte noch . . .	BRIN-gen zee meer BIT-teh nohkh . . .
_⅛ liter glass.	_ein Achtel.	_ine AHKH-tel.
_¼ liter glass.	_ein Viertel.	_ine FEER-tel.
_bottle.	_eine Flasche.	_INE-eh FLAHSH-eh.

BEER

Breweries abound all over German-speaking Europe—even small towns often have their own—producing an amazing variety of brews. When enjoying this popular beverage "at the source," so to speak, it helps to know some of the terms Germans apply to their favorite drink. The two main categories are *helles* [HEHL-ehs] (light—in color) and *dunkles* [DUNK-lehs] (dark) *Bier,* which can be ordered *vom Fass* (literally: from the barrel) by the glass or, if you're thirsty, by *Maß* (one liter mug). Ordering is easy: *Ein Bier, bitte* (A beer, please). If you want to be more precise:

I'd like a small/large glass of beer.	Ich hätte gern ein kleines/großes Bier.	ikh HEHT-teh gehrn ine KLINE-es/GROHS-ehs beer.

Some types of German beer:

Altbier [AHLT-beer]	Bitter, light beer with high hops (*Hopfen*) content
Bockbier, Doppelbock, Märzen-, Starkbier [BOK-beer, DOP-pehl-bok, MEHR-tsen-, SHTAHRK-beer]	Beers high in alcohol and malt content
Malzbier [MAHLTS-beer]	Dark, sweet beer, low in alcohol, high in calories
Pilsener [PIL-zeh-ne(r)]	Light beer with pronounced hops aroma
Radlermaß [RAAD-le(r)-maas]	Light beer with a dash of lemonade; called *Alsterwasser* [AHL-ste(r)-vahs-e(r)] in Northern Germany
Weißbier, Weizenbier [VICE-beer, VITE-sen-beer]	Light ale brewed from wheat, popular in Berlin as a *Berliner Weiße mit Schuss*—*Weizenbier* with a shot of *Himbeersaft* (raspberry juice)

OTHER BEVERAGES

To cap off your meal, you may want to try a little *Schnaps* (shnahps) or German brandy, *Weinbrandt* (VINE-brahnt) (brandy). The many varieties of brandies often have names ending in *-schnaps*, *-wasser*, or *-geist*. Some of the traditional favorites:

Apfelschnaps [AHP-fehl-shnahps]	Apple brandy
Birnenschnaps [BEER-nen-shnahps]	Pear brandy
Bommerlunder, Kümmel [bom-me(r)-LUN-de(r), KEWM-mel]	Caraway-flavored brandies
Doornkaat, Steinhäger [DORN-kaat, SHTINE-hay-ge(r)]	German gin, juniper berry brandies
Himbeergeist [HIM-bayr-geyst]	Raspberry brandy
Kirschwasser [KIRSH-vahs-se(r)]	Cherry brandy

Kräuterlikör [KROY-te(r)-li-ku(r)r]   Herbal liqueur

Zwetschgenwasser   Plum brandy
[TSVEHTSH-gen-vahs-se(r)]

Should you wish to inquire about local spirits:

Are there any special alcoholic drinks from this region?	Gibt es aus dieser Gegend besondere Spirituosen?	gipt ehs ows DEE-ze(r) GAY-gehnt beh-ZOHN-deh-reh spi-ri-too-OH-zen?

Some nonalcoholic drinks you may want to order:

I'd like a/an . . .	Ich hätte gern . . :	ikh HEHT-teh gehrn . . .
_mineral water.	_ein Mineralwasser.	_ine mi-neh-RAAL-vahs-se(r).
_fruit juice.	_einen Obstsaft.	_INE-en OPST-zahft.
_apple juice.	_einen Apfelsaft.	_INE-en AHP-fehl-zahft.
_orange juice.	_einen Orangensaft.	_INE-en o-RAHN-zhehn-zahft.
_lemonade.	_eine Limonade.	_INE-eh lee-mo-NAA-deh.
_iced tea.	_einen Eistee.	_INE-en ICE-tay.
_Coke/Pepsi.	_ein Cola/Pepsi Cola.	_ine KOH-lah/PEHP-si KOH-lah.
_hot chocolate.	_eine heiße Schokolade.	_INE-eh HICE-seh sho-ko-LAA-deh.
_cup/pot of coffee.	_eine Tasse/Portion Kaffee.	_INE-eh TAHS-seh/por-TSIOHN KAH-feh.
_with cream.	_mit Sahne.	_mit ZAA-neh.
_black/decaffein-ated coffee.	_einen schwarzen/koffeinfreien Kaffee.	_INE-en SHVAHRT-sen/kof-feh-EEN-frey-en KAH-feh.
_espresso.	_einen Expresso.	_INE-en ehs-SPREHSsoh.
_tea with lemon/milk.	_einen Tee mit Zitrone/Milch.	_INE-en tay mit tsi-TROH-neh/milkh.
_herbal tea.	_einen Kräutertee.	_INE-en KROY-te(r)-tay.

8 SOCIALIZING

Meeting people and discovering a new culture through personal contacts can be one of the most rewarding travel experiences. Europeans are generally more reserved than Americans, but with a little patience, good will, and curiosity, behavioral as well as linguistic barriers are easily overcome. A genuine interest in the people and culture of your host country is perhaps the best way into the German-speaking world.

When meeting or taking leave, German speakers usually shake hands; close friends often embrace, while women exchange kisses on the cheek. There is a somewhat complex set of rules for switching from the formal *Sie* to the familiar *du* form of address, and these rules may vary from one locale to another, so to be on the safe side and not risk offending anyone, wait for the native speaker to offer or suggest using the *du* form. (*Warum duzen wir uns nicht?* Why don't we use the "*du*" form with each other?) Younger Germans, students in particular, tend to use first names and *du* with strangers of their own age. When adults address children under the age of 16, they use the *du* form.

DIALOGUE Introductions (Sich Vorstellen)

Karen Jackson:	Guten Abend. Darf ich mich vorstellen? Ich heiße Karen Jackson.	GOO-ten AA-behnt. dahrf ikh mikh FOR-shtehl-len? ikh HICE-seh "Karen Jackson."
Klaus Schulz:	Sehr erfreut. Ich heiße Klaus Schulz.	zehr ehr-FROYT. ikh HICE-seh klows shults.
Karen Jackson:	Ich freue mich sehr, Sie kennen-zulernen.	ikh FROY-eh mikh zehr, zee KEHN-nen-tsoo-lehr-nen.
Klaus Schulz:	Sind Sie hier in der Schweiz auf Urlaubsreise?	zint zee heer in dehr shvites owf OOR-lowps-rye-zeh?
Karen Jackson:	Ja, ich bleibe noch eine Woche.	yaa, ikh BLYE-beh nohkh INE-eh VOKH-eh.

| Klaus Schulz: | **Ich hoffe, Sie amüsieren sich gut. Auf Wiedersehen.** | ikh HOF-feh, zee ah-mew-ZEE-ren sikh goot. owf VEE-de(r)-zay-en. |
| Karen Jackson: | **Vielen Dank und auf Wiedersehen.** | FEE-len dahnk unt owf VEE-de(r)-zay-en. |

Karen Jackson: Good evening. May I introduce myself? My name is Karen Jackson.

Klaus Schulz: Pleased to meet you. My name is Klaus Schulz.

Karen Jackson: I am very pleased to meet you.

Klaus Schulz: Are you here in Switzerland on vacation?

Karen Jackson: Yes, I'll be here for one more week.

Klaus Schulz: I hope you have a good time. Good-bye.

Karen Jackson: Thanks a lot and good-bye.

FIRST CONVERSATION

I'd like to introduce you to . . .	Ich möchte Ihnen ____ vorstellen.	ikh MU(R)KH-teh EE-nen ____ FOR-shtehl-len.
May I introduce . . .	**Darf ich ____ vorstellen?**	dahrf ikh ____ FOR-shtehl-len?
_my husband?	_meinen Mann	_MINE-en mahn
_my wife?	_meine Frau	_MINE-eh frow
_my colleague?	_meinen Kollegen/meine Kollegin	_MINE-en ko-LAY-gehn/MINE-eh ko-LAY-gin
_my friend?	_meinen Freund/meine Freundin*	_MINE-en froynt/MINE-eh FROYN-din
Pleased to meet you.	**Sehr erfreut.**	zehr ehr-FROYT.

*These terms are not used as casually in German as "friend" in English; in male/female relationships, they indicate boyfriend/girlfriend. For more casual relationships, Germans use the word *Bekannte(r)* (acquaintance).

May I introduce myself?	Darf ich mich vorstellen?	dahrf ikh mikh FOR-shtehl-len?
What's your name?	**Wie heißen Sie?**	vee HICE-sen zee?
My name is . . .	Ich heiße ____ /Mein Name ist . . .	ikh HICE-seh ____ /mine NAA-meh ist . . .
How are you?/How do you do?	**Wie geht es Ihnen?**	vee gayt ehs EE-nen?
Fine, thanks, and you?	**Danke, gut. Und Ihnen?**	**DAHN-keh, goot. unt EE-nen?**
How are you?*	Wie geht's?*	vee-gayts?

WHERE ARE YOU FROM?

Are you German/ Swiss/ Austrian?	Sind Sie aus Deutschland/ der Schweiz/ Österreich?	zint zee ows DOYCH-lahnt/dehr shvites/U(R)-steh-ryekh?
Where are you from?	**Woher kommen Sie?**	voh-HEHR KOM-men zee?
I'm from . . .	Ich bin aus . . .	ikh bin ows . . .
_the United States.	_den Vereinigten Staaten.	_dehn fehr-INE-ikh-ten SHTAA-ten.
_Canada.	_Kanada.	_KAH-nah-dah.
_England.	_England.	_EHNG-lahnt.
_Australia.	_Australien.	_ows-TRAAL-yen.
Where do you live?	Wo wohnen Sie?	voh VOH-nen zee?
I live in . . .	**Ich wohne in . . .**	ikh VOH-neh in . . .
_New England.	_Neuengland.	_noy-EHNG-lahnt.
_the Middle West.	_dem Mittelwesten.	_dehm MIT-tel-vehs-ten.
_Boston.	**_Boston.**	**_BOS-ton.**
_California.	_Kalifornien.	_kah-lee-FORN-yen.
How long have you been here?	Wie lange sind Sie schon hier?	vee LAHNG-eh zint zee shohn heer?
We've been here a week.	Wir sind schon seit einer Woche hier.	veer zint shohn zite INE-e(r) VOKH-eh heer.

*Informal expression to be used with "*du*" friends (see page 90).

92

How do you like . . .	Wie gefällt Ihnen . . .	vee geh-FEHLT EE-nen . . .
_Germany?	_Deutschland?	_DOYCH-lahnt?
_Switzerland?	_die Schweiz?	_dee shvites?
_Austria?	_Österreich?	_U(R)-steh-ryekh?
I don't know yet.	Ich weiß noch nicht.	ikh vice nohkh nikht.
I just arrived.	Ich bin gerade erst angekommen.	ikh bin geh-RAA-deh ehrst AHN-geh-kom-men.
I like it a lot here.	**Mir gefällt* es hier sehr gut.**	**meer geh-FEHLT ehs heer zehr goot.**
I like ____ a lot.	Mir gefällt/ gefallen* ____ sehr.	meer geh-FEHLT/geh-FAHL-len ____ zehr.
_the landscape	_die Landschaft	_dee LAHNT-shahft
_the cities	_die Städte	_dee SHTEH-teh
_the people	_die Menschen	_dee MEHN-shen
Everything is so . . .	Alles ist so . . .	AH-lehs ist zoh . . .
_interesting.	_interessant.	_in-teh-rehs-SAHNT.
_different.	_anders.	_AHN-dehrs.
_beautiful.	_schön.	_shu(r)n.

CONTINENTS AND COUNTRIES

I'm from . . .	Ich komme aus** . . .	ikh KOM-eh ows . . .
Africa	Afrika	AAF-ree-kah
Asia	Asien	AHZ-yen
Australia	Australien	aw-STRAA-lyen
Europe	Europa	oy-ROH-pah
North America	Nordamerika	NORT-ah-meh-ri-kah

*The verb *gefallen* (to please) agrees with the object of the translated English sentence. "*Mir gefallen die Städte*" (I like the cities) means literally: "The cities are pleasing to me."

**Because of the preposition *aus* (from), which requires the dative case, those countries taking a definite article, like *die Schweiz* (Switzerland), will appear different in this construction: *Ich komme aus der Schweiz.*

South America	Südamerika	ZEWT-ah-meh-ri-kah
Argentina	Argentinien	ahr-gehn-TEEN-yen
Austria	Österreich	U(R)-stehr-ryekh
Belgium	Belgien	BEHL-gyen
Brazil	Brasilien	brah-ZEEL-yen
Canada	Kanada	KAH-nah-dah
China	China	KHEE-nah
Czech Republic	die Tschechische Republik	dee tsheh-kheesheh ree-poo-BLEEK
Denmark	Dänemark	DAY-neh-mahrk
England	England	EHNG-lahnt
Finland	Finnland	FIN-lahnt
France	Frankreich	FRAHNK-ryekh
Germany	Deutschland	DOYCH-lahnt
Great Britain	Großbritannien	grohs-bri-TAHN-yen
Greece	Griechenland	GREE-khen-lahnt
Holland/the Netherlands	Holland/die Niederlande	HOL-lahnt/dee NEE-de(r)-lahn-deh
Hungary	Ungarn	UN-gahrn
India	Indien	IN-dyen
Ireland	Irland	EER-lahnt
Israel	Israel	IS-rah-el
Italy	Italien	ee-TAAL-yen
Japan	Japan	YAA-pahn
Korea	Korea	ko-RAY-ah
Liechtenstein	Liechtenstein	LEEKH-ten-shtine
Luxembourg	Luxemburg	LUK-sehm-boork
Mexico	Mexiko	MEHK-see-koh
New Zealand	Neuseeland	noy-ZAY-lahnt
Norway	Norwegen	NOR-vay-gen
Poland	Polen	POH-len
Portugal	Portugal	POR-too-gaal
Russia	Russland	RUS-lahnt

Scotland	Schottland	SHOT-lahnt
Slovakia	die Slowakei	dee sloh-vah-KYE
South Africa	Südafrika	ZEWT-aaf-ree-kah
Spain	Spanien	SHPAH-nyen
Sweden	Schweden	SHVAY-den
Switzerland	die Schweiz	dee shvites
Turkey	die Türkei	dee tewr-KYE
United States	die Vereinigten Staaten	dee fehr-EYE-nikh-ten SHTAA-ten

WHAT DO YOU DO?

What do you do?	**Was machen Sie beruflich?**	**VAHS MAH-khen zee buh-ROOF-likh?**
I'm a businessman/ woman.	Ich bin Geschäftsmann/ -frau.	ikh bin geh-SHEHFTS-mahn/-frow.
I'm on a business trip now.	Ich bin jetzt auf Geschäftsreise.	ikh bin yehtst owf geh-SHEHFTS-rye-zeh.
I'm retired.	**Ich bin pensioniert.**	**ikh bin pehn-zioh-NEERT.**

JOBS AND OCCUPATIONS*

accountant	der Buchhalter	dehr BOOKH-hahl-te(r)
architect	der Architekt	dehr ahr-khee-TEHKT
artist	der Künstler	dehr KEWNST-le(r)
baker	der Bäcker	dehr BEH-ke(r)
butcher	der Metzger/ Fleischer	dehr MEHTS-ge(r)/ FLYE-she(r)
cardiologist	der Kardiologe	dehr kahr-dyoh-LOH-geh
carpenter	der Tischler	dehr TISH-le(r)
cook	der Koch	dehr kokh
dentist	der Zahnarzt	dehr TSAAN-ahrtst

*The feminine forms are derived in most cases by adding the suffix -in and by placing an umlaut over the main vowel; for example, *der Arzt, die Ärztin* (doctor); *der Koch, die Köchin* (cook). As with nationalities, here too the indefinite article *ein(e)* is not used; for example, *Ich bin Lehrer* (I'm a teacher).

doctor	der Arzt	dehr ahrtst
electrician	der Elektriker	dehr eh-LEHK-tri-ke(r)
engineer	der Ingenieur	dehr in-zheh-NYUR
eye doctor	der Augenarzt	dehr OW-gen-ahrtst
lawyer	der Rechtsanwalt	dehr REHKHTS-ahn-vahlt
hotel maid	das Zimmer-mädchen	dahs TSIM-e(r)-mayt-khen
nurse	die Krankenschwester	dee KRAHN-ken-shvehs-te(r)
painter	der Maler	dehr MAA-le(r)
plumber	der Klempner	dehr KLEHMP-ne(r)
salesperson	der Verkäufer	dehr fehr-KOY-fe(r)
secretary	der Sekretär	dehr zeh-kreh-TAYR
	die Sekretärin	dee zeh-kreh-TAYR-in
shopkeeper	der Ladenbesitzer	dehr LAA-den-beh-zits-e(r)
teacher	der Lehrer	dehr LEHR-e(r)
waiter	der Kellner	dehr KEHL-ne(r)
waitress	die Kellnerin	dee KEHL-neh-rin
writer	der Schriftsteller	dehr SHRIFT-shtehl-le(r)

MAKING FRIENDS

May I invite you . . .	Darf ich Sie ____ einladen?	dahrf ikh zee ____ INE-laa-den?
_for a cup of tea?	_zu einer Tasse Tee	_tsoo INE-e(r) TAHS-seh tay
_for a glass of wine?	_zu einem Glas Wein	_tsoo INE-em glaas vine
_to lunch/dinner?	_zum Mittagessen/ Abendessen	_tsoom MIT-taak-ehs-sen/AA-behnt-ehs-sen
Can I get you a drink?	Möchten Sie etwas trinken?	MU(R)KH-ten zee EHT-vahs TRIN-ken?
Are you married?	Sind Sie verheiratet?	zint zee fehr-HYE-raa-tet?
No, I'm . . .	Nein, ich bin . . .	nine, ikh bin . . .
_single.	_ledig.	_LAY-dikh.
_divorced.	_geschieden.	_geh-SHEE-den.

_a widow(er).	_Witwe/Witwer.	_VIT-veh/VIT-ve(r).
Are you traveling alone?	**Reisen Sie allein?**	**RYE-zen zee ah-LINE?**
I'm here with friends.	**Ich bin mit Freunden hier.**	**ikh bin mit FROYN-den heer.**
My family is traveling with me.	**Meine Familie reist auch mit.**	**MINE-eh fah-MEEL-yeh reyst owkh mit.**
Are you free this evening/ tomorrow?	**Sind Sie heute Abend**/morgen **frei?**	**zint zee HOY-teh AA-behnt/MOR-gen frye?**
May I telephone you?	**Darf ich Sie anrufen?**	**dahrf ikh zee AHN-roo-fen?**
What's your phone number?	**Wie ist Ihre Telefonnummer?**	**vee ist EE-reh tay-lay-FOHN-num-me(r)?**
What's your address?	**Wie ist Ihre Adresse?**	**vee ist EE-reh ah-DREHS-seh?**
Can you join us for a drink this evening?	**Kommen Sie heute Abend auf ein Gläschen zu uns?**	**KOM-men zee HOY-teh AA-behnt owf ine GLEHS-khen tsoo uns.**
With pleasure, thanks.	**Mit Vergnügen, danke.**	**mit fehrk-NEW-gen, DAHN-keh.**
Thanks very much, but I have no time.	**Vielen Dank, aber ich habe keine Zeit.**	**FEE-len dahnk, AA-be(r) ikh HAA-beh KINE-eh tsite.**
Would you like to go with us . . .	**Möchten Sie mit uns ___ gehen?**	**MU(R)KH-ten zee mit uns ___ GAY-en?**
_to the movies?	_ins Kino	_ins KEE-noh
_to a party?	**_zu einer Party**	**_tsoo INE-e(r) PAAR-tee**
Thanks for the invitation.	**Danke für die Einladung.**	**DAHN-keh fewr dee INE-laa-dung.**
Great. I'd love to come.	**Prima. Ich komme sehr gerne mit.**	**PREE-mah. ikh KOM-meh zehr GEHR-neh mit.**
May I bring a friend?	**Darf ich einen Freund/eine Freundin mitbringen?**	**dahrf ikh INE-en froynt/INE-eh FROYN-din MIT-brin-gen?**

Where shall we meet?	Wo treffen wir uns?	voh TREHF-fen veer uns?
I'll wait here for you.	Ich warte hier auf Sie.	ikh VAHR-teh heer owf zee.
I'll pick you up at your hotel.	Ich hole Sie von Ihrem Hotel ab.	ikh HOH-leh zee fon EE-rem ho-TEL ahp.
It's getting late.	Es wird spät.	ehs virt shpayt.
I must be getting back.	Ich muss schon langsam zurück.	ikh mus shohn LAHNG-sahm tsoo-REWK.
May I take you home?	Darf ich Sie nach Hause bringen?	dahrf ikh zee nahkh HOW-zeh BRIN-gen?
Thanks for everything.	Vielen Dank für alles.	FEE-len dahnk fewr AH-lehs.
It's been a wonderful evening.	Es war ein wunderbarer Abend.	ehs vahr ine VUN-de(r)-baa-re(r) AA-behnt.

THE FAMILY

I'm traveling without/with my family.	Ich reise ohne die/mit der* Familie.	ikh RYE-zeh OH-neh dee/mit dehr fah-MEEL-yeh.
My family lives in Milwaukee.	Meine Familie wohnt in Milwaukee.	MINE-eh fah-MEEL-yeh vohnt in "Milwaukee."
My family is spread out.	Meine Familie wohnt weit auseinander.	MINE-eh fah-MEEL-yeh vohnt vite ows-ine-AHN-de(r).
I have . . .	**Ich habe . . .**	**ikh HAA-beh . . .**
_a large/small family.	**_eine große/kleine Familie.**	**_INE-eh GROHS-seh/KLINE-eh fah-MEEL-yeh.**
_many (German) relatives.	**_viele (deutsche) Verwandte.**	**_FEE-leh (DOY-cheh) fehr-VAHN-teh.**
_a husband/a wife.	**_einen Mann/eine Frau.**	**_INE-en mahn/INE-eh frow.**

*When referring to relatives and parts of the body, German speakers often use the definite article _der, die, das_ (the) instead of the possessive pronouns _mein, dein_ (my, your), etc.

_two children.	_zwei Kinder.	_tsvye KIN-de(r).
_a daughter/two daughters.	_eine Tochter/zwei Töchter.	_INE-eh TOHKH-te(r)/tsvye TU(R)KH-te(r).
_a son/two sons.	_einen Sohn/zwei Söhne.	_INE-nen zohn/tsvye ZU(R)-neh.
_a baby.	_ein Baby.	_ine BAY-bee.
_a brother/two brothers.	_einen Bruder/zwei Brüder.	_INE-en BROO-de(r)/tsvye BREW-de(r).
_a sister/two sisters.	_eine Schwester/zwei Schwestern.	_INE-eh SHVEHS-te(r)/tsvye SHVEHS-te(r)n.
_three siblings.	_drei Geschwister.	_drye geh-SHVIS-te(r).
_a grandmother.	_eine Großmutter.	_INE-eh GROHS-MUT-te(r).
_a grandfather.	_einen Großvater.	_INE-en GROHS-faa-te(r).
_grandparents.	_Großeltern.	_GROHS-ehl-tern.
_a grandson/granddaughter.	_einen Enkel/eine Enkelin.	_INE-en EHNG-kel/INE-eh EHNG-keh-lin.
_an aunt/two aunts.	_eine Tante/zwei Tanten.	_INE-eh TAHN-teh/tsvye TAHN-ten.
_an uncle/two uncles.	_einen Onkel/zwei Onkel.	_INE-en ONG-kel/tsvye ONG-kel.
_a cousin (male).	_einen Vetter.	_INE-en FEHT-te(r).
_a cousin (female).	_eine Kusine.	_INE-eh koo-ZEE-neh.
_a niece/a nephew.	_eine Nichte/einen Neffen.	_INE-eh NIKH-teh/INE-en NEH-fehn.
My mother/father/parents live in Europe.	Meine Mutter/mein Vater/meine Eltern wohnen in Europa.	MINE-eh MUT-te(r)/mine FAA-te(r)/MINE-eh EHL-tern VOH-nehn een oy-ROH-pah.
How old are your children?	Wie alt sind Ihre Kinder?	vee aalt zint EE-reh KIN-de(r)?

Peter is five years old.	Peter ist fünf Jahre alt.	PAY-te(r) ist fewnf YAA-reh aalt.
He's older/younger than Paul.	Er ist älter/jünger als Paul.	ehr ist EHL-te(r)/YEWN-ge(r) ahls powl.
He's my oldest/youngest son.	Er ist mein ältester/jüngster Sohn.	ehr ist mine EHL-tehs-te(r)/YEWN-gste(r) zohn.

IN THE HOME

We have a/an . . .	Wir haben . . .	veer HAA-ben . . .
_apartment/flat.	_eine Wohnung.	_INE-eh VOH-nung.
_condominium.	_eine Eigentums-wohnung.	_INE-eh EYE-gen-tooms-voh-nung.
_house.	_ein Haus.	_ine hows.
_town house/row house.	_ein Reihenhaus.	_ine RYE-en-hows.
_vacation house.	_ein Ferienhaus.	_FEHR-yen-hows.
Make yourself at home.	**Fühlen Sie sich wie zu Hause.**	**FEW-len zee zikh vee tsoo HOW-zeh.**
Please, take a seat.	Setzen Sie sich, bitte.	ZEHT-sen zee zikh, BIT-teh.
Make yourself comfortable.	Machen Sie es sich bequem.	MAHKH-en zee ehs zikh beh-KVAYM.
What a lovely house you have!	Was für ein schönes Haus haben Sie!	vahs fewr ine SHU(R)-nehs hows HAA-ben zee!
We also like this neighborhood a lot.	Uns gefällt auch diese Nachbarschaft sehr.	uns geh-FEHLT owkh DEE-zeh NAHKH-baar-shahft zehr.
At my house . . .	Bei mir . . .	bye meer . . .
At your house . . .	Bei Ihnen/bei dir . . .	bye EE-nen/bye deer . . .
At our house . . .	Bei uns* . . .	bye uns . . .

*This and the preceding two expressions can be understood in a larger geographic sense, that is, "at home in our country," "in our hometown," "in our neighborhood."

Would you like to see the house?	Möchten Sie das Haus sehen?	MU(R)KH-ten zee dahs hows ZAY-en?
Here is . . .	Hier ist . . .	heer ist . . .
_the living room.	_das Wohnzimmer.	_dahs VOHN-tsim-me(r).
_the dining room.	_das Speisezimmer.	_dahs SHPYE-zeh-tsim-me(r).
_the kitchen.	_die Küche.	_die KEW-kheh.
_the bedroom.	_das Schlafzimmer.	_dahs SHLAHF-tsim-me(r).
_the bathroom.	_das Badezimmer.	_dahs BAA-deh-tsim-me(r).
_the attic.	_der Dachboden.	_dehr DAHKH-boh-den.
_the cellar.	_der Keller.	_dehr KEHL-le(r).
_the study.	_das Arbeitszimmer.	_dahs AHR-bites-tsim-me(r).
_the sofa.	_das Sofa.	_dahs ZOH-fah.
_the armchair.	_der Sessel.	_dehr SEHS-sel.
_the table.	_der Tisch.	_dehr tish.
_the chair.	_der Stuhl.	_dehr shtool.
_the lamp.	_die Lampe.	_dee LAHM-peh.
_the door.	_die Tür.	_dee tewr.
_the rug.	_der Teppich.	_dehr TEHP-pikh.
_the carpeting.	_der Teppichboden.	_dehr TEHP-pikh-boh-den.
_the ceiling.	_die Decke.	_dee DEH-keh.
_the floor.	_der Boden.	_dehr BOH-den.
Thanks for inviting us to your home.	Danke für die Einladung, Sie zu Hause zu besuchen.	DAHN-keh fewr dee INE-lah-dung, zee tsoo HOW-zeh tsoo beh-ZOO-khen.
You must come to visit us sometime.	Sie müssen uns mal besuchen.	zee MEWS-sen uns maal beh-ZOO-khen.

TALKING ABOUT LANGUAGE

Do you speak . . .	Sprechen Sie . . .	SHPREH-khen zee . . .
_English?	_Englisch?	_EHN-glish?
_Spanish?	_Spanisch?	_SHPAHN-ish?
_French?	_Französisch?	_frahn-ZU(R)-zish?
_Arabic?	_Arabisch?	_ah-RAA-bish?
_Chinese?	_Chinesisch?	_khee-NAY-zish?
_German?	_Deutsch?	_doych?
_Japanese?	_Japanisch?	_yaa-PAH-nish?
_Portuguese?	_Portugiesisch?	_por-too-GEE-zish?
_Russian?	_Russisch?	_ROO-sish?
I speak only English.	Ich spreche nur Englisch.	ikh SHPREH-kheh noor EHN-glish.
I speak only a little German.	**Ich spreche nur ein bisschen Deutsch.**	**ikh SHPREH-kheh noor ine BIS-khen doych.**
My German is bad/weak.	**Mein Deutsch ist schlecht/ schwach.**	**mine doych ist shlehkht/shvahkh.**
That's not true. You speak very well.	Das stimmt nicht. Sie sprechen sehr gut.	dahs shtimt nikht. zee SHPREH-khen zehr goot.
I'm trying to learn German.	Ich versuche, Deutsch zu lernen.	ikh fehr-ZOO-kheh, doych tsoo LEHR-nen.
I (don't) understand.	**Ich verstehe (nicht).**	**ikh fehr-SHTEH-eh (nikht).**
I understand more than I can speak.	Ich verstehe mehr als ich sprechen kann.	ikh fehr-SHTEH-eh mehr ahls ikh SHPREH-khen kahn.
Can you understand me?	Können Sie mich verstehen?	KU(R)-nen zee mikh fehr-SHTAY-en?
Repeat that, please.	**Wiederholen Sie das, bitte.**	**vee-de(r)-HOH-len zee dahs BIT-teh.**
Please speak more slowly.	**Bitte, sprechen Sie langsamer.**	**BIT-teh SHPRE-khen zee LAHNG-zahm-me(r).**

What do you call this/that in German?	Wie heißt dies/das auf Deutsch?	vee heyst dees/dahs owf doych?
What does that mean?	Was bedeutet das?	vahs beh-DOY-tet dahs?
How do you say . . .	Wie sagt man . . .	vee zahgt mahn . . .
_in German?	_auf Deutsch?	_owf doych?
_in English?	_auf Englisch?	_owf EHN-glish?
Could you translate this for me/us?	Könnten Sie mir/uns das übersetzen?	KU(R)N-ten zee meer/uns dahs ew-be(r)-ZEHT-sen?
Is there anyone here who speaks English?	Gibt es hier jemanden, der Englisch spricht?	gipt ehs heer YAY-mahn-ten, dehr EHN-glish shprikht?

9 PERSONAL CARE

DIALOGUE
At the Hairdresser's (Beim Damenfriseur)

Friseur:	Was kann ich für Sie tun?	vahs kahn ikh fewr zee toon?
Kundin:	Haare schneiden, bitte.	HAA-reh SHNYE-den, BIT-teh.
Friseur:	Wie möchten Sie Ihr Haar haben?	vee MU(R)KH-ten zee eer haar HAA-ben?
Kundin:	Hinten lang, aber an den Seiten etwas kürzer.	HIN-ten lahng, AH-be(r) ahn dehn ZITE-en EHT-vahs KEWR-tse(r).
Friseur:	Schön. Möchten Sie auch eine Dauerwelle haben?	shu(r)n. MU(R)KH-ten zee owkh INE-neh DOW-e(r)-vehl-leh HAA-ben?
Kundin:	Nein, aber Waschen und Legen, bitte.	nine, AH-be(r) VAHSH-en unt LAY-gen, BIT-teh.
Friseur:	In Ordnung. Nehmen Sie hier Platz, bitte.	in ORT-nung. NAY-mehn zee heer plahts, BIT-teh.

....

Hairdresser:	What can I do for you?
Client:	A haircut, please.
Hairdresser:	How would you like your hair?
Client:	Long in back, but a little shorter on the sides.
Hairdresser:	Fine. Would you like a permanent too?
Client:	No, but a shampoo and set, please.
Hairdresser:	Fine. Take a seat here, please.

AT THE BARBERSHOP

Is there a barbershop nearby?	Gibt es hier in der Nähe einen Herrenfriseur?	gipt ehs heer in dehr NAY-eh INE-en HEH-ren-fri-zur?
I need a haircut, please.	**Würden Sie mir bitte die Haare schneiden.**	**WU(R)-den zee meer BIT-teh dee HAA-reh SHNYE-den.**

Long in front, (not too) short in back.	Vorne lang, hinten (nicht zu) kurz.	FOR-neh lahng, HIN-ten [nikht tsoo] koorts.
Leave it longer/take a little off . . .	Lassen Sie es ____ länger/ Nehmen Sie ____ etwas weg.	LAHS-en zee ehs ____ LEHN-ge(r)/ NAY-men zee ____ EHT-vahs vehk.
_on top.	_oben	_OH-ben
_on the sides.	_an den Seiten	_ahn dehn ZITE-en
_on the neck.	_im Nacken	_im NAH-ken
That's enough.	**Das genügt.**	**dahs geh-NEWKT.**
I'd like a shave, please.	**Rasieren, bitte.**	**rah-ZEE-ren, BIT-teh.**
Please trim my . . .	Stutzen Sie mir bitte . . .	SHTUT-sen zee meer BIT-teh . . .
_beard.	_den Bart.	_dehn baart.
_moustache.	_den Schnurbart.	_dehn SHNOOR-baart.
_sideburns.	_die Koteletten.	_dee kot-LEHT-ten.

AT THE BEAUTY SALON

Is there a hairdresser's/ beauty salon in the hotel?	Gibt's einen Friseur/ Damensalon im Hotel?	gipts INE-en fri-ZUR/DAA-men-zaa-lon im ho-TEL?
Do I need an appointment?	Muss ich mich anmelden?	mus ikh mikh AHN-mehl-den?
Can I make an appointment for today/tomorrow?	Kann ich für heute/morgen einen Termin haben?	kahn ikh fewr HOY-teh/MOR-gen INE-en tehr-MEEN HAA-ben?
I need a haircut, please.	Haare schneiden, bitte.	HAA-reh SHNYE-den, BIT-teh.
Don't cut it too short.	**Nicht zu kurz schneiden.**	**nikht tsoo koorts SHNYE-den.**
Show me photos of new hairstyles, please.	Zeigen Sie mir bitte Fotos von neuen Frisuren.	TSYE-gen zee meer BIT-teh FOH-tohs fon NOY-en fri-ZOOR-en.
I'd like . . .	**Ich möchte . . .**	**ikh MU(R)KH-teh . . .**

_just a shampoo and set.	_nur Waschen und Legen.	_noor VAHSH-en unt LAY-gen.
_a permanent.	_eine Dauer-welle.	_INE-eh DOW-e(r)-vehl-leh.
_a new hairdo.	_eine neue Frisur.	_INE-eh NOY-eh fri-ZOOR.
_a touch-up.	_eine Auffrischung.	_INE-eh OWF-frish-ung.
_a manicure.	_eine Manikūre.	_INE-eh MAH-ni-kew-reh.
_a color rinse.	_eine Farbspülung.	_INE-eh FAHRP-shpew-lung.
Do you have a color chart?	Haben Sie eine Farbtabelle?	HAA-ben zee INE-eh FAHRP-tah-beh-leh?
This time I'd like . . .	Diesmal möchte ich . . .	DEES-maal MU(R)KH-teh ikh . . .
_light/dark blond.	_hell-/dunkel-blond.	_HEHL-/DUN-kel-blont.
_brunette/auburn.	_braun/kas-tanien-braun.	_brown/kah-STAA-nyen-brown.
_a lighter/darker color.	_eine hellere/dunklere Farbe.	_INE-eh HEHL-lehr-eh/DUN-klehr-eh FAHR-beh.
(No) hair spray, please.	(Kein) Haarspray, bitte.	[kine] HAAR-shpray, BIT-teh.
That's fine, thank you.	So ist es schön, danke.	zoh ist ehs shu(r)n, DAHN-keh.

LAUNDRY AND DRY CLEANING

Is there____ nearby?	Gibt es ____ in der Nähe?	gipt ehs ____ in dehr NAY-eh?
_a laundry	_eine Wäscherei	_INE-eh vehsh-eh-RYE
_a dry cleaner's	_eine (chemi-sche) Reinigung	_INE-eh (KHAY-mi-sheh) RYE-ni-gung
_a laundromat	_einen Waschsalon	_INE-en VAHSH-zaa-lon

I want to have these clothes . . .	Ich möchte diese Kleider ____ lassen.	ikh MU(R)KH-teh DEE-zeh KLYE-de(r) ____ LAHS-sen.
_washed.	_waschen	_VAHSH-en
_dry-cleaned.	_reinigen	_RYE-ni-gen
_ironed/pressed.	_bügeln/dampf-bügeln	_BEW-geln/DAHMPF-bew-geln
When will they be ready?	Wann sind sie fertig?	vahn zint zee FEHR-tikh?
I need them . . .	Ich brauche sie . . .	ikh BROW-kheh zee . . .
_as soon as possible.	_so bald wie möglich.	_zoh bahlt vee MU(R)-glikh.
_today/tonight.	_heute/heute Abend.	_HOY-teh/HOY-teh AA-behnt.
Can you . . .	Können Sie . . .	KU(R)-nen zee . . .
_sew on this button?	_diesen Knopf annähen?	_DEE-zen knopf AHN-nay-en?
_remove this stain?	_diesen Fleck entfernen?	_DEE-zen flehk ehnt-FEHR-nen?
Is my laundry ready?	Ist meine Wäsche fertig?	ist MINE-eh VEHSH-eh FEHR-tikh?
Something is missing.	Es fehlt etwas.	ehs fehlt EHT-vahs.
This piece isn't mine.	Dieses Stück gehört mir nicht.	DEE-zehs shtewk geh-HU(R)RT meer nikht.

10 HEALTH CARE

Medical facilities and services in Germany, Switzerland, and Austria are modern and efficient. For minor problems, you can rely on a local pharmacist for advice.

DIALOGUE   At the Pharmacy (In Der Apotheke)

Apotheker:	Womit kann ich Ihnen dienen?	voh-MIT kahn ikh EE-nen DEE-nen?
Reisende:	Haben Sie etwas gegen Husten?	HAA-ben zee EHT-vahs GAY-gen HOOS-ten?
Apotheker:	Sicher. Hätten Sie lieber Hustensaft oder Hustenbonbons?	HEHT-ten zee LEE-be(r) HOOS-ten-zahft OH-de(r) HOOS-ten-bong-bongs?
Reisende:	Was würden Sie empfehlen?	vahs VU(R)R-den zee ehm-PFAY-len?
Apotheker:	Wie schwer ist der Husten?	vee shvehr ist dehr HOOS-ten?
Reisende:	Er ist relativ leicht.	ehr ist ray-lah-TEEF lyekht.
Apotheker:	Dann probieren Sie diese Bonbons.	dahn pro-BEER-en zee DEE-zeh bong-BONGS.

Pharmacist:	How can I help you?
Traveler:	Do you have something for a cough?
Pharmacist:	Of course. Would you prefer cough syrup or cough drops?
Traveler:	What would you recommend?
Pharmacist:	How bad is the cough?
Traveler:	It's relatively light.
Pharmacist:	Then try these drops.

AT THE PHARMACY

A typical *Apotheke* (pharmacy) in German-speaking countries will be more specialized than its American counterpart and will deal primarily with prescription and over-the-counter drugs, as well as other health products, including herbal teas and remedies. You'll find toiletries, household articles, and nonprescription medicines at a *Drogerie* (drug store). All larger towns have an all-night pharmacy, and the address is posted on the door or window of every pharmacy in town—and in the local phone book.

Where can I find an (all-night) pharmacy?	Wo finde ich eine Apotheke (mit Nachtdienst)?	voh FIN-deh ikh INE-eh ah-poh-TAY-keh [mit NAHKHT-deenst]?
When does it open/close?	Wann öffnet/ schließt sie?	vahn U(R)F-net/shleest zee?
I need something for . . .	**Ich brauche etwas gegen . . .**	**ikh BROW-kheh EHT-vahs GAY-gen . . .**
_a cold.	_eine Erkältung.	_INE-eh ehr-KEHL-tung.
_a sore throat.	_Halsschmerzen.	_HAHLS-shmehr-tsen.
_a cough.	_Husten.	_HOOS-ten.
_constipation.	_Verstopfung.	_fehr-SHTOP-fung.
_diarrhea.	_Durchfall.	_DURKH-fahl.
_fever.	_Fieber.	_FEE-be(r).
_a hangover.	_Kater.	_KAA-te(r).
_hay fever.	_Heuschnupfen.	_HOY-shnup-fen.
_headache.	**_Kopfschmerzen.**	**_KOPF-shmehr-tsen.**
_indigestion.	**_Magenverstimmung.**	**_MAA-gen-fehr-shtim-mung.**
_insect bites.	_Insektenstiche.	_in-ZEHK-ten-shtikh-eh.
_motion sickness.	_Reisekrankheit.	_RYE-zeh-krahnk-hite.
_sunburn.	_Sonnenbrand.	_ZON-nen-brahnt.
_a toothache.	_Zahnschmerzen.	_TSAAN-shmehrt-sen.
Can you fill this prescription for me?	Können Sie mir dieses Rezept anfertigen?	KU(R)-nen zee meer DEE-zehs reh-TSEHPT AHN-fehr-tig-en?

I'll wait for it.	Ich warte darauf.	ikh VAAR-teh dah-ROWF.
It's urgent.	Es ist dringend.	ehs ist DRING-ent.
I need . . .	**Ich brauche . . .**	**ikh BROW-kheh . . .**
_an antacid.	_ein Antiacidum.	_ine ahn-tee-AA-si-doom.
_an antiseptic.	_ein Antiseptikum.	_ine ahn-tee-ZEHP-ti-koom.
_antiseptic cream.	_Wundsalbe.	_VUNT-zaal-beh.
_aspirin.	_Aspirin.	_ah-spi-REEN.
_bandages.	_Verbandzeug.	_fehr-BAHNT-tsoyk.
_Band-Aids.	**_Heftpflaster.**	**_HEHFT-pflahs-te(r).**
_contact lens solution.	_Kontaktlinsen-flüssigkeit.	_kon-TAHKT-lin-zen-flews-ikh-kite.
_contraceptives.	**_Verhütungsmittel.**	**_fehr-HEW-tungs-mit-tel.**
_corn cushions.	_Hühneraugen-pflaster.	_HEW-nehr-ow-gen-pflahs-te(r).
_cotton balls.	_Watte.	_VAH-teh.
_cough drops/syrup.	_Hustenbonbons/-saft.	_HOOS-ten-bong-bongs/-zahft.
_disinfectant.	_Desinfektions-mittel.	_deh-sin-fehk-TSIOHNS-mit-tel.
_eardrops.	_Ohrentropfen.	_OHR-en-trop-fen.
_eyedrops.	_Augentropfen.	_OW-gen-trop-fen.
_insect repellent/spray.	_Insektenschutz/Insektizid.	_in-ZEHK-ten-shuts/in-zehk-ti-TSEET.
_iodine.	_Jod.	_yoht.
_a laxative.	_ein Abführmittel.	_ine AHP-fewr-mit-tel.
_mouthwash.	_Mundwasser.	_MUNT-vahs-se(r).
_a pain killer/analgesic.	_ein Schmerzmittel.	_ine SHMEHRTS-mit-tel.
_sanitary napkins.	**_Damenbinden.**	**_DAA-men-bin-den.**
_sleeping pills.	_Schlaftabletten.	_SHLAAF-tah-bleht-ten.
_suppositories.	_Zäpfchen.	_TSEHPF-khen.

_tampons.	_Tampons.	_TAHM-pongs.
_a thermometer.	_ein Thermometer.	_ine tehr-mo-MAY-te(r).
_throat lozenges.	_Halspastillen.	_HAHLS-pahs-til-en.
_a tranquillizer.	_ein Beruhigungs-mittel.	_ine beh-ROO-i-gungs-mit-tel.
_vitamins.	_Vitamine.	_vee-taa-MEE-neh.

FINDING A DOCTOR

In an emergency, you can call the *ärztlicher Notdienst* (emergency medical service), listed at the beginning of every telephone directory. Otherwise your hotel or the *Fremdenverkehrsbüro* (tourist information office) should be able to refer you to a doctor.

I need a doctor right away.	Ich brauche schnell einen Arzt.	ikh BROW-kheh shnehl INE-en ahrtst.
Can you call me a doctor?	Können Sie mir einen Arzt rufen?	KU(R)-nen zee meer INE-en ahrtst ROO-fen?
Is there a doctor here who speaks English?	Gibt es hier einen Arzt, der Englisch spricht?	gipt ehs heer INE-en ahrtst, dehr EHN-glish shprikht?
Can he/she see me here in the hotel?	Kann er/sie mich hier im Hotel sehen?	kahn ehr/zee mikh heer im ho-TEL ZAY-en?
Can you recommend a/an . . .	Können Sie mir einen _____ empfehlen?	KU(R)-nen zee meer INE-en _____ ehm-PFAY-len?
_general practitioner?	_praktischen Arzt	_PRAHK-tish-en ahrtst
_pediatrician?	_Kinderarzt	_KIN-de(r)-ahrtst
_gynecologist?	_Frauenarzt	_FROW-en-ahrtst
_eye doctor?	_Augenarzt	_OW-gen-ahrtst
Where's the doctor's office?	Wo ist die Arztpraxis?	voh ist dee AHRTST-prahk-sis?
When are the office hours?	Wann sind die Sprechstunden?	vahn zint dee SHPREKH-shtun-den?

111

Can I have an appointment . . .	Kann ich ____ einen Termin haben?	kahn ikh ____ INE-en tehr-MEEN HAA-ben?
_as soon as possible?	_so bald wie möglich	_zoh bahlt vee MU(R)G-likh
_today/tomorrow?	_heute/morgen	_HOY-teh/MOR-gen

TALKING TO THE DOCTOR

I don't feel well.	Ich fühle mich nicht wohl.	ikh FEW-leh mikh nikht vohl.
I'm sick.	Ich bin krank.	ikh bin krahnk.
I don't know what's wrong with me.	Ich weiß nicht, was mir fehlt.	ikh vice nikht, vahs meer fehlt.
I have a fever/no fever.	Ich habe (kein) Fieber.	ikh HAA-beh (kine) FEE-be(r).
I'm dizzy/nauseated.	Mir ist schwindlig/übel.	meer ist SHVIND-likh/EW-bel.
I've been vomiting.	Ich habe mich übergeben.	ikh HAA-beh mikh ew-be(r)-GAY-ben.
I'm constipated.	Ich habe Verstopfung.	ikh HAA-beh fehr-SHTOP-fung.
I have diarrhea.	Ich habe Durchfall.	ikh HAA-beh DURKH-fahl.
I can't sleep.	Ich kann nicht schlafen.	ikh kahn nikht SHLAA-fen.
I have . . .	Ich habe . . .	ikh HAA-beh . . .
_an abscess.	_einen Abszess.	_INE-en ahps-TSEHS.
_asthma.	_Asthma.	_AHST-mah.
_a backache.	_Rücken-schmerzen.	_REW-ken-shmehrt-sen.
_a broken leg.	_einen Beinbruch.	_INE-en BINE-brukh.
_a bruise.	_eine Quetschung.	_INE-eh KVEHTSH-ung.
_a burn.	_eine Brandwunde.	_INE-eh BRAHNT-vun-deh.
_a cold.	_eine Erkältung.	_INE-eh ehr-KEHL-tung.

_a cough.	_Husten.	_HOOS-ten.
_cramps.	_Krämpfe.	_KREHM-pfeh.
_a cut.	_eine Schnittwunde.	_INE-eh SHNIT-vun-deh.
_an earache.	_Ohrenschmerzen.	_OHR-en-shmehrt-sen.
_something in my eye.	_etwas im Auge.	_EHT-vahs im OW-geh.
_the flu.	_Grippe.	_GRIP-peh.
_a fracture.	_einen Knochenbruch.	_INE-en KNOKH-en-brukh.
_a headache.	_Kopfschmerzen.	_KOPF-shmehrt-sen.
_a lump/swelling.	_eine Beule/ Schwellung.	_INE-eh BOY-leh/SHVEHL-lung.
_rheumatism.	_Rheuma.	_ROY-mah.
_a sore throat.	_Halsschmerzen.	_HAHLS-shmehrt-sen.
_a stiff neck.	_einen steifen Nacken.	_INE-en SHTYE-fen NAH-ken.
_a stomachache.	_Magen-schmerzen.	_MAA-gen-schmehrt-sen.
_sunstroke.	_einen Sonnenstich.	_INE-en ZON-nen-shtikh.
_a sty.	_einen Augen-liederbrand.	_INE-en OW-gen-lee-de(r)-brahnt.
I'm (not) allergic to penicillin.	**Ich bin gegen** Penizillin (nicht) **allergisch.**	i(h)h bin GAY-gen peh-ni-tsil-LEEN [nikht] ah-LEHR-gish.
I'm a diabetic and take insulin/this medicine.	**Ich bin Diabetiker und nehme Insulin**/dieses Medikament.	ikh bin dee-ah-BEH-ti-ke(r) unt NAY-meh in-zoo-LEEN/DEE-zehs meh-di-kah-MEHNT.
I have heart trouble.	Ich bin herzkrank.	ikh bin HEHRTS-krahnk.
I had a heart attack four years ago.	Vor vier Jahren erlitt ich einen Herzanfall.	for feer YAA-ren ehr-LIT ikh INE-en HEHRTS-ahn-fahl.

I've had this pain for two days.	Seit zwei Tagen habe ich diese Schmerzen.	zite tsvye TAA-gen HAA-beh ikh DEE-zeh SHMEHRT-sehn.
I have menstrual pains.	Ich habe Menstruations-beschwerden.	ikh HAA-beh mehn-stru-ah-TSIOHNS-beh-shvehr-den.
I'm four months' pregnant.	Ich bin im vierten Monat schwanger.	ikh bin im FEER-ten MOH-naat SHVAHNG-e(r).

PARTS OF THE BODY

My ____ hurts.	Mir tut/tun* ____ weh.	meer toot/toon ____ vay.
_ankle	_der Knöchel	_dehr KNU(R)-khel
_appendix	_der Blind-darm	_dehr BLINT-dahrm
_arm	**_der Arm**	**_dehr ahrm**
_back	_der Rücken	_dehr REW-ken
_bladder	_die Blase	_dee BLAA-zeh
_bowels	_der Darm	_dehr dahrm
_breast	**_die Brust**	**_dee broost**
_buttocks	_das Gesäß	_dahs geh-SEHS
_chest	**_der Brustkorb**	**_dehr BROOST-korp**
_ear	_das Ohr	_dahs ohr
_eye/eyes	_das Auge/die Augen	_dahs OW-geh/dee OW-gen
_face	_das Gesicht	_dahs geh-ZIKHT
_finger	_der Finger	_dehr FIN-ge(r)
_foot/feet	_der Fuß/die Füße	_dehr foos/dee FEWS-seh
_gland	_die Drüse	_dee DREW-zeh
_hand	_die Hand	_dee hahnt
_head	_der Kopf	_dehr kopf

*Tun is the plural form of the verb, as in Mir tun die Augen weh (literally, my eyes hurt me).

_heart	_das Herz	_dash hehrts
_hip	_die Hüfte	_dee HEWF-teh
_jaw	_der Kiefer	_dehr KEE-fe(r)
_joint	_das Gelenk	_dahs geh-LEHNK
_kidney(s)	_die Niere(n)	_dee NEER-eh/NEER-en
_knee	_das Knie	_dahs knee
_leg	_das Bein	_dahs bine
_lip	_die Lippe	_dee LIP-peh
_liver	_die Leber	_dee LAY-be(r)
_lung(s)	_die Lunge(n)	_dee LUNG-eh/LUNG-en
_mouth	_der Mund	_dehr munt
_muscle	_der Muskel	_dehr MUS-kel
_neck	_der Hals	_dehr hahls
_nose	_die Nase	_dee NAA-zeh
_penis	_der Penis	_dehr PAY-nis
_rib(s)	_die Rippe(n)	_die RIP-peh/RIP-pen
_shoulder	_die Schulter	_dee SHUL-te(r)
_skin	_die Haut	_dee howt
_spine	_die Wirbelsäule	_dee VEER-bel-zoy-leh
_stomach	**_der Magen**	**_dehr MAA-gen**
_tendon	_die Sehne	_dee ZAY-neh
_thigh	_der Schenkel	_dehr SHEHN-kel
_throat	**_der Hals**	**_dehr hahls**
_thumb	_der Daumen	_dehr DOW-men
_toe(s)	_die Zehe (n)	_dee TSEH-eh/TSEH-en
_tooth/teeth	_der Zahn/die Zähne	_dehr TSAAN/dee TSAY-neh
_tongue	_die Zunge	_dee TSUN-geh
_tonsils	_die Mandeln	_dee MAHN-deln
_vagina	_die Scheide	_dee SHYE-deh
_vein	_die Vene	_dee VAY-neh
_wrist	_das Handgelenk	_dahs HAHNT-geh-lehnk

115

What You'll Hear From the Doctor

Wo haben Sie Schmerzen?	voh HAA-ben zee SHMEHRT-sen?	Where does it hurt?
Seit wann haben sie diese Schmerzen?	zite vahn HAA-ben zee DEE-zeh SHMEHRT-sen?	How long have you had these pains?
Welche Symptome haben Sie?	VEHL-kheh ZOOMP-toh-meh HAA-ben zee?	What symptoms do you have?
Wie werden Sie behandelt?	vee VEHR-den zee beh-HAHN-delt?	How are you being treated?
Welche Medikamente nehmen Sie?	VEHL-kheh meh-di-kah-MEHN-teh NAY-men zee?	What medicines are you taking?
Ziehen Sie sich aus/an.	TSEE-en zee zikh ows/ahn.	Undress/Get dressed.
Machen Sie den Oberkörper frei.	MAHKH-en zee dehn OH-be(r)-ku(r)r-pe(r) frye.	Undress to the waist.
Legen Sie sich hierhin.	LAY-gen zee zikh heer-HIN.	Lie down here.
Öffnen Sie den Mund.	U(R)F-nen zee dehn munt.	Open your mouth.
Zeigen Sie die Zunge.	TSYE-gen zee dee TSUN-geh.	Stick our your tongue.
Husten Sie.	HOOS-ten zee.	Cough.
Tief durchatmen.	teef DURKH-aht-men.	Breathe deeply.
Zeigen Sie mir, wo es weh tut.	TSYE_gen zee meer, voh ehs vay toot.	Show me where it hurts.
Ich werde ____ messen.	ikh VEHR-deh ____ MEHS-sen.	I'm going to take . . .
_Ihre Temperatur	_EE-reh tehm-pay-raa-TOOR	_your temperature.
_Ihren Blutdruck/Puls	_EE-ren BLOOT-druk/puls	_blood pressure/pulse.
Ich brauche eine . . .	ikh BROW-kheh INE-eh . . .	I need a . . .
_Blutprobe.	_BLOOT-proh-beh.	_blood sample.

_Urinprobe.	_oo-REEN-proh-beh.	_urine sample.
_Stuhlprobe.	_SHTOOL-proh-beh.	_stool sample.
Ich gebe Ihnen eine Spritze.	ikh GAY-beh EE-nen INE-eh SHPRIT-seh.	I'm giving you an injection.
Sie müssen . . .	zee MEWS-en . . .	You have to . . .
_sich röntgen lassen.	_zikh RU(R)NT-gen LAHS-sen.	_be X-rayed.
_einen Facharzt sehen.	_INE-en FAHKH-ahrtst ZAY-en.	_see a specialist.
_drei Tage im Bett bleiben.	_drye TAA-geh im beht BLYE-ben.	_stay in bed for three days.
_ins Kranken-haus gehen.	_ins KRAHN-ken-hows GAY-en.	_go to the hospital.
Es ist (nicht) ernst.	ehs ist [nikht] ehrnst.	It's (not) serious.
Es ist . . .	ehs ist . . .	It's . . .
_gebrochen.	_geh-BROKH-en.	_broken.
_verrenkt.	_fehr-REHNKT.	_dislocated.
_verstaucht.	_fehr-SHTOWKHT.	_sprained.
_gerissen.	_geh-RIS-sen.	_torn.
_infiziert.	_in-fi-TSEERT.	_infected.
Sie haben (eine) . . .	zee HAA-ben [INE-eh] . . .	You have (a/an) . . .
_Blasenentzün-dung.	_BLAA-zen-ehn-tsewn-dung.	_bladder infection.
_Blinddarm-entzündung.	_BLINT-dahrm-ehn-tswen-dung.	_appendicitis.
_Gelbsucht.	_GEHLP-sukht.	_jaundice.
_Geschlechts-krankheit.	_geh-SHLEHKHTS-krahnk-hite.	_venereal disease.
_Grippe.	_GRIP-peh.	_the flu.
_Hepatitis.	_heh-pah-TEE-tis.	_hepatitis.
_einen Knochen-bruch.	_IFH-nen KNOKH-en-brukh.	_fracture.
_Lebensmit-telvergiftung.	_LAY-bens-mi-tel-fehr-gif-tung.	_food poisoning.
_Lungenentzün-dung.	_LUNG-en-ehn-tsewn-dung.	_pneumonia.

| _Magenentzün-dung. | _MAA-gen-ehn-tsewn-dung. | _gastritis. |
| _Masern. | _MAH-zern. | _measles. |

Patients' Questions

Is it serious/contagious?	Ist es ernst/ansteckend?	ist ehs ehrnst/AHN-shteh-kehnt
What exactly is wrong with me?	**Was genau fehlt mir?**	**vahs geh-NOW fehlt meer?**
How long should I stay in bed?	Wie lange soll ich im Bett bleiben?	vee LAHNG-eh zol ik im beht BLYE-ben?
When can I travel again?	Wann kann ich wieder reisen?	vahn kahn ik VEE-de(r) RYE-zen?
Do I need a prescription?	**Brauche ich ein Rezept?**	**BROW-kheh ik ine reh-TSEHPT?**
Could you please fill out this medical form?	Könnten Sie mir bitte dieses Krankenkasse-formular aus-füllen?	KU(R)N-ten zee meer BIT-teh DEE-zehs KRAHN-ken-kahs-seh-for-moo-lahr OWS-few-len?
May I have a receipt for my insurance?	Kann ich eine Quittung für meine Krankenkasse haben?	kahn ik INE-eh KVIT-tung fewr MINE-eh KRAHN-ken-kahs-seh HAA-ben?

AT THE HOSPITAL

Help me!	Helfen Sie mir!	HEHL-fen zee meer!
It's an emergency.	**Es ist ein Notfall.**	**ehs ist ine NOHT-fahl.**
Call a doctor/ambulance immediately.	Rufen Sie sofort einen Arzt/Krankenwagen.	ROO-fen zee zoh-FORT INE-en ahrtst/KRAHN-ken-vaa-gen.
Get me (him/her) to the hospital as fast as possible.	Bringen Sie mich (ihn/sie) so schnell wie möglich ins Krankenhaus.	BRIN-gen zee mikh [een/zee] zoh shnehl vee MU(R)G-likh ins KRAHN-ken-hows.

I was in an accident.	Ich hatte einen Unfall.	ikh HAA-teh INE-en UN-fahl.
I need first aid.	Ich brauche erste Hilfe.	ikh BROW-kheh EHRS-teh HIL-feh.
I'm (she/he is) bleeding.	Ich blute (sie/er blutet).	ikh BLOO-teh [zee/ehr BLOO-tet].
I've (she/he has) lost a lot of blood.	Ich habe (sie/er hat) viel Blut verloren.	ikh HAA-beh [zee/ehr haht] feel bloot fehr-LOH-ren.
She's/he's unconscious.	Sie/er ist bewusstlos.	zee/ehr ist beh-VUST-lohs.
I'm afraid something is broken/ dislocated.	Ich fürchte, es ist etwas gebrochen/ verrenkt.	ikh FEWRKH-teh, ehs ist EHT-vahs geh-BROKH-en/fehr-REHNKT.
I can't move my arm/leg.	Ich kann den Arm/das Bein nicht bewegen.	ikh kahn dehn ahrm/dahs bine nikht beh-VAY-gen.
She/he burned herself/himself.	Sie/er hat sich verbrannt.	zee/ehr haht zikh fehr-BRAHNT.
I ate something poisonous.	Ich habe mich vergiftet.	ikh HAA-beh mikh fehr-GIF-tet.
Where's the doctor/nurse?	Wo ist der Arzt/ die Kranken-schwester?	voh ist dehr ahrtst/dee KRAHN-ken-shvehs-te(r)?
I'm in pain.	Ich habe Schmerzen.	ikh HAA-beh SHMEHRT-sen.
I can't eat/sleep.	Ich kann nicht essen/schlafen.	ikh kahn nikht EHS-sen/SHLAA-fen.
How long will I have to stay in the hospital?	Wie lange muss ich im Krankenhaus bleiben?	vee LAHNG-eh mus ikh im KRAHN-ken-hows BLYE-ben?
Please notify my family.	Benachrichtigen Sie bitte meine Familie.	beh-NAHKH-rikh-ti-gen zee BIT-teh MINE-eh fah-MEEL-yeh.
What are the visiting hours?	Wann sind die Besuchszeiten?	vahn zint dee beh-ZOOKS-tsye-ten?

THE DENTIST

Can you recommend a good dentist?	Können Sie mir einen guten Zahnarzt empfehlen?	KU(R)-nen zee meer INE-en GOO-ten TSAAN-ahrtst ehm-PFAY-len?
I need an (urgent) appointment to see Dr. . . .	Ich brauche einen (dringenden) Termin bei Herrn/Frau Dr. . . .	ikh BROW-kheh INE-en [DRING-en-den] tehr-MEEN bye hehrn/frow DOK-tor . . .
I have a (terrible) toothache.	**Ich habe (furchtbare) Zahnschmerzen.**	**ikh HAA-beh (FOORKHT-bahr-eh) TSAAN-shmehrt-sen.**
My gums are bleeding.	Das Zahnfleisch blutet.	dahs TSAAN-fleysh BLOO-tet.
I've lost a filling/crown.	**Ich habe eine Plombe**/Krone verloren.	**ikh HAA-beh INE-eh PLOM-beh**/KROH-neh fehr-LOH-ren.
I've broken a tooth.	Ich habe einen Zahn ausgebissen.	ikh HAA-beh INE-en tsaan OWS-geh-bis-sen.
Is it . . .	Ist es . . .	ist ehs . . .
_an abcess?	_ein Abszess?	_ine ahps-TSEHS?
_an infection?	_eine Infektion?	_INE-eh in-fehk-TSYOHN?
_a cavity?	_ein Zahn mit Karies?	_ine tsaan mit KAH-ree-ehs?
Can the tooth be saved?	Ist der Zahn noch zu retten?	ist dehr tsaan nohkh tsoo REH-ten?
I don't want to have it pulled.	Ich will ihn nicht ziehen lassen.	ikh vil een nikht TSEE-en LAHS-en.
Can you fix it temporarily?	Können Sie ihn provisorisch behandeln?	KU(R)-nen zee een pro-vi-ZOR-ish beh-HAHN-deln?
Can you fill it with silver/gold?	**Können Sie ihn mit Silberamalgam/** Gold **plombieren?**	**KU(R)-nen zee een mit ZIL-be(r)-ah-maal-gam**/gohlt plom-**BEER-en?**

Please give me a local anesthetic.	Geben Sie mir bitte eine Spritze.	GAY-ben zee mer BIT-teh INE-eh SHPRIT-seh.
Can you fix my denture/bridge?	Können Sie mein Gebiss/meine Brücke reparieren?	KU(R)-nen zee mine geh-BIS/MINE-eh BREW-keh reh-pah-REE-ren?
Do I need another appointment?	Brauche ich noch einen Termin?	BROW-kheh ikh nohkh INE-en tehr-MEEN?

THE OPTICIAN

Can you repair these glasses?	**Können Sie diese Brille reparieren?**	**KU(R)-nen zee DEE-zeh BRIL-leh reh-pah-REER-en?**
The frame/one lens is broken.	Das Gestell/eine Linse ist zerbrochen.	dahs geh-SHTEHL/INE-eh LIN-zeh ist tsehr-BROKH-en.
I've lost a contact lens.	**Ich habe eine Kontaklinse verloren.**	**ikh HAA-beh INE-eh kon-TAHKT-lin-zeh fehr-LOH-ren.**
Can you replace it?	Können Sie sie ersetzen?	KU(R)-nen zee zee ehr-ZEHT-sen?
How long will it take?	Wie lange dauert es?	vee LAHNG-eh DOW-ehrt ehs?
I'd like . . .	Ich hätte gern . . .	ikh HEHT-teh gehrn . . .
_contact lens solution	_Kontaktlinsenflüssigkeit.	_kon-TAHKT-lin-zen-flews-ikh-kite.
_a pair of sunglasses.	_eine Sonnenbrille.	_INE-eh ZON-nen-bril-leh.

11 ON THE ROAD

CAR RENTALS

Most major U.S. car-rental agencies have branches in German-speaking countries, and it is easier and usually more economical to make rental arrangements before you arrive. Be sure to specify a car with automatic transmission if you don't know how to drive one with a stick shift. You can use your U.S. driver's license to drive and, if you're over 21, to rent a car. If you're planning a long trip, however, an International Driver's License is a good idea. It's available at a nominal charge from the Canadian and American Automobile Associations, and in the United Kingdom from the Automobile Association or the Royal Automobile Club.

DIALOGUE
At the Car-Rental Agency (Bei Der Autovermietung)

Reisender:	Ich möchte einen preiswerten Kleinwagen mieten.	ikh MU(R)KH-teh INE-en PRICE-vehr-ten KLINE-vaagen MEE-ten.
Angestellte:	Wir Können Ihnen einen VW Golf mit Automatik anbieten.	veer KU(R)-nen EE-nen INE-en fow vay gohlf mit ow-toh-MAH-tik AHN-bee-ten.
Reisender:	Kann ich ihn nur über das Wochenende nehmen?	kahn ikh een noor EW-be(r) dahs VOHKH-en-ehn-deh NAY-men?
Angestellte:	Sicher. So bekommen Sie einen Sonderpreis, inklusive unbegrenzter Kilometerzahl.	ZIKH-e(r). zoh beh-KOM-men zee INE-en ZON-de(r)-price, in-klu-SEE-veh un-beh-GREHNTS-te(r) kee-loh-MAY-te(r)-tsaal.
Reisender:	Wunderbar. Abgemacht.	VUN-de(r)-baar. AHP-geh-mahkht.
Angestellte:	Schön. Darf ich Ihren Pass und Führerschein sehen?	shu(r)n. dahrf ikh EE-ren pahs unt FEW-re(r)-shine ZAY-en?

Traveler:	I'd like to rent an economical subcompact car.
Employee:	We can offer you a VW Golf with automatic transmission.
Traveler:	Can I take it just for the weekend?
Employee:	Of course. That way you get a special price, including unlimited milage.
Traveler:	Great. It's a deal.
Employee:	Fine. May I see your passport and driver's license?

Is there a car rental agency in this town?	Gibt es eine Autovermietung in dieser Stadt?	gipt ehs INE-eh OW-toh-fehr-MEE-tung in DEE-ze(r) shtaht?
I'd like to rent . . .	Ich möchte ____ mieten.	ikh MU(R)KH-teh ____ MEE-ten.
_a small/ subcompact car.	_einen Kleinwagen	_INE-en KLINE-vaa-gen
_a midsize car.	_einen Mittelklassewagen	_INE-en MIT-tel-klahs-se-vaa-gen
_a large car.	_einen großen Wagen	_INE-en GROHS-sen VAA-gen
_a station wagon.	_einen Kombiwagen	_INE-en KOM-bee-vaa-gen
_a car with automatic transmission.	_einen Wagen mit Automatik	_INE-en VAA-gen mit ot-toh-MAH-tik
_your least expensive car.	_Ihren preiswertesten Wagen	_EE-ren PRICE-vehr-tehs-ten VAA-gen
How much is it per . . .	Wieviel kostet es pro . . .	VEE-feel KOS-tet ehs proh . . .
_day/week/month?	_Tag/Woche/Monat?	_taak/VOHKH-eh/MOH-naat?
_kilometer?	_Kilometer?	_kee-loh-MAY-te(r)?
I'd like comprehensive insurance.	Ich möchte eine Vollkaskover-sicherung.	ikh MU(R)KH-teh INE-eh VOL-kahs-koh-vehr-sikh-eh-rung.

123

Does the rental price include unlimited milage?	Ist unbegrenzte Kilometerzahl im Mietpreis inbegriffen?	ist un-beh-GREHNTS-teh kee-loh-MAY-te(r)-tsaal im MEET-price IN-beh-grif-en?
Can I leave the car in another city?	Kann ich den Wagen anderswo zurückgeben?	kahn ikh dehn VAA-gen AHN-dehrs-voh tsoo-REWK-gay-ben?
Will I be charged extra for this?	Muss ich dafür extra bezahlen?	mus ikh DAH-fewr EHKS-trah beh-TSAA-len?
Do you need . . .	Brauchen Sie . . .	BROW-khen zee . . .
_my driver's license?	_meinen Führerschein?	_MINE-en FEW-re(r)-shine?
_a deposit?	_eine Kaution?	_INE-eh kow-TSYOHN?

DRIVING

Germany, Austria, and Switzerland all have extensive, well-maintained highway networks and roads, though you may find exceptions in eastern Germany. To use the *Autobahn* (super-highway) in Switzerland or Austria, you must purchase a *Vignette* (sticker) for your windshield. Buy these stickers from the Austrian and Swiss Automobile Associations before you arrive or, afterward, from gas stations and tobacconists. The speed of some drivers on the German *Autobahn*, where 130 km (80 mi) per hour is only the recommended speed limit, may take your breath away, so you may prefer to plan your route along the more scenic, secondary highways. Always try to avoid rush hour in and around cities and the seasonal peak traffic periods during school holidays.

Besides lots and meters, larger towns and cities also have Blue Zones, where you need a *Parkscheibe* (parking disk), available at no cost from tourist offices, gas stations, automobile clubs, and hotels. This honor-system parking option requires you to set your arrival time on the disk, display it on your windshield, and leave within an allotted time.

Asking Directions

| Excuse me. | Entschuldigen Sie, bitte. | ehnt-SHOOL-di-gen zee, BIT-teh. |

I've lost my way.	Ich habe mich verfahren.	ikh HAA-beh mikh fehr-FAA-ren.
Can you tell me how I get to Salzburg?	**Können Sie mir sagen, wie ich nach Salzburg komme?**	**KU(R)-nen zee meer ZAA-gen, vee ikh nahkh ZALTZ-boorg KOM-meh?**
Is this the road to ____?	Führt diese Straße nach ____?	fewrt DEE-zeh SHTRAAS-eh nahkh ____?
How far is it to the next town/to ____?	Wie weit ist es bis zur nächsten Stadt/bis zu ____?	vee vite ist ehs bis tsoor NAYKH-sten staht/bis tsoo ____?
Is there a better/faster/less congested road?	Gibt es eine bessere/schnellere/weniger befahrene Straße?	gibt ehs INE-eh BEHS-seh-reh/SHNEHL-leh-reh/VAY-nikh-er beh-FAA-reh-neh-SHTRAAS-seh?
Should I drive straight ahead/to the left/right?	Soll ich geradeaus/links/rechts fahren?	zol ikh geh-RAA-deh ows/links/rehkhts FAA-ren?
Where should I turn?	**Wo soll ich abbiegen?**	**voh zol ikh AHP-bee-gen?**
Where can I get a good road map?	Wo bekomme ich eine gute Straßenkarte?	voh beh-KOM-meh ikh INE-eh GOO-teh SHTRAAS-sen-kahr-teh?
May I park here?	**Darf ich hier parken?**	**dahrf ikh heer PAHR-ken?**
Is there a parking lot near here?	Gibt es in der Nähe einen Parkplatz?	gipt ehs in dehr NAY-eh INE-en PAHRK-plahts?
Do you have change for the parking meter?	Haben Sie Kleingeld für die Parkuhr?	HAA-ben zee KLINE-gehlt fewr dee PAHRK-oor?

DISTANCES AND LIQUID MEASURES

On the Continent, distances are expressed in kilometers and liquid measures (gas and oil, for example) in liters.* The following formulas and charts tell how to make conversions.

*In Europe, gas mileage is calculated not in miles per gallon, but in liters per 100 km.

DISTANCE CONVERSIONS		LIQUID MEASURE CONVERSIONS	
1 kilometer (km.) =.62 miles		1 liter (l) = .26 gallon	
1 mile = 1.61 km.		1 gallon = 3.78 liters	
Kilometers	**Miles**	**Liters**	**Gallons**
1	0.62	10	2.6
5	3.1	15	4.0
8	5.0	20	5.3
10	6.2	30	7.9
15	9.3	40	10.6
20	12.4	50	13.2
50	31.0	60	15.8
75	46.6	70	18.5
100	62.1		

THE SERVICE STATION

Where's the nearest gas station (with service/with self service)?	Wo ist die nächste Tankstelle [mit Bedienung/mit Selbstbedienung (SB)]?	voh ist dee NAYKH-steh TAHNK-shtehl-eh [mit beh-dee-nung/mit ZEHLPST-beh-dee-nung]?
Fill it, please, with . . .	**Volltanken, bitte, mit . . .**	**FOL-tahn-ken, BIT-teh, mit . . .**
_regular/super.	_Normal/Super.	_nor-MAAL/ZOO-pe(r).
_unleaded.	_bleifreiem Benzin.	_BLYE-frye-em behn-TSEEN.
_diesel.	_Diesel.	_DEE-zel.
Give me 40 liters super.	**Geben Sie mir vierzig Liter Super.**	**GAY-ben zee meer FEER-tsikh LEE-te(r) ZOO-pe(r).**
Please check the . . .	**Prüfen Sie bitte . . .**	**PREW-fen zee BIT-teh . . .**
_oil.	_den Ölstand.	_dehn U(R)L-shtahnt.
_water.	_das Wasser.	_dahs VAHS-se(r).
_battery.	_die Batterie.	_dee bah-teh-REE.
_brake fluid.	_die Brems-flüssigkeit.	_dee BREHMS-flews-sikh-kite.

_tire pressure.	_den Reifendruck.	_dehn REY-fen-druk.
_spare tire.	_den Ersatzreifen.	_dehn ehr-ZAHTS-rye-fen.
_lights.	_die Beleuchtung.	_dee beh-LOYKH-tung.
Please change the . . .	Wechseln Sie bitte . . .	VEHK-seln zee BIT-teh . . .
_oil.	_das Motoröl.	_dahs moh-TOHR-u(r)l.
_tire.	_den Reifen.	_dehn RYE-fen.
_fan belt.	_den Keilriemen.	_dehn KILE-ree-men.
_spark plugs.	_die Zündkerzen.	_TSEWNT-kehr-tsen.
_wipers.	_die Scheibenwischer.	_dee SHYE-ben-vishe(r).
Please clean the windshield.	Reinigen Sie bitte die Windschutzscheibe.	RYE-ni-gen zee BIT-teh dee VINT-shuts-shye-beh.

EMERGENCIES AND CAR PROBLEMS

Where's the nearest garage (for repairs)?	Wo ist die nächste Reparaturwerkstatt?	voh ist dee NAYKH-steh reh-pah-rah-TOOR-vehrk-shtaht?
I need a mechanic/tow truck.	Ich brauche einen Mechaniker/Abschleppwagen.	ikh BROW-kheh INE-en meh-KHAH-ni-ke(r)/AHP-shlehp-vaa-gen.
My car has broken down.	Mein Wagen hat eine Panne.	mine VAA-gen haht INE-eh PAHN-eh.
It won't start.	Er springt nicht an.	ehr shpringt nikht ahn.
The battery is dead.	Die Batterie ist leer.	dee bah-teh-REE ist layr.
I have a flat tire.	Ich habe einen Platten.	ikh HAA-beh INE-en PLAHT-ten.
The engine overheats.	Der Motor läuft zu heiß.	dehr moh-TOHR loyft tsoo hice.
I've run out of gas.	Der Tank ist leer.	dehr tahnk ist layr.
I've locked the keys inside the car.	Ich habe die Schlüssel im Wagen eingeschlossen.	ikh HAA-beh dee SHLEWS-sel im VAA-gen INE-geh-shlos-sen.

This is broken.	Das ist kaputt.	dahs ist kah-POOT.
The engine is making a funny sound.	Der Motor macht ein komisches Geräusch.	dehr moh-TOHR mahkt ine KOH-mish-es geh-ROYSH.
Something is wrong with the . . .	. . . ist/sind nicht in Ordnung.	. . . ist/zint nikht in ORT-nung.
_directional signals.	_Die Blinklichter	_dee BLINK-likh-te(r)
_headlights.	_Die Scheinwerfer	_dee SHINE-vehr-fe(r)
_the electrical system.	_Die elektrische Anlage	_dee eh-LEHK-trish-eh AHN-laa-geh
_the ignition.	_Die Zündung	_dee TSEWN-dung
_the starter.	_Der Anlasser	_dehr AHN-lahs-se(r)
_carburetor.	_Der Vergaser	_dehr vehr-GAA-ze(r)
_fuel pump.	_Die Benzinpumpe	_dee behn-TSEEN-pum-peh
_brakes.	_Die Bremsen	_dee BREHM-zen
_radiator.	_Der Kühler	_dehr KEW-le(r)
_exhaust pipe.	_Der Auspuff	_dehr OWS-puf
_transmission.	_Das Getriebe	_dahs geh-TREE-beh
_wheels.	_Die Räder	_dee RAY-de(r)
Is it serious?	Ist es etwas Ernstes?	ist ehs EHT-vahs EHRN-stress?
Do you have the parts?	Haben Sie die Ersatzteile?	HAA-ben zee dee ehr-ZAHTS-tile-eh?
Can you repair it temporarily?	**Können Sie es provisorisch reparieren?**	**KU(R)-nen zee ehs pro-vee-ZOH-rish reh-pah-REE-ren?**
How long will it take?	**Wie lange dauert es?**	**vee LAHNG-eh DOW-ert ehs?**
How much will it cost?	Wieviel wird es kosten?	VEE-feel wirt ehs KOS-ten?
Can I have an itemized bill for my insurance?	Kann ich eine detaillierte Rechnung für meine Versicherung haben?	kahn ikh INE-eh deh-tah-YEER-teh REHKH-nung fewr MINE-eh fehr-ZIKH-eh-rung HAA-ben?

128

ROAD SIGNS

Ausfahrt	Exit
Ausfahrt frei halten	Don't Block Exit (Driveway)
Blaue Zone	Blue Parking Zone (requires parking disk)
Durchgangsverkehr	Through Traffic
Einbahnstrasse	One-Way Street
Einfahrt	Entrance
Einordnen	Get in Lane
Ende des Parkverbots	End of No-Parking Zone
Frostschäden	Frost Damage
Fussgängerzone	Pedestrian Zone
Gefährliches Gefälle	Dangerous Descent
Glatteis	Ice Conditions
Halt, Polizei	Stop, Police
Hupen verboten	No Horn Honking
Kurzparkzone	Limited Parking Zone
Langsam fahren	Drive Slowly
Lawinengefahr	Avalanche Danger
Links fahren	Keep Left
LKW	Trucks/Truck Route
Notausfahrt	Emergency Exit
Nur für Anlieger	Access Only for Residents
Parken verboten	No Parking
Rechts fahren	Keep Right
Sackgasse	Dead-End Street
Schlechte Fahrbahn	Bad Road Surface
Schule	School
Stadtmitte	Center of Town
Stau	Traffic Jam
Steinschlag	Falling Rocks
Strassenarbeit auf 3 KM	Road Work for the Next 3 km
Umleitung	Detour

Verkehrsstau auf 10 KM	Traffic Backup for the Next 10 km
. . . verboten	No . . .
Vorfahrt gewähren	Yield
Vorsicht	Caution
Zoll	Customs/Border Crossing

NO ENTRY FOR MOTOR VEHICLES

DANGEROUS INTERSECTION AHEAD

STOP

NO ENTRY

MINIMUM SPEED (km/hr)

SPEED LIMIT (km/hr)

DIRECTION TO BE FOLLOWED (at the next intersection)

OVERHEAD CLEARANCE (meters)

ROTARY

NO PASSING

END OF NO PASSING ZONE

END OF RESTRICTION

NO LEFT TURN

NO U-TURN

NO PARKING

131

ONE WAY

DEAD END

PARKING

SUPERHIGHWAY

YIELD

GAS

DANGER AHEAD

DANGEROUS
DESCENT

BUMPS

ROAD NARROWS

LEVEL (RAILROAD)
CROSSING

TWO-WAY
TRAFFIC

SLIPPERY ROAD

CAUTION—
SHARP CURVE

PEDESTRIAN
CROSSING

TELEPHONES

The easiest way to make a telephone call is from your hotel, but hotels levy hefty surcharges. You'll save money by using the public phones, which are relatively easy to operate and usually have multilingual instructions posted inside. Most operators speak English. Most post offices have public phones and sometimes fax machines. From these and from most other public phones, you can place direct-dial long-distance and international calls. Throughout Germany and Switzerland and in Austrian cities, many telephone booths require a phone card instead of coins. The cards come in varying denominations and can be purchased at post offices, train stations, tobacconists, and the like. Newer pay phones make change and also indicate on long-distance calls when you must insert more coins.

Telephone numbers are quoted in pairs, and *zwei* over the phone becomes *zwo* [tsvoh]. When spelling out words over the phone, use the alphabet and pronunciation method described on pages 6–7.

DIALOGUE   On the Telephone (Am Telefon)

Birgit Lenz:	Firma Beck und Böttger, Lenz*, guten Tag†.	FIR-mah behk unt BU(R)T-ge(r), lehnts, GOO-ten taak.
Bernd Pohl:	Guten Morgen. Hier spricht Bernd Pohl aus Hamburg. Darf ich Herrn Beck sprechen?	GOO-ten MOR-gen. heer shprikht behrnt pohl ows HAHM-boork. dahrf ikh hehrn behk SHPREHKH-en?
Birgit Lenz:	Einen Augenblick, bitte. . . . Es tut mir leid, er ist im Moment außer Haus.	INE-en OW-gen-blik, BIT- teh. . . . ehs toot meer light, ehr ist im mo-MEHNT OWS-e(r) hows.

*When answering the phone, German speakers usually identify themselves with last names only.

†Some people might adjust their greeting to the time of day, and use *guten Morgen* or *guten Abend* instead.

Bernd Pohl:	**Wann kommt er zurück?**	vahn kohmt ehr tsoo-REWK?
Birgit Lenz:	**Um drei Uhr ungefähr.**	oom drye oor UN-ge-fayr.
Bernd Pohl:	**Sagen Sie ihm bitte, dass ich angerufen habe.**	ZAA-gen zee ihm BIT-teh, dahs ikh AHN-ge-roo-fen HAA-beh.
Birgit Lenz:	**Ich werde es ihm ausrichten. Soll er Sie zurückrufen?**	ikh VEHR-deh ehs ihm OWS-rikh-ten. zol ehr zee tsoo-REWK-roo-fen?
Bernd Pohl:	**Ja, bitte. Die Nummer hat er.**	yaa, BIT-teh. dee NUM-me(r) haht ehr.
Birgit Lenz:	**Es geht in Ordnung. Auf Wiederhören.**	ehs gayt in ORT-nung. owf VEE-de(r)-hu(r)-ren.
Bernd Pohl:	**Vielen Dank und auf Wiederhören.**	FEE-len dahnk unt owf VEE-de(r)-hu(r)-ren.

....

Birgit Lenz:	Hello. This is Birgit Lenz at Beck and Böttger.
Bernd Pohl:	Good morning. This is Bernard Pohl calling from Hamburg. May I speak to Mr. Beck?
Birgit Lenz:	Just a moment. . . . I'm sorry, he's away right now.
Bernd Pohl:	When will be be back?
Birgit Lenz:	Around three.
Bernd Pohl:	Please tell him I called.
Birgit Lenz:	I'll give him the message. Should he call you back?
Bernd Pohl:	Yes, please. He has my number.
Birgit Lenz:	I'll see that he calls you. Good-bye.
Bernd Pohl:	Thank you and good-bye.

| Where's a telephone/ telephone directory? | Wo ist ein Telefon/ Telefonbuch? | voh ist ine tay-lay-FOHN/tay-lay-FOHN-bookh? |
| Is there a phone booth near here? | Gibt es in der Nähe eine Telefonzelle? | gipt ehs in dehr NAY-eh INE-eh tay-lay-FOHN-tsehl-leh? |

May I use your phone?	Darf ich Ihr Telefon benutzen?	dahrf ikh eer tay-lay-FOHN beh-NUT-sen?
How much/what coins do I need for a local call?	Wieviel/welche Münzen brauche ich für ein Ortsgespräch?	VEE-feel/VEHL-kheh MEWN-tsen BROW-kheh ikh fewr ine ORTS-geh-shpraykh?
What's the area code for Stuttgart?	**Welche Vorwahlnummer hat Stuttgart?**	**VEHL-kheh FOHR-vaal-num-me(r) haht SHTOOT-gart?**
How do I reach the (international) operator?	Wie wahle ich die (internationale) Vermittlung?	vee VAY-leh ikh dee [in-tehr-nah-tsyo-NAA-leh] fehr-MIT-lung?
Hello. I'd like . . .	**Guten Tag. Ich möchte . . .**	**GOO-ten taak. ikh MU(R)KH-teh . . .**
_Stuttgart 14-43-70.	_Stuttgart 14-43-70.	_SHTOOT-gart [FEER-tsayn DRYE-unt-feer-zikh-ZEEP-zikh].
_(international) information.	_die (internationale) Auskunft.	_dee [in-tehr-nah-tsyo-NAA-leh] OWS-koonft.
_to place a long-distance call to London.	**_ein Ferngespräch nach London.**	**_ine FEHRN-geh-shpraykh nahkh LON-don.**
_a person-to-person call.	_ein Gespräch mit Voranmeldung.	_ine geh-SHPRAYKH mit FOHR-ahn-mehl-dung.
_a collect call.	_ein R-Gespräch.	_ine EHR-geh-shpraykh.
Please help me reach this number.	Helfen Sie mir bitte, diese Nummer zu erreichen.	HEHL-fen zee meer BIT-teh, DEE-zeh NUM-me(r) tsoo ehr-RYEKH-en.
Can I dial direct?	**Kann ich durchwählen?**	**Kahn ikh DURKH-vay-len?**
Connect me with the number/extension . . .	Verbinden Sie mich mit der Nummer/dem Nebenan-schluss . . .	fehr-BIN-den zee mikh mit dehr NUM-me(r)/dehm NAY-ben-ahn-shlus . . .

135

You gave me the wrong number.	Sie haben mich falsch verbunden.	zee HAA-ben mikh fahlsh fehr-BUN-den.
The connection is bad.	Die Verbindung ist schlecht.	dee vehr-BIN-dung ist shlehkht.
We were cut off.	Wir sind unterbrochen worden.	veer zint un-te(r)-BROKH-en VOR-den.
May I speak to Mr./Mrs. Munter?	Darf ich Herrn/Frau Munter sprechen?	dahrt ikh hehrn/frow MOON-ter SHPREHKH-EN?
Speaking.	Am Apparat.	ahm ah-pah-RAAT.
Please speak louder/more slowly.	Sprechen Sie bitte lauter/langsamer.	SHPREHKH-en zee BIT-teh LOW-te(r)/LAHNG-zaa-me(r).
Please repeat.	Wiederholen Sie, bitte.	vee-de(r)-HOH-len zee BIT-teh.
May I leave a message for Mr./Mrs. ____?	Darf ich Herrn/Frau ____ eine Nachricht hinterlassen?	dahrf ikh hehrn/frow ____ INE-eh NAKH-rikht HIN-ter-lahs-sen?

Phrases You'll Hear Over the Phone

Wer ist am Apparat?	vehr ist ahm ah-pah-RAAT?	Who's calling?
Wen wollen Sie sprechen?	vehn VOL-len zee SHPREHKH-en?	Whom do you want to speak to?
Bleiben Sie am Apparat.	BLYE-ben zee ahm ah-pah-RAAT.	Hold the line.
Es meldet sich niemand.	ehs MEHL-det zikh NEE-mahnt.	There's no answer.
Die Leitung ist besetzt.	dee LYE-tung ist beh-ZEHTST.	The line is busy.
Sie sind falsch verbunden.	zee zint fahlsh fehr-BUN-den.	You have the wrong number.
Ein Anruf für Sie.	ine AHN-roof fewr zee.	You have a call.

Welche Nummer haben Sie gewählt?	VEHL-kheh NUM-me(r) HAA-ben zee geh-VAYLT?	What number did you dial?
Sie/er ist im Moment nicht da.	zee/ehr ist im mo-MEHNT nikht daa.	She/he is not here at the moment.
Kann ich etwas ausrichten?	kahn ikh EHT-vahs OWS-rikh-ten?	Can I take a message?
Können Sie später zurückrufen?	KU(R)-nen zee SHPAY-te(r) tsoo-REWK-roo-fen?	Can you call back later?

THE POST OFFICE

The hours of Germany's *Bundespost* (Federal Postal Service) are from 8:30 AM to 6:30 PM on weekdays, and Saturday from 8:30 AM to 1:30 PM. Austrian post offices are generally open weekdays from 8 AM to noon and from 2 to 6 PM, and on Saturday from 8 to 10 AM. In Switzerland, post offices are open weekdays from 8 AM to 5:30 PM with no lunch break. Main post offices in large cities have extended hours. Mailboxes in all three countries are yellow, sometimes blue in Austria. Stamps are available at newsstands and kiosks, as well as at post offices in Switzerland and Austria, but in Germany only at post offices and postal stamp automats. All post offices receive and distribute *postlagernd*—in Switzerland *poste restante*—(general delivery) mail.

I want to mail this letter.	Ich will diesen Brief aufgeben.	ikh vil DEE-zen breef OWF-gay-ben.
Where's the nearest mailbox?	Wo ist der nächste Briefkasten?	voh ist dehr NAYKH-steh BREEF-kahs-ten?
I'm looking for the post office.	Ich suche das Postamt.	ikh ZOO-kheh dahs POST-ahmt.
Where is the window for . . .	Wo ist der Schalter für . . .	voh ist dehr SHAHL-te(r) fewr . . .
_stamps?	_Briefmarken?	_BREEF-mahr-ken?
_packages?	_Pakete?	_pah-KAY-teh?
_money orders?	_Postanweisungen?	_POST-ahn-vye-zung-en?
_telegrams?	_Telegramme?	_tay-lay-GRAAM-meh?
_general delivery?	_postlagernde Sendungen?	_POST-laa-gehrn-deh ZEHN-dung-en?

137

How much postage do I need on ____ to Canada/England/ the U.S.?	Was kostet ____ nach Kanada/ England/**in die USA?**	vahs KOS-tet ____ nahkh KAA-nah-dah/EHNG-lahnt/ in dee oo-ehs-aa?
_a letter	_ein Brief	_ine breef
_a postcard	_eine Postkarte	_INE-eh POST-kahr-teh
_an airmail letter	_ein Luftpostbrief	_ine LUFT-post-breef
_an express (special delivery) letter	_ein Eilbrief	_ine ILE-breef
_a registered letter	_ein Einschrei-bebrief	_ine INE-shrye-be-breef
_this package	_dieses Paket	_DEE-zehs pah-KAYT
When will it arrive?	Wann wird es ankommen?	vahn virt ehs AHN-kom-men?
I'd like to insure this letter/package.	Ich möchte diesen Brief/dieses Paket versich-ern lassen.	ikh MU(R)KH-teh DEE-zen breef/DEE-zehs pah-KAYT fehr-ZIKH-ern LAHS-en.
Do you have commemorative stamps for stamp collectors?	Haben Sie Sondermarken für Briefmarken-sammler?	HAA-ben zee ZOHN-de(r)-mahr-ken fewr BREEF-mahr-ken-zahm-le(r)?
May I please have . . .	**Geben Sie mir bitte . . .**	**GAY-ben zee meer BIT-teh . . .**
_ten (airmail) stamps.	_zehn (Luftpost) Briefmarken.	_tsayn (LUFT-post) BREEF-mahr-ken.
_three envelopes.	_drei Briefumschläge.	_drye BREEF-oom-shlay-geh.
Is there any mail for me?	Ist Post für mich da?	ist post fewr mikh daa?
Here's my passport.	Hier ist mein Pass.	heer ist mine pahs.

SENDING A FAX

Can I fax this to you?	Kann ich Ihnen das zufaxen?	Kahn ikh EE-nen dahs TSOO-fahksen?

138

What number do I dial?	Welche Nummer muß ich wählen?	VEHL-khuh NOO-muhr muhss ikh VAY-len?
I'd like to send a fax to . . .	Ich möchte ein Fax nach _____ aufgeben.	ikh MU(R)KH-teh ine fahks nahkh _____ OWF-gay-ben.
May I use your fax?	Darf ich bitte Ihr Faxgerät benutzen?	DARF ikh BIH-tuh eer FAHKS-geh-rayt beh-NOOTZ-en?
Could you help me dial?	Könnten Sie mir bitte helfen die Nummer zu wählen?	KUH(R)N-ten zee meer BIH-tuh HEHL-fen dee NOO-muhr tsoo VAY-len?

E-MAIL AND THE INTERNET

You'll find Internet cafés all over Europe; Munich, an e-commerce hub, is especially well-connected. Check with visitor information desks in train stations, or ask your hotel concierge, for the exact whereabouts of Internet stations.

Where is the computer?	Wo ist der Computer?	VOH ist dayr kohm-PYOO-ter?
I need to send an e-mail.	Ich muss eine E-mail verschicken.	ikh muss ine-uh EE-mayl fayr-SHIK-en.
Can I get get on the Internet?	Kann ich ins Internet gehen?	KAHN ikh ins IN-ter-net GAY-en?
Do you have a Web site?	Haben Sie eine Website?	HAH-ben zee INE-uh WEHB-site?

THE MEDIA

In the larger cities of German-speaking Europe, newspapers and magazines from all over the world are available; look for an international press dealer at the train station. Should you have trouble locating them, look in the Yellow Pages for international or English-language bookstores and newsstands. BBC and AFN (American Forces Network) radio broadcasts can be received all over Europe, and American and British TV programs are becoming increasingly available through cable and satellite hookups. Video rental shops, most of them including a large selection of English-language films, are also proliferating rapidly. You may want to tune in to German-language radio and

TV, especially news broadcasts, as this is an excellent way to improve your language skills.

Publications

Do you have ____ in English?	Haben Sie ____ in Englisch?	HAA-ben zee ____ in EHNG-lish?
_newspapers	_Zeitungen	_TSITE-ung-en
_magazines	_Zeitschriften	_TSITE-shrif-ten
_books/publications	_Bücher/Veröffentlichungen	_BEW-khe(r)/fehr-U(R)F-ehnt-likh-ung-en

Radio and TV

Are there any English-language ____ here?	Gibt es hier englischsprachige . . .	gipt ehs heer EHNG-lish-shprahkh-i-geh . . .
_radio stations	_Radiosender?	_RAA-dee-oh-zehn-de(r)?
_TV channels	_Fernsehprogramme?	_FEHRN-zay-proh-GRAAM-meh?
What is the dial setting/channel number?	Auf welcher Frequenz?/Welches Programm?	owf VEHL-khe(r) fray-KVEHNTS?/VEHL-khess proh-GRAAM?
Do you have a TV guide?	Haben Sie ein Fernsehprogramm?*	HAA-ben zee ine FEHRN-zay-proh-graam?

*The word for TV channel and TV guide is the same in German.

Before your trip, you should read something about the countries you are visiting. In addition to guidebooks, your travel agent or national tourist offices can provide information that will help you plan an itinerary. The Internet is also very useful for research. You'll find a plethora of links to the Web sites of local tourist offices, publications, attractions, and booking services on www.fodors.com. Once you reach your destination, ask your hotel concierge for a map and guide to the city.

DIALOGUE   Touring the City (Stadtbeisichtigung)

Reisender:	Was für Sehenswürdigkeiten gibt es in dieser Stadt?	vahs fewr SAY-ens-vewr-dikh-kite-en gipt ehs in DEE-ze(r) shtaht?
Hotelangestellte:	Hier gibt es eine Menge interessante Sachen zu sehen.	heer gipt ehs INE-eh MEHNG-eh in-teh-reh-SAHKH-teh ZAHKH-en tsoo ZAY-en.
Reisender:	Und wo liegen sie?	unt voh LEE-gen zee?
Hotelangestellte:	Die meisten liegen in der Altstadt.	dee MICE-ten LEE-gen in dehr AHLT-shtaht.
Reisender:	Ist es leicht, dahin zu kommen?	ist ehs lyekht dah-HIN tsoo KOM-men?
Hotelangestellte:	Ja, sicher. Der dreier Bus, der hier an der Ecke hält, fährt direkt in die Altstadt.	yaa, ZIKH-e(r). dehr DRYE-e(r) bus, dehr heer ahn dehr EH-keh hehlt, fehrt dee-REHKT in dee AHLT-shtaht.
Reisender:	Gibt es da einen Dom?	gipt ehs da INE-en dohm?
Hotelangestellte:	Ja, sogar einen sehr berühmten spätgotischen Dom und dazu mehrere Museen.	yaa, zoh-GAHR INE-en zehr beh-REWM-ten SHPAYT-goh-tish-en dohm unt dah-TSOO MEH-rehr-eh moo-ZAY-en.

Reisender:	**Vielen Dank für die Hinweise.**	FEE-len dahnk fewr dee HIN-vye-zeh.
Traveler:	What kind of sites worth seeing are there in this town?	
Hotel clerk:	There are many interesting things to see here.	
Traveler:	And where are they?	
Hotel clerk:	Most of them are in the old part of the city.	
Traveler:	Is it easy to get there?	
Hotel clerk:	Yes, of course. The number three bus that stops here on the corner goes right there.	
Traveler:	Is there a cathedral there?	
Hotel clerk:	Yes, in fact a very famous late Gothic cathedral and several museums as well.	
Traveler:	Thanks very much for the tips.	

FINDING THE SIGHTS

Where is the tourist office?	**Wo ist das Fremden-verkehrsbüro?**	voh ist dahs FREHM-den-fehr-kehrs-bew-roh?
What are the most important things to see?	**Was sind die wichtigsten Sehenswür-digkeiten?**	vahs zint dee VIKH-tikh-sten ZAY-ens-vewr-dikh-kite-en?
Do you have . . .	**Haben Sie . . .**	HAA-ben zee . . .
_a map of the town?	_einen Stadtplan?	_INE-en SHTAHT-plaan?
_a guidebook for the town/area (in English)?	_einen Stadtführer/Reiseführer für die Gegend (auf Englisch)?	_INE-en SHTAHT-few-re(r)/RYE-zeh-few-re(r) fewr dee GAY-gehnt [owf EHNG-lish]?
Can you recommend a tour of the town/an excursion?	Können Sie eine Stadtrundfahrt/einen Ausflug empfehlen?	KU(R)-nen zee INE-eh SHTAHT-runt-faart/INE-en OWS-floog ehm-PFAY-len?

Does the tour guide speak English?	Spricht der Fremdenführer Englisch?	shprikht dehr FREHM-den-few-re(r) EHNG-lish?
When/Where does the tour start?	Wann/Wo beginnt die Rundfahrt?	vahn/voh beh-GINT dee RUNT-faart?
How long does it last?	Wie lange dauert sie?	vee LAHNG-eh DOW-ert zee?
How much does it cost?	Was kostet sie?	vahs KOS-tet zee?
Does that include lunch?	Ist das Mittagessen inbegiffen?	ist dahs MIT-taag-ehs-sen IN-beh-grif-en?
We'd like an English-speaking guide for . . .	Wir möchten einen englisch-sprechenden Fremdenführer für . . .	veer MU(R)KH-ten INE-en EHNG-lish-shprehkh-en-den FREHM-den-few-re(r) fewr . . .
_an afternoon.	_einen Nachmittag.	_INE-en NAHKH-mit-taak.
_a day.	_einen Tag.	_INE-en taak.
Where is/are the . . .	**Wo ist/wo sind . . .**	**voh ist/voh zint . . .**
_abbey?	_die Abtei?	_dee ahp-TYE?
_amusement park?	_der Vergnü-gungspark?	_dehr fehrg-NEW-gungks-paark?
_aquarium?	_das Aquarium?	_dahs ah-KVAH-ree-oom?
_art galleries?	**_die Kunstgalerien?**	**_die KUNST-gah-leh-ree-en?**
_artists' quarter?	_das Künstlerviertel?	_dahs KEWNST-lehr-feer-tel?
_botanical gardens?	_der botanische Garten?	_dehr bo-TAA-nish-eh GAAR-ten?
_castle?	_das Schloss/die Burg?	_dahs shlos/dee boork?
_cathedral?	**_der Dom/die Kathedrale?**	**_dehr dohm/dee kaa-tay-DRAA-leh?**
_caves?	_die Höhlen?	_dee HU(R)-len?
_cemetery?	_der Friedhof?	_dehr FREET-hohf?

_chapel?	_die Kapelle?	_dee kah-PEHL-leh?
_church?	_die Kirche?	_dee KEER-kheh?
_city center/ downtown?	**_die Stadtmitte**/das Zentrum/die Innenstadt?	_dee SHTAHT-mit-teh/dahs TSEHN-trum/dee IN-nen-shtaht?
_city/town hall?	_das Rathaus?	_dahs RAAT-hows?
_city walls/ ramparts?	_die Stadtmauern?	_dee SHTAHT-mow-ern?
_commercial district?	_das Geschäftsviertel?	_dahs geh-SHEHFTS-feer-tel?
_concert hall?	_die Konzerthalle?	_dee kon-TSEHRT-hahl-leh?
_convent/ monastery?	_das Kloster?	_dahs KLOHS-te(r)?
_convention hall?	_die Kongresshalle?	_dee kon-GREHS-hahl-leh?
_courthouse?	_das Gericht?	_dahs geh-RIKHT?
_exhibition center?	_die Ausstellungshalle?	_dee OWS-shtehl-lungs-hahl-leh?
_factory?	_die Fabrik?	_dee fah-BRIK?
_fair (trade fair)?	_die (Handels-) Messe?	_dee [HAHN-dels-] MEHS-seh?
_flea market?	_der Flohmarkt?	_dehr FLOH-mahrkt?
_fortress?	_die Burg?	_dee boork?
_fountain?	_der (Spring-) Brunnen?	_dehr [SHPRING-] BRUN-nen?
_gardens?	_die Gärten/ Grünanlagen?	_dee GEHR-ten/GREWN-ahn-laa-gen?
_grave/tomb of ____?	_das Grab von ____?	_dahs grahp fon ____?
_harbor?	_der Hafen?	_dehr HAA-fen?
_library?	_die Bibliothek?	_dee bib-lee-oh-TAYK?
_main square?	**_der Hauptplatz?**	_dehr HOWPT-plahts?

144

_market?	_der Markt?	_dehr mahrkt?
_memorial/monument?	_das Denkmal?	_dahs DEHNK-maal?
_museum?	_das Museum?	_dahs moo-ZAY-um?
_old town?	**_die Altstadt?**	_dee AHLT-shtaht?
_open-air stage?	_die Freilichtbühne?	_dee FRYE-likht-bew-neh?
_opera house?	_das Opernhaus/die Oper?	_dahs OH-pehrn-hows/dee OH-pe(r)?
_palace?	_der Palast/das Schloss?	_dehr pah-LAHST/dahs shlos?
_park?	_der Park?	_dehr pahrk?
_planetarium?	_das Planetarium?	_dahs plah-neh-TAA-ree-um?
_river?	_der Fluss?	_dehr flus?
_ruins?	_die Ruinen?	_dee roo-EE-nen?
_shopping district?	_das Einkaufsviertel?	_dahs INE-kowfs-feer-tel?
_stadium?	_das Stadion?	_dahs SHTAA-dee-ohn?
_statue?	_die Statue?	_dee SHTAA-too-eh?
_stock exchange?	_die Börse?	_dee BU(R)-zeh?
_synagogue?	_die Synagoge?	_dee zew-nah-GOH-geh?
_theater?	_das Theater?	_dahs tay-AA-te(r)?
_tower?	_der Turm?	_dehr toorm?
_university?	_die Universität?	_dee u-nee-vehr-zi-TAYT?
_zoo?	_der Zoo?	_dehr tsoh?
How old is that building?	Wie alt ist das Gebäude?	vee ahlt ist dahs geh-BOY-deh?
Who built it?	Wer hat es gebaut?	vehr haht ehs geh-BOWT?
What monument is that?	Was für ein Denkmal ist das?	vahs fewr ine DEHNK-maal ist dahs?

145

| Where can I get souvenirs? | Wo kann man Andenken kaufen? | voh kahn mahn AHN-dehn-ken KOW-fen? |

AT THE MUSEUM

When does the museum open/close?	Wann öffnet/schließt das Museum?	vahn U(R)F-net/shleest dahs moo-ZAY-um?
How much is the admission for . . .	Was kostet der Eintritt für . . .	vahs KOS-tet dehr INE-trit fewr . . .
_an adult?	_einen Erwachsenen?	_INE-en ehr-VAHK-seh-nen?
_a child?	_ein Kind?	_ine kint?
_a senior?	_einen Rentner?	_INE-en REHNT-ne(r)?
Is there a group discount?	Gibt es eine Gruppener-mäßigung?	gipt ehs INE-eh GRUP-pen-ehr-MAYS-i-gung?
Do you have . . .	Haben Sie . . .	HAA-ben zee . . .
_a guidebook (in English)?	_einen Museumsführer (in Englisch)?	_INE-en moo-ZAY-ums-few-re(r) [in EHNG-lish]?
_an audiocassette guide to the museum?	_einen Tonband-begleiter für das Museum?	_INE-en TOHN-bahnt-beh-GLITE-e(r) fewr dahs moo-ZAY-um?
May I take (flash) pictures?	Darf man (mit Blitz) fotografieren?	dahrf mahn [mit blits] foh-toh-grah-FEE-ren?
Where can I buy reproductions/catalogs?	Wo kann man Reproduktionen/Kataloge kaufen?	woh kahn mahn ray-pro-duk-TSYOH-nen/kah-tah-LOH-geh KOW-fen?
I'm interested in . . .	Ich interessiere mich für . . .	ikh in-teh-rehs-SEER-reh mikh fewr . . .
_antiques.	_Antiquitäten.	_ahn-tik-vee-TAY-ten.
_anthropology.	_Anthropologie.	_ahn-tro-po-lo-GEE.
_archaeology.	_Archäologie.	_ahr-keh-o-lo-GEE.
_classical art.	_klassische Kunst.	_KLAHS-ish-eh kunst.
_medieval art.	_mittelalterliche Kunst.	_MIT-tel-ahl-te(r)-likh-eh kunst.

146

_Renaissance art.	_Renaissance* Kunst.	_ruh-nay-SAH[N]S* kunst.
_modern art.	_moderne Kunst.	_mo-DEHR-neh kunst.
_impressionist art.	_impressionistische Kunst.	_im-prehs-yoh-NIS-tish-eh kunst.
_expressionist art.	_expressionistische Kunst.	_ehk-sprehs-yoh-NIS-tish-eh kunst.
_surrealist art.	_surrealistische Kunst.	_sur-reh-aa-LIS-tish-eh kunst.
_ceramics.	_Keramik.	_keh-RAA-mik.
_fine arts.	_bildende Künste.	_BIL-den-deh KEWN-steh.
_furniture.	_Möbel.	_MU(R)-bel.
_geography.	_Geographie.	_gay-o-grah-FEE.
_geology.	_Geologie.	_gay-o-lo-GEE.
_handicrafts.	_Kunsthandwerk.	_KUNST-hahnt-vehrk.
_history.	_Geschichte.	_geh-SHIKH-teh.
_musical instruments.	_musikalische Instrumente.	_moo-zee-KAH-lish-eh in-stroo-MEHN-teh.
_natural history.	_Naturkunde.	_nah-TOOR-kun-deh.
_painting.	_Malerei.	_maa-leh-RYE.
_pottery.	_Töpferei.	_tu(r)p-feh-RYE.
_sculpture.	_Bildhauerei.	_BILT-how-eh-rye.
_zoology.	_Zoologie.	_tsoh-o-lo-GEE.
Who is the . . .	Wer ist der . . .	vehr ist dehr . . .
_artist?	_Künstler?	_KEWNST-le(r)?
_architect?	_Architekt?	_ahr-khi-TEHKT?
_painter?	_Maler?	_MAA-le(r)?
_sculptor?	_Bildhauer?	_BILT-how-e(r)?
Who painted that picture?	Wer hat das Bild gemalt?	vehr haht dahs bilt geh-MAALT?

---

*German speakers use the French pronunciation, nasalizing the final *n*.

When was it painted?	Wann wurde es gemalt?	vahn VOOR-deh ehs geh-MAALT?
I think it's . . .	Ich finde es . . .	ikh FIN-deh ehs . . .
_beautiful.	_schön.	_shu(r)n.
_exceptional.	_außerordentlich.	_ows-e(r)-OR-dehnt-likh.
_impressive.	_eindrucksvoll.	_INE-druks-fol.
_(un)interesting.	_(un)interessant.	_[UN-] in-teh-rehs-SAHNT.
_strange.	_merkwürdig.	_MEHRK-vu(r)-dikh.
_ugly.	_hässlich.	_HEHS-likh.

IN THE COUNTRY

Where are the most beautiful/interesting landscapes?	Wo sind die schönsten/interessantesten Landschaften?	voh zint dee SHU(R)N-sten/in-teh-rehs-SAHN-tehs-ten LAHNT-shahf-ten?
How far is it to ____?	Wie weit ist es bis ____?	vee vite ist ehs bis ____?
Is there a bus from here?	Gibt es von hier einen Bus dahin?	gipt ehs fon heer INE-en bus dah-HIN?
How long does the trip take?	Wie lange dauert die Fahrt?	vee LAHNG-eh DOW-ert dee faart?
barn	die Scheune	dee SHOY-neh
beach	der Strand	dehr shtrahnt
bridge	die Brücke	dee BREW-keh
cliff	der Felsen	dehr FEHL-zen
farm	der Bauernhof	dehr BOW-ehrn-hohf
field	das Feld	dahs fehlt
flowers	die Blumen	dee BLOO-men
footpath	der Fußweg	dehr FOOS-vehk
forest/wood	der Wald	dehr vahlt
garden	der Garten	dehr GAAR-ten
hill	der Hügel	dehr HEW-gel

inn	das Gasthaus	dahs GAHST-hows
lake	der See	dehr zay
meadow	die Wiese	dee VEE-zeh
mountain pass	der Pass	dehr pahs
pond	der Teich	dehr tyekh
river	der Fluss	dehr flus
sea	die See/das Meer	dee zay/dahs mayr
valley	das Tal	dahs taal
village	das Dorf	dahs dorf
vineyard	der Weinberg	dehr VINE-behrk
waterfall	der Wasserfall	dehr VAHS-se(r)-fahl

RELIGIOUS SERVICES

Austria and southern Germany are predominantly Roman Catholic, northern Germany is mostly Protestant, and the Swiss population is evenly divided between the two religions; but in the larger cities of all three countries you will find other denominations and religions well represented. Most churches are open to the public, but visitors should be careful not to disturb any services in progress.

Is there a _____ nearby?	Gibt es eine _____ in der Nähe?	gipt ehs INE-eh _____ in dehr NAY-eh?
_Protestant church	_evangelische Kirche	_ay-vahn-GAY-lish-eh KEER-kheh
_Catholic church	_katholische Kirche	_kah-TOH-lish-eh KEER-kheh
_synagogue	_Synagoge	_zew-nah-GOH-geh
_mosque	_Moschee	_mo-SHAY
When does the mass/service begin?	Wann beginnt die Messe/der Gottesdienst?	vahn beh-GINT dee MEHS-eh/dehr GOT-tehs-deenst?
Is there a service in English?	Gibt es einen Gottesdienst in Englisch?	gipt ehs INE-en GOT-ehs-deenst in EHNG-lish?

I'm looking for a ____ who speaks English.	Ich suche einen ____, der Englisch spricht.	ikh ZOO-kheh INE-en ____, dehr EHNG-lish shprikht.
_minister	_Pfarrer	_PFAH-re(r)
_priest	_Priester	_PREES-te(r)
_rabbi	_Rabbi(ner)	_rah-BEE-ne(r)
_mullah	_Mullah	_MOO-lah

In Germany, Switzerland, and Austria shops open between 8 and 10 AM and close between 6 and 8 PM weekdays. Department stores maintain longer opening hours than smaller shops, which sometimes close for an hour or two at lunchtime. On Saturday most shops in Germany close before 4 PM; shops in Austria and Switzerland stay open as late as 5 PM. In Switzerland, many shop owners take Monday mornings off. Most stores in all three countries are closed on Sunday. The best bet for late-night or emergency purchases is in a train station (or airport), where the stores—including groceries—stay open until 11 PM.

You will pay a hefty *Mehrwertsteuer,* or value-added tax, on purchases made in Germany (16%), Austria (10%–20%), and Switzerland (5.3%). On certain purchases, you may be able to get a refund for the tax you've paid; ask the shopkeeper for the proper forms.

DIALOGUE
At the Department Store (Im Kaufhaus)

Kunde:	Guten Tag. Ich suche Schuhe. Bin ich hier richtig?	GOO-ten taak. ikh ZOO-kheh shoo-eh. bin ikh heer RIKH-tikh?
Verkäuferin:	Jawohl. Womit kann ich Ihnen dienen?	yah-VOHL. voh-MIT kahn ikh EE-nen DEE-nen?
Kunde:	Ich brauche sehr bequeme Schuhe zum Wandern.	ikh BROW-kheh zehr beh-KVAY-meh SHOO-eh tsoom VAHN-dern.
Verkäuferin:	Möchten Sie vielleicht Wanderstiefel?	MU(R)KH-ten zee fee-LYEKHT VAHN-de(r)-shtee-fel?
Kunde:	Nein, lieber nor-male Lederschuhe mit Gummisohlen, die ich auch in der Stadt tragen kann.	nine, LEE-be(r) nor-MAA-leh LAY-der-shoo-eh mit GOO-mee-soh-len, dee ikh owkh in dehr shtaht TRAA-gen kahn.

Verkäuferin:	**Welche Größe? Und welche Farbe hätten Sie gern?**	**VEHL-kheh GRU(R)S-eh? unt VEHL-kheh FAHR-beh HEH-ten zee gehrn?**
Kunde:	**Dreiundvierzig und dunkelbraun, bitte.**	**DRYE-unt-feer-tsikh unt DUN-kel-brown, BIT-teh.**

Shopper: Hello, I'm looking for shoes. Am I in the right place?

Salesperson: Yes, indeed. What can I do for you?

Shopper: I need very comfortable shoes for hiking.

Salesperson: Perhaps you'd like hiking boots?

Shopper: No, I'd rather have normal leather shoes with rubber soles that I can also wear in town.

Salesperson: What size? And what color would you like?

Shopper: Forty-three and dark brown, please.

TYPES OF STORES

I'm looking for . . .	Ich suche . . .	ikh ZOO-kheh . . .
_an antique shop.	_ein Antiquitätengeschäft.	_ine ahn-tik-vee-TAY-ten-geh-shehft.
_an art dealer.	_einen Kunsthändler.	_INE-en KUNST-hehnt-le(r).
_a bakery.	_eine Bäckerei.	_INE-eh beh-keh-RYE.
_a bookstore.	_eine Buchhandlung.	_INE-eh BOOKH-hahnt-lung.
_a butcher shop.	_eine Metzgerei.	_INE-eh mehts-geh-RYE.
_a camera shop.	_ein Fotogeschäft.	_ine FOH-toh-geh-shehft.
_a candy store.	_einen Süßwarenladen.	_INE-en SEWS-vaa-ren-laa-den
_a cheese shop.	_ein Käsegeschäft.	_ine KAY-zeh-geh-shehft.
_a china shop.	_einen Porzellanladen.	_INE-en por-tsehl-LAAN-laa-den.

_a clothing store.	_ein Beklei-dungsgeschäft.	_ine beh-KLYE-dungs-geh-sheft.
for women.	Damenbeklei-dungsgeschäft.	DAA-men-beh-KLYE-dungs-geh-sheft.
for men.	Herrenbeklei-dungsgeschäft.	HEH-ren-beh-KLYE-dungs-geh-sheft.
for children.	Kinderbeklei-dungsgeschäft.	KIN-de(r)-beh-KLYE-dungs-geh-sheft.
_a dairy store.	_ein Milchgeschäft.	_ine MILKH-geh-sheft.
_a delicatessen.	_ein Delikates-sengeschäft.	_ine deh-li-kah-TEHS-sen-geh-sheft.
_a department store.	_ein Kaufhaus.	_ine KOWF-hows.
_a drugstore.	_eine Drogerie/Apotheke.*	_INE-eh dro-geh-REE/ah-poh-TAY-keh.
_a drycleaner's.	_eine chemische Reinigung.	_INE-eh KHAY-mish-eh RYE-ni-gung.
_an electrical (appliance) store.	_ein Elektrogeschäft.	_ine ay-LEHK-troh-geh-sheft.
_a fish market.	_eine Fischhandlung.	_INE-eh FISH-hahnt-lung.
_a flea market.	_einen Flohmarkt.	_INE-en FLOH-mahrkt.
_a flower shop.	_ein Blumengeschäft.	_ine BLOO-men-geh-sheft.
_a furrier.	_ein Pelzgeschäft.	_ine PEHLTS-geh-sheft.
_a furniture store.	_ein Möbelgeschäft.	_ine MU(R)-bel-geh-sheft.
_a gourmet grocery.	_ein Feinkost-geschäft.	_ine FINE-kost-geh-sheft.
_a grocery store.	_ein Lebensmit-telgeschäft.	_ine LAY-bens-mit-tel-geh-sheft.
_a hardware store.	_eine Eisenwaren-handlung.	_INE-eh EYE-zen-vaa-ren-hahnt-lung.

*A *Drogerie* specializes in nonprescription drugs and toiletries, an *Apotheke* in prescription medicines.

_a health food store.	_ein Reformhaus.	_ine ray-FORM-hows.
_a jewelry store.	_einen Juwelier.	_INE-en yu-veh-LEER.
_a laundromat.	_einen Waschsalon.	_INE-en VAHSH-zaa-long.
_a laundry.	_eine Wäscherei.	_INE-eh vehsh-eh-RYE.
_a liquor store.	_eine Spirituosen-handlung.	_INE-eh shpee-ree-tu-OH-zen-hahnt-lung.
_a market.	_einen Markt.	_INE-en mahrkt.
_a newsstand.	_einen Zeitungsstand.	_INE-en TSYE-tungs-shtahnt.
_an optician.	_einen Optiker.	_INE-en OP-tik-e(r).
_a pastry shop.	_eine Konditorei.	_INE-eh kon-dee-to-RYE.
_a photographer.	_einen Fotografen.	_INE-en foh-toh-GRAA-fen.
_a produce shop.	_eine Gemüse-handlung.	_INE-eh geh-MEW-zeh-hahnt-lung.
_a record store.	_ein Schallplat-tengeschäft.	_ine SHAHL-plah-ten-geh-shehft.
_a secondhand shop.	_einen Gebraucht-warenladen.	_INE-en geh-BROWKHT-vaa-ren-laa-den.
_a shoe repair shop.	_einen Schuhmacher.	_INE-en SHOO-mahkh-e(r).
_a shoe store.	_ein Schuhgeschäft.	_ine SHOO-geh-shehft.
_a shopping center.	_ein Einkaufszentrum.	_ine INE-kowfs-tsehn-trum.
_a souvenir (gift) shop.	_einen Andenkenladen.	_INE-en AHN-dehn-ken-laa-den.
_a sporting goods shop.	_ein Sportgeschäft.	_ine SHPORT-geh-shehft.
_a stationery shop.	_ein Schreib-warengeschäft.	_ine SHRYEP-vaa-ren-geh-shehft.

_a supermarket.	_einen Supermarkt.	_INE-en ZOO-pe(r)-mahrkt.
_a tailor.	_einen Schneider.	_INE-en SHNYE-de(r).
_a tobacco shop.	_einen Tabak-laden.	_INE-en tah-BAHK-laa-den.
_a toy shop.	_ein Spielwaren-geschäft.	_ine SHPEEL-vaa-ren-geh-shehft.
_a travel agency.	_ein Reisebüro.	_ine RYE-zeh-bew-roh.
_a watchmaker.	_einen Uhrmacher.	_INE-en OOR-mahkh-e(r).
_a wine shop.	_eine Weinhandlung.	_INE-eh VINE-hahnt-lung.

GENERAL SHOPPING EXPRESSIONS

Where can I find . . . ?	Wo finde ich . . . ?	voh FIN-deh ikh . . . ?
Can you help me?	**Können Sie mir helfen?**	**KU(R)-nen zee meer HEHL-fen?**
I'm just browsing.	**Ich schaue mich nur um.**	**ikh SHOW-eh mikh noor oom.**
I'd like to buy . . .	Ich möchte ____ kaufen.	ikh MU(R)KH-teh ____ KOW-fen.
Do you sell/stock ____?	Verkaufen/Führen Sie ____?	fehr-KOW-fen/FEW-ren zee ____?
Where is the ____ department?	Wo ist die ____ -abteilung?	voh ist dee ____ -ahp-tile-ung?
Can you show me . . .	**Können Sie mir ____ zeigen?**	**KU(R)-nen zee meer ____ TSYE-gen?**
_this/that?	_das da/das dort	_dahs daa/dahs dort
_the one in the window/in the display case?	_das im Schaufenster/in der Vitrine	_dahs im SHOW-fehn-ste(r)/in dehr vi-TREE-neh
_some more?	_noch andere	_nohkh AHN-deh-reh
_something less costly/cheaper?	_etwas Preiswerteres/Billigeres	_EHT-vahs PRICE-vehr-teh-rehs/BIL-likh-e(r)-rehs

_something better?	_etwas Besseres	_EHT-vahs BEHS-seh-rehs
_something larger/smaller?	_etwas Größeres/Kleineres	_EHT-vahs GRU(R)S-eh-rehs/KLINE-eh-rehs
I prefer something . . .	Ich hätte lieber etwas . . .	ikh HEHT-teh LEE-ber EHT-vahs . . .
_handmade.	_Handgemachtes.	_HAHNT-geh-mahkh-tehs.
_more typical.	_Typischeres.	_TEW-pish-eh-rehs.

Deciding and Paying

How much is this (in dollars)?	Wieviel kostet das (in Dollar)?	VEE-feel KOS-tet dahs [in DOL-lahr]?
Please write it down.	Schreiben Sie es bitte auf.	SHRYE-ben zee ehs BIT-teh owf.
I'll take it/two.	Ich nehme es/zwei.	ikh NAY-meh ehs/tsvye.
Do you have it in stock?	Haben Sie es auf Lager?	HAA-ben zee ehs owf LAA-ge(r)?
Can you please . . .	Können Sie es mir bitte . . .	KU(R)-nen zee ehs meer BIT-teh . . .
_order it for me?	_bestellen?	_beh-SHTEHL-len?
_send it to me?	_schicken?	_SHIK-en?
_deliver it to my hotel?	_ins Hotel liefern?	_ins ho-TEL LEE-fern?
How long will it take?	Wie lange dauert es?	vee LAHNG-eh DOW-ert ehs?
Where do I pay?	Wo ist die Kasse?	voh ist dee KAHS-seh?
Can I pay with . . .	Kann ich mit ____ bezahlen?	kahn ikh mit ____ beh-TSAA-len?
_traveler's checks?	_Reiseschecks	_RYE-zeh-shehks
_this credit card?	_dieser Kreditkarte	_DEE-ze(r) kray-DEET-kahr-teh
_dollars/pounds?	_Dollar/Pfund	_DOL-lahr/pfunt

Do I have to pay the value-added tax?	Muss ich die Mehrwertsteuer bezahlen?	mus ikh dee MEHR-vehrt-shtoy-e(r) beh-TSAA-len?
Do you have forms for the return of this tax?	Haben Sie Formulare für die Rückgabe dieser Steuer?	HAA-ben zee for-moo-LAH-reh fewr dee REWK-gaa-beh DEE-ze(r) SHTOY-e(r)?
May I please have a bag/plastic sack?	Kann ich bitte eine Tragetasche/Plastiktüte haben?	kahn ikh BIT-teh INE-eh TRAA-geh-tahsh-eh/PLAHS-tik-tew-teh HAA-ben?
Could you please gift wrap this?	Können Sie das bitte als Geschenk verpacken?	KU(R)-nen zee dahs BIT-teh ahls geh-SHEHNK fehr-PAH-ken?
Can I exchange this?	Kann ich das umtauschen?	kahn ikh dahs OOM-tow-shen?
I'd like to return this.	Ich möchte das zurückgeben.	ikh MU(R)KH-teh dahs tsoo-REWK-gay-ben.
Here's my receipt.	Hier ist die Quittung.	heer ist dee KVIT-tung.

CLOTHING (*KLEIDUNG*)

I'd like a/an/some . . .	Ich hätte gern . . .	i(h)h HEHT-teh gehrn . . .
_a bathrobe.	_einen Bademantel.	_INE-en BAA-deh-mahn-tel.
_a bathing cap.	_eine Badekappe.	_INE-eh BAA-deh-kah-peh.
_a bathing suit.	_einen Badeanzug.	_INE-en BAA-deh-ahn-tsook.
_belt.	_einen Gürtel.	_INE-en GEWR-tel.
_blouse.	**_eine Bluse.**	**_INE-eh BLOO-zeh.**
_bow tie.	_eine Fliege.	_INE-eh FLEE-geh.
_brassiere.	_einen Büstenhalter.	_INE-en BEWS-ten-hahl-te(r).
_cap.	_eine Mütze.	_INE-eh MEW-tseh.
_coat.	**_einen Mantel.**	**_INE-en MAHN-tel.**
_dress.	_ein Kleid.	_ine klite.

_dressing gown.	_einen Morgenrock.	_INE-en MOR-gen-rok.
_evening dress/gown.	_ein Abendkleid.	_ine AA-behnt-klite.
_fur coat.	_einen Pelzmantel.	_INE-en PEHLTS-mahn-tel.
_girdle.	_einen Hüfthalter.	_INE-en HEWFT-hahl-te(r).
_gloves.	_Handschuhe.	_HAHNT-shoo-eh.
_handbag.	_eine Handtasche.	_INE-eh HAHNT-tahsh-eh.
_handkerchief.	_ein Taschentuch.	_ine TAHSH-en-tookh.
_hat.	**_einen Hut.**	**_INE-en hoot.**
_jacket.	_eine Jacke.	_INE-en YAH-keh.
_jeans.	_Jeans.	_"jeans."
_leather pants.	_eine Lederhose.	_INE-eh LAY-de(r)-hoh-zeh.
_lingerie.	_Damenunter-wäsche.	_DAA-men-un-te(r)-vehsh-eh.
_overalls.	_einen Overall.	_INE-en OH-ver-ahl.
_panties.	_einen Schlüpfer.	_INE-en SHLEWP-fe(r).
_pants/trousers.	_eine Hose.	_INE-eh HOH-zeh.
_panty hose.	_eine Strumpfhose.	_INE-eh SHTRUMPF-hoh-zeh.
_pullover.	_einen Pullover.	_INE-en pu-LOH-ve(r).
turtleneck.	mit Rollkragen.	mit ROL-kraa-gen.
V-neck.	mit V-Ausschnitt.	mit FOW-ows-shnit.
_pajamas.	_einen Pyjama.	_INE-en pi-JAA-maa.
_raincoat.	**_einen Regenmantel.**	**_INE-en RAY-gen-mahn-tel.**
_scarf.	_ein Halstuch.	_ine HAHLS-tookh.
_shirt.	_ein Hemd.	_ine hehmt.
with long/ short sleeves.	mit langen/ kurzen Ärmeln.	mit LAHN-gen/koort-sen EHR-meln.

sleeveless shirt.	ein ärmelloses Hemd.	ine EHR-mehl-loh-zehs hehmt.
_(a pair of) shoes.	_(ein Paar) Schuhe.	_[ine paar] SHOO-eh.
_shorts.	_Shorts.	_"shorts."
_skirt.	_einen Rock.	_INE-en rok.
_slip.	_einen Unterrock.	_INE-en UN-te(r)-rok.
_socks.	_Socken.	_ZOK-en.
_sports coat/jacket.	_einen Sportsakko.	_INE-en SHPORT-zah-koh.
_stockings.	_Strümpfe.	_SHTREWM-pfeh.
_suit (man's).	_einen Anzug.	_INE-en AHN-tsook.
_suit (woman's).	_ein Kostüm.	_ine kos-TEWM.
_suspenders/ braces.	_Hosenträger.	_HOH-zen-tray-ge(r).
_sweater.	_einen Pullover.	_INE-en pull-OH-ver.
_sweater blouse.	_eine Strickbluse.	_INE-eh SHTRIK-bloo-zeh.
_swimming trunks.	_eine Badehose.	_INE-eh BAA-deh-hoh-zeh.
_tie.	_eine Krawatte.	_INE-eh krah-VAHT-teh.
_tights.	_eine Strumpfhose.	_INE-eh SHTRUMPF-hoh-zeh.
_trench coat.	_einen Trenchcoat.	_INE-en "trench coat."
_umbrella.	_einen Regenschirm.	_INE-en RAY-gen-sheerm.
_underpants.	_eine Unterhose.	_INE-eh UN-te(r)-hoh-zeh.
_undershirt.	_ein Unterhemd.	_ine UN-te(r)-hehmt.
_underwear.	_Unterwäsche.	_UN-te(r)-vehsh-eh.
_vest.	_eine Weste.	_INE-eh VEHS-teh.

Materials and Fabrics

I don't like this material.	Der Stoff gefällt mir nicht.	dehr shtof geh-fehlt meer nikht.

159

I prefer natural fibers.	Ich hätte lieber etwas aus natürlichen Fasern.	ikh HEHT-teh LEE-be(r) EHT-vahs ous nah-TEWR-likh-en FAA-zern.
Is this fabric . . .	Ist dieser Stoff . . .	ist DEE-ze(r) shtof . . .
_pure wool?	_reine Wolle?	_RINE-eh VOL-leh?
_synthetic?	_aus Kunststoff?	_ows KUNST-shtof?
_wash-and-wear?	_bügelfrei?	_BEW-gel-frye?
Will it shrink?	Läuft das noch ein?	loyft dahs nokh ine?
I want something . . .	Ich möchte etwas . . .	ikh MU(R)KH-teh EHT-vahs . . .
_thicker/thinner.	_Dickeres/Dünne-res.	_DIK-eh-rehs-DEWN-neh-rehs.
_of better quality.	_von besserer Qualität.	_fon BEHS-eh-re(r) kvah-li-TAYT.
Do you have anything in . . .	**Haben Sie etwas in . . .**	**HAA-ben zee EHT-vahs in . . .**
_corduroy?	_Kordsamt?	_KORT-zahmt?
_cotton?	**_Baumwolle?**	**_BOWM-vol-leh?**
_crepe?	_Krepp?	_krehp?
_denim?	_Jeansstoff?	_DSHEENS-shtof?
_felt?	_Filz?	_filts?
_flannel?	_Flanell?	_flah-NEHL?
_gabardine?	_Gabardine?	_GAH-bahr-din?
_lace?	_Spitze?	_SHPIT-seh?
_leather?	_Leder?	_LAY-de(r)?
_linen?	_Leinen?	_LINE-en?
_nylon?	_Nylon?	_NYE-lon?
_poplin?	_Popline?	_po-peh-LEEN?
_rayon?	_Kunstseide?	_KUNST-zye-deh?
_satin?	_Satin?	_zah-TEHNG?
_silk?	**_Seide?**	**_ZYE-deh?**
_suede?	_Wildleder?	_VILT-lay-de(r)?
_velvet?	_Samt?	_zahmt?
_wool?	**_Wolle?**	**_VO-leh?**

160

Colors and Patterns

I'd like something . . .	Ich möchte etwas . . .	ikh MU(R)KH-teh EHT-vahs . . .
_lighter/darker.	_Helleres/ Dunkleres	_HEHL-leh-rehs/ DUNK-leh-rehs.
_in a different color.	_in einer anderen Farbe.	_in INE-e(r) AHN-deh-ren FAHR-beh.
_to match this.	_hierzu Passendes.	_HEER-tsoo PAHS-sen-dehs.
_colorfast.	_Farbechtes.	_FAHRP-ehkt-tehs.
Do you have it in . . .	**Haben Sie es in . . .**	**HAA-ben zee ehs in . . .**
_beige?	_beige?	_bayzh?
_black?	**_schwarz?**	_shvahrts?
_blue?	**_blau?**	_blow?
_brown?	_braun?	_brown?
_gray?	_grau?	_grow?
_green?	_grün?	_grewn?
_orange?	_orange?	_o-RAHNG-zheh?
_pink?	_rosa?	_ROH-zah?
_purple?	_violett?	_vee-oh-LEHT?
_red?	_rot?	_roht?
_silver?	_silbern?	_ZIL-bern?
_white?	**_weiß?**	_vice?
_yellow?	_gelb?	_gehlp?
I'd rather have it . . .	Ich hätte es lieber . . .	ikh HEHT-teh ehs LEE-be(r) . . .
_in a solid color.	_uni.	_U-nee.
_with stripes.	_gestreift.	_geh-SHTRYEFT.
_with polka dots.	_mit Punktmuster	_mit PUNKT-mus-te(r). _in plaid/
_checkered.	_kariert.	_kah-REERT.

161

Sizes and Fitting

I'm a size 40.	Ich trage Größe vierzig.	ikh TRAA-geh GRU(R)-S-eh FEER-tsikh.
I don't know my size.	Ich kenne meine Größe nicht.	ikh KEH-neh MINE-eh GRU(R)S-seh nikht.
May I try it on?	Kann ich es anprobieren?	kahn ikh ehs AHN-pro-beer-en?
Is there a mirror?	Gibt es einen Spiegel?	gipt ehs INE-en SHPEE-gel?
It fits very well.	Es passt/sitzt sehr gut.	ehs pahst/zitst zehr goot.
It doesn't fit.	Es passt nicht.	ehs pahst nikht.
Can you alter it?	Können Sie es ändern?	KU(R)-nen zee ehs EHN-dern?

SHOES

I need a pair of . . .	Ich brauche ein Paar . . .	ikh BROW-kheh ine paar . . .
_boots/rain boots.	_Stiefel/Regen-stiefel.	_SHTEE-fel/RAY-gen-shtee-fel.
_flats.	_flache Schuhe.	_FLAH-kheh SHOO-eh.
_high heels.	_Schuhe mit hohen Absätzen.	_SHOO-eh mit HOH-en AHP-zeht-sen.
_sandals/shoes.	_Sandalen/Schuhe.	_zahn-DAA-len/SHOO-eh.
_slippers.	_Hausschuhe.	_HOWS-shoo-eh.
_sneakers.	_Turnschuhe.	_TURN-shoo-eh.
Do you have any with leather/rubber soles?	Haben Sie welche mit Leder-/Gummisohlen?	HAA-ben zee VEHL-kheh mit LAY-de(r)-/GOOM-mee-zoh-len?
These are too . . .	Diese sind zu . . .	DEE-zeh zint tsoo . . .
_small/large.	_klein/groß.	_kline/grohs.
_narrow/wide.	_eng/weit.	_ehng/vite.

WOMEN'S CLOTHING SIZES

Coats, dresses, suits, skirts, slacks

U.S.	4	6	8	10	12	14	16
Europe	36	38	40	42	44	46	48

Blouses/Sweaters

U.S.	32/6	34/8	36/10	38/12	40/14	42/16
Europe	38/2	40/3	42/4	44/5	46/6	48/7

Shoes

U.S.	4	4½	5	5½	6	6½	7	7½	8	8½	9	9½	10
Europe	35	35	36	36	37	37	38	38	39	39	40	40	41

MEN'S CLOTHING SIZES

Suits/Coats

U.S.	34	36	38	40	42	44	46	48
Europe	44	46	48	50	52	54	56	58

Sweaters

U.S.	XS/36	S/38	M/40	L/42	XL/44	
Europe	42/2	44/3	46–48/4	50/5	52–54/6	

Shirts

U.S.	14	14½	15	15½	16	16½	17	17½	18
Europe	36	37	38	39	40	41	42	43	44

Slacks

U.S.	30	31	32	33	34	35	36	37	38	39
Europe	38	39–40	41	42	43	44–45	46	47	48–49	50

Socks

U.S.	9½	10	10½	11	11½	12	13
Europe	36–37	38–39	40–41	42–43	44–45	46–47	48–49

Shoes

U.S.	7	7½	8	8½	9	9½	10	10½	11
Europe	39	40	41	42	43	43	44	44	45

THE JEWELRY STORE (*BEIM JUWELIER*)

What kind of jewelry/watches do you have?	Was für Schmucksachen/ Uhren haben Sie?	vahs fewr SHMUK-zahkh-en/OOR-en HAA-ben zee?
I'm looking for a/an/some . . .	Ich suche . . .	ikh ZOO-kheh . . .
_alarm clock.	_einen Wecker.	_INE-en VEHK-e(r).
_antique jewelry.	_alten Schmuck.	_AHL-ten shmuk.
_bracelet.	_ein Armband.	_ine AHRM-bahnt.
_brooch.	_eine Brosche.	_INE-eh BROSH-eh.
_chain.	_eine Kette.	_INE-eh KEHT-teh.
_cufflinks.	_Manschetten-knöpfe.	_mahn-SHEHT-ten-knu(r)p-feh.
_earrings.	_Ohrringe.	_OHR-ring-eh.
_gem.	_einen Edelstein.	_INE-en AY-del-shtine.
_jewelry box.	_ein Schmuck-Kästchen.	_ine SHMUK-kehst-khen.
_necklace.	_eine Halskette.	_INE-eh HAHLS-keht-teh.
_pin.	_eine Anstecknadel.	_INE-eh AHN-shtehk-naa-del.
_ring.	_einen Ring.	_INE-en ring.
_engagement ring.	_einen Verlobungsring.	_INE-en fehr-LOH-bungs-ring.
_wedding ring.	_einen Ehering.	_INE-en AY-eh-ring.
_tiepin.	_eine Krawattennadel.	_INE-eh krah-VAHT-ten-naa-del.
_wristwatch.	_eine Armbanduhr.	_INE-eh AHRM-bahnt-oor.
What do you have in . . .	Was haben Sie in . . .	vahs HAA-ben zee in . . .
_gold?	_Gold?	_golt?
_platinum?	_Platin?	_plah-TEEN?
_silver?	_Silber?	_ZIL-be(r)?
_stainless steel?	_Edelstahl?	_AY-del-shtahl?

164

What's this made of?	Aus welchem Metall ist das?	ows VEHL-khem meh-TAHL ist dahs?
Is this solid gold or just gold plate?	Ist das massives Gold oder nur vergoldet?	ist dahs mah-SEE-vehs golt OH-de(r) noor fehr-GOL-det?
How many karats is it?	Wieviel Karat hat es?	VEE-feel kah-RAAT haht ehs?
Can you repair this watch/jewelry?	Können Sie diese Uhr/dieses Schmuckstück reparieren?	KU(R)-nen zee DEE-zeh oor/DEE-zehs SHMUK-shtewk reh-pah-REE-ren?
Show me please your selection of . . .	Zeigen Sie mir bitte Ihre Auswahl von . . .	TSYE-gen zee meer BIT-teh EE-reh OWS-vaal fon . . .
_amber.	_Bernstein.	_BEHRN-shtine.
_amethyst.	_Amethyst.	_ah-meh-TEWST.
_crystal.	_Kristall.	_kris-TAHL.
_diamonds.	_Diamanten.	_dee-ah-MAHN-ten.
_emeralds.	_Smaragden.	_smah-RAHK-ten.
_hematite.	_Hämatiten.	_hay-mah-TEE-tehn.
_ivory.	_Elfenbein.	_EHL-fen-bine.
_jade.	_Jade.	_YAA-deh.
_onyx.	_Onyx.	_OH-niks.
_pearls.	_Perlen.	_PEHR-len.
_rubies.	_Rubinen.	_ru-BEE-nen.
_sapphires.	_Saphiren.	_zah-FEE-ren.
_topazes.	_Topasen.	_toh-PAA-zen.
_turquoises.	_Türkisen.	_tewr-KEE-zen.

THE PHOTO SHOP (*DAS FOTOGESCHÄFT*)

I need film for this camera/movie camera.	Ich brauche einen Film für diese Kamera/Filmkamera.	ikh BROW-kheh INE-en film fewr DEE-zeh KAH-meh-raa/FILM-kah-meh-raa.
I'd like a roll of . . .	Ich möchte einen . . .	ikh MU(R)KH-teh INE-en . . .

_35-mm color film.	_fünfunddreißig Millimeter Farbfilm.	_FEWNF-unt-drye-sikh mi-lee-MAY-te(r) FAHRP-film.
_black-and-white film.	_Schwarzweiß-film.	_shvahrts-VICE-film.
_color slide film.	_Film für Farbdias.	_film fewr FAHRP-dee-ahs.
_daylight film.	_Tageslichtfilm.	_TAA-gehs-likht-film.
_artificial light film.	_Kunstlichtfilm.	_KUNST-likht-film.
24/36 exposures, please.	Vierundzwanzig/ sechsunddreißig Aufnahmen, bitte.	FEER-unt-TSVAHN-tsikh/zehks-unt-drye-sikh OWF-naa-men, BIT-teh.
How much does developing cost?	Was kostet das Entwickeln?	vahs KOS-tet dahs ehnt-VIK-eln?
I'd like . . .	Ich möchte . . .	ikh MU(R)KH-teh . . .
_one/two prints of each negative.	_einen Abzug/zwei Abzüge von jedem Negativ.	_INE-en AHP-tsook/tsvye AHP-tsew-geh fon YEH-dem NEH-gah-teef.
_matte/glossy prints.	_matt/Hochglanz-abzüge.	_maht/HOHKH-glahnts-AHP-tzew-geh.
_enlargements.	_Vergrößerungen.	_fehr-GRU(R)S-eh-rung-en.
When will they be ready?	Wann sind sie fertig?	vahn zint see FEHR-tikh?
Do you sell ____ cameras?	Verkaufen Sie ____ Kameras?	fehr-KOW-fen zee ____ KAH-meh-raas?
_automatic	_automatische	_ow-to-MAH-ti-sheh
_simple	_einfache	_INE-fah-khe
_single lens reflex	_Spiegelreflex	_SHPEE-gel-reh-flehks
_movie	_Film	_film
Do you carry . . .	Führen Sie . . .	FEW-ren zee . . .
_batteries?	_Batterien?	_bah-teh-REE-en?
_filters?	_Filter?	_FIL-te(r)?
_lens caps?	_Objektivdeckel?	_ob-yehk-TEEF-deh-kel?

166

BOOKS, MAGAZINES, AND PAPER GOODS (*BÜCHER, ZEITSCHRIFTEN, UND PAPIER-WAREN*)

Larger bookstores in German-speaking countries will often stock English-language and other foreign-language publications. Newspapers, magazines, and postcards are readily available at a newsstand (*Zeitungsstand* or *Kiosk*).

Where can I find English-language . . .	Wo finde ich englisch-sprachige . . .	voh FIN-deh ikh EHNG-lish-shprahkh-i-geh . . .
_newspapers?	_Zeitungen?	_TSITE-ung-en?
_magazines?	_Zeitschriften?	_TSITE-shrif-ten?
_books/publications?	_Bücher/Veröffentlich-ungen?	_BEW-khe(r)/fehr-U(R)F-ehnt-likh-ung-en?
Where's the section for . . .	Wo stehen die . . .	voh SHTAY-en dee . . .
_books in English?	_Bücher in Englisch?	_BEW-khe(r) in EHNG-lish?
_dictionaries?	_Wörterbücher?	_VUR-te(r)-bew-khe(r)?
_guidebooks?	_Reiseführer?	_RYE-zeh-few-re(r)?
_secondhand books?	_antiquarischen Bücher?	_ahn-ti-KVAA-rish-en-BEW-khe(r)?
Do you have . . .	Haben Sie . . .	HAA-ben zee . . .
_a German-English pocket dictionary?	_ein deutsch-englisches Taschen-wörterbuch?	_ine doych-EHNG-lish-ehs TAHSH-en-vur-te(r)-bookh?
_the novel ____ by ____ in English?	_den Roman ____ von ____ in Englisch?	_dehn roh-MAAN ____ fon ____ in EHNG-lish?
I'd like a/an/some . . .	Ich möchte . . .	ikh MU(R)KH-teh . . .
_adhesive tape.	_Klebeband.	_KLAY-beh-bahnt.
_ballpoint pen.	_einen Kugel-schreiber.	_INE-en KOO-gel-shrye-be(r).

167

_calendar.	_einen Kalender.	_INE-en kah-LEHN-de(r).
_carbon paper.	_Kohlepapier.	_KOH-leh-pah-peer.
_crayons.	_Buntstifte.	_BUNT-shtif-teh.
_drawing paper.	_Zeichenpapier.	_TSYE-khen-pah-peer.
_envelopes.	_Briefum-schläge.	_BREEF-oom-shlay-geh.
_eraser.	_einen Radiergummi.	_INE-en rah-DEER-goom-mee.
_felt-tip.	_einen Filzstift.	_INE-en FILTS-shtift.
_fountain pen.	_einen Füllfeder-halter.	_INE-en FEWL-fay-de(r)-hahl-te(r).
_glue.	_Leim.	_lime.
_ink.	_Tinte.	_TIN-teh.
_labels.	_Etiketten.	_eh-ti-KEH-tehn.
_notebook.	_ein Notizheft.	_ine no-TEETS-hehft.
_paper clips.	_Büro-klammern.	_bew-ROH-klahm-mern.
_pencil.	_einen Bleistift.	_INE-en BLYE-shtift.
_pencil sharpener.	_einen Bleistift-spitzer.	_INE-en BLYE-shtift-shpit-se(r).
_playing cards.	_Spielkarten.	_SHPEEL-kahr-ten.
_pocket calculator.	_einen Taschen-rechner.	_INE-en TAHSH-en-rehkh-ne(r).
_postcards.	_Ansichtskarten.	_AHN-zikhts-kahr-ten.
_ruler.	_ein Lineal.	_ine lee-neh-AAL.
_Scotch tape.	_Tesafilm.	_TAY-zah-film.
_stapler.	_eine Drahtheft-maschine.	_INE-eh DRAHT-heft-mah-shee-neh.

_staples.	_Heftklammern.	_HEHFT-klahm-mern.
_string.	_Schnur.	_shnoor.
_(airmail) stationery.	_(Luftpost) Briefpapier.	_[LUFT-post] BREEF-pah-peer.
_thumbtacks.	_Reißzwecken.	_RICE-tsveh-ken.
_typing paper.	_Schreibmaschinenpapier.	_SHRIPE-mah-shee-nen-pah-peer.
_writing pad.	_einen Schreibblock.	_INE-en SHRIPE-blok.

ELECTRICAL APPLIANCES (*ELEKTROGERÄTE*)

Standard household current throughout continental Europe is 220 volts, 50-cycle A.C. Many appliances are now equipped with dual-voltage capacity. Make sure about this before you buy an appliance overseas; otherwise you will need a transformer, as well as adapter plugs, to use it in the United States.

What's the voltage on this appliance?	Welche Spannung hat dieses Gerät?	VEHL-kheh SHPAHN-nung haht DEE-zehs geh-RAYT?
Show me how it works, please.	Zeigen Sie mir bitte, wie es funktioniert.	TSYE-gen zee meer BIT-teh, vee ehs funk-tsyo-NEERT.
Do you have batteries for this?	Haben Sie hierfür Batterien?	HAA-ben zee HEER-fewr bah-teh-REE-en?
It's broken. Can you fix it?	Es ist kaputt. Können Sie es reparieren?	ehs ist kah-PUT. KU(R)-nen zee ehs reh-pah-REE-ren?
I need a/an/some . . .	Ich brauche . . .	ikh BROW-kheh . . .
_adapter plug.	_einen Zwischenstecker.	_INE-en TSVISH-en-shteh-ke(r).
_bulb.	_eine Glühbirne.	_INE-eh GLEW-beer-neh.
_cassette recorder.	_einen Kassettenrecorder.	_INE-en kah-SEHT-ten-reh-kor-de(r).
_clock radio.	_einen Radiowecker.	_INE-en RAA-dee-oh-veh-ke(r).

169

_extension cord.	_eine Ver-längerungs-schnur.	_INE-eh fehr-LEHNG-eh-rungs-shnoor.
_hair dryer.	_einen Haartrockner.	_INE-en HAAR-trok-ne(r).
_travel iron.	_ein Reisebügeleisen.	_ine RYE-zeh-bew-gel-eye-zen.
_lamp.	_eine Lampe.	_INE-eh LAHM-peh.
_plug.	_einen Stecker.	_INE-en SHTEH-ke(r).
_(portable) radio.	_ein (Koffer-) Radio.	_ine [KO-fe(r)-] RAA-dee-oh.
_record/CD player.	_einen Platten-/CD-Spieler.	_INE-en PLAHT-ten-/TSEH-DEH-SHPEE-lehr.
_shaver.	_einen Rasierapparat.	_INE-en rah-ZEER-ah-pah-raat.
_cassette recorder.	_ein Kassettenrecorder	_ine kah-SEHT-ten reh-kohr-dehr
_(color) TV.	_einen (Farb-) Fernseher.	_INE-en [FAHRP-] FEHRN-zay-er.
_transformer.	_einen Transfor-mator.	_INE-en trahns-for-MAA-tor.
_VCR.	_einen Video-recorder.	_INE-en VEE-deh-oh-reh-kor-de(r).
_DVD player.	_DVD-Spieler.	_deh-fow-DEH SHPEE-lehr.

THE RECORD STORE (*PLATTENGESCHÄFT*)

Do you have any recordings by____?	Haben Sie Auf-nahmen von ____?	HAA-ben zee OWF-naa-men fon ____?
May I listen to this DEE-zeh CD?	Darf ich diese CD hören?	dahrf ikh TSEH-DEH HU(R)-en?
Do you sell . . .	Verkaufen Sie . . .	fehr-KOW-fen zee . . .
_audiocassettes?	_Kassetten?	_kah-SEHT-ten?
_videocassettes?	_Videokassetten?	_VEE-deh-oh-kah-seht-ten?
_CDs?	_CD?	_tseh-DEH

_LPs (33 rpm)?	_Langspiel-platten?	_LAHNG-shpeel-plaht-ten?
Where's the section for . . .	Wo finde ich . . .	voh FIN-deh ikh . . .
_chamber music?	_die Kammermusik?	_dee KAHM-me(r)-moo-zeek?
_classical music?	_die klassische Musik?	_dee KLAHS-sish-eh moo-ZEEK?
_folk music/folk songs?	_die Volksmusik/Volkslieder?	_dee FOLKS-moo-zeek/FOLKS-lee-de(r)?
_jazz?	_den Jazz?	_dehn jazz?
_opera?	_die Opermusik?	_dee OH-pe(r)-moo-zeek?
_pop music/hits?	_die Popmusik/Schlager?	_dee POP-moo-zeek/SHLAA-ge(r)?

TOILETRIES (*TOILETTENARTIKEL*)

The following list of items can be found at a *Drogerie* (drug store) or department store. Prescription medicines are available only at an *Apotheke* (pharmacy; see At the Pharmacy, in Chapter 10).

I'd like a/an/some . . .	Ich hätte gern . . .	ikh HEHT-teh gehrn . . .
_aftershave lotion.	_ein Rasierwasser.	_ine rah-ZEER-vahs-se(r).
_bobby pins.	_Haarnadeln.	_HAAR-naa-dehln.
_bath salts.	_Badesalz.	_BAA-deh-zahlts.
_bubble bath.	_ein Schaumbad.	_ine SHOWM-baat.
_cleansing cream.	_eine Reinigungs-creme.	_INE-eh RYE-ni-gungs-kraym.
_cologne.	_Kölnisch Wasser.	_KU(R)L-nish VAHS-se(r).
_condoms.	**_Kondome.**	**_kon-DOH-meh.**
_comb.	_einen Kamm.	_INE-en kahm.
_curlers.	_Lockenwickler.	_LOK-en-vik-le(r).

171

_deodorant.	_ein De(s)odorant.	_ine deh-(z)oh-doh-RAHNT.
_diapers.	_Windeln.	_VIN-deln.
_emery board.	_eine Nagelfeile.	_INE-eh NAA-gel-fye-leh.
_eyebrow pencil.	_einen Augen-brauenstift.	_INE-en OW-gen-brow-en-shtift.
_eyeliner.	_einen Lidstift.	_INE-en LEET-shtift.
_eye shadow.	_einen Lidschatten.	_INE-en LEET-shaht-ten.
_face powder.	_Gesichtspuder.	_geh-ZIKHTS-poo-de(r).
_foot powder.	_Fußpuder.	_FOOS-poo-de(r).
_hairbrush.	_eine Haarbürste.	_INE-eh HAAR-bewr-steh.
_hair spray.	_ein Haarspray.	_INE HAAR-shpray.
_hand cream.	_Handcreme.	_HAHNT-kraym.
_lip balm.	_eine Lippenbalsam.	_INE-eh LIP-pen-bahl-sahm.
_lipstick.	_einen Lippenstift.	_INE-en LIP-pen-shtift.
_mascara.	_Wimperntusche.	_VIM-pern-tush-eh.
_mirror.	_einen Spiegel.	_INE-en SHPEE-gel.
_moisturizing cream.	_Feuchtigkeits-creme.	_FOYKH-tikh-kites-kraym.
_mouthwash.	_ein Mundwasser.	_ine MUNT-vahs-se(r).
_nail clippers.	_eine Nageltrimmer.	_INE-eh NAA-gel-tree-mehr.
_nail polish (remover).	_Nagellack (-entferner).	_NAA-gel-lahk [-ehnt-fehr-ne(r)].
_nail scissors.	_eine Nagelschere.	_INE-eh NAA-gel-shay-reh.
_perfume.	_ein Parfüm.	_ine pahr-FEWM.
_razor.	_einen Rasierapparat.	_INE-en rah-ZEER-ahp-pah-raat.

_razor blades.	_Rasierklingen.	_rah-ZEER-kling-en.
_rouge.	_Rouge/Schminke.	_roozh/SHMIN-keh.
_safety pins.	_Sicherheits- nadeln.	_ZIKH-e(r)-hites-NAA- deln.
_sanitary napkins.	**_Damenbinden.**	**_DAA-men-bin-den.**
_scissors.	_eine Schere.	_INE-eh SHAY-reh.
_setting lotion.	_einen Haarfestiger.	_INE-en HAAR-fehs-ti- ge(r).
_shampoo.	_ein Haarwasch- mittel.	_ine HAAR-vahsh-mit- tel.
_shaving cream.	_Rasiercreme.	_rah-ZEER-kraym.
_soap.	_eine Seife.	_INE-eh ZYE-feh.
_sponge.	_einen Schwamm.	_INE-en shvahm.
_suntan lotion/oil.	_Sonnencreme/ -öl.	_ZON-en-kraym/ u(r)l.
_talcum powder.	_Talkumpuder.	_TAAL-kum-poo-de(r).
_tampons.	_Tampons.	_TAHM-pongs.
_tissues.	_Papiertücher.	_pah-PEER-tew- khe(r).
_toilet paper.	_Toilettenpapier.	_toy-LEHT-ten-pah- peer.
_toilet water.	_ein Toilettenwasser.	_ine toy-LEHT-ten- vahs-se(r).
_toothbrush.	**_eine Zahnbürste.**	**_INE-eh TSAAN- bewr-steh.**
_toothpaste.	**_Zahnpasta.**	**_TSAAN-pahs-tah.**
_towels.	_Handtücher.	_HAHNT-tew-khe(r).
_tweezers.	_eine Pinzette.	_INE-eh pin-TSEHT- teh.

FOOD SHOPPING (*LEBENSMITTELEINKAUF*)

The standard unit of weight for purchasing produce, cheese, and sausage is the kilogram (*Kilo*), fractions thereof, or 100-gram units (*einhundert, zweihundert Gramm,* etc.) for smaller amounts. You'll also hear the term *Pfund* (pound), which is equal to half a kilo or 500 grams. Take along your own shopping bag or basket, since not all shops and markets provide bags—and those that do commonly charge a small fee for them.

I'd like a loaf of dark bread, please.	Ich hätte gern ein Bauernbrot, bitte.	ikh HEHT-teh gehrn ine BOW-ern-broht, BIT-teh.
May I have a tasting sample of this cheese/sausage?	Darf ich eine Kostprobe von diesem Käse/ dieser Wurst haben?	dahrf ikh INE-eh KOST-proh-beh fon DEE-zem KAY-zeh/DEE-ze(r) voorst HAA-ben?
May I help myself?	Darf ich mich selbst bedienen?	dahrf ikh mikh zehlpst beh-DEE-nen?
Please give me . . .	**Geben Sie mir, bitte . . .**	**GAY-ben zee meer, BIT-teh . . .**
_a kilo of potatoes.	_ein Kilo Kartoffeln.	_ine KEE-loh kahr-TOF-feln.
_half a kilo of tomatoes.	_ein halbes Kilo Tomaten.	_ine HAHL-behs KEE-loh to-MAA-ten.
_a pound (500 grams) of butter.	_ein Pfund Butter.	_ine pfunt BUT-te(r).
_200 grams of cheese.	_zweihundert Gramm Käse.	_TSVYE-hun-dert graam KAY-zeh.
_100 grams of liverwurst.	_hundert Gramm Leberwurst.	_HUN-dert gram LAY-be(r)-voorst.
_three slices of ham.	**_drei Scheiben Schinken.**	**_drye SHYE-ben SHIN-ken.**
_half a dozen eggs.	_ein halbes Dutzend Eier.	_ine HAHL-behs DUT-sehnt EYE-e(r).
_a liter of milk.	**_einen Liter Milch.**	**_INE-en LEE-te(r) milkh.**
_a bottle of fruit juice.	**_eine Flasche Obstsaft.**	**_INE-eh FLAHS-eh OPST-sahft.**
_a package of coffee.	_eine Packung Kaffee.	_INE-eh PAHK-ung KAH-fay.
_a jar of jam.	_ein Glas Marmelade.	_ine glaas mahr-meh-LAA-deh.
_a can of beans.	_eine Büchse Bohnen.	_INE-eh BEWK-seh BOH-nen.
_a cup of yogurt.	_einen Becher Yogurt.	_INE-en BEHKH-e(r) YO-gurt.

WEIGHTS AND MEASURES

METRIC WEIGHT	U.S.
1 gram (g)	0.035 ounce
28.35 grams	1 ounce
100 grams	3.5 ounce
454 grams	1 pound
1 kilogram (kilo)	2.2 pounds

LIQUIDS	U.S.
1 liter (l)	4.226 cups
1 liter	2.113 pints
1 liter	1.056 quarts
3.785 liters	1 gallon

DRY MEASURE	U.S.
1 litre	0.908 quart
1 decalitre	1.135 pecks
1 hectolitre	2.837 bushels

One inch = 2.54 centimeters
One centimeter = .39 inch

inches	feet	yards	
1 mm.	0.039	0.003	0.001
1 cm.	0.39	0.03	0.01
1 dm.	3.94	0.32	0.10
1 m.	39.40	3.28	1.09

.39 (# of centimeters) = (# of inches)
2.54 (# of inches) = (# of centimeters)

inches	feet	yards	
1 mm.	0.039	0.003	0.001
1 cm.	0.39	0.03	0.01
1 dm.	3.94	0.32	0.10
1 m.	39.40	3.28	1.09

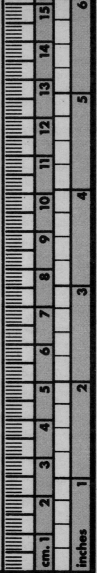

Larger cities offer a variety of nightclubs, discos, cabarets, and gambling casinos. In terms of cultural entertainment and diversions, such as theater, cinema, opera, ballet, musical concerts, and festivals, the richness and high quality of the productions from this part of the world are difficult to match. Those traveling with children will find the German-speaking world quite *kinderfreundlich* (friendly to children), with its modern, well-kept playgrounds, amusement parks, children's museums, aquariums, and zoos. Berlin and Hamburg boast two of the world's most famous zoos. A special treat for young and old are the many marionette and puppet shows, part of a long and rich German tradition and usually performed outdoors during the summer.

In addition, Germany, Austria, and Switzerland offer a wide array of sports activities, both spectator and participatory.

DIALOGUE   Swimming (Schwimmen)

Helmut:	Die Sonne sticht heute! Mir ist wahnsinnig heiß.	dee ZON-eh shtikht HOY-teh! meer ist WAAN-zin-nikh hice.
Linda:	Mir auch. Gehen wir baden.	meer owkh. GAY-en veer BAA-den.
Helmut:	Gute Idee. Gehen wir ins Schwimmbad oder zum Strand?	GOO-teh ee-DAY. GAY-en veer ins SHVIM-baat OH-de(r) tsoom shtrahnt?
Linda:	Lieber zum Strand. Ich mag das Chlorwasser im Schwimmbad nicht.	LEE-be(r) tsoom shtrahnt. ikh mahk dahs KLOR-vahs-se(r) im SHVIM-baat nikht.
Helmut:	Wie wär's denn mit dem Strand am Waldsee?	vee vehrs den mit dehm shtrahnt ahm VAHLT-zee?
Linda:	Schön. Treffen wir uns da in einer halben Stunde.	shu(r)n. TREHF-en veer uns daa in INE-e(r) HAHL-ben SHTUN-deh.

Helmut:	**Abgemacht. Vergiss dein Sonnenöl nicht. Sonst bekommst du* einen Sonnenbrand.**	AHP-geh-mahkht. fehr-GIS dine ZON-en-u(r)l nikht. zonst beh-KOMST doo INE-en ZON-en-brahnt.

Helmut:	The sun is so strong today! I'm really hot.
Linda:	Me too. Let's go swimming.
Helmut:	Good idea. Shall we go to a swimming pool or to the beach?
Linda:	I'd prefer the beach. I don't like the chlorinated water in the pool.
Helmut:	How about the beach at the forest lake?
Linda:	Fine. Let's meet there in half an hour.
Helmut:	Agreed. Don't forget your suntan oil. Otherwise you'll get sunburned.

*Note here the use of the familiar form of address *du*. For the rules regarding its use, see pages 48 and 183.

PARTICIPATORY SPORTS

Swimming

Is there a swimming pool/thermal pool (spa) near here?	**Gibt es ein Schwimmbad/ Thermalbad in der Nähe?**	gipt ehs ine SHVIM-baat/tayr-MAAL-baat in dehr NAY-eh?
Is it . . .	**Ist es . . .**	ist ehs . . .
_outdoors/**indoors?**	_ein Freibad/ **Hallenbad?**	_ine FRYE-baat/HAHL-en-baat?
_heated/crowded?	_geheizt/über-füllt?	_geh-HYETST/ew-be(r)-FEWLT?
Is there a lifeguard?	Gibt es einen Rettungsdienst?	gipt ehs INE-en REHT-tungs-deenst?

At the Beach

Can you swim in this lake/ pond/river?	Kann man in diesem See/Teich/Fluss baden?	kahn mahn in DEE-zem zee/tyekh/flus BAA-den?

177

Is it dangerous for children?	Ist es für Kinder gefährlich?	ist ehs fewr KIN-de(r) geh-FEHR-likh?
Can you recommend a . . .	Können Sie uns (einen) ____ empfehlen?	KU(R)-nen zee uns [INE-en] ____ ehm-PFAY-len?
_sandy beach?	_Sandstrand	_ZAHNT-shtrahnt
_quiet beach?	_ruhigen Strand	_ROO-i-gen shtrahnt
_nudist beach?	_FKK* Strand	_EHF-KAH-KAH shtrahnt
_beach resort?	_ein Strandbad	_ine SHTRAHNT-baat
_seaside resort?	_ein Seebad	_ine ZEE-baat
How are the waves/surf?	Wie ist der Wellengang/die Brandung?	vee ist dehr VEHL-len-gahng/dee BRAHN-dung?
Is the water cold/warm?	Ist das Wasser kalt/warm?	ist dahs VAHS-se(r) kahlt/vahrm?
Where can I rent/buy . . .	Wo kann ich ____ mieten/kaufen?	voh kahn ikh ____ MEE-ten/KOW-fen?
_an air mattress?	_eine Luftmatratze	_INE-eh LUFT-mah-traht-seh
_a beach chair?	_einen Liegestuhl	_INE-en LEE-geh-shtool
_a beach towel?	_ein Strandtuch	_ine SHTRAHNT-tookh
_a canopied beach chair?	_einen Strandkorb	_IHN-en-SHTRAHNT-korp
_a rowboat?	_ein Ruderboot	_ine ROO-de(r)-boht
_a sailboat?	_ein Segelboot	_ine ZAY-gel-boht
_skin-diving equipment?	_eine Taucher-ausrüstung	_INE-eh TOW-khe(r)-ows-rews-tung
_a surfboard?	_ein Surfbrett	_ine SURF-breht
_an umbrella?	_einen Sonnen-schirm	_INE-en ZON-en-shirm

*FKK = abbreviation of *Freikörperkultur,* which means, literally, free body culture. This nudist movement has a long tradition in Germany, and its beaches are quite popular, especially in the north.

_water skis?	*Wasserskier*	_VAHS-se(r)-shee-e(r)
What's the fee per hour/day/week?	Was kostet es pro Stunde/Tag/ Woche?	vahs KOS-tet ehs proh SHTUN-deh/taak/ VOKH-eh?

Other Active Sports

My favorite sports are . . .	Meine Lieblings- sportarten sind . . .	MINE-eh LEEP-lings- shport-ahr-ten zint . . .
_basketball	_Basketball	_BAAS-keht-bahl
_bowling	_Kegeln	_KAY-geln
_boxing	_Boxen	_BOKS-en
_cycling	_Radfahren	_RAAT-faa-ren
_golf	_Golf	_golf
_horseback riding	_Reiten	_RYE-ten
_mountain climbing	_Bergsteigen	_BEHRK-shyte-gen
_skiing	_Skifahren	_SHEE-faa-ren
_soccer	_Fußball	_FOOS-bahl
_swimming	_Schwimmen	_SHVIM-men
_tennis	_Tennis	_TEHN-is
_volleyball	_Volleyball	_VOL-lee-bahl
I'm looking for . . .	Ich suche . . .	ikh ZOO-kheh . . .
_a golf course.	_einen Golfplatz.	_INE-en GOLF-plahts.
_a soccer field.	_ein Fußballfeld.	_INE FOOS-bahl-fehlt.
_tennis courts.	_Tennisplätze.	_TEHN-nis-pleht-seh.
Are there rackets for rent?	Gibt es Tennisschlä- ger zu mieten?	gipt ehs TEHN-is-shlay- ge(r) tsoo MEE-ten?
We also need balls.	Wir brauchen auch Bälle.	veer BROW-khen owkh BEHL-leh.
You play very well.	Sie spielen sehr gut.	zee SHPEE-len zehr goot.

*In German, *Ski* is sometimes spelled *Schi*, and always pronounced SHEE.

Winter Sports

How far is the nearest ski area?	Wie weit ist das nächste Skigebiet?	vee vite ist dahs NAYKH-steh SHEE-geh-beet?
Can you get there by train?	Kann man mit der Bahn dahin?	kahn mahn mit dehr baan dah-HIN?
What are the skiing conditions like now?	Wie sind jetzt die Skiverhältnisse?	vee zint yehtst dee SHEE-fehr-hehlt-nis-seh?
Are there . . .	Gibt es . . .	gipt ehs . . .
_ski lifts?	_Skilifts?	_SHEE-lifts?
_beginners' slopes?	_Pisten für Anfänger?	_PIS-ten fewr AHN-fehn-ge(r)?
_skiing lessons?	_Skiunterricht?	_SHEE-un-tehr-rikht?
_cross-country ski trails?	_Wege für Langlauf-Skifahrer?	_VAY-geh fewr LAHNG-lawf-shee-faa-re(r)?
Is there an (artificial) skating rink there?	Gibt es dort eine (Kunst-) Eisbahn?	gipt ehs dort INE-eh [KUNST-] ICE-baan?
Can you rent . . .	Kann man ____ mieten?	kahn mahn ____ MEE-ten?
_skiing equipment?	_eine Skiausrüstung?	_INE-eh SHEE-ows-rews-tung?
_downhill skis?	_Abfahrtsskier?	_AHP-faarts-shee-e(r)?
_cross-country skis?	_Langlaufskier?	_LAHNG-lawf-shee-e(r)?
_poles/boots?	_Skistöcke/ Stiefel?	_SHEE-shtu(r)-keh/ SHTEE-fel?
_skates?	_Schlittschuhe?	_SHLIT-shoo-eh?
_a sled?	_einen Schlitten?	_INE-en SHLIT-ten?

SPECTATOR SPORTS

| Is there a soccer game this weekend? | Gibt es am Wochenende ein Fußballspiel? | gipt ehs ahm VOKH-en-ehn-deh ine FOOS-bahl-shpeel? |

Which teams are playing?	Welche Mannschaften spielen?	VEHL-kheh MAHN-shahf-ten SHPEE-len?
Where's the stadium?	Wo ist das Stadion?	voh ist dahs SHTAA-dee-ohn?
When does the game start?	Wann beginnt das Spiel?	vahn beh-GINT dahs shpeel?
How much are the tickets?	Was kosten die Eintrittskarten?	vahs KOS-ten dee INE-trits-kahr-ten?
Can you get me a ticket?	Können Sie mir eine Karte besorgen?	KU(R)-nen zee meer INE-eh KAHR-teh beh-ZOR-gen?
I'd like to see . . .	Ich habe Lust, ____ zu sehen.	ikh HAA-beh loost, ____ tsoo ZAY-en.
_a boxing match.	_einen Boxkampf	_INE-en BOKS-kahmpf
_car racing.	_ein Autorennen	_ine OW-toh-rehn-nen
_a golf tournament.	_ein Golfturnier	_ine GOLF-toor-neer
_horse racing.	_ein Pferderennen	_ine PFEHR-deh-rehn-nen
_a tennis tournament.	_ein Tennisturnier	_ine TEHN-nis-toor-neer

MOVIES

Foreign films are usually dubbed into German, but some movie houses will show them at certain times with the original sound track and German subtitles. This will be indicated by the letters OF (*Originalfassung* = original version), OmU (*Original mit Unter-titel* = original with subtitles); or OV, *Originalversion*. In large cities, there are usually one or two theaters that show all films in the original version. Films are shown on a fixed schedule, so tickets can be purchased in advance.

Let's go to the movies tonight.	Komm, gehen wir heute abend ins Kino.	kohm, GAY-en veer HOY-tehAA-behnt ins KEE-noh.
I want to see the new film by ____ with ____.	Ich will den neuen Film von ____ mit ____sehen.	ikh vil dehn NOY-en film fon ____ mit ____ ZAY-en.

What kind of film is it?	Was für ein Film ist es?	vahs fewr ine film ist ehs?
Is it dubbed?	Ist er synchronisiert?	ist ehr sin-kro-nee-ZEERT?
Who is the leading actor/actress?	Wer spielt die Hauptrolle?	vehr shpeelt dee HOWPT-rol-leh?
Who's the director?	Wer ist der Regisseur?	vehr ist dehr reh-zhis-SUR?
Where/When is it playing?	Wo/Wann spielt er?	voh/vahn shpeelt ehr?
I'd rather see . . .	Ich möchte lieber ____ sehen.	ikh MU(R)KH-teh LEE-be(r) ____ ZAY-en.
_the original version with subtitles.	_die Originalfassung mit Untertiteln	_dee o-ri-gi-NAAL-fahs-sung mit UN-te(r)-tee-teln
_a comedy.	_eine Komödie	_INE-eh ko-MU(R)-dyeh
_a musical.	_ein Musical	_ine "musical"
_a thriller.	_einen Krimi	_INE-en KREE-mee
_a Western.	_einen Western	_INE-en VEHST-ern
I'd like tickets (now) for this evening.	Ich möchte jetzt Karten für heute abend.	ikh MU(R)KH-teh yehtst KAHR-ten fewr HOY-teh AA-behnt.

THEATER, CONCERTS, OPERA, AND BALLET

Non-German operas, operettas, and stage plays are usually performed in German translations. The same is true even for well-known non-German musicals. Music, dance, and pantomime performances are of course the most accessible for non-German speakers, but those with an interest in theater and some grasp of German may find it worthwhile to venture into theater and opera productions in German. Often the music, sets, and staging are so impressive that they can be enjoyed in and of themselves.

Can you recommend a/an . . .	Können Sie mir ____ empfehlen?	KU(R)-nen zee meer ____ ehm-PFAY-len?
_ballet?	_ein Ballett	_ine bah-LEHT
_concert?	_ein Konzert	_ine kon-TSEHRT

_opera?	_eine Oper	_INE-eh OH-pe(r)
_operetta?	_eine Operette	_INE-eh oh-peh-REHT-teh
_play?	_ein Theaterstück	_ine tay-AA-te(r)-shtewk
Where's the theater/opera house/concert hall?	Wo ist das Theater/das Opernhaus/die Konzerthalle?	voh ist dahs tay-AA-te(r)/dahs OH-pern-hows/dee kon-TSEHRT-hahl-eh?
What's being performed?	**Was wird gespielt?**	**vahs virt geh-SHPEELT?**
Who's it by?	Von wem ist das?	fon vehm ist dahs?
Which orchestra is playing?	Welches Orchester spielt?	VEHL-khes or-KEHS-te(r) shpeelt?
Who's conducting/ singing/dancing?	**Wer dirigiert/ singt/tanzt?**	**vehr di-ree-GEERT/ zinkt/tahntst?**
I'd like . . .	Ich möchte . . .	ikh MU(R)KH-teh . . .
_an orchestra seat toward the middle.	_einen Platz im Parkett in der Mitte.	_INE-en plahts im pahr-KEHT in dehr MIT-teh.
_a balcony seat not too far back.	_einen Platz im Balkon nicht zu weit hinten.	_INE-en plahts im baal-KON nikht tsoo vite HIN-ten.

CLUBS AND DISCOS

Is there _____ in this town?	**Gibt es in dieser Stadt _____**	**gipt ehs in DEE-ze(r) shtaht . . .**
_a good disco	_eine gute Diskothek?	_INE-eh GOO-teh dis-koh-TAYK?
_an interesting nightclub	_ein interessantes Nachtlokal?	_ine in-teh-rehs-SAHN-tehs NAHKHT-loh-kaal?
Is there a floor show?	**Gibt es Attraktionen?**	**gipt ehs aht-trahk-TSYOH-nen?**
Are reservations necessary?	Muss man reservieren lassen?	mus mahn reh-zeh-VEER-en LAHS-en?

English	German	Pronunciation
Is evening dress required?	Wird Abendgarderobe verlangt?	virt AA-behnt-gaar-deh-roh-beh fehr-LAHNKT?
Is there a cover charge?	Gibt es eine Mindestgebühr?	gipt ehs INE-eh MIN-dehst-geh-bewr?
Would you like to dance?	**Möchten Sie tanzen?**	**MU(R)KH-ten zee TAHN-tsen?**

GRAMMAR IN BRIEF

NOUNS AND ARTICLES

All German nouns begin with a capital letter and fall into one of three gender catagories: masculine, feminine, or neuter. Although there are some rules to determine grammatical gender from the spelling and meaning of a word, it is largely unpredictable and should be learned together with the noun in question. The definite articles, *der, die, das* (the), and the indefinite articles, *ein, eine* (a/an), are determined by the gender of a noun. The changes from singular to plural noun forms are complex and include the addition of umlauts and the endings *-e, -er, -en, -s;* in some cases, there is no change at all. The plural definite article, *die,* is the same for all three genders.

Definite Articles:

Singular

masculine	der Vater	the father
feminine	die Mutter	the mother
neuter	das Mädchen	the girl

Plural

masculine	die Väter	the fathers
feminine	die Mütter	the mothers
neuter	die Mädchen	the girls

Indefinite Articles:

Singular

masculine	ein Tisch	a table
feminine	eine Tasse	a cup
neuter	ein Messer	a knife

Singular

masculine	kein Tisch	no table
feminine	keine Tasse	no cup
neuter	kein Messer	no knife

Plural

masculine	keine Tische	no tables
feminine	keine Tassen	no cups
neuter	keine Messer	no knives

Note: the indefinite article *ein* has no plural form. To translate "I need (some) cups," you would say "*Ich brauche Tassen.*" The negative *kein* does have a plural form and takes the same endings in the singular as the indefinite article.

ADJECTIVES AND DECLENSIONS

Predicate adjectives like *neu* in this sentence, *Der Wagen ist neu* (The car is new), are not declined, that is, they have no endings and appear as in the dictionary. When they precede the noun they modify, as in *Der neue Wagen fährt gut* (The new car drives well). Adjectives take endings, like articles, according to the gender of the noun and its case or use in the sentence. The four cases are: subject (nominative), direct object (accusative), indirect object (dative), and possessive (genitive). The following charts illustrate how articles, adjectives, and nouns are declined.

	Masculine Singular	Masculine Plural
subject	der alte Freund (the old friend)	die alten Freunde
direct object	den alten Freund	die alten Freunde
indirect object	dem alten Freund	den alten Freuden
possessive	des alten Freundes	der alten Freunde

	Feminine Singular	Feminine Plural
subject	die schwarze Katze (the black cat)	die schwarzen Katzen
direct object	die schwarze Katze	die schwarzen Katzen
indirect object	der schwarzen Katze	den schwarzen Katzen
possessive	der schwarzen Katze	der schwarzen Katzen

	Neuter Singular	Neuter Plural
subject	das kleine Buch (the small book)	die kleinen Bücher
direct object	das kleine Buch	die kleinen Bücher
indirect object	dem kleinen Buch	den kleinen Büchern
possessive	des kleinen Buches	der kleinen Bücher

When the adjective is preceded by the indefinite article, the adjective endings are somewhat different.

	Masculine Singular	Feminine Singular
subject	ein alter Freund (an old friend)	eine schwarze Katze (a black cat)
direct object	einen alten Freund	eine schwarze Katze
Indirect object	einem alten Freund	einer schwarzen Katze
possessive	eines alten Freundes	einer schwarzen Katze

	Neuter Singular	Negative Plural
subject	ein kleines Buch (a small book)	keine* kleinen Bücher (no small books)
direct object	ein kleines Buch	keine kleinen Bücher
indirect object	einem kleinen Buch	keinen kleinen Büchern
possessive	eines kleinen Buches	keiner kleinen Bücher

When modifying adjectives are not preceded by an article, they have the same endings as the definite article, except for the seldom-occurring masculine and neuter singular possessives, which become *-en* instead of *-es*. More common examples: *Er trinkt nur kaltes Bier* (He drinks only cold beer); *Mir schmeckt heiße Suppe* (I like hot soup).

Demonstrative Adjectives

Referred to sometimes as "*der* words," the demonstrative adjectives *dieser* (this), *jener* (that), *jeder* (every), *mancher* (some), *welcher* (which) follow the same declension as the definite article, *der, die, das.* Examples: *Dieses Brot schmeckt gut* (This bread

---

*See Note, under Nouns and Articles.

tastes good); *Mit welchem Bus fahren Sie*? (With which bus are you traveling?). In conversation *jener* (that) is usually replaced by the definite article, which is then given special stress. Example: *Dieser Sessel ist bequem, der Stuhl aber gar nicht*. (This armchair is comfortable, but that chair isn't comfortable at all.)

Possessive Adjectives

The endings on these parts of speech agree with the gender and number of the noun they modify, regardless of the possessor's gender. Examples: *ihr Vater* (her father), *seine Mutter* (his mother). In the singular possessive, adjectives are declined like the indefinite article, *ein* and are thus sometimes called "*ein* words." The plural forms follow the declension pattern of the definite article.

mein	my	unser	our
dein	your (familiar singular)	euer	your (familiar plural)
Ihr	your (polite singular)	Ihr	your (polite plural)
ihr	her	ihr	their
sein	his/its		

Note that *Ihr*, the polite form of your, is capitalized and the same in both singular and plural, while *ihr* can mean either her or their—only context will clarify which; for example, *Anna verwöhnt ihr Kind* (Anna spoils her child); *Die Eltern verwöhnen ihr Kind*. (The parents spoil their child.)

Comparative and Superlative Adjective Forms

The comparative is formed by adding *-er*, the superlative by adding *-st* or *-est* to the adjective. Single syllable adjectives usually add an umlaut where possible. For example:

hart (hard)	härter (harder)	härtest (hardest)
aggressiv (aggressive)	aggressiver (more aggressive)	aggressivst (most aggressive)
groß (large)	größer (larger)	größt (largest)

Regular adjective endings are added to these forms: *das härteste Holz* (the hardest wood), *mit dem aggressiveren Spieler* (with the more aggressive player). Predicate superlatives take this form: *Dieser Baum ist am größten.* (This tree is the largest.)

ADVERBS

Most adverbs are derived from adjectives in their undeclined form; for example, *Sie ist schön* (She is beautiful), *Sie singt schön* (She sings beautifully). The suffix *-lich* corresponds to our *-ly* ending. As in English, however, some of the most commonly used adverbs have unique forms and must be learned individually; for example: *fast* = almost, *sehr* = very, *ziemlich* = rather.

PRONOUNS

Personal pronouns are declined as follows:

Subject	Direct Object	Indirect Object
ich (I)	mich (me)	mir (to me)
du (you, familiar singular)	dich (you)	dir (to you)
er (he/it)	ihn (him/it)	ihm (to him/it)
sie (she/it)	sie (her/it)	ihr (to her/it)
es (it)	es (it)	ihm (to it/him/her)
wir (we)	uns (us)	uns (to us)
ihr (you, familiar plural)	euch (you)	euch (to you)
sie (they)	sie (them)	ihnen (to them)
Sie (you, polite plural and singular)	Sie (you)	Ihnen (to you)

Examples:

Er leiht *es mir* (He lends it to me);

Wir schicken *ihn euch* (We send him/it to you).

When both direct and indirect objects are pronouns, as above, the direct object precedes the indirect. When both are nouns (*Wir schicken Hans den Brief*—We send Hans the letter), the order is reversed. When they are mixed, the pronoun precedes the noun:

Wir schicken ihn Hans (We send it to Hans).

Wir schicken ihm den Brief (We send him the letter).

As with the possessive adjectives, the polite forms of you (*Sie, Ihnen*) are capitalized to distinguish them from *sie* (she, her, they, them) and *ihnen* (to them). Other pronouns with identical forms (e.g., *ihm* [to him, or, to it]) can be differentiated only through context. Personal pronouns reflect the grammatical gender of the nouns they replace.

The familiar you forms, *du* and *ihr*, should be used only when addressing relatives, close friends, young children, and animals. For all others, use *Sie*; otherwise, you may offend the person.

Reflexive Pronouns

These pronouns are used in combination with reflexive verbs to express the idea of "oneself." They have the same forms as the personal pronouns, except for the third person singular (*er, sie, es*), plural (*sie*), and polite second person (*Sie*), which as direct and indirect objects all take the reflexive form *sich*. Reflexive verbs are usually listed in the dictionary together with this pronoun *sich*. Examples:

sich setzen (to sit down), *Er setzt <u>sich</u>* (He sits [himself] down).

sich putzen (to clean oneself), *Ich putze <u>mir</u> die Zähne* (I clean my teeth).

VERBS

German, like English, has regular and irregular verbs; some of the latter follow the same vowel shift patterns as their English cognates: *trinken, trank, getrunken* (drink, drank, drunk). In English perfect tenses are formed with the auxiliary verb "have," while German uses two different ones. Most verbs are conjugated with *haben* (to have), but those of motion or change of state (e.g., *laufen* [to run], *wachsen* [to grow]) take *sein* (to be). Future tense uses the auxiliary *werden* (to become).

There is no equivalent in German for the continuous tenses in English. The present continuous, I am working, is rendered by the simple present: *Ich arbeite*. The past continuous, I was working, by either the simple past, *Ich arbeitete* (I worked) or the present perfect, *I habe gearbeitet* (I have worked). The latter two tenses are equivalent in German, but in conversation, where English speakers would use the simple past, such as "I spoke," Germans prefer the present perfect: *Ich habe gesprochen* (I have spoken). As in English, the German present tense is often used to express the future: *Wir fahren morgen ab* (We leave [will leave] tomorrow). Here are the conjugations of two regular and two irregular verbs in four of the most frequently used tenses.

Regular			Irregular	
Infinitive:	sagen (to say)	arbeiten (to work)	denken (to think)	fahren (to travel)

Present

ich	sage	arbeite	denke	fahre
du	sagst	arbeitest	denkst	fährst
es/sie/es	sagt	arbeitet	denkt	fährt
wir	sagen	arbeiten	denken	fahren
ihr	sagt	arbeitet	denkt	fahrt
sie/Sie	sagen	arbeiten	denken	fahren

Past (Imperfect)

ich	sagte	arbeitete	dachte	fuhr
du	sagtest	arbeitetest	dachtest	fuhrst
er/sie/es	sagte	arbeitete	dachte	fuhr
wir	sagten	arbeiteten	dachten	fuhren
ihr	sagtet	arbeitetet	dachtet	fuhrt
sie/Sie	sagten	arbeiteten	dachten	fuhren

Present Perfect (auxiliary **haben**) · (auxiliary **sein**)

ich	habe gesagt	gearbeitet	gedacht	bin gefahren
du	hast gesagt	gearbeitet	gedacht	bist gefahren
er/sie/es	hat gesagt	gearbeitet	gedacht	ist gefahren
wir	haben gesagt	gearbeitet	gedacht	sind gefahren
ihr	habt gesagt	gearbeitet	gedacht	seid gefahren
sie/Sie	haben gesagt	gearbeitet	gedacht	sind gefahren

Future (auxiliary **werden**)

ich	werde sagen	arbeiten	denken	fahren
du	wirst sagen	arbeiten	denken	fahren
er/sie/es	wird sagen	arbeiten	denken	fahren
wir	werden sagen	arbeiten	denken	fahren
ihr	werdet sagen	arbeiten	denken	fahren
sie/Sie	werden sagen	arbeiten	denken	fahren

Note that in the endings of *arbeiten* and other regular verbs whose stem ends in *-t* or *-d* (e.g., *reden* = to talk, *retten* = to save), extra *e*'s are added for reasons of pronunciation in the first three tenses. The verb *denken* has a mixture of regular and irregular traits: the vowel and stem change from present to past, from *denk* to *dach*, is irregular, but the past participle, *gedacht*, has a regular form, that is, the ending is *-t* instead of *-en*. Other verbs that follow this same pattern are: *brennen* (to burn), *bringen* (to bring), *nennen* (to name), *rennen* (to run), *senden* (to send). The so-called modal verbs, *dürfen* (to be allowed), *können* (to be able to), *mögen* (to like), *müssen* (to have to), and *sollen* (to be supposed to), also belong to this hybrid category.

Separable Prefixes

Certain verbs can be combined with prefixes, which are separated from the main verb in simple tenses. Example: *ziehen* (to pull) has these reflexive forms: *sich <u>an</u>ziehen* (to dress oneself), *sich <u>aus</u>ziehen* (to undress oneself), *sich <u>um</u>ziehen* (to change dress), *Ich ziehe mich <u>um</u>* (I'm changing).

The past participle of such verbs is formed by inserting the *ge-* syllable between the two parts of the verb: *Ich habe mich <u>umge</u>zogen* (I have changed).

WORD ORDER

German sentences follow the same basic pattern as English—subject, verb, predicate—but the second position of the verb in German is more fixed, so that if anything besides the subject precedes it, the subject-verb order is reversed:

Heute sprechen wir Deutsch (Today we speak German).

Suspended word order, with the verb or parts of the verb at the end of a clause, occurs often in subordinate clauses:

Ich glaube, dass der Preis zu hoch <u>ist</u> (I think that the price is too high).

And with participle and infinitive constructions:

Er <u>hat</u> den Film schon <u>gesehen</u> (He has already seen the film).

Er <u>möchte</u> den Film morgen <u>sehen</u> (He would like to see the film tomorrow).

Questions and Commands

Here the normal word order is simply reversed:

Gehen Sie ins Kino? (Do you go/Are you going to the movies?)

Gehen Sie ins Kino! (Go to the movies!)

Gehen Sie nicht ins Kino! (Don't go to the movies!)

In German there is no equivalent for the English auxiliary verb "do" in questions and commands.

NEGATIVE SENTENCES

Sentences are negated by either *nicht* or *kein*. *Nicht* is often suspended at the end of the sentence:

Ich verstehe die Frage <u>nicht</u> (I don't understand the question).

Er will mich <u>nicht</u> verstehen (He doesn't want to understand me).

Ich habe <u>keine</u> Fragen (I have no questions).

ENGLISH/GERMAN DICTIONARY

List of Abbreviations

m. *masculine*
f. *feminine*

n. *neuter*
pl. *plural*

A

a, an ein(-e) *[ine, INE-eh]*
abbey Abtei, f. *[ahp-TYE]*
abbreviation Abkürzung, f. *[AHP-kewrt-sung]*
able, to be kann *[kahn]*; können *[KU(R)-nen]*
about ungefähr *[UN-geh-fayr]*
above oben *[OH-ben]*
abroad im Ausland *[im OWS-lahnt]*
abscess Abszess, m. *[ahps-TSEHS]*
absolutely unbedingt *[UN-beh-dinkt]*
accelerator Gaspedal, n. *[GAHS-peh-daal]*
accept, to annehmen *[AHN-nay-men]*
accident Unfall, m. *[UN-fahl]*
accommodation Unterkunft, f. *[UN-te(r)-kunft]*
accompany, to begleiten *[beh-GLYE-ten]*
account Konto, n. *[KON-toh]*
ache Schmerz, m. *[shmehrts]*
acid Säure, f. *[ZOY-reh]*
acquaintance Bekannte, m., f. *[beh-KAHN-teh]*
across (movement) über *[EW-be(r)]*; durch *[durkh]*
across gegenüber *[gay-gen-EW-be(r)]*
actually eigentlich *[EYE-gehnt-likh]*
address Adresse, f. *[ah-DREHS-seh]*

adhesive tape Heftpflaster, n. *[HEHFT-pflahs-te(r)]*
adjust, to einstellen *[INE-shtehl-len]*
admire, to bewundern *[beh-VOON-dern]*
admission Eintritt, m. *[INE-trit]*; Zutritt, m. *[TSOO-trit]*
admission fee Eintrittsgeld, n. *[INE-trits-gehlt]*
adult Erwachsene, m./f. *[ehr-VAHK-seh-neh]*
advertising Werbung, f. *[VEHR-bung]*
afraid of something, to be vor etwas Angst haben *[for EHT-vahs ahngst HAA-ben]*
after nach *[nahkh]*
afternoon Nachmittag, m. *[NAHKH-mit-taak]*
aftershave lotion Raiserwasser, n. *[rah-ZEER-vahs-se(r)]*
afterward nachher *[NAHKH-hehr]*
again noch einmal *[nohkh INE-maal]*; wieder *[VEE-de(r)]*
against gegen *[GAY-gen]*
age Alter, n. *[AHL-te(r)]*
agency Büro, n. *[bew-ROH]*
ago vor *[for]*
agreed einverstanden *[INE-fehr-shtahn-den]*
air Luft, f. *[luft]*
air-conditioned klimatisiert *[klee-mah-ti-ZEERT]*

air conditioner Klimaanlage, f. [KLEE-mah-ahn-laa-geh]

airline Fluggesellschaft, f. [FLOOK-geh-zehl-shahft]

airmail mit Luftpost [mit LUFT-post]

air mattress Luftmatraze, f. [LUFT-mah-trah-tseh]

airplane Flugzeug, n. [FLOOK-tsoyk]

airport Flughafen, m. [FLOOK-haa-fen]

alarm clock Wecker, m. [VEH-ke(r)]

all alle(-s) [AH-leh(s)]

all right in Ordnung [in ORT-nung]

allergic allergisch [ah-LEHR-gish]

allowed erlaubt [ehr-LOWPT]

almond Mandel, f. [MAHN-del]

almost fast [fahst]

alone allein [ah-LINE]

aloud laut [lowt]

Alps Alpen, pl. [AHL-pen]

already schon [shon]

also auch [owkh]

always immer [IM-me(r)]

A.M. vormittags [FOR-mit-tahks]

amazing erstaunlich [ehr-SHTOWN-likh]

ambulance Krankenwagen, m. [KRAHN-ken-vaa-gen]

America Amerika, n. [ah-MEH-ri-kah]

American Amerikaner(-in), m., f. [ah-meh-ri-KAH-ne(r), (-neh-rin)]

American amerikanisch [ah-meh-ri-KAH-nish]

among unter [UN-te(r)]; zwischen [TSVISH-en]

amount Betrag, m. [beh-TRAHK]

amuse, to unterhalten [un-te(r)-HAAL-ten]; vergnügen [fehrk-NEW-gen]

and und [unt]

angel Engel, m. [EHN-gel]

angry wütend [VEW-tehnt]; böse [BU(R)-zeh]

animal Tier, n. [teer]

ankle Knöchel, m. [KNU(R)-khel]

annoy ärgern [EHR-gern]

another ein anderer [ine AHN-deh-re(r)]; noch ein(-e) [nohkh ine/INE-eh]

answer Antwort, f. [AHNT-vort]

answer, to antworten [AHNT-vor-ten]

antibiotic Antibiotikum, n. [ahn-ti-bee-OH-ti-koom]

antique Antiquität, f. [ahn-tik-vee-TAYT]

antiseptic Antiseptikum, n. [ahn-ti-ZEHP-ti-koom]

any etwas [EHT-vahs]; einige [INE-i-geh]

anybody, anyone (irgend)jemand [(IR-gehnt) YAY-mahnt]

anything (irgend)etwas [(IR-gehnt)EHT-vahs]

anyway jedenfalls [YAY-den-fahls]

anywhere irgendwo [IR-gehnt-voh]

apartment Wohnung, f. [VOH-nung]

apology Entschuldigung, f. [ehnt-SHOOL-di-gung]

apologize, to sich entschuldigen [zikh ehnt-SHOOL-di-gen]

appendicitis Blinddarmentzündung, f. [BLINT-dahrm-ehnt-tsewn-dung]

appetizer Vorspeise, f. [FOR-shpye-zeh]

apple Apfel, m. [AHP-fel]

appliance Gerät, n. *[geh-RAYT]*

appointment Verabredung, f. *[fehr-AHP-ray-dung]*

approximately ungefähr *[UN-geh-fayr]*

apricot Aprikose, f. *[ahp-ri-KOH-zeh]*

April April, m. *[ah-PRIL]*

area Gebiet, n. *[geh-BEET]*; Gegend, f. *[GAY-gehnt]*

area code Vorwahlnummer, f. *[FOR-vaal-num-me(r)]*

arrest, to verhaften *[fehr-HAHF-ten]*

arm Arm, m. *[ahrm]*

armchair Sessel, m. *[ZEHS-sel]*

around um *[um]*; herum *[heh-RUM]*

arrival Ankunft, f. *[AHN-kunft]*

arrive, to ankommen *[AHN-kom-men]*

art Kunst, f. *[kunst]*

article Artikel, m. *[ahr-TEE-kel]*

artificial künstlich *[KEWNST-likh]*

artist Künstler, m. *[KEWNST-le(r)]*

as als *[ahls]*; wie *[vee]*

ashtray Aschenbecher, m. *[AHSH-en-behkh-e(r)]*

ask, to fragen *[FRAA-gen]*; bitten *[BIT-ten]*

asparagus Spargel, m. *[SH-PAHR-gel]*

aspirin Aspirin, n. *[ahs-pi-REEN]*

asthma Asthma, n. *[AHST-mah]*

at an *[ahn]*; bei *[bye]*

at least mindestens *[MIN-dehs-tens]*

at once sofort *[zoh-FORT]*

attention Achtung, f. *[AHKH-tung]*; Aufmerksamkeit, f. *[OWF-mehrk-saam-kite]*

attorney Rechtsanwalt, m. *[REHKHTS-ahn-vahlt]*

attraction (sightseeing) Sehenswürdigkeit, f. *[ZAY-ens-vewr-dikh-kite]*

attractive schön *[shu(r)n]*; anziehend *[AHN-tsee-ent]*

August August, m. *[ow-GUST]*

aunt Tante, f. *[TAHN-teh]*

Austria Österreich, n. *[U(R)S-teh-ryekh]*

Austrian Österreicher(-in), m., f. *[U(R)S-teh-ryekh-e(r), {-eh-rin}]*

Austrian österreichisch *[U(R)S-teh-rye-ish]*

automatic automatisch *[ow-toh-MAH-tish]*

autumn Herbst, m. *[hehrpst]*

avenue Allee, f. *[ah-LAY]*

average durchschnittlich *[DURKH-shnit-likh]*

avoid, to vermeiden *[fehr-MYE-den]*

away weg *[vehk]*

awful scheußlich *[SHOYS-likh]*; schrecklich *[SHREHK-likh]*

B

baby Baby, n. *[BAY-bee]*

baby food Säuglingsnahrung, f. *[SOYK-lings-naa-rung]*

baby-sitter Babysitter, m. *[BAY-bee-sit-e(r)]*

back (body part) Rücken, m. *[REWK-en]*

back (direction) zurück *[tsoo-REWK]*

back, to be zurück sein *[tsoo-REWK zine]*

backache Rücken-
schmerzen, pl. *[REWK-en-
shmehrt-sen]*
bacon Speck, m. *[shpehk]*
bad schlecht *[shlehkht]*
bag Tasche, f. *[TAHSH-eh];*
Tüte, f. *[TEW-teh]*
baggage Gepäck, n. *[geh-
PEHK]*
baggage car Gepäckwa-
gen, m. *[geh-PEHK-vaa-gen]*
baggage check Gepäckkontrolle, f. *[geh-PEHK-kon-trol-
leh]*
baggage checkroom
Gepäckaufbewahrung, f.
[geh-PEHK-owf-beh-vaa-rung]
baggage claim Gepäckausgabe, f. *[geh-PEHK-ows-gaa-
beh]*
baggage locker Schließfach, n. *[SHLEES-fahkh]*
bake, to backen *[BAH-ken]*
baked gebacken *[geh-BAH-
ken]*
bakery Bäckerei, f. *[beh-keh-
RYE]*
balcony Balkon, m. *[bahl-
KON]*
ball Ball, m. *[bahl]*
ballet Ballett, n. *[bah-LEHT]*
band Musikkapelle, f. *[moo-
ZEEK-kah-pehl-leh]*
bandage Verband, m. *[fehr-
BAHNT]*
bank (finance) Bank, f.
[bahnk]
banknote Schein, m. *[shine]*
barber Friseur, m. *[fri-ZUR]*
bargain Sonderangebot, n.
[ZON-de(r)-ahn-geh-boht]
basement Untergeschoss, n.
[UN-te(r)-geh-shos]
basket Korb, m. *[korp]*
bath, bathroom Bad, n.
[baat]
bathe, to baden *[BAA-den]*

bathing suit Badeanzug, m.
[BAA-deh-ahn-tsook]
bathtub Badewanne, f.
[BAA-deh-vah-neh]
battery Batterie, f. *[bah-teh-
REE]*
be, to sein *[zine]*
beach Strand, m. *[shtrahnt]*
bean Bohne, f. *[BOH-neh]*
beard Bart, m. *[bahrt]*
beautiful schön *[shu(r)n]*
beauty salon Schönheitssalon, m. *[SHU(R)N-hites-zah-
lohng]*
because weil *[vile]*
bed Bett, n. *[beht]*
bed-and-breakfast Übernachtung mit Frühstück
*[ew-be(r)-NAHKH-tung mit
FREW-shtewk]*
bedroom Schlafzimmer, n.
[SHLAHF-tsim-me(r)]
beef Rindfleisch, n. *[RINT-
flyshe]*
beer Bier, n. *[beer]*
beer garden Biergarten, m.
[BEER-gahr-ten]
beer stein Bierkrug, m.
[BEER-krook]
beet (root) rote Bete, f.
[ROH-teh BAY-teh]
before vor *[for]*
begin, to beginnen *[beh-GIN-
nen]*
beginner Anfänger, m.
[AHN-fehn-ge(r)]
beginning Anfang, m. *[AHN-
fahng]*
behind hinten *[HIN-ten]*
believe, to glauben *[GLOW-
ben]*
bell (door) Klingel, f. *[KLING-
el]*
bellhop Hotel-page, m. *[ho-
TEL-pah-sheh]*
belong, to gehören *[geh-
HU(R)-en]*
below unten *[UN-ten]*

belt Gürtel, m. *[GEWR-tel]*

beside neben *[NAY-ben]*

best beste *[BEHS-teh]*

bet, to wetten *[VEHT-ten]*

better besser *[BEHS-se(r)]*

beverage Getränk, n. *[geh-TREHNK]*

between zwischen *[TSVISH-en]*

beyond jenseits *[YEHN-zites]*

bicycle Fahrrad, n. *[FAAR-raat]*

big groß *[grohs]*

bill (restaurant) Rechnung, f. *[REHKH-nung]*

billion Milliarde, f. *[mil-YAAR-deh]*

binoculars Fernglas, n. *[FEHRN-glaas]*

bird Vogel, m. *[FOH-gel]*

birthday Geburtstag, m. *[geh-BURTS-taak]*

bite, to beißen *[BICE-sen]*

bitter bitter *[BIT-te(r)]*

black schwarz *[shvahrts]*

bladder Blase, f. *[BLAA-zeh]*

blade (razor) Klinge, f. *[KLING-eh]*

blanket Decke, f. *[DEH-keh]*

bleed, to bluten *[BLOO-ten]*

blond blond *[blont]*

blood Blut, n. *[bloot]*

blood pressure Blutdruck, m. *[BLOOT-druk]*

blouse Bluse, f. *[BLOO-zeh]*

blue blau *[blow]*

boardinghouse Pension, f. *[pehn-ZYON]*

boarding pass Bordkarte, f. *[BOHRT-kahr-teh]*

boat Schiff, n. *[shif]*; Boot, n. *[boht]*

body Körper, m. *[KU(R)R-pe(r)]*

boiled gekocht *[geh-KOKHT]*

bone Knochen, m. *[KNOKH-en]*

book Buch, n. *[bookh]*

book, to reservieren lassen *[reh-zehr-VEER-en LAHS-sen]*; buchen *[BOO-khehn]*

bookstore Buchhandlung, f. *[BOOKH-hahnd-lung]*

boots Stiefel, pl. *[SHTEE-fel]*

booth Telefonzelle, f. *[tay-lay-FON-tsehl-leh]*

border Grenze, f. *[GREHN-tseh]*

born geboren *[geh-BOR-en]*

borrow, to borgen *[BOR-gen]*

boss Chef, m. *[shehf]*

botanical garden Botanischer Garten, m. *[bo-TAA-nish-e(r) GAAR-ten]*

both beide, *[BYE-deh]*

bother, to ärgern *[EHR-gern]*

bottle Flasche, f. *[FLAHSH-eh]*

box Schachtel, f. *[SHAHKH-tel]*

box office Kasse, f. *[KAHS-seh]*

boy Junge, m. *[YUN-geh]*

bra BH, m. *[bay-hah]*; Büstenhalter, m. *[BEWS-ten-hahl-te(r)]*

bracelet Armband, n. *[AHRM-bahnt]*

brain Gehirn, n. *[geh-HEERN]*

brakes Bremsen, pl. *[BREHM-zen]*

bread Brot, n. *[broht]*

break, to zerbrechen *[tsehr-BREHKH-en]*

breakdown Panne, f. *[PAHN-eh]*

breakfast Frühstück, n. *[FREW-shtewk]*

breast Brust, f. *[broost]*

breathe, to atmen *[AAT-men]*

bridge Brücke, f. *[BREW-keh]*

briefcase Aktentasche, f. *[AAK-ten-tah-sheh]*

bring, to bringen *[BRIN-gen]*

British Brite; Britin, m., f. *[BRI-teh; BRI-tin]*

broil, to grillen *[GRIL-len]*

198

broken gebrochen *[geh-BROKH-en]*; kaputt *[kah-PUT]*
brooch Broche, f. *[BRO-sheh]*
brother Bruder, m. *[BROO-de(r)]*
brother-in-law Schwager, m. *[SHVAA-ge(r)]*
brown braun *[brown]*
bruise Quetschung, f. *[KVEHT-chung]*
brush Bürste, f. *[BEWR-steh]*
brush, to bürsten *[BEWR-sten]*
buckle Schnalle, f. *[SHNAHL-leh]*
building Gebäude, n. *[geh-BOY-deh]*
bulb (electric) (Glüh)birne, f. *[{GLEW}-BEER-neh]*
bump, to stoßen *[SHTOHS-sen]*
bumper (car) Stoßstange, f. *[SHTOHS-shtahng-eh]*
burn Brandwunde, f. *[BRAHNT-vun-deh]*
burn, to brennen *[BREHN-nen]*
bus Bus, m. *[bus]*
bus stop Bushaltestelle, f. *[BUS-hahl-teh-shtehl-leh]*
bus tour Rundfahrt, f. *[RUNT-faart]*
business Geschäft, n. *[geh-SHEHFT]*
business trip Geschäftsreise, f. *[geh-SHEHFTS-rye-zeh]*
busy beschäftigt *[beh-SHEHF-tikht]*
but aber *[AA-be(r)]*
butcher Fleischer, m. *[FLYE-she(r)]*; Metzger, m. *[MEHTS-ge(r)]*
butcher shop Fleischerei, f. *[flye-sheh-RYE]*; Metzgerei, f. *[mehts-geh-RYE]*
butter Butter, f. *[BUT-te(r)]*
button Knopf, m. *[knopf]*
buy, to kaufen *[KOW-fen]*
by durch *[durkh]*; von *[fon]*

C

cab Taxi, n. *[TAHK-see]*
cabbage Kohl, m. *[kohl]*
cable (telegram) Telegramm, n. *[tay-lay-GRAAM]*
café Café, n. *[kah-FAY]*
cake Kuchen, m. *[KOO-khen]*
call (telephone) Anruf, m. *[AHN-roof]*
call, to (telephone) anrufen *[AHN-roo-fen]*
calm ruhig *[ROO-ikh]*
camera Fotoapparat, m. *[FOH-toh-ah-pah-raat]*
camp, to zelten *[TSEHL-ten]*
campsite Campingplatz, m. *[KAHM-ping-plahts]*
can (container) Dose, f. *[DOH-zeh]*; Büchse, f. *[BEWK-seh]*
can (to be able) können *[KU(R)-nen]*
can opener Büchsenöffner, m. *[BEWK-sen-u(r)f-ne(r)]*
cancel, to absagen *[AHP-zaa-gen]*
candle Kerze, f. *[KEHRT-seh]*
candy Bonbon, n. *[bong-BONG]*
cap Kappe, f. *[KAH-peh]*; Mütze, f. *[MEWT-seh]*
capital Hauptstadt, f. *[HOWPT-shtaht]*
car Wagen, m. *[VAA-gen]*; Auto, n. *[OW-toh]*
car breakdown Autopanne, f. *[OW-toh-pahn-neh]*
car rental agency Autovermietung, f. *[OW-toh-fehr-mee-tung]*
carburetor Vergaser, m. *[fehr-GAA-ze(r)]*
card (Post)karte, f. *[{POST}-KAHR-teh]*
careful! Vorsicht! *[FOR-zikht]*

careful sorgfältig *[ZORK-fehl-tikh]*

careful, to be aufpassen *[OWF-pahs-sen]*

carpet Teppich, m. *[TEHP-pikh]*

carrot Karotte, f. *[kah-ROT-teh]*

carry, to tragen *[TRAA-gen]*

carry-on luggage Handgepäck, n. *[HAHNT-geh-pehk]*

cassette recorder kassetten-recorder, m. *[kah-SET-ehn-reh-kohr-dehr]*

cash Bargeld, n. *[BAAR-gehlt]*

cash, to einlösen *[INE-lu(r)-zen]*

cash desk Kasse, f. *[KAHS-seh]*

castle Schloss, n. *[shlos]*

cat Katze, f. *[KAHT-seh]*

catch, to fangen *[FAHNG-en]*

cathedral Dom, m. *[dohm]*; Kathedrale, f. *[kah-teh-DRAAL-eh]*

Catholic katholisch *[kah-TOH-lish]*

cauliflower Blumenkohl, m. *[BLOO-men-kohl]*

caution Vorsicht, f. *[FOR-zikht]*

cave Höhle, f. *[HU(R)-leh]*

CD CD, f. *[TSEH-deh]*

CD player CD-Spieler *[TSEH-deh-SHPEE-lehr]*

ceiling Decke, f. *[DEH-keh]*

celery Sellerie, m. *[ZEHL-eh-ree]*

cell Zelle, f. *[TSEHL-leh]*

cemetery Friedhof, m. *[FREET-hohf]*

center Zentrum, n. *[TSEHN-trum]*

century Jahrhundert, n. *[YAAR-hun-dert]*

certain sicher *[ZIKH-e(r)]*; gewiß *[geh-VIS]*

certainly bestimmt *[beh-SHTIMT]*; sicher *[ZIKH-e(r)]*

certificate Zeugnis, n. *[TSOYK-nis]*

chain Kette, f. *[KEHT-teh]*

chair Stuhl, m. *[shtool]*

change (money) Kleingeld, n. *[KLINE-gehlt]*

change, to wechseln *[VEHK-seln]*

change, to (bus, train) umsteigen *[OOM-shtye-gen]*

chapel Kapelle, f. *[kah-PEHL-leh]*

charge Gebühr, f. *[ge-BEWR]*

charge, to berechnen *[beh-REHKH-nen]*

cheap billig *[BIL-likh]*

check Scheck, m. *[shehk]*; Rechnung, f. *[REHKH-nung]*

check, to (über)prüfen *[{EW-be(r)}-PREW-fen]*

check, to (luggage) aufgeben *[OWF-gay-ben]*

checkbook Scheckbuch, n. *[SHEHK-bookh]*

checkroom Gepäckaufbe-wahrung, f. *[geh-PEHK-owf-beh-vaa-rung]*

checkroom (theater) Garderobe, f. *[gar-deh-ROH-beh]*

cheek Wange, f. *[VAHN-geh]*

cheese Käse, m. *[KAY-zeh]*

cherry Kirsche, f. *[KIR-sheh]*

chest (part of body) Brust, f. *[broost]*

chestnut Kastanie, f. *[kah-STAHN-yeh]*

chewing gum Kaugummi, m. *[KOW-goom-mee]*

chicken Huhn, n. *[hoon]*

child Kind, n. *[kint]*

chill, to kühlen *[KEW-len]*

chin Kinn, n. *[kin]*

chocolate Schokolade, f. *[sho-ko-LAA-deh]*

choice Wahl, f. *[vaal]*

choose, to   (aus)wählen
[{OWS}-VAY-len]

chop   Kotelett, n. [kot-LEHT]

Christmas   Weihnachten, f.
[VYE-nahkh-ten]

church   Kirche, f. [KIR-kheh]

cider   Apfelmost, m. [AHP-
fehl-mohst]

cigar   Zigarre, f. [tsi-GAA-
reh]

cigarette   Zigarette, f. [tsi-
gaa-REHT-teh]

cigarette lighter   Feuerzeug,
n. [FOY-e(r)-tsoyk]

cinema   Kino, n. [KEE-noh]

citizen   Bürger, m. [BEWR-
ge(r)]

city   Stadt, f. [shtaht]

city hall   Rathaus, n. [RAAT-
hows]

class   Klasse, f. [KLAHS-seh]

classic   klassisch [KLAHS-sish]

clean   sauber [ZOW-be(r)]

clean, to   reinigen [RYE-ni-
gen]

cleaner's   Reinigung, f. [RYE-
nee-gung]

clear   klar [klahr]

clear (not blocked)   frei [frye]

client   Kund(-e), (-in), m./f.
[KUN-deh; KUN-din]

cliff   Felsen, m. [FEHL-zen]

climb   steigen [SHTYE-gen]

clock   Uhr, f. [oor]

close (near)   nahe [NAA-heh]

close, to   schließen [SHLEES-
sen]

closed   geschlossen [geh-
SHLOS-sen]

closet   Schrank, m. [shrahnk]

cloth   Stoff, m. [shtof]

clothes   Kleider, pl. [KLIDE-
e(r)]

cloud   Wolke, f. [VOL-keh]

cloudy   bewölkt [beh-VU(R)KT]

club   Klub, m. [kloop]

clutch (car)   Kupplung, f.
[KUP-lung]

coach   Bus, m. [bus]

coast   Küste, f. [KEWS-teh]

coat   Mantel, m. [MAHN-tel]

coffee   Kaffee, m. [KAH-feh]

coin   Münze, f. [MEWN-tseh]

cold   kalt [kahlt]

cold (sick)   erkältet [ehr-KEHL-
tet]

collar   Kragen, m. [KRAA-gen]

collect, to   sammeln [ZAHM-
eln]

colleague   Kolleg(-e), (-in),
m., f. [kol-LAY-geh; kol-LAY-
gin]

collect call   R-Gespräch, n.
[EHR-geh-shpraykh]

color   Farbe, f. [FAHR-beh]

color film   Farbfilm, m.
[FAHRP-film]

comb   Kamm, m. [kahm]

come, to   kommen [KOM-men]

come back, to   zurückkommen [tsoo-REWK-kom-men]

comedy   Komödie, f. [ko-
MU(R)-dyeh]

comfortable   bequem [beh-
KVEHM]

commission   Gebühr, f. [geh-
BEWR]

company   Gesellschaft, f.
[geh-ZEHL-shahft]

compare, to   vergleichen
[vehr-GLYE-khen]

compartment   Abteil, n.
[AHP-tile]

complaint   Reklamation, f.
[reh-klah-mah-TSIOHN];
Beschwerde, f. [beh-
SHVEHR-deh]

concert   Konzert, n. [kon-
TSEHRT]

conductor (orchestra)   Dirigent, m. [di-ri-GEHNT]

confirm, to   bestätigen [beh-
SHTAY-ti-gen]

connection (train)   Anschluss,
m. [AHN-shloos]

confused   verwirrt [fehr-VIRT]

consulate Konsulat, n. *[kon-zu-LAHT]*

contact lenses Kontaktlinsen, pl. *[kon-TAHKT-lin-zen]*

contents Inhalt, m. *[IN-hahlt]*

continue, to fortsetzen *[FORT-zeht-sen]*

convent Kloster, n. *[KLOH-ste(r)]*

conversation Gespräch, n. *[geh-SHPRAYKH]*

cook, to kochen *[KOKH-en]*

cooked gekocht *[geh-KOKHT]*

cookies Kekse, pl. *[KAYK-seh]*

cool kühl *[kewl]*

copper Kupfer, n. *[KUP-fe(r)]*

corduroy Kordsamt, m. *[KORT-zahmt]*

corkscrew Korkenzieher, m. *[KOR-ken-tsee-e(r)]*

corn Mais, m. *[mice]*

corn (foot) Hühnerauge, n. *[HEW-ne(r)-ow-geh]*

corner Ecke, f. *[EH-keh]*

costs Kosten, pl. *[KOS-ten]*

cost, to kosten *[KOS-ten]*

cotton Baumwolle, f. *[BOWM-vol-leh]*

cotton wool Watte, f. *[VAHT-teh]*

cough Husten, m. *[HOOS-ten]*

cough, to husten *[HOOS-ten]*

could könnte *[KU(R)N-teh]*

count, to zählen *[TSAY-len]*

country Land, n. *[lahnt]*

countryside Landschaft, f. *[LAHNT-shahft]*

course (meal) Gang, m. *[gahng]*

court Gericht, n. *[geh-RIKHT]*

courtyard Hinterhof, m. *[HIN-te(r)-hohf]*

cousin Kusine, f. *[koo-ZEE-neh]*; Vetter, m. *[FEHT-te(r)]*

cover, to (be)decken *[(beh)-DEHK-en]*

cramp Krampf, m. *[krahmpf]*

cranberry Preiselbeere f. *[PRICE-ehl-bay-reh]*

crazy verrückt *[fehr-REWKT]*

cream Sahne, f. *[ZAA-neh]*

cream (cosmetic) Creme, f. *[kraym]*

credit card Kreditkarte, f. *[kray-DEET-kahr-teh]*

crime Verbrechen, n. *[fehr-BREHKH-en]*

crisp knusprig *[KNOOS-prikh]*

cross Kreuz, n. *[kroyts]*

cross, to überqueren *[ew-be(r)-KVAY-ren]*

crossroads Kreuzung, f. *[KROY-tsung]*

crosswalk Zebrastreifen, m. *[TSAY-brah-shtrye-fen]*

crust Kruste, f. *[KROOS-teh]*

cry, to weinen *[VINE-en]*

cucumber Gurke, f. *[GOOR-keh]*

cuisine Küche, f. *[KEW-kheh]*

cup Tasse, f. *[TAHS-seh]*

curl Locke, f. *[LO-keh]*

curler Lockenwickler, m. *[LO-ken-vik-le(r)]*

currency Währung, f. *[VAY-rung]*

currency exchange office Wechselstube, f. *[VEHK-sehl-shtoo-beh]*

curtain Vorhang, m. *[FOR-hahng]*

curve Kurve, f. *[KOOR-veh]*

customer Kunde, m. *[KUN-deh]*

customs Zoll, m. *[tsol]*

cut (wound) Schnittwunde, f. *[SHNIT-vun-deh]*

cut, to schneiden *[SHNYE-den]*

cutlet Kotelett, n. *[kot-LEHT]*

cycling Radfahren, n. *[RAAT-faa-ren]*

Czech Republic Tschechische Republik, f. *[CHEH-khee-sheh ree-poo-BLEEK]*

D

daily täglich *[TAYG-likh]*
daily (newspaper)
  Tageszeitung, f. *[TAA-gehs-tsye-tung]*
dairy Molkerei, f. *[mohl-keh-RYE]*
damp feucht *[foykht]*
dance Tanz, m. *[tahnts]*
dance, to tanzen *[TAHN-tsen]*
danger Gefahr, f. *[geh-FAAR]*
dangerous gefährlich *[geh-FEHR-likh]*
dark dunkel *[DUN-kel]*
date (calendar) Datum, n. *[DAA-tum]*
daughter Tochter, f. *[TOKH-te(r)]*
day Tag, m. *[taak]*
day after tomorrow übermorgen *[EW-be(r)-mor-gen]*
day before yesterday vorgestern *[FOR-gehs-tern]*
dead tot *[toht]*
dead end Sackgasse, f. *[ZAHK-gaas-seh]*
deaf taub *[towp]*
death Tod, m. *[toht]*
dear lieb *[leep]*
debt Schuld, f. *[shoolt]*
decade Jahrzehnt, n. *[YAAR-tsehnt]*
decaffeinated koffeinfrei *[kof-feh-EEN-frye]*
December Dezember, m. *[deh-TSEHM-be(r)]*
decide, to entscheiden *[ehnt-SHIDE-en]*
declare, to (custom) verzollen *[fehr-TSOL-len]*
deep tief *[teef]*
delay Verspätung, f. *[fehr-SHPAY-tung]*
delicatessen Feinkostgeschäft, n. *[FINE-kost-geh-shehft]*

delicious köstlich *[KU(R)ST-likh]*
deliver, to liefern *[LEE-fern]*
delivery Lieferung, f. *[LEE-feh-rung]*
demand, to verlangen *[fehr-LAHNG-en]*
Denmark Dänemark, n. *[DEH-neh-mahrk]*
dentist Zahnarzt, m. *[TSAAN-ahrtst]*
denture Gebiss, n. *[geh-BIS]*
department Abteilung, f. *[ahp-TILE-ung]*
department store Kaufhaus, n. *[KOWF-hows]*
departure Abflug, m. *[AHP-flook]*; Abfahrt, f. *[AHP-faart]*
desire Wunsch, m. *[voonsh]*
desk Schreibtisch, m. *[SHRIPE-tish]*
despite trotz *[trots]*
dessert Nachtisch, m. *[NAHKH-tish]*
detour (traffic) Umleitung, f. *[OOM-lye-tung]*
develop, to entwickeln *[ehnt-VIK-eln]*
devil Teufel, m. *[TOY-fel]*
diabetes Zuckerkrankheit, f. *[TSU-ke(r)-krahnk-hite]*
diabetic Diabetiker, m. *[dee-ah-BAY-ti-ke(r)]*
dial, to wählen *[VAY-len]*
diaper Windel, f. *[VIN-del]*
diarrhea Durchfall, m. *[DURKH-fahl]*
dictionary Wörterbuch, n. *[VU(R)-te(r)-bookh]*
diesel fuel Dieselöl, n. *[DEE-zel-u(r)]*
diet Diät, f. *[dee-AYT]*
different verschieden *[fehr-SHEE-den]*
difficult schwer *[shvehr]*
difficulty Schwierigkeit, f. *[SHVEE-rikh-kite]*

dining car Speisewagen, m.
[SHPYE-zeh-vaa-gen]

dining room Esszimmer, n.
[EHS-tsim-me(r)]; Speisesaal,
m. *[SHPYE-zeh-zaal]*

dinner Abendessen, n. *[AA-behnt-ehs-sen]*

direct direkt *[dee-REHKT]*

direction Richtung, f. *[RIKH-tung]*

directions, to give den Weg
zeigen *[dehn vehk TSYE-gen]*

directory (telephone) Telefonbuch, n. *[tay-lay-FON-bookh]*

dirty schmutzig *[SHMUT-tsikh]*

disabled Behinderte, m., f.
[beh-HIN-dehr-teh]

disappointed enttäuscht
[ehnt-TOYSHT]

discount Rabatt, m. *[raa-BAHT]*

discover, to entdecken *[ehnt-DEHK-en]*

disease Krankheit, f.
[KRAHNK-hite]

dish (food) Gericht, n. *[geh-RIKHT]*

disinfect, to desinfizieren
[dehs-in-fi-TSEE-ren]

dissatisfied unzufrieden
[UN-tsoo-free-den]

distance Entfernung, f. *[ehnt-FEHR-nung]*

district Bezirk, m. *[beh-TSIRK]*

disturb, to stören *[SHTU(R)-en]*

divorced geschieden *[geh-SHEE-den]*

dizzy schwindlig *[SHVINT-likh]*

do, to tun *[toon]*

dock Hafenanlage, f. *[HAA-fen-ahn-laa-geh]*

doctor Arzt, m. *[ahrtst]*;
Ärztin, f. *[EHR-stin]*

document Dokument, n. *[do-koo-MEHNT]*

dog Hund, m. *[hunt]*

doll Puppe, f. *[PUP-peh]*

dollar Dollar, m. *[DOL-lahr]*

door Tür, f. *[tewr]*

doorman Portier, m. *[por-TYAY]*

double bed Doppelbett, n.
[DOP-pehl-beht]

double room Doppelzimmer, n. *[DOP-pehl-tsim-me(r)]*

down hinunter *[hin-UN-te(r)]*

downstairs unten *[UN-ten]*

downtown Zentrum, n.
[TSEHN-trum]

dozen Dutzend, n. *[DUT-sehnt]*

drama Drama, n. *[DRAA-mah]*

drawer Schublade, f.
[SHOOP-laa-deh]

drawing paper Zeichenpapier, n. *[TSYE-khen-pah-peer]*

dress Kleid, n. *[klite]*

dress, to (oneself) sich
anziehen *[zikh AHN-tsee-en]*

dressing gown Morgenrock,
m. *[MOR-gen-rok]*

dried getrocknet *[geh-TROK-net]*

drink Getränk, n. *[geh-TREHNK]*

drink, to trinken *[TRIN-ken]*

drinking water Trinkwasser,
n. *[TRINK-vahs-se(r)]*

drive, to fahren *[FAA-ren]*

driver Fahrer, m. *[FAA-re(r)]*

driver's license
Führerschein, n. *[FEWR-e(r)-shine]*

drops Tropfen, pl. *[TROP-fen]*

drug Medikament, n. *[meh-di-kah-MEHNT]*

drugstore Drogerie, f. *[dro-geh-REE]*

drunk betrunken *[beh-TRUN-ken]*

dry trocken *[TRO-ken]*

dry cleaning chemische Reinigung, f. *[KHAY-mish-eh RYE-ni-gung]*
duck Ente, f. *[EHN-teh]*
during während *[VAY-rehnt]*
dust Staub, m. *[shtowp]*
duty (customs) Zoll, m. *[tsol]*
duty-free zollfrei *[TSOL-frye]*
DVD player DVD-Spieler, m. *[deh-fow-DEH SHPEE-lehr]*
dye Farbstoff, m. *[FAHRP-shtof]*

E

each jede(-r, -s) *[YAY-deh {-e(r), -ehs}]*
ear Ohr, n. *[ohr]*
earache Ohrenschmerzen, pl. *[OH-ren-shmehrt-sen]*
early früh *[frew]*
earn, to verdienen *[fehr-DEE-nen]*
earring Ohrring, m. *[OHR-ring]*
east Osten, m. *[OS-ten]*
Easter Ostern, pl. *[OS-tern]*
easy leicht *[lyekht]*
eat, to essen *[EHS-sen]*
eel Aal, m. *[aal]*
eggs Eier, pl. *[EYE-e(r)]*
eggplant Aubergine, f. *[o-ber-ZHEE-neh]*
eight acht *[ahkht]*
eighteen achtzehn *[AHKH-tsayn]*
eighth achte(-r; -s) *[AHKH-teh {-te(r), -tehs}]*
eighty achtzig *[AHKH-tsikh]*
elbow Ellbogen, m. *[EHL-boh-gen]*
electric elektrisch *[eh-LEHK-trish]*
elevator Lift, m. *[lift]*
eleven elf *[ehlf]*
embassy Botschaft, f. *[BOHT-shahft]*

emergency Notfall, m. *[NOHT-fahl]*
emergency exit Notausgang, m. *[NOHT-ows-gahng]*
empty leer *[lehr]*
end Ende, n. *[EHN-deh]*
end, to beenden *[beh-EHN-den]*
engaged (betrothed) verlobt *[fehr-LOHPT]*
engine Motor, m. *[moh-TOHR]*
England England, n. *[EHNG-lahnt]*
English englisch *[EHNG-lish]*
enjoy genießen *[geh-NEES-sen]*
enlargement Vergrößerung, f. *[fehr-GRU(r)s-eh-rung]*
enough genug *[geh-NOOK]*
entrance Eingang, m. *[INE-gahng]*
entrance fee Eintrittsgeld, n. *[INE-trits-gehlt]*
envelope Umschlag, m. *[OOM-shlahk]*
environment Umwelt, f. *[OOM-vehlt]*
equal gleich *[glyekh]*
equipment Ausrüstung, f. *[OWS-rews-tung]*
error Fehler, m. *[FAY-le(r)]*
escalator Rolltreppe, f. *[ROL-trehp-peh]*
especially besonders *[beh-ZON-dehrs]*
estimate, to schätzen *[SHE-HTS-en]*
Europe Europa *[oy-ROH-pah]*
even selbst *[zehlpst]*
evening Abend, m. *[AA-behnt]*
evening gown Abendkleid, n. *[AA-behnt-klite]*
ever jemals *[YAY-maals]*
every jede(-r, -s) *[YAH-deh {-de(r), -dehs}]*
everything alles *[AH-lehs]*

everywhere überall *[EW-be(r)-ahl]*

example Beispiel, n. *[BYE-shpeel]*

excellent ausgezeichnet *[OWS-geh-tsyekh-net]*

exchange Austausch, m. *[OWS-towsh]*

exchange, to wechseln *[VEHK-seln]*

exchange rate Wechselkurs, m. *[VEHK-sel-koors]*

excursion Ausflug, m. *[OWS-flook]*

excuse Ausrede, f. *[OWS-ray-deh]*

excuse, to entschuldigen *[ehnt-SHOOL-di-gen]*

exhaust (car) Abgase, pl. *[AHP-gaa-zeh]*

exhausted erschöpft *[ehr-SHU(R)PFT]*

exhibition Ausstellung, f. *[OWS-shtehl-lung]*

exit Ausgang, m. *[OWS-gahng]*

expect, to erwarten *[ehr-VAAR-ten]*

expenses Spesen, pl. *[SHPAY-zen]*

expensive teuer *[TOY-e(r)]*

experience Erfahrung, f. *[ehr-FAA-rung]*

explain, to erklären *[ehr-KLEHR-en]*

express train Schnellzug, m. *[SHNEHL-tsook]*

extra zusätzlich *[TSOO-zehts-likh]*; extra *[EHK-strah]*

eye Auge, n. *[OW-geh]*

eyebrow Augenbraue, f. *[OW-gen-brow-eh]*

eyeglasses Brille, f. *[BRIL-leh]*

eyelash Augenwimper, f. *[OW-gen-vim-pe(r)]*

eyelid Augenlid, n. *[OW-gen-leet]*

F

fabric Stoff, m. *[shtof]*

face Gesicht, n. *[ge-ZIKHT]*

face cream Gesichtscreme, f. *[geh-ZIKHTS-kraym]*

factory Fabrik, f. *[fah-BREEK]*

fall (autumn) Herbst, m. *[hehrpst]*

fall, to fallen *[FAHL-len]*

false falsch *[fahlsh]*

familiar with, to be vertraut sein mit *[fehr-TROWT zine mit]*

family Familie, f. *[fah-MEEL-yeh]*

fan Ventilator, m. *[vehn-ti-LAA-tor]*

far weit *[vite]*

fare (fee) Fahrpreis, m. *[FAAR-price]*

farm Bauernhof, m. *[BOW-ehrn-hohf]*

fashion Mode, f. *[MOH-deh]*

fast schnell *[shnehl]*

fat dick; Fett, n. *[dik; feht]*

father Vater, m. *[FAA-te(r)]*

father-in-law Schwiegervater, m. *[SHVEE-ge(r)-faa-te(r)]*

faucet Wasserhahn, m. *[VAHS-se(r)-hahn]*

favor Gefallen, m. *[geh-FAHL-len]*

fear Angst, f. *[ahngst]*

fear, to Angst haben *[ahngst HAA-ben]*

February Februar, m. *[FAY-broo-aar]*

feel, to sich fühlen *[zikh FEW-len]*

felt (cloth) Filz, m. *[filts]*

fender Kotflügel, m. *[KOHT-flew-gel]*

ferry Fähre, f. *[FEH-reh]*

festival Fest, n. *[fehst]*

fever Fieber, n. *[FEE-be(r)]*

few wenige; einige *[VEH-ni-geh; INE-i-geh]*

field Feld, n. *[fehlt]*

fifteen fünfzehn *[FEWNF-tsayn]*

fifty fünfzig *[FEWNF-tsikh]*

fig Feige, f. *[FYE-geh]*

file Feile, f. *[FYE-leh]*

fill in, to ausfüllen *[OWS-fewl-len]*

fill up, to volltanken *[FOL-tahn-ken]*

fillet Filet, n. *[fee-LAY]*

filling (tooth) Plombe, f. *[PLOM-beh]*

filling station Tankstelle, f. *[TAHNK-stehl-leh]*

film Film, m. *[film]*

find, to finden *[FIN-den]*

fine (quality) fein *[fine]*

fine (penalty) Geldstrafe, f. *[GEHLT-shtrah-feh]*

fine arts bildende Künste, pl. *[BIL-den-deh KEWN-steh]*

finger Finger, m. *[FIN-ge(r)]*

finish, to erledigen *[ehr-LAY-di-gen]*

fire Feuer, n. *[FOY-e(r)]*

fire department Feuerwehr, f. *[FOY-e(r)-vehr]*

first erste (-r, -s) *[EHR-steh {-ste(r), -stehs}]*

first aid kit Verbandkasten, m. *[fehr-BAHNT-kahs-ten]*

fish Fisch, m. *[fish]*

fish, to angeln *[AHN-geln]*

five fünf *[fewnf]*

fit, to passen *[PAHS-sen]*

fix, to reparieren *[reh-pah-REE-ren]*

flash (on camera) Blitzlicht, n. *[BLITS-likht]*

flashlight Taschenlampe, f. *[TAHSH-en-lahm-peh]*

flat flach *[flahkh]*

flat tire Reifenpanne, f. *[RYE-fen-pahn-neh]*

flavor Geschmack, m. *[geh-SHMAHK]*

flea market Flohmarkt, m. *[FLOH-mahrkt]*

flight Flug, m. *[flook]*

floor Boden, m. *[BOH-den];* Stock, m. *[shtok]*

florist Blumengeschäft, n. *[BLOO-men-geh-shehft]*

flour Mehl, n. *[mayl]*

flow fließen *[FLEES-sen]*

flower Blume, f. *[BLOO-meh]*

flu Grippe, f. *[GRIP-peh]*

fluid Flüssigkeit, f. *[FLEWS-sikh-kite]*

fly, to fliegen *[FLEE-gen]*

fog Nebel, m. *[NAY-bel]*

folding chair Klappstuhl, m. *[KLAHP-shtool]*

folk music Volksmusik, f. *[FOLKS-moo-zeek]*

follow, to folgen *[FOL-gen]*

food Essen, n. *[EHS-sen]*

foot Fuß, m. *[foos]*

footpath Fußweg, m. *[FOOS-vehk]*

foot powder Fußpuder, m. *[FOOS-poo-de(r)]*

for für *[fewr]*

forbidden verboten *[fehr-BOH-ten]*

forehead Stirn, f. *[shteern]*

foreign fremd *[frehmt]*

foreigner Ausländer, (-in), m., f. *[OWS-lehn-de(r), {-deh-rin}]*

forest Wald, m. *[vahlt]*

forget, to vergessen *[fehr-GEHS-sen]*

fork Gabel, f. *[GAA-bel]*

form Formular, n. *[for-moo-LAHR]*

format Format, n. *[for-MAAT]*

fortress Burg, f. *[boork];* Festung, f. *[FEHS-tung]*

fortune Vermögen, n. *[fehr-MU(R)-gen]*

forty vierzig *[FEER-tsikh]*

forward vorwärts [FOR-vehrts]

fountain Brunnen, m. [BRUN-nen]

fountain pen Füllfederhalter, m. [FEWL-fay-de(r)-hahl-te(r)]

four vier [feer]

fourteen vierzehn [FEER-tsayn]

fourth vierte (-r, -s) [FEER-teh {-te(r), -tehs}]

fowl Geflügel, n. [geh-FLEW-gel]

fox Fuchs, m. [fooks]

fracture Bruch, m. [brukh]

frame Rahmen, m. [RAA-men]

France Frankreich, n. [FRAHNK-ryekh]

free frei [frye]

freeze, to frieren [FREE-ren]

frequent häufig [HOY-fikh]

fresh frisch [frish]

Friday Freitag, m. [FRYE-taak]

fried gebraten [geh-BRAA-ten]

friend Freund, (-in), m., f. [FROYNT, FROYN-din]

friendly freundlich [FROYNT-likh]

frog Frosch, m. [frohsh]

from von [fon]

front vorne [FOR-neh]

frost Frost, m. [frost]

frozen gefroren [geh-FROH-ren]

fruit Obst, n. [opst]

fry, to braten [BRAA-ten]

full voll [fol]

fun, to have Spaß haben [shpahs HAA-ben]

funny komisch [KOH-mish]

furniture Möbel, pl. [MU(R)-bel]

furs Pelze, pl. [PEHL-tseh]

future Zukunft, f. [TSOO-kunft]

G

gallery Galerie, f. [gah-leh-REE]

gain weight, to zunehmen [TSOO-nay-men]

game Spiel, n. [shpeel]

gamble, to spielen [SHPEE-len]

garage Garage, f. [gah-RAH-zheh]

garbage Abfall, m. [AHP-fahl]

garden Garten, m. [GAAR-ten]

garlic Knoblauch, m. [KNOH-blowkh]

gas Gas, n. [gahs]

gasoline Benzin, n. [behn-TSEEN]

gas station Tankstelle, f. [TAHNK-shtehl-leh]

gear (car) Gang, m. [gahng]

general allgemein [AHL-geh-mine]

general delivery post-lagernd [POST-laa-gehrnt]

generous großzügig [GROHS-tsew-gikh]

gentleman Herr, m. [hehr]

genuine echt [ehkht]

German deutsch [doych]

Germany Deutschland, n. [DOYCH-lahnt]

get, to (obtain) bekommen [beh-KOM-men]

get, to (fetch) holen [HOH-len]

get back, to zurück sein [tsoo-REWK zine]

get dressed, to sich anziehen [zikh AHN-tsee-en]

get off (out), to aussteigen [OWS-shtye-gen]

get up, to aufstehen [OWF-shteh-en]

gift Geschenk, n. [geh-SHEHNK]

208

gin (drink) Gin, m. *[jin]*
ginger Ingwer, m. *[ING-vehr]*
girl Mädchen, n. *[MAYT-khen]*
give, to geben *[GAY-ben]*
glad froh *[froh]*
gladly gern *[gehrn]*
glass Glas, n. *[glaas]*
glasses (eye) Brille, f. *[BRIL-leh]*
glove Handschuh, m. *[HAHNT-shoo]*
go, to gehen *[GAY-en]*
go away, to weggehen *[VEHK-gay-en]*
go home, to nach Hause gehen *[nahkh HOW-zeh GAY-en]*
god Gott, m. *[got]*
gold Gold, n. *[golt]*
golf course Golfplatz, m. *[GOLF-plahts]*
good gut *[goot]*
good-bye auf Wiedersehen *[owf VEE-de(r)-zay-en]*
goose Gans, f. *[gahns]*
gourmet Feinschmecker, m. *[FINE-shmehk-e(r)]*
gram Gramm, n. *[graam]*
grammar Grammatik, f. *[grah-MAH-tik]*
grandparents Großeltern, pl. *[GROHS-ehl-tern]*
grape (Wein)traube, f. *[{VINE} TROW-beh]*
grapefruit Pampelmuse, f. *[pahm-pehl-MOO-zeh]*
grass Gras, n. *[grahs]*
grave Grab, n. *[grahp]*
gray grau *[grow]*
great groß *[grohs]*
green grün *[grewn]*
greeting Gruß, m. *[groos]*
grilled gegrillt *[geh-GRILT]*
grocery store Lebensmittelgeschäft, n. *[LAY-bens-mit-tel-geh-shehft]*
ground Boden, m. *[BOH-den]*

ground floor Erdgeschoss, n. *[EHRT-geh-shos]*
guidebook Reiseführer, m. *[RYE-zeh-few-re(r)]*
guided tour Führung, f. *[FEW-rung]*

H

habit Gewohnheit, f. *[geh-VOHN-hite]*
hair Haar, n. *[haar]*
hairbrush Haarbürste, f. *[HAAR-bewr-steh]*
haircut Frisur, f. *[fri-ZOOR]*
hairdresser Friseur, m. *[fri-ZUR]*; Friseuse, f. *[fri-ZOY-seh]*
hair dryer Haartrockner, m. *[HAAR-trok-ne(r)]*
hairpin Haarnadel, f. *[HAAR-naa-dehl]*
half Hälfte, f. *[HEHLF-teh]*; halb *[hahlp]*
hall Halle, f. *[HAHL-leh]*
ham Schinken, m. *[SHIN-ken]*
hammer Hammer, m. *[HAHM-me(r)]*
hand Hand, f. *[hahnt]*
handbag Handtasche, f. *[HAHNT-tahsh-eh]*
handicapped behindert *[beh-HIN-dert]*
handkerchief Taschentuch, n. *[TAHSH-en-took]*
handmade handgearbeitet *[HAHNT-geh-ahr-bye-tet]*
hanger (clothes) Kleiderbügel, m. *[KLIDE-e(r)-bew-gel]*
hangover Kater, m. *[KAA-te(r)]*
happy glücklich *[GLEWK-likh]*
harbor Hafen, m. *[HAA-fen]*
hard (difficult) schwer *[shvehr]*
hard (tough) hart *[hahrt]*

hardware store Eisenwaren-handlung, f. *[EYE-zen-vaa-ren-hahnt-lung]*
harmful schädlich *[SHAYT-likh]*
hat Hut, m. *[hoot]*
hay fever Heuschnupfen, m. *[HOY-shnup-fen]*
have, to haben *[HAA-ben]*
he er *[ehr]*
head Kopf, m. *[kopf]*
headache Kopfschmerzen, pl. *[KOPF-shmehrt-sen]*
headlight Scheinwerfer, m. *[SHINE-vehr-fe(r)]*
head waiter Oberkellner, m. *[OH-be(r)-kehl-ne(r)]*
health Gesundheit, f. *[geh-ZUNT-hite]*
health food store Re-formhaus, n. *[reh-FORM-hows]*
health insurance Krankenkasse, f. *[KRAHN-ken-kahs-seh]*
hear, to hören *[HU(R)-en]*
heart Herz, n. *[hehrts]*
heart trouble Herzkrankheit, f. *[HEHRTS-krahnk-hite]*
heat Hitze, f. *[HIT-seh]*
heater Heizgerät, n. *[HITES-geh-rayt]*
heaven Himmel, m. *[HIM-mel]*
heavy schwer *[shvehr]*
heel Ferse, f. *[FEHR-zeh]*
heel (of shoe) Absatz, m. *[AHP-zahts]*
height Höhe, f. *[HU(R)-eh]*
hell Hölle, f. *[HU(R)-leh]*
hello! (phone) Hallo! *[HAH-loh]*
help Hilfe, f. *[HIL-feh]*
help, to helfen *[HEHL-fen]*
herbs Kräuter, pl. *[KROY-te(r)]*
here hier *[heer]*
high hoch *[hohkh]*

high school Oberschule, f. *[OH-be(r)-shoo-leh]*
high tide Flut, f. *[floot]*
highway Landstraße, f. *[LAHNT-shtrahs-seh]*
hike Wanderung, f. *[VAHN-deh-rung]*
hill Hügel, m. *[HEW-gel]*
hip Hütte, f. *[HEWF-teh]*
hire, to (rent) mieten *[MEE-ten]*
history Geschichte, f. *[geh-SHIKH-teh]*
hit, to schlagen *[SHLAA-gen]*
hitchhiker Anhalter, m. *[AHN-hahl-te(r)]*
hold, to halten *[HAAL-ten]*
hole Loch, n. *[lohkh]*
holiday Feiertag, m. *[FYE-e(r)-taak]*
holidays Ferien, pl. *[FEHR-yen]*; Urlaub, m. *[OOR-lowp]*
holy heilig *[HYE-likh]*
home Heim, n. *[hime]*; Haus, n. *[hows]*
home, to go nach Hause gehen *[nahkh HOW-zeh GAY-en]*
(at) home zu Hause *[tsoo HOW-zeh]*
home address Heimatadresse, f. *[HYE-maat-ah-drehs-seh]*
honey Honig, m. *[HOH-nikh]*
hope Hoffnung, f. *[HOF-nung]*
horn (car) Hupe, f. *[HOO-peh]*
horse Pferd, n. *[pfehrt]*
hospital Krankenhaus, n. *[KRAHN-ken-hows]*
hospitality Gastfreund-schaft, f. *[GAHST-froynt-shahft]*
host Gastgeber, m. *[GAHST-gay-be(r)]*
hot heiß *[hice]*
hotel Hotel, n. *[ho-TEL]*

hour Stunde, f. *[SHTUN-deh]*
house Haus, n. *[hows]*
how wie *[vee]*
how much wieviel *[VEE-feel]*
hundred hundert *[HUN-dert]*
Hungary Ungarn, n. *[UN-gahrn]*
hunger Hunger, m. *[HUN-ge(r)]*
hungry, to be Hunger haben *[HUN-ge(r) HAA-ben]*
hurry, to eilen *[EYE-len]*
hurry, to be in a es eilig haben *[ehs EYE-likh HAA-ben]*
hurt, to weh tun *[vay toon]*; schmerzen *[SHMEHRT-sen]*
hurt, to (oneself) sich verletzen *[zikh fehr-LEHT-sen]*
husband Mann, m. *[mahn]*; Ehemann, m. *[AY-eh-mahn]*
hut Hütte, f. *[HEW-teh]*

I

ice Eis, n. *[ice]*
ice cream Eis, n. *[ice]*
ice cube Eiswürfel, m. *[ICE-vewr-fel]*
identity card Ausweis, m. *[OWS-vice]*
if wenn *[vehn]*; ob *[op]*
ignition Zündung, f. *[TSEWN-dung]*
ill krank *[krahnk]*
illness Krankheit, f. *[KRAHNK-hite]*
immediately sofort *[zoh-FORT]*
important wichtig *[VIKH-tikh]*
impossible unmöglich *[un-MU(R)-glikh]*
impressive eindrucksvoll *[INE-druks-fol]*
in in *[in]*
included inbegriffen *[IN-beh-grif-fen]*

increase, to erhöhen *[ehr-HU(R)-en]*
indigestion Magenverstim-mung, f. *[MAA-gen-fehr-shtim-ung]*
inexpensive preiswert *[PRICE-vehrt]*
infection Infektion, f. *[in-fehk-TSYOHN]*
inflation Inflation, f. *[in-flah-TSYOHN]*
information Auskunft, f. *[OWS-kunft]*
injection Spritze, f. *[SHPRI-tseh]*
injure, to verletzen *[fehr-LEHT-sen]*
ink Tinte, f. *[TIN-teh]*
inn Gasthaus, n. *[GAHST-hows]*
insect repellent Insekten-schutz, m. *[in-ZEHK-ten-shuts]*
inside drinnen *[DRIN-nen]*
instead of statt *[shtaht]*
insurance Versicherung, f. *[fehr-ZIKH-eh-rung]*
interest Interesse, n. *[in-teh-REHS-seh]*
interested in, to be sich in-teressieren für *[zikh in-teh-rehs-SEE-ren fewr]*
interesting interessant *[in-teh-rehs-SAHNT]*
intersection Kreuzung, f. *[KROY-tsung]*
introduce, to vorstellen *[FOR-shtehl-len]*
invite einladen *[INE-laa-den]*
iodine Jod, n. *[yoht]*
iron (metal) Eisen, n. *[EYE-zen]*
iron (flatiron) Bügeleisen, n. *[BEW-gel-eye-zen]*
iron, to bügeln *[BEW-geln]*
island Insel, f. *[IN-zel]*
ivory Elfenbein, n. *[EHL-fen-bine]*

J

jack (car) Wagenheber, m. *[VAA-gen-hay-be(r)]*
jacket Jacke, f. *[YAH-keh]*
jam Marmelade, f. *[mahr-meh-LAA-deh]*
January Januar, m. *[YAH-noo-aar]*
Japan Japan, n. *[YAH-pahn]*
jar Glas, n. *[glaas]*
jaw Kiefer, m. *[KEE-fe(r)]*
jeweler Juwelier, m. *[yoo-veh-LEER]*
jewelry Schmuck, m. *[shmuk]*
Jewish jüdisch *[YEW-dish]*
job (employment) Stelle, f. *[SHTEHL-leh]*
job (task) Aufgabe, f. *[OWF-gaa-beh]*
joint Gelenk, n. *[geh-LEHNK]*
joke Witz, m. *[vits]*
journey Fahrt, f. *[faart]*
joy Freude, f. *[FROY-deh]*
juice Saft, m. *[zahft]*
July Juli, m. *[YOO-lee]*
June Juni, m. *[YOO-nee]*
just (only) nur *[noor]*

K

keep, to behalten *[beh-HAAL-ten]*
key Schlüssel, m. *[SHLEWS-sel]*
kidney Niere, f. *[NEE-reh]*
kilogram Kilo(gramm), n. *[KEE-loh {GRAAM}]*
kilometer Kilometer, m. *[kee-loh-MAY-te(r)]*
kind (nice) nett *[neht]*
kind (type) Art, f. *[ahrt]*
kiss Kuss, m. *[kus]*
kiss, to küssen *[KEWS-sen]*
kitchen Küche, f. *[KEW-kheh]*
knee Knie, n. *[knee]*
knife Messer, m. *[MEHS-se(r)]*

knock, to klopfen *[KLOP-fen]*
know, to (be familiar with) kennen *[KEHN-nen]*
know, to (facts) wissen *[VIS-sen]*
kosher koscher *[KOH-she(r)]*

L

label Etikett, f. *[eh-ti-KEHT]*
lace Spitze, f. *[SHPIT-seh]*
laces (shoe) Schuhbänder, pl. *[SHOO-behn-de(r)]*
ladder Leiter, f. *[LITE-e(r)]*
ladies' room Damentoilette, f. *[DAA-men-toy-leh-teh]*
lady Dame, f. *[DAA-meh]*
lake See, m. *[zay]*
lamb Lammfleisch, n. *[LAHM-flyshe]*
lamp Lampe, f. *[LAHM-peh]*
land Land, n. *[lahnt]*
land, to landen *[LAHN-den]*
landscape Landschaft, f. *[LAHNT-shahft]*
language Sprache, f. *[SH-PRAHKH-eh]*
large groß *[grohs]*
last letzte *[LEHTS-teh]*
last, to dauern *[DOW-ern]*
late spät *[shpayt]*
laugh, to lachen *[LAHKH-en]*
laundromat Waschsalon, m. *[VAHSCH-zaa-long]*
laundry Wäscherei, f. *[veh-sheh-RYE]*
lawyer Rechtsanwalt, m. *[REHKHTS-ahn-vahlt]*
lawn Rasen, m. *[RAA-zen]*
laxative Abführmittel, n. *[AHP-fewr-mit-tel]*
lead, to führen *[FEW-ren]*
lead (stage) Hauptrolle, f. *[HOWPT-rol-leh]*
leak, to lecken *[LEHK-en]*
learn, to lernen *[LEHR-nen]*

least, at wenigstens *[VAY-nikh-stens]*

leather Leder, n. *[LAY-de(r)]*

leave, to (behind) lassen *[LAHS-sen]*

leave, to (depart) abfahren *[AHP-faa-ren]*

left links *[links]*

leg Bein, n. *[bine]*

lemon Zitrone, f. *[tsi-TROH-neh]*

lemonade Limonade, f. *[lee-moh-NAA-deh]*

lend, to leihen *[LYE-en]*

length Länge, f. *[LEHNG-eh]*

lens (camera) Objektiv, n. *[op-yehk-TEEF]*

lens (glasses) Glas, n. *[glaas]*

less weniger *[VAY-neh-ge(r)]*

lesson Aufgabe, f. *[OWF-gaa-beh]*

let, to lassen *[LAHS-sen]*

letter Brief, m. *[breef]*

letter box Briefkasten, m. *[BREEF-kahs-ten]*

lettuce Kopfsalat, m. *[KOPF-zah-laat]*

level Ebene, f. *[AY-beh-neh]*

library Bibliothek, f. *[bib-lee-oh-TAYK]*

license (driver's) Führerschein, m. *[FEW-re(r)-shine]*

lie, to (down) sich hinlegen *[zikh HIN-lay-gen]*

life Leben, n. *[LAY-ben]*

lifeguard Rettungsschwimmer, m. *[REH-tungs-shvim-me(r)]*

lift, to heben *[HAY-ben]*

light (weight) leicht *[lyekht]*

light Licht, n. *[likht]*

light, to anzünden *[AHN-tsewn-den]*

lighter Feuerzeug, n. *[FOY-e(r)-tsoyk]*

lightning Blitz, m. *[blits]*

like (as) wie *[vee]*

like, to gern haben *[gehrn HAA-ben]*; mögen *[MU(R)-gen]*; gefallen *[geh-FAHL-len]*

lime Limone, f. *[li-MOH-neh]*

limit Begrenzung, f. *[beh-GREHN-tsung]*

line Linie, f. *[LEEN-yeh]*

line (of people) Schlange, f. *[SHLAHNG-eh]*

linen Leinen, n. *[LINE-en]*

lip Lippe, f. *[LIP-peh]*

lipstick Lippenstift, m. *[LIP-pen-shtift]*

liqueur Likör, m. *[li-KUR]*

liquor Alkohol, m. *[AHL-koh-hol]*

list Liste, f. *[LIS-teh]*

listen, to (zu)hören *[(TSOO)HU(R)-ren]*

liter Liter, m. *[LEE-te(r)]*

little klein *[kline]*

live, to leben *[LAY-ben]*

liver Leber, f. *[LAY-be(r)]*

living room Wohnzimmer, n. *[VOHN-tsim-me(r)]*

lobby Eingangshalle, f. *[INE-gahngs-hahl-leh]*

lobster Hummer, m. *[HUM-me(r)]*

local hiesig *[HEE-zikh]*

local train Nahverkehrszug, m. *[NAA-fehr-kehrs-tsook]*

local phone call Ortsgespräch, n. *[ORTS-geh-spraykh]*

lock, to abschließen *[AHP-shlees-en]*

long lang *[lahng]*

long-distance call Ferngespräch, n. *[FEHRN-geh-spraykh]*

look at, to ansehen *[AHN-zay-en]*

look for, to suchen *[ZOO-khen]*

look out, to aufpassen *[OWF-pahs-sen]*

lose, to verlieren *[fehr-LEER-en]*

lose weight, to abnehmen *[AHP-nay-men]*

loss Verlust, m. *[fehr-LOOST]*

lost verloren *[fehr-LOR-en]*

lost and found Fundbüro, n. *[FUNT-bew-roh]*

a lot eine Menge *[INE-eh MEHNG-eh]*

lotion Lotion, f. *[loh-TSYOHN]*

love Liebe, f. *[LEE-beh]*

love, to lieben *[LEE-ben]*

low niedrig *[NEE-drikh]*

low tide Ebbe, f. *[EHB-eh]*

luck Glück, n. *[glewk]*

good luck viel Glück *[feel glewk]*

luggage Gepäck, n. *[geh-PEHK]*

lunch Mittagessen, n. *[MIT-taak-ehs-sen]*

lung Lunge, f. *[LUNG-eh]*

luxury Luxus, m. *[LUKS-us]*

M

machine Maschine, f. *[mah-SHEE-neh]*

magazine Zeitschrift, f. *[TSITE-shrift]*

maid Zimmermädchen, n. *[TSIM-e(r)-mayt-khen]*

mail Post, f. *[post]*

mail, to aufgeben *[OWF-gay-ben]*

mailbox Briefkasten, m. *[BREEF-kahs-ten]*

make, to machen *[MAHKH-en]*

man Mann, m. *[mahn]*

manager Geschäftsführer, m. *[geh-SHEHFTS-few-re(r)]*

manicure Maniküre, f. *[mah-ni-KEW-reh]*

many viele *[FEE-leh]*

map Karte, f. *[KAHR-teh]*; Plan, m. *[plaan]*

March März, m. *[mehrts]*

market Markt, m. *[mahrkt]*

married verheiratet *[fehr-HYE-raa-tet]*

mass (church) Messe, f. *[MEHS-seh]*

massage Massage, f. *[mah-SAA-zheh]*

match Streichholz, n. *[SHTRYEKH-hohlts]*

material (fabric) Stoff, m. *[shtof]*

mattress Matratze, f. *[mah-TRAHT-tseh]*

May Mai, m. *[mye]*

maybe vielleicht *[fee-LYEKHT]*

meal Mahlzeit, f. *[MAAL-tsite]*

mean, to bedeuten *[beh-DOY-ten]*

meaning Bedeutung, f. *[beh-DOY-tung]*

means Mittel, n. *[MIT-tel]*

measure, to messen *[MEHS-sen]*

meat Fleisch, n. *[flyshe]*

mechanic Mechaniker, m. *[meh-KHAH-ni-ke(r)]*

medical ärztlich *[EHRTS-likh]*

medicine Medikament, n. *[meh-di-kah-MEHNT]*

meet, to treffen *[TREHF-fen]*

meeting Versammlung, f. *[fehr-ZAHM-lung]*

melon Melone, f. *[meh-LOH-neh]*

mend, to flicken *[FLIK-en]*

men's room Herrentoilette, f. *[HEHR-ren-toy-leht-teh]*

menstrual pains Menstruationsbeschwerden, pl. *[mehn-stru-ah-TSYOHNS-beh-shvehr-den]*

mention, to erwähnen *[ehr-VAY-nen]*

menu Speisekarte, f.
[SHPYE-zeh-kahr-teh]

merry fröhlich [FRU(R)-likh]

mess Unordnung, f. [UN-ort-nung]

message Nachricht, f.
[NAKHK-rikht]

meter (length) Meter, m.
[MAY-te(r)]

middle Mitte, f. [MIT-teh]

middle-class bürgerlich
[BEWR-ge(r)-likh]

midnight Mitternacht, f.
[MIT-te(r)-nahkht]

mild mild [milt]

milk Milch, f. [milkh]

million Million, f. [mil-YOHN]

mind Geist, m. [geyst]

mineral water Mineral-wasser, n. [mi-neh-RAAL-vahs-se(r)]

minister (clergyman) Pfarrer,
m. [PFAHR-e(r)]

mint Minze, f. [MIN-tseh]

minute Minute, f. [mi-NOO-teh]

mirror Spiegel, m. [SHPEE-gel]

Miss Fräulein, n. [FROY-line]

miss, to versäumen [fehr-ZOY-men]

missing, to be verschwun-den sein [fehr-SHVUN-den zine]

mistake Irrtum, m. [EER-toom]

modern modern [mo-DEHRN]

moment Augenblick, m.
[OW-gen-blik]

monastery Kloster, n.
[KLOHS-te(r)]

Monday Montag, m.
[MOHN-taak]

money Geld, n. [gehlt]

money order Postan-weisung, f. [POST-ahn-vye-zung]

month Monat, m. [MOH-naat]

monument Denkmal, n.
[DEHNK-maal]

moon Mond, f. [mohnt]

more mehr [mehr]

morning Morgen, m. [MOR-gen]

mosque Moschee, f. [mo-SHAY]

mother Mutter, f. [MUT-te(r)]

mother-in-law Schwiegermutter, f. [SHVEE-ge(r)-MUT-te(r)]

motion sickness Reisekrankheit, f. [RYE-zeh-krahnk-hite]

motor Motor, m. [moh-TOHR]

motorcycle Motorrad, n.
[moh-TOHR-raat]

mountain Berg, m. [behrk]

mountain pass Paß, m.
[pahs]

mouth Mund, m. [munt]

mouthwash Mundwasser, n.
[MUNT-vahs-se(r)]

move (to change residence) umziehen [OOM-tsee-en]

movie Film, m. [film]

movie theater Kino, n. [KEE-noh]

Mr. Herr, m. [hehr]

Mrs., Ms. Frau, f. [frow]

much viel [feel]

muscle Muskel, m. [MUS-kel]

museum Museum, n. [moo-ZAY-um]

mushroom Pilz, m. [pilts]

music Musik, f. [moo-ZEEK]

mussels Muscheln, pl.
[MOO-shehln]

must, to müssen [MEWS-sen]

mustache Schnurrbart, m.
[SHNOOR-bahrt]

mustard Senf, m. [zehnf]

myself selbst [zehlpst]

215

N

nail (finger) Nagel, m. *[NAA-gel]*

nail polish Nagellack, m. *[NAA-gel-lahk]*

naked nackt *[nahkt]*

name Name, m. *[NAA-meh]*

named, to be heißen *[HICE-sen]*

napkin Serviette, f. *[sehr-VYEHT-teh]*

narrow eng *[ehng]*

nationality Staatsange-hörigkeit, f. *[SHTAATS-ahn-geh-hu(r)-rikh-kite]*

native einheimisch *[INE-hye-mish]*

nature Natur, f. *[nah-TOOR]*

nausea Übelkeit, f. *[EW-bel-kite]*

near nah *[naa]*

nearby in der Nähe *[in dehr NAY-eh]*

nearly fast *[fahst]*

necessary nötig *[NU(R)-tikh]*

neck Hals, m. *[hahls]*

necklace Halskette, f. *[HAHLS-keht-teh]*

necktie Krawatte, f. *[krah-VAHT-teh]*

need, to brauchen *[BROW-khen]*

needle Nadel, f. *[NAA-del]*

neighbor Nachbar, m. *[NAHKH-baar]*

neighborhood Nach-barschaft, f. *[NAHKH-baar-shahft]*

nerve Nerv, m. *[nehrf]*

never nie *[nee]*

never mind macht nichts *[mahkht nikhts]*

new neu *[noy]*

New Year Neujahr, n. *[NOY-yaar]*

newspaper Zeitung, f. *[TSITE-ung]*

newspaper stand Zeitungs-stand, m. *[TSITE-ungs-shtahnt]*

next nächst *[naykhst]*

nice nett *[neht]*

night Nacht, f. *[nahkht]*

nightclub Nachtlokal, n. *[NAHKHT-loh-kaal]*

nightgown Nachthemd, n. *[HAHKHT-hehmt]*

nine neun *[noyn]*

nineteen neunzehn *[NOYN-tsayn]*

ninety neunzig *[NOYN-tsikh]*

ninth neunte *[NOYN-teh]*

no nein *[nine]*

no one niemand *[NEE-mahnt]*

noise Lärm, m. *[lehrm]*

noisy laut *[lowt]*

none kein *[kine]*

nonsmoker Nichtraucher, m. *[NIKHT-row-khe(r)]*

noodles Nudeln, pl. *[NOO-deln]*

noon Mittag, m. *[MIT-taak]*

north Norden, m. *[NOR-den]; nördlich [NU(R)RT-likh]*

nose Nase, f. *[NAA-zeh]*

not nicht *[nikht]*

not at all gar nicht *[gaar nikht]*

notebook Notizheft, n. *[no-TEETS-hehft]*

nothing nichts *[nikhts]*

notice Anzeige, f. *[AHN-tsye-geh]*

notice, to bemerken *[beh-MEHR-ken]*

novel Roman, m. *[roh-MAAN]*

November November, m. *[no-VEHM-be(r)]*

now jetzt *[yehtst]*

number Nummer, f. *[NUM-me(r)]*

nurse Krankenschwester, f. *[KRAHN-ken-shvehs-te(r)]*

nut Nuss, m. *[noos]*

O

object Gegenstand, m. *[GAY-gen-shtahnt]*

obtain, to bekommen *[beh-KOM-men]*

occupation Beruf, m. *[beh-ROOF]*

occupied besetzt *[beh-ZEHTST]*

ocean Ozean, m. *[OH-tsay-ahn]*

October Oktober, m. *[ok-TOH-be(r)]*

odd (number) ungerade *[UN-geh-raa-deh]*

of von *[fon]*

of course natürlich *[nah-TEWR-likh]*

offer, to anbieten *[ahn-BEE-ten]*

office Büro, n. *[bew-ROH]*; Amt, n. *[ahmt]*

often oft *[oft]*

oil Öl, n. *[u(r)l]*

okay okay *[o-kay]*

old alt *[ahlt]*

olive Olive, f. *[o-LEE-veh]*

omelet Omelett, n. *[om-LEHT]*

on an *[ahn]*; auf *[owf]*

on foot zu Fuß *[tsoo foos]*

on time pünktlich *[PEWNKT-likh]*

once einmal *[INE-maal]*

one eins *[ines]*

one-way ticket einfache Fahrkarte, f. *[INE-fahkh-eh FAAR-kahr-teh]*

one-way street Einbahn-straße, f. *[INE-baan-shtrahs-eh]*

onion Zwiebel, f. *[TSVEE-bel]*

only nur *[noor]*

open offen *[OF-fen]*

open, to öffnen *[U(R)F-nen]*; aufmachen *[OWF-mahkh-en]*

opera Oper, f. *[OH-pe(r)]*

operation Operation, f. *[o-peh-rah-TSYOHN]*

operator (phone) Vermitt-tlung, f. *[fehr-MIT-lung]*

opportunity Gelegenheit, f. *[geh-LAY-gen-hite]*

opposite Gegenteil, n. *[GAY-gen-tile]*

opposite (across from) gegenüber *[gay-gen-EW-be(r)]*

optician Optiker, m. *[OP-ti-ke(r)]*

or oder *[OH-de(r)]*

orange Orange, f. *[oh-RAHN-zheh]*

orange juice Orangensaft, m. *[oh-RAHN-zhen-sahft]*

orchestra Orchester, n. *[or-KEHS-te(r)]*

order Bestellung, f. *[beh-SHTEH-lung]*

order, to bestellen *[beh-SHTEHL-len]*

ordinary gewöhnlich *[geh-VU(R)N-likh]*

other andere *[AHN-deh-reh]*

otherwise sonst *[zonst]*

out aus *[ows]*

out of order außer Betrieb *[OWS-se(r) beh-TREEP]*

outdoors draußen *[DROWS-sen]*

outlet (electrical) Steckdose, f. *[SHTEHK-doh-zeh]*

outfit Ausrüstung, f. *[OWS-rews-tung]*

outside of außerhalb *[OWS-se(r)-hahlp]*

oven Ofen, m. *[OH-fen]*

over (above) über *[EW-be(r)]*

over (finished) aus *[ows]*; zu Ende *[tsoo EHN-deh]*

overcoat Mantel, m. *[MAHN-tel]*

overdone zu stark gebraten *[tsoo shtahrk geh-BRAA-ten]*

overdose Überdosis, f. *[EW-be(r)-doh-zis]*

overheat, to (motor) heißlaufen *[HICE-low-fen]*

overnight (stay) eine Nacht *[INE-eh nahkht]*

overrun überlaufen *[ew-be(r)-LOW-fen]*

overtime Überstunden, pl. *[EW-be(r)-shtun-den]*

owe, to schulden *[SHOOL-den]*

own, to besitzen *[beh-ZIT-sen]*

owner Besitzer, m. *[beh-ZIT-se(r)]*

oyster Auster, f. *[OW-ste(r)]*

P

pack, to packen *[PAH-ken]*

package Paket, n. *[pah-KAYT]*

pain Schmerz, m. *[shmehrts]*

painter Maler, m. *[MAA-le(r)]*

painting Bild, n. *[bilt]*; Gemälde, n. *[geh-MEHL-deh]*

painted gemalt *[geh-MAALT]*

pair Paar, n. *[paar]*

pajamas Pyjama, m. *[pi-JAA-maa]*

palace Palast, m. *[pah-LAHST]*; Schloss, m. *[shlos]*

pancake Pfannkuchen, m. *[PFAHN-koo-khen]*

panties Schlüpfer, m. *[SHLEWP-fer]*

pants Hose, f. *[HOH-zeh]*

panty hose Strumpfhose, f. *[SHTRUMPF-hoh-zeh]*

paper Papier, n. *[pah-PEER]*

parcel Paket, n. *[pah-KAYT]*

pardon Verzeihung, f. *[fehr-TSYE-ung]*; Wie bitte? *[vee BIT-teh]*

park Park, m. *[pahrk]*

park, to parken *[PAHR-ken]*

parking disk Parkscheibe, f. *[PAHRK-shye-beh]*

parking lot Parkplatz, m. *[PAHRK-plahts]*

parking meter Parkuhr, f. *[PAHRK-oor]*

parking prohibited Parken verboten *[PAHR-ken fehr-BOH-ten]*

parsley Petersilie, f. *[pay-te(r)-ZEEL-yeh]*

part Teil, m. *[tile]*

part, to (separate) trennen *[TREHN-en]*

party (celebration) Party, f. *[PAHR-tee]*

pass (permit) Ausweis, m. *[OWS-vice]*

pass, to (car) überholen *[EW-be(r)-hoh-len]*

passenger Fahrgast, m. *[FAAR-gahst]*

passport (Reise-)Pass, m. *[(RYE-zeh-)pahs]*

past Vergangenheit, f. *[fehr-GAHNG-en-hite]*

pasta Teigwaren, pl. *[TIKE-vaa-ren]*

pastry Gebäck, n. *[geh-BEHK]*

pastry shop Konditorei, f. *[kon-dee-to-RYE]*

path Pfad, m. *[pfaat]*

pay, to bezahlen *[beh-TSAA-len]*

pea Erbse, f. *[EHRP-seh]*

peach Pfirsich, m. *[PFIR-zikh]*

peak Gipfel, m. *[GIP-fel]*

pear Birne, f. *[BEER-neh]*

pedestrian Fußgänger, m. *[FOOS-gehng-e(r)]*

pedestrian zone Fußgängerzone, f. *[FOOS-gehng-e(r)-tsoh-neh]*

pediatrician Kinderarzt, m. *[KIN-de(r)-ahrtst]*

pen (ball point) Kugelschreiber, m. *[KOO-gel-shrye-be(r)]*

penknife Taschenmesser, n. *[TAHSH-en-mehs-se(r)]*

pencil Bleistift, m. *[BLYE-shtift]*

people Leute, pl. *[LOY-teh]*

pepper Pfeffer, m. *[PFEH-fe(r)]*

perfect perfekt *[pehr-FEHKT]*

performance Vorstellung, f. *[for-SHTEHL-lung]*

perfume Parfüm, n. *[pahr-FEWM]*

perhaps vielleicht *[fee-LYEKHT]*

period (menstrual) Periode, f. *[peh-ree-OH-deh]*

permanent wave Dauerwelle, f. *[DOW-e(r)-vehl-leh]*

permit (pass) Genehmigung, f. *[geh-NAY-mi-gung]*

permit, to erlauben *[ehr-LOW-ben]*

person Person, f. *[pehr-ZOHN]*

personal persönlich *[pehr-ZU(R)N-likh]*

personal check Barscheck, m. *[BAAR-shehk]*

person-to-person call Gespräch mit Voranmeldung *[geh-SHPRAYKH mit FOHR-ahn-mehl-dung]*

persuade, to überzeugen *[ew-be(r)-TSOY-gen]*

pharmacy Apotheke, f. *[ah-poh-TAY-keh]*

phone Telefon, n. *[tay-lay-FON]*

photocopy Fotokopie, f. *[fot-toh-koh-PEE]*

photograph Foto, n. *[FOH-toh]*

photograph, to fotografieren *[fot-toh-grah-FEE-ren]*

phrase Ausdruck, m. *[OWS-druk]*

piano Klavier, m. *[klah-VEER]*

pickle saure Gurke, f. *[SOW-reh GOOR-keh]*

pick up, to abholen *[AHP-hoh-len]*

picnic Picknick, n. *[PIK-nik]*

picture Bild, n. *[bilt]*

pie Torte, f. *[TOR-teh]*

piece Stück, n. *[shtewk]*

pier Pier, m. *[peer]*

pig Schwein, n. *[shvine]*

pigeon Taube, f. *[TOW-beh]*

pill Pille, f. *[PIL-eh]*

pillow Kopfkissen, n. *[KOPF-kis-sen]*

pillowcase Kopfkissenbezug, m. *[KOPF-kis-sen-beh-tsook]*

pilot Pilot, m. *[pee-LOHT]*

pin Stecknadel, f. *[SHTEHK-naa-del]*

pineapple Ananas, f. *[AH-nah-nahs]*

pink rosa *[ROH-zah]*

pipe Pfeife, f. *[PFIFE-eh]*

pipe tobacco Pfeifentabak, m. *[PFIFE-en-tah-bahk]*

pitcher Krug, m. *[krook]*

pity!, What a Wie schade! *[vee SHAA-deh]*

place Platz, m. *[plahts]*; Ort, n. *[ort]*

place, to stellen *[SHTEHL-len]*

plan Plan, m. *[plaan]*

plan, to planen *[PLAA-nen]*

planetarium Planetarium, n. *[plah-neh-TAH-ree-oom]*

plate Teller, m. *[TEHL-le(r)]*

platform (station) Bahnsteig, m. [BAAN-shtyek]

play (stage) Stück, n. [shtewk]

play, to spielen [SHPEE-len]

playground Spielplatz, m. [SHPEEL-plahts]

playing cards Spielkarten, pl. [SHPEEL-kahr-ten]

pleasant angenehm [AHN-geh-naym]

please bitte [BIT-teh]

pleasure Vergnügen, n. [fehrk-NEW-gen]

pliers Zange, f. [TSAHNG-eh]

plug (electrical) Steckdose, f. [SHTEHK-doh-zeh]

plum Pflaume, f. [PFLOW-meh]

pocket Tasche, f. [TAHSH-eh]

pocketbook Brieftasche, f. [BREEF-tahsh-eh]

point, to zeigen [TSYE-gen]

poison Gift, n. [gift]

Poland Polen, n. [POH-len]

police Polizei, f. [po-lee-TSYE]

police station Polizeiwache, f. [po-lee-TSYE-vahkh-eh]

policeman Polizist, m. [po-lee-TSIST]

polish, to polieren [po-LEE-ren]

polite höflich [HU(R)F-likh]

pond Teich, m. [tyekh]

pool (game) Billard, n. [BIL-yahrt]

poor arm [ahrm]

pork Schweinefleisch, n. [SHVINE-eh-flyshe]

port Hafen, m. [HAA-fen]

porter Gepäckträger, m. [geh-PEHK-tray-ge(r)]

portion Portion, f. [por-TSYOHN]

possible möglich [MU(R)G-likh]

postage Porto, n. [POR-toh]

postcard Postkarte, f. [POST-kahr-teh]

post office Postamt, n. [POST-ahmt]

post office box Postfach, n. [POST-fahkh]

potato Kartoffel, f. [kahr-TOF-fel]

pottery Keramik, f. [keh-RAH-mik]

pour, to einschenken [INE-shehn-ken]

powder Puder, m. [POO-de(r)]; Pulver, n. [POOL-ve(r)]

powerful kräftig [KREHF-tikh]

practical praktisch [PRAHK-tish]

practice, to üben [EW-ben]

prefer, to vorziehen [FOR-tsee-en]; lieber haben [LEE-be(r) HAA-ben]

pregnant schwanger [SHVAHNG-e(r)]

prepare, to vorbereiten [FOR-beh-rye-ten]

prescription Rezept, n. [reh-TZEHPT]

present (gift) Geschenk, n. [geh-SHEHNK]

present, to übergeben [ew-be(r)-GAY-ben]

press (media) Presse, f. [PREHS-seh]

press, to drücken [DREWK-en]

pressure Druck, m. [druk]

pretty hübsch [hewpsh]

price Preis, m. [price]

price range Preisskala, f. [PRICE-skah-lah]

priest Priester, m. [PREES-te(r)]

print (photo) Abzug, m. [AHP-tsook]

print, to drucken [DRUK-en]

private privat [pri-VAAT]

private lessons Privatunterricht, m. [pri-VAAT-un-teh-rikht]

profession Beruf, m. *[beh-ROOF]*

prohibit, to verbieten *[fehr-BEE-ten]*

program Programm, n. *[proh-GRAAM]*

promise, to versprechen *[fehr-SHPREHKH-en]*

pronunciation Aussprache, f. *[OWS-shprahkh-eh]*

property Besitz, m. *[beh-ZITS]*; Grundstück, n. *[GROONT-shtewk]*

protect, to beschützen *[beh-SHEWT-sen]*

Protestant evangelisch *[ay-fahn-GAY-lish]*

prune Backpflaume, f. *[BAHK-pflow-meh]*

public öffentlich *[U(R)F-ehnt-likh]*

pull, to ziehen *[TSEE-en]*

pump (fuel) Pumpe, f. *[PUM-peh]*

puncture (flat tire) Reifen-panne, f. *[RIFE-en-pahn-eh]*

purchases Einkäufe, pl. *[INE-koy-feh]*

purple violett *[vee-oh-LEHT]*

purse Handtasche, f. *[HAHNT-tahsh-eh]*

push, to (a button) drücken *[DREWK-en]*

push, to (a car) schieben *[SHEE-ben]*

put, to stellen *[SHTEHL-len]*

put on, to (dress) anziehen *[AHN-tsee-en]*

Q

quality Qualität, f. *[kvah-li-TAYT]*

quantity Menge, f. *[MEHNG-eh]*

quarter Viertel, n. *[FEER-tel]*

question Frage, f. *[FRAA-geh]*

quiche Quiche, f. *[keesh]*

quick(ly) schnell *[shnehl]*

quiet ruhig *[ROO-ikh]*

quite ziemlich *[TSEEM-likh]*

R

rabbi Rabbi(ner), m. *[rah-BEE-ne(r), rah-BEE]*

rabbit Kaninchen, s. *[kah-NEEN-khen]*; Hase, f. *[HAA-zeh]*

rabies Tollwut, f. *[TOL-voot]*

racetrack Rennbahn, f. *[REHN-baan]*

radiator Heizkörper, m. *[HITES-ku(r)-pe(r)]*; (car) Küh-ler, m. *[KEW-le(r)]*

radio Radio, n. *[RAA-dee-oh]*

radish Radieschen, n. *[raa-DEES-khen]*

railroad Eisenbahn, f. *[EYE-zen-baan]*

railroad station Bahnhof, m. *[BAAN-hohf]*

rain Regen, m. *[RAY-gen]*

raincoat Regenmantel, m. *[RAY-gen-mahn-tel]*

raisins Rosinen, pl. *[roh-ZEE-nen]*

rare selten *[ZEHL-ten]*

rare (uncooked) blutig *[BLOO-tikh]*

raspberry Himbeere, f. *[HIM-bay-reh]*

rate Tarif, m. *[tah-REEF]*

rate of exchange Wech-selkurs, m. *[VEHK-sel-koors]*

rather lieber *[LEE-be(r)]*

rather (quite) ziemlich *[TSEEM-likh]*

raw roh *[roh]*

razor Rasierapparat, n. *[rah-ZEER-ah-pah-raat]*

razor blade Rasierklinge, f. *[rah-ZEER-kling-eh]*

read, to lesen *[LAY-zen]*

221

ready bereit *[beh-RITE]*

ready, to be fertig sein *[FEHR-tikh zine]*

real echt *[ehkht]*

really wirklich *[VIRK-likh]*

rear hinten *[HIN-ten]*

reason Grund, m. *[groont]*

reasonable vernünftig *[fehr-NEWNF-tikh]*

receipt Quittung, f. *[KVIT-tung]*

receive, to erhalten *[ehr-HAAL-ten];* empfangen *[ehm-PFAHNG-en]*

receiver (letter) Empfänger, m. *[ehm-PFEHNG-e(r)]*

receiver (phone) Hörer, m. *[HU(R)-e(r)]*

recently kürzlich *[KEWRTS-likh]*

recommend, to empfehlen *[ehm-PFAY-len]*

recording Aufnahme, f. *[OWF-naa-meh]*

recover, to sich erholen *[zikh ehr-HOH-len]*

red rot *[roht]*

reduction (price) Ermäßigung, f. *[ehr-MAYS-si-gung]*

refreshing erfrischend *[ehr-FRISH-ent]*

refund Rückerstattung, f. *[REWK-ehr-shtaht-tung]*

refuse, to ablehnen *[AHP-lay-nen]*

regards Grüße, pl. *[GREWS-seh]*

register, to sich eintragen *[zikh INE-traa-gen]*

registered mail per Einschreiben *[pehr INE-shrye-ben]*

regret, to bedauern *[beh-DOW-ern]*

regular normal *[nor-MAAL];* regelmäßig *[RAY-gel-mays-ikh]*

relative Verwandte, m., f. *[fehr-VAHN-teh]*

religion Religion, f. *[ray-li-GYOHN]*

religious service Gottesdienst, m. *[GOT-tehs-deenst]*

remain, to bleiben *[BLYE-ben]*

remedy Heilmittel, n. *[HILE-mit-tel]*

remember, to sich erinnern *[zikh eh-RIN-ern]*

rent Miete, f. *[MEE-teh]*

rent, to vermieten *[fehr-MEE-ten]*

repair Reparatur, f. *[reh-pah-rah-TOOR]*

repair, to reparieren *[reh-pah-REE-ren]*

repeat, to wiederholen *[vee-de(r)-HOH-len]*

replace, to ersetzen *[ehr-ZEHT-sen]*

represent, to vertreten *[fehr-TRAY-ten]*

request, to bitten *[BIT-ten]*

require, to verlangen *[fehr-LAHNG-en]*

resemble, to ähneln *[AY-neln]*

reservation Reservierung, f. *[reh-zehr-VEE-rung]*

reserve, to reservieren (lassen) *[reh-zehr-VEE-ren {LAHS-en}]*

reserved vorbestellt *[FOR-beh-shtehlt]*

responsibility Verantwortung, f. *[fehr-AHNT-vor-tung]*

resort (place) Ferienort, m. *[FEHR-yen-ort]*

rest Ruhe, f. *[ROO-eh]*

rest, to sich ausruhen *[zikh OWS-roo-en]*

restaurant Restaurant, n. *[rehs-to-RAHNT]*

rest room Toilette, f. *[toy-LEHT-teh]*

result Ergebnis, n. *[ehr-GAYP-nis]*

retirement Ruhestand, m. *[ROO-eh-shtahnt]*

return, to (something) zurückgeben *[tsoo-REWK-gay-ben]*

return to (come back) zurückkommen *[tsoo-REWK-kom-men]*

rib Rippe, f. *[RIP-peh]*

ribbon Band, n. *[bahnt]*

rice Reis, m. *[rice]*

rich reich *[ryekh]*

ride Fahrt, f. *[faart]*

ride, to fahren *[FAA-ren]*

ride, to (a horse) reiten *[RITE-en]*

right (correct) richtig *[RIKH-tikh]*

right (direction) rechts *[rehkhts]*

right, to be Recht haben *[rehkht HAA-ben]*

right away gleich *[glyekh]*

right-handed rechtshändig *[REHKHTS-hehn-dikh]*

ring Ring, m. *[ring]*

ring, to klingeln *[KLING-eln]*

rinse, to spülen *[SHPEW-len]*

risk Risiko, n. *[REE-zee-koh]*

river Fluss, m. *[floos]*

road Straße, f. *[SHTRAHS-seh]*

road map Straßenkarte, f. *[SHTRAHS-sen-kahr-teh]*

roast, to braten *[BRAA-ten]*

roasted gebraten *[geh-BRAA-ten]*

robbery Raub, m. *[rowp]*

robe Badermantel, m. *[BAA-deh-mahn-tel]*

role (stage) Rolle, f. *[ROL-leh]*

roll (film) Filmrolle, f. *[FILM-rol-leh]*

roll, to rollen *[ROL-len]*

rolls (bread) Brötchen, pl. *[BRU(R)T-khen]*

roof Dach, n. *[dahkh]*

room Zimmer, n. *[TSIM-me(r)]*

room service Zimmerbedienung, f. *[TSIM-me(r)-beh-dee-nung]*

root Wurzel, f. *[VUR-tsel]*

rope Seil, n. *[zile]*

rose Rose, f. *[ROH-zeh]*

rosé wine Rosé, m. *[roh-ZAY]*

rouge Rouge, n. *[roozh]*

round rund *[runt]*

round-trip ticket Rückfahrkarte, f. *[REWK-faar-kahr-teh]*

row (theatre) Reihe, f. *[RYE-eh]*

rowboat Ruderboot, n. *[ROO-de(r)-boht]*

rubber Gummi, m. *[GOOM-mee]*

rubber eraser Radiergummi, m. *[rah-DEER-goom-mee]*

rubber band Gummiband, n. *[GOOM-mee-bahnt]*

rug Teppich, m. *[TEHP-pikh]*

ruins Ruinen, pl. *[roo-EE-nen]*

rule Regel, f. *[RAY-gel]*

ruler Lineal, n. *[lee-nay-AAL]*

run, to laufen *[LOW-fen]*

running water fließendes Wasser, n. *[FLEES-sen-dehs VAHS-se(r)]*

runway (plane) Piste, f. *[PIS-teh]*

rush hour Stoßzeit, f. *[SHTOHS-tsite]*

rye bread Roggenbrot, n. *[ROG-gen-broht]*

S

sad traurig *[TROW-rikh]*

safe sicher *[ZIKH-e(r)]*

safety pin Sicherheitsnadel, f. *[ZIKH-e(r)-hites-naa-del]*

salad Salat, m. *[zah-LAAT]*

sale Verkauf, m. *[fehr-KOWF]*

sale (low prices) Ausverkauf, m. *[OWS-fehr-kowf]*

salesman Verkäufer, m.
[fehr-KOY-fe(r)]

saleswoman Verkäuferin, f.
[fehr-KOY-feh-rin]

salt Salz, n. *[zahlts]*

salty salzig *[ZAHL-tsikh]*

same selbe *[ZEHL-beh]*; gleiche *[GLYE-kheh]*

sand Sand, m. *[zahnt]*

sandwich Sandwich, n.
[SAHNT-vitch]

sanitary napkin Damenbinde, f. *[DAA-men-bin-deh]*

Saturday Samstag, m.
[ZAHMS-taak]; Sonnabend,
m. *[ZON-aa-behnt]*

sauce Soße, f. *[ZOH-zeh]*

saucer Untertasse, f. *[UN-
te(r)-tahs-seh]*

sausage Wurst, f. *[voorst]*

save, to (money) sparen
[SHPAA-ren]

save, to (person) retten
[REHT-ten]

say, to sagen *[ZAA-gen]*

scarf Schal, m. *[shahl]*

scenic route landschaftlich
schöne Straße, f. *[LAHNT-
shahft-likh SHU(R)-neh
SHTRAHS-eh]*

schedule Fahrplan, m.
[FAAR-plaan]

school Schule, f. *[SHOO-leh]*

scissors Schere, f. *[SHAY-reh]*

scrambled eggs Rühreier,
pl. *[REWR-eye-e(r)]*

screwdriver Schraubenzieher, m. *[SHROW-ben-tsee-
e(r)]*

sculpture Skulptur, f. *[skulp-
TOOR]*

sea Meer, n. *[mayr]*

seafood Meeresfrüchte, pl.
[MAY-rehs-frewkh-teh]

seasick seekrank *[ZAY-
krahnk]*

season Jahreszeit, f. *[YAA-
rehs-tsite]*

seasoning Würze, pl.
[VEWR-tseh]

seat Platz, m. *[plahts]*

seat belt Sicherheitsgurt, m.
[ZIKH-e(r)-hites-gurt]

second zweite *[TSVITE-teh]*

second (time) Sekunde, f.
[zeh-KOON-deh]

secondhand gebraucht *[geh-
BROWKHT]*

secretary Sekretär(in),
m./f. *[zeh-kreh-TAYR{-in}]*

see, to sehen *[ZAY-en]*

seem, to scheinen
[SHINE-en]

selection Auswahl, f. *[OWS-
vaal]*

sell, to verkaufen *[fehr-KOW-
fen]*

send, to schicken *[SHIK-en]*;
senden *[ZEHN-den]*

sender (mail) Absender, m.
[AHP-zehn-de(r)]

senior citizen's pass Seniorenpass, m. *[zehn-YOR-
en-pahs]*

sentence (grammar) Satz, m.
[zahts]

September September, m.
[zehp-TEHM-be(r)]

serious ernst *[ehrnst]*

serve, to dienen *[DEE-nen]*;
servieren *[zehr-VEE-ren]*

service Bedienung, f. *[beh-
DEE-nung]*

service station Tankstelle, f.
[TAHNK-shtehl-leh]

seven sieben *[ZEE-ben]*

seventeen siebzehn *[ZEEP-
tsayn]*

seventh siebte *[ZEEP-teh]*

seventy siebzig *[ZEEP-
tsikh]*

several mehrere *[MEH-reh-
reh]*

sew, to nähen *[NAY-en]*

shade, shadow Schatten, m.
[SHAHT-ten]

shampoo Haarwaschmittel, n. *[HAAR-vahsh-mit-tel]*; Shampoo, n. *[shahm-POO]*

share, to teilen *[TILE-en]*

shave, to rasieren *[rah-ZEE-ren]*

shaving cream Rasiercreme, f. *[rah-ZEER-kraym]*

shaver Rasierapparat, n. *[rah-ZEER-ah-pah-raat]*

shawl Tuch, n. *[tookh]*

she sie *[zee]*

sheep Schaf, n. *[shahf]*

sheet Bettlaken, n. *[BEHT-lah-ken]*

shelf Regal, n. *[ray-GAAL]*

shell Schale, f. *[SHAH-leh]*

shine, to (shoes) putzen *[PUT-sen]*; polieren *[po-LEE-ren]*

ship Schiff, n. *[shif]*

ship, to verschiffen *[fehr-SHIF-fen]*

shirt Hemd, n. *[hehmt]*

shoe Schuh, m. *[shoo]*

shoelaces Schnürsenkel, pl. *[SHNEWR-zehn-kel]*

shop Geschäft, n. *[geh-SHEHFT]*; Laden, m. *[LAA-den]*

shopping, to go einkaufen gehen *[INE-kow-fen GAY-en]*

shopping center Einkaufszentrum, n. *[INE-kowfs-tsehn-trum]*

short kurz *[koorts]*

shorts (underwear) Unterhosen, pl. *[UN-te(r)-hoh-zen]*

shoulder Schulter, f. *[SHOO-te(r)]*

show (art) Ausstellung, f. *[OWS-shtehl-lung]*

show (performance) Vorstellung, f. *[FOR-shtehl-lung]*

show, to zeigen *[TSYE-gen]*

show window Schaufenster, n. *[SHOW-fehn-ste(r)]*

shower Dusche, f. *[DOO-sheh]*

shrimp Garnele, f. *[gahr-NAY-leh]*

shrink, to einlaufen *[INE-low-fen]*

shut, to schließen *[SHLEES-sen]*

shutter Fensterladen, m. *[FEHN-ste(r)-laa-den]*

shutter (camera) Verschluss, m. *[fehr-SHLUS]*

sick krank *[krahnk]*

sickness Krankheit, f. *[KRAHNK-hite]*

side Seite, f. *[ZITE-eh]*

sidewalk Bürgersteig, m. *[BEWR-ge(r)-shtike]*

sight-seeing Besichtigung, f. *[beh-ZIKH-ti-gung]*

sign Schild, n. *[shilt]*

sign, to unterschreiben *[un-te(r)-SHRYE-ben]*

silk Seide, f. *[ZYE-deh]*

silver Silber, n. *[ZIL-be(r)]*

silverware Besteck, n. *[beh-SHTEHK]*

since seit *[zite]*

sincerely (yours) mit freundlichen Grüßen *[mit FROYNT-likh-en GREWS-en]*

sing, to singen *[ZING-en]*

single (unmarried) ledig *[LAY-dikh]*

single room Einzelzimmer, n. *[INE-tsel-tsim-me(r)]*

sink Waschbecken, n. *[VAHSH-beh-ken]*

sister Schwester, f. *[SHVEHS-te(r)]*

sister-in-law Schwägerin, f. *[SHVAY-geh-rin]*

sit down, to sich setzen *[zikh ZEHT-sen]*

site Stelle, f. *[SHTEHL-leh]*

six sechs *[zehks]*

sixteen sechzehn *[ZEHKH-tsayn]*

sixty sechzig *[ZEHKH-tsikh]*

size Größe, f. *[GRU(R)S-eh]*

skating rink Eisbahn, f. *[ICE-baan]*

ski Ski, m. *[shee]*

ski equipment Skiausrüstung, f. *[SHEE-ows-rews-tung]*

ski lift Skilift, m. *[SHEE-lift]*

skiing skifahren *[SHEE-faa-ren]*

skiing, cross-country Langlaufski fahren *[LAHNG-lowf-shee faa-ren]*

skin Haut, f. *[howt]*

skirt Rock, m. *[rok]*

sky Himmel, m. *[HIM-mel]*

sleep, to schlafen *[SHLAH-fen]*

sleeping bag Schlafsack, m. *[SHLAHF-zahk]*

sleeping car Schlafwagen, m. *[SHLAHF-vaa-gen]*

sleeve Ärmel, m. *[EHR-mel]*

slice Scheibe, f. *[SHYE-beh]*

slide (photo) Dia, n. *[DEE-ah]*

slip Unterrock, m. *[UN-te(r)-rok]*

slippers Hausschuhe, pl. *[HOWS-shoo-eh]*

slippery rutschig *[RUT-shikh]*

Slovakia Slowakei, f. *[sloh-vah-KYE]*

slow(ly) langsam *[LAHNG-zahm]*

slow down, to langsam fahren *[LAHNG-zahm FAA-ren]*

small klein *[kline]*

smile, to lächeln *[LEH-kheln]*

smoke, to rauchen *[ROW-khen]*

smoked geräuchert *[geh-ROY-khert]*

smoking section Raucherabteil *[ROW-khe(r)-ahp-tile]*

smooth glatt *[glaht]*

snack bar Schnellimbiss, m. *[SHNEHL-im-bis]*

snail Schnecke, f. *[SHNEH-keh]*

snow Schnee, m. *[shnay]*

snow, to schneien *[SHNYE-en]*

soap Seife, f. *[ZYE-feh]*

sober nüchtern *[NEWKH-tern]*

soccer Fußball, m. *[FOOS-bahl]*

socks Socken, pl. *[ZO-ken]*

sofa Sofa, n. *[ZOH-fah]*

soft weich *[vyekh]*

soft drink alkoholfreies Getränk, n. *[AHL-koh-hohl-frye-ehs geh-TREHNK]*

sold out ausverkauft *[OWS-fehr-kowft]*

sole (shoe) Sohle, f. *[ZOH-leh]*

solid massiv *[mah-SEEF]*

some einige *[INE-eh-geh]*; etwas *[EHT-vahs]*

someone jemand *[YAY-mahnt]*

something etwas *[EHT-vahs]*

sometimes manchmal *[MAHNCH-maal]*

somewhere irgendwo *[EER-gehnt-voh]*

son Sohn, m. *[zohn]*

song Lied, n. *[leet]*

soon bald *[bahlt]*

sore throat Halsschmerzen, pl. *[HAHLS-shmehrt-sen]*

sorrow Leid, n. *[lite]*

sorry, I am es tut mir leid *[ehs toot meer lite]*

sort (type) Sorte, f. *[ZOR-teh]*

soup Suppe, f. *[ZOOP-peh]*

sour sauer *[ZOW-e(r)]*

south Süden, m. *[ZEW-den]*

souvenir Andenken, n. *[AHN-dehn-ken]*

spa Kurort, m. *[KOOR-ort]*

spare parts Ersatzteile, pl. *[ehr-ZAHTS-tile-eh]*

spare tire Ersatzreifen, m. *[ehr-ZAHTS-rye-fen]*

spark plug Zündkerze, f. *[TSEWNT-kehr-tseh]*

sparkling wine Schaumwein, m. *[SHOWM-vine]*

speak, to sprechen *[SH-PREHKH-en]*

speaker (stereo) Lautsprecher, m. *[LOWT-sprehkh-e(r)]*

special besondere *[beh-ZON-deh-reh]*

specialty Spezialität, f. *[shpeh-tsee-ah-lee-TAYT]*

speed Geschwindigkeit, f. *[geh-SHVIN-dikh-kite]*

speed limit Geschwindigkeitsbegrenzung, f. *[geh-SHVIN-dikh-kites-beh-GREHN-tsung]*

spell, to buchstabieren *[bookh-shtah-BEE-ren]*

spend, to (money) ausgeben *[OWS-gay-ben]*

spend, to (time) verbringen *[fehr-BRIN-gen]*

spice Gewürz, n. *[geh-VEWRTS]*

spinach Spinat, m. *[shpi-NAAT]*

sponge Schwamm, m. *[shvahm]*

spoon Löffel, m. *[LU(R)F-el]*

spouse Gatte, m. *[GAHT-teh]*; Gattin, f. *[GAHT-tin]*

sprain, to verstauchen *[fehr-SHTOW-khen]*

spring (mechanical) Feder, f. *[FAY-de(r)]*

spring (of water) Quelle, f. *[KVEHL-leh]*

spring (season) Frühling, m. *[FREW-ling]*

square (geometric) Quadrat, n. *[kvah-DRAHT]*

square (town) Platz, m. *[plahts]*

stadium Stadion, n. *[SHTAA-dee-ohn]*

stain Fleck, m. *[flehk]*

staircase Treppenhaus, n. *[TREHP-pen-hows]*

stairs Treppe, f. *[TREHP-peh]*

stamp (postage) Briefmarke, f. *[BREEF-mahr-keh]*

stand, to stehen *[SHTAY-en]*

stand in line, to Schlange stehen *[SHLAHNG-eh shtay-en]*

stand up, to aufstehen *[OWF-shtay-en]*

star Stern, m. *[shtehrn]*

starch (laundry) Stärke, f. *[SHTEHR-keh]*

start, to beginnen *[beh-GIN-nen]*

start, to (a car) anspringen *[AHN-spring-en]*

starter (car) Anlasser, m. *[AHN-lahs-se(r)]*

state Staat, m. *[shtaat]*; Land, n. *[lahnt]*

station Bahnhof, m. *[BAAN-hohf]*

stationery Schreibwaren, pl. *[SHRIPE-vaa-ren]*

statue Statue, f. *[SHTAH-too-eh]*

stay Aufenthalt, m. *[OWF-ehnt-hahlt]*

stay, to (lodge) übernachten *[EW-be(r)-nahkh-ten]*

stay, to (remain) bleiben *[BLYE-ben]*

steak Steak, m. *[shtayk]*

steal, to stehlen *[SHTEH-len]*

steel Stahl, m. *[shtahl]*

steering wheel Lenkrad, n. *[LEHNK-raat]*

stew Eintopf, m. *[INE-topf]*

stewardess Stewardess, f. *[SHTOO-ahr-dehs]*

stick (pole) Stock, m. *[shtok]*

still noch *[nokh]*

stock exchange Börse, f. *[BU(R)-zeh]*

stocking Strumpf, m. *[shtrumpf]*

stomach Magen, m. *[MAA-gen]*

stomachache Magen-
schmerzen, pl. *[MAA-gen-
shmehr-tsen]*
stone Stein, m. *[shtine]*
stop (along the way) anhal-
ten *[AHN-hahl-ten]*
stop, to stehenbleiben
[SHTAY-en-blye-ben]
stoplight Ampel, m. *[AHM-
pel]*
store Laden, m. *[LAA-den];*
Geschäft, n. *[geh-SHEHFT]*
storm Sturm, m. *[shtoorm]*
story (floor) Etage, f. *[eh-
TAH-zheh]*
story (tale) Erzählung, f.
[ehr-TSAY-lung]
straight gerade *[geh-RAA-
deh]*
strange seltsam *[ZEHLT-zahm]*
strap Riemen, m. *[REE-men]*
straw Stroh, n. *[shtroh]*
strawberry Erdbeere, f.
[EHRT-bay-reh]
street Straße, f. *[SHTRAHS-
eh]*
streetcar Straßenbahn, f.
[SHTRAHS-sen-baan]
string Schnur, f. *[shnoor]*
stripe Streifen, m. *[SHTRIFE-
en]*
strong stark *[shtahrk]*
student Student, m. *[shtu-
DEHNT]*
study, to studieren *[shtu-DEE-
ren]*
style (fashion) Stil, m. *[shteel]*
suburb Vorort, m. *[FOR-ort]*
subway Untergrundbahn, f.
[UN-te(r)-grunt-baan]
subway station Ubahnsta-
tion, f. *[OO-baan-shtah-
tsyohn]*
success Erfolg, m. *[ehr-FOLK]*
suddenly plötzlich *[PLU(R)TS-
likh]*
suede Wildleder, n. *[VILT-
lay-de(r)]*

sugar Zucker, m. *[TSU-ke(r)]*
suit Anzug, m. *[AHN-tsook]*
suitcase Koffer, m. *[KOF-fe(r)]*
sum Summe, f. *[ZOOM-meh]*
summer Sommer, m. *[ZOM-
me(r)]*
sun Sonne, f. *[ZON-nen]*
Sunday Sonntag, m. *[ZON-
taak]*
sunglasses Sonnenbrille, f.
[ZON-nen-bril-leh]
sunny sonnig *[ZON-nikh]*
suntan lotion Sonnenöl, n.
[ZON-nen-u(r)l]
supermarket Supermarkt,
m. *[ZOO-pe(r)-mahrkt]*
supper Abendessen, n. *[AA-
behnt-ehs-sen]*
suppository Zäpfchen, n.
[TSEHPF-khen]
sure sicher *[ZIKH-e(r)]*
surgery Chirurgie, f. *[khee-
roor-GEE]*
swallow schlucken *[SHLUK-
en]*
sweater Pullover, m. *[pul-
LOH-ve(r)]*
sweet süß *[zews]*
swell, to anschwellen *[AHN-
shvehl-len]*
swim, to schwimmen
[SHVIM-men]
swimming suit Badeanzug,
m. *[BAA-deh-ahn-tsook]*
swimming pool Schwimmbad, n. *[SHVIM-baat]*
Swiss schweizerisch *[SHVYE-
tseh-rish]*
switch Schalter, m. *[SHAHL-
te(r)]*
Switzerland die Schweiz
[dee shvites]
swollen angeschwollen
[AHN-geh-shvol-len]
symptom Symptom, n.
[zewmp-TOHM]
synagogue Synagoge, f.
[zew-nah-GOH-geh]

228

syrup (cough) Sirup, m. *[ZEE-rup]*

system System, n. *[zews-TAYM]*

T

table Tisch, m. *[tish]*

tablecloth Tischdecke, f. *[TISH-deh-keh]*

tablespoon Esslöffel, m. *[EHS-lu(r)-fel]*

tailor Schneider, m. *[SHNYE-de(r)]*

take, to nehmen *[NAY-men]*

take a photo, to ein Foto machen *[ine FOH-toh MAHKH-en]*

take time, to dauern *[DOW-ern]*

talk, to reden *[RAY-den]*

tall groß *[grohs]*

tan hellbraun *[HEHL-brown]*

tangerine Mandarine, f. *[mahn-dah-REE-neh]*

tap Wasserhahn, m. *[VAHS-se(r)-haan]*

tape Band, n. *[bahnt]*

taste, to schmecken *[SHMEHK-en]*

tasty schmackhaft *[SHMAHK-hahft]*

tax-free steuerfrei *[STOY-e(r)-frye]*

taxi Taxi, n. *[TAHK-see]*

tea Tee, m. *[tay]*

team Mannschaft, f. *[MAHN-shahft]*

teaspoon Teelöffel, m. *[TAY-lu(r)-fel]*

teach, to lehren *[LEHR-en]*

tear, to reißen *[RICE-sen]*

telegram Telegram, n. *[tay-lay-GRAAM]*

telephone Telefon, n. *[tay-lay-FON]*

telephone, to anrufen *[AHN-roo-fen]*

telephone booth Telefonzelle, f. *[tay-lay-FON-tsehl-leh]*

telephone directory Telefon-buch, n. *[tay-lay-FON-bookh]*

television (set) Fernseher, m. *[FEHRN-zay-e(r)]*

telex, to ein Telex schicken *[ine TAY-lehks SHIK-en]*

tell, to erzählen *[ehr-TSAY-len]*

teller (bank) Kassierer, (-in), m., f. *[kah-SEE-re(r), {-reh-rin}]*

temple Tempel, m. *[TEHM-pel]*

temporary provisorisch *[pro-vee-ZOH-rish]*

ten zehn *[tsayn]*

tender zart *[tsahrt]*

tense gespannt *[geh-SHPAHNT]*

tent Zelt, n. *[tsehlt]*

tenth zehnte *[TSAYN-teh]*

than als *[ahls]*

thank, to danken *[DAHN-ken]*

thank you very much vielen Dank *[FEE-len dahnk]*

that jene (-r, -s) *[YEH-neh, {-ne(r), -nehs}]*

that (which) dass *[dahs]*

the der, die, das *[dehr, dee, dahs]*

theater Theater, n. *[tay-AA-te(r)]*

then dann *[dahn]*

there da *[daa]*; dort *[dort]*

there are (is) es gibt *[ehs gipt]*

therefore also *[AHL-zoh]*

thermometer Thermometer, n. *[tehr-mo-MAY-te(r)]*

they sie *[zee]*

thick dick *[dik]*

thief Dieb, m. *[deep]*

thigh Schenkel, m. *[SHEHN-kel]*

thin dünn *[dewn]*

thing Ding, n. *[ding]*; Sache, f. *[ZAHKH-eh]*

think, to denken *[DEHN-ken]*

think, to (belive) glauben *[GLOW-ben]*

third dritte, -r, -s *[DRIT-teh, (-te(r), -tehs)]*

thirsty, to be Durst haben *[durst HAA-ben]*

thirteen dreizehn *[DRYE-tsayn]*

thirty dreißig *[DRYE-sikh]*

this, these diese *[DEE-zeh, (-ze(r), -zehs)]*

thousand tausend *[TOW-zehnt]*

thread Faden, m. *[FAA-den]*

three drei *[drye]*

throat Hals, m. *[hahls]*

through durch *[durkh]*

thumb Daumen, m. *[DOW-men]*

thunder Donner, m. *[DON-ne(r)]*

Thursday Donnerstag, m. *[DON-nehrs-taak]*

ticket Karte, f. *[KAHR-teh]*

tie Krawatte, f. *[krah-VAHT-teh]*

tights Strumpfhose, f. *[SHTRUMPF-hoh-zeh]*

till bis *[bis]*

time Zeit, f. *[tsite]*; Mal, n. *[maal]*

timetable Fahrplan, m. *[FAAR-plaan]*

tip Trinkgeld, m. *[TRINK-gehlt]*

tire (car) Reifen, m. *[RIFE-en]*

tired müde *[MEW-deh]*

tissue Papiertuch, n. *[pah-PEER-tookh]*

to zu *[tsoo]*; nach *[nahkh]*

toast Toast, m. *[tohst]*

tobacco Tabak, m. *[TAH-bahk]*

tobacco shop Tabakladen, m. *[tah-BAHK-laa-den]*

today heute *[HOY-teh]*

toe Zehe, f. *[TSEH-eh]*

together zusammen *[tsoo-ZAHM-men]*

toilet Toilette, f. *[toy-LEHT-teh]*

toilet paper Toilettenpapier, n. *[toy-LEHT-ten-pah-peer]*

toll Gebühr, f. *[geh-BEWR]*

tomato Tomate, f. *[toh-MAH-teh]*

tomb Grab, n. *[grahp]*

tomorrow morgen *[MOR-gen]*

tongue Zunge, f. *[TSUN-geh]*

tonight heute Abend *[HOY-teh AA-behnt]*

too (also) auch *[owkh]*

too bad! schade! *[SHAA-deh]*

tool Werkzeug, n. *[VEHRK-tsoyk]*

tooth Zahn, m. *[tsaan]*

toothache Zahnschmerzen, pl. *[TSAAN-shmehrt-sen]*

toothbrush Zahnbürste, f. *[TSAAN-bewr-steh]*

toothpaste Zahnpasta, f. *[TSAAN-pahs-tah]*

top Spitze, f. *[SHPIT-seh]*

touch, to berühren *[beh-REW-ren]*

tough zäh *[tsay]*

tour Rundfahrt, f. *[RUNT-faart]*

tourism Tourismus, m. *[too-RIS-moos]*

tourist Tourist, m. *[too-RIST]*

tourist office Fremden-verkehrsbüro, n. *[FREHM-den-fehr-kehrs-bew-roh]*

toward(s) gegen *[GAY-gen]*

towel Handtuch, n. *[HAHNT-tookh]*

tower Turm, m. *[toorm]*

town Stadt, f. *[shtaht]*

town hall Rathaus, n. *[RAAT-hows]*

toy Spielzeug, n. *[SHPEEL-tsoyk]*

toy shop Spielwarenladen, n. *[SHPEEL-vaa-ren-laa-den]*

track (train) Gleis, n. *[glice]*

traffic Verkehr, m. *[fehr-KEHR]*

traffic jam Stau, m. *[shtow]*

traffic light Ampel, f. *[AHM-pel]*

trailer Wohnwagen, m. *[VOHN-vaa-gen]*

train Zug, m. *[tsook]*

train station Bahnhof, m. *[BAAN-hohf]*

transfer, to überweisen *[ew-be(r)-VYE-zen]*

translate, to übersetzen *[ew-be(r)-ZEHT-sen]*

transmission Getriebe, n. *[geh-TREE-beh]*

trash Abfall, m. *[AHP-fahl]*

travel, to reisen *[RYE-zen]*

travel agency Reisebüro, n. *[RYE-zeh-bew-roh]*

traveler's check Reisescheck, m. *[RYE-zeh-shehk]*

treasure Schatz, m. *[shahts]*

treat, to behandeln *[beh-HAHN-deln]*

treatment Behandlung, f. *[beh-HAHNT-lung]*

tree Baum, m. *[bowm]*

trip Reise, f. *[RYE-zeh]*

trousers Hose, f. *[HOH-zeh]*

trout Forelle, f. *[fo-REHL-leh]*

truck Lastwagen, m. *[LAHST-vaa-gen]*

true wahr *[vaar]*

trunk (car) Kofferraum, m. *[KOF-fe(r)-rowm]*

try, to versuchen *[fehr-ZOO-khen]*; probieren *[pro-BEER-en]*

try on, to anprobieren *[AHN-pro-beer-en]*

tube Tube, f. *[TOO-beh]*

Tuesday Dienstag, m. *[DEENS-taak]*

turkey Truthahn, m. *[TROOT-haan]*

turn Kurve, f. *[KOOR-veh]*

turn, to drehen *[DREH-en]*

turn, to (direction) abbiegen *[AHP-bee-gen]*

turn signal Blinker, m. *[BLIN-ke(r)]*

tuxedo Smoking, m. *[SMOH-king]*

twelve zwölf *[tsvu(r)lf]*

twenty zwanzig *[TSVAHN-tsikh]*

twice zweimal *[TSVYE-maal]*

two zwei *[tsvye]*

type (sort) Art, f. *[ahrt]*; Sorte, f. *[ZOR-teh]*

typewriter Schreibmaschine, f. *[SHRIPE-mah-shee-neh]*

typical typisch *[TEW-pish]*

U

ugly hässlich *[HEHS-likh]*

ulcer Geschwür, n. *[geh-SHVEWR]*

umbrella Regenschirm, m. *[RAY-gen-shirm]*

uncle Onkel, m. *[OHN-kel]*

uncomfortable unbequem *[UN-beh-kvaym]*

unconscious bewusstlos *[beh-VUST-lohs]*

under unter *[UN-te(r)]*

underdone nicht durchgebraten *[nikht durkh-geh-BRAA-ten]*

underpants Unterhose, f. *[UN-te(r)-hoh-zeh]*

undershirt Unterhemd, n. *[UN-te(r)-hehmt]*

understand, to verstehen *[fehr-SHTAY-en]*

underwear Unterwäsche, f. *[UN-te(r)-veh-sheh]*

unfortunately leider *[LYE-de(r)]*

231

unhappy unglücklich *[UN-glewk-likh]*

unique einzigartig *[INE-tsikh-ahr-tikh]*

United Kingdom das Vereinigte Königreich *[dahs fehr-eye-nikh-teh KU(R)-nikh-ryekh]*

United States die Vereinigten Staaten (von Amerika) *[dee fehr-EYE-nikh-ten SHTAA-ten {fon ah-MEH-ri-kah}]*

university Universität, f. *[u-nee-vehr-zi-TAYT]*

until bis *[bis]*

up oben *[OH-ben]*; hinauf *[hin-OWF]*

upper obere *[OH-beh-reh]*

upside down verkehrt herum *[vehr-KEHRT hehr-ROOM]*

upset stomach Magenverstimmung, f. *[MAA-gen-fehr-shtim-nung]*

urgent dringend *[DRING-ent]*

use (purpose) Verwendung, f. *[fehr-VEHN-dung]*

use, to benutzen *[beh-NUT-sen]*

used gebraucht *[geh-BROWKHT]*

useful nützlich *[NEWTS-likh]*

usual gewöhnlich *[geh-VU(R)N-likh]*

V

vacant frei *[frye]*

vacation Ferien, pl. *[FEHR-yen]*

valid gültig *[GEWL-tikh]*

valley Tal, n. *[taal]*

value Wert, m. *[vehrt]*

valuable wertvoll *[VEHRT-fol]*

value-added tax Mehrwertsteuer, f. *[MEHR-vehrt-shtoy-e(r)]*

veal Kalbfleisch, n. *[KAHLP-flyshe]*

vegetable Gemüse, n. *[geh-MEW-zeh]*

vegetarian vegetarisch *[veh-geh-TAH-rish]*

velvet Samt, m. *[zahmt]*

verify, to bestätigen *[beh-SHTAY-tig-en]*

vertical senkrecht *[ZEHNK-rehkht]*

very sehr *[zehr]*

vest Weste, f. *[VEHS-teh]*

veterinarian Tierarzt, m. *[TEER-ahrtst]*

via über *[EW-be(r)]*

Vienna Wien, n. *[veen]*

vice versa umgekehrt *[OOM-geh-kehrt]*

view Aussicht, f. *[OWS-zikht]*

village Dorf, n. *[dorf]*

vinegar Essig, m. *[EHS-sikh]*

vineyard Weinberg, m. *[VINE-behrk]*

visa Visum, n. *[VEE-zoom]*

visit Besuch, m. *[beh-ZOOKH]*

visit, to besuchen *[beh-ZOO-khen]*

voice Stimme, f. *[SHTIM-meh]*

voltage Stromspannung, f. *[SHTROHM-shpah-nung]*

vomit, to sich erbrechen *[zikh ehr-BREHKH-en]*

W

wait, to warten *[VAAR-ten]*

waiter Kellner, m. *[KEHL-ner]*

waiting room Wartesaal, m. *[VAAR-teh-zaal]*

waitress Kellnerin, f. *[KEHL-neh-rin]*

wake, to wecken *[VEHK-en]*

wake up, to aufwachen *[OWF-vahkh-en]*

walk Spaziergang, m. *[shpah-TSEER-gahng]*

walk, to (zu Fuß) gehen [{tsoo foos} GAY-en]

wall (exterior) Mauer, f. [MOW-e(r)]

wall (interior) Wand, f. [vahnt]

wallet Brieftasche, f. [BREEF-tahsh-eh]

want, to wollen [VOL-len]

war Krieg, m. [kreek]

warm warm [vahrm]

wash, to waschen [VAHSH-en]

wash-and-wear bügelfrei [BEW-gel-frye]

washbasin Waschbecken, n. [VAHSH-beh-ken]

waste of time Zeitver-schwendung, f. [TSITE-vehr-shvehn-dung]

watch Uhr, f. [oor]

watch, to beobachten [beh-OH-bahkh-ten]

watchmaker Uhrmacher, m. [OOR-mahkh-e(r)]

watch out, to aufpassen [OWF-pahs-sen]

water Wasser, n. [VAHS-e(r)]

waterfall Wasserfall, m. [VAHS-se(r)-fahl]

waterproof wasserdicht [VAHS-se(r)-dikht]

wave Welle, f. [VEHL-leh]

way Weg, m. [vehk]

we wir [veer]

weak schwach [shvahkh]

wear, to tragen [TRAA-gen]

weather Wetter, n. [VEHT-te(r)]

weather forecast Wetter-bericht, m. [VEHT-te(r)-beh-rikht]

wedding Hochzeit, f. [HOKH-tsite]

Wednesday Mittwoch, m. [MIT-vokh]

week Woche, f. [VOKH-eh]

weekend Wochenende, n. [VOKH-en-ehn-deh]

weigh, to wiegen [VEE-gen]

weight Gewicht, n. [geh-VIKHT]

well gut [goot]; wohl [vohl]

well Brunnen, m. [BRUN-nen]

well-done (meat) gut durchgebraten [goot durkh-geh-BRAA-ten]

well-known bekannt [beh-KAHNT]

west West(en), m. [VEHST {-en}]

wet nass [nahs]

what was [vahs]

wheel Rad, n. [raat]

when wann [vahn]; wenn [vehn]

where wo [voh]

which welche (-r, -s) [VEHL-kheh, {-khe(r), -khehs}]

white weiß [vice]

who wer [vehr]

whole ganz [gahnts]

why warum [vah-ROOM]

wide breit [brite]; weit [vite]

widow Witwe, f. [VIT-veh]

widower Witwer, m. [VIT-ve(r)]

wife Frau, f. [frow]; Ehefrau, f. [AY-eh-frow]

wild wild [vilt]

win, to gewinnen [geh-VIN-nen]

wind Wind, m. [vint]

window Fenster, n. [FEHN-ste(r)]

windshield Wind-schutzscheibe, f. [VINT-shuts-shye-beh]

wine Wein, m. [vine]

wine list Weinkarte, f. [VINE-kahr-teh]

wine shop Weinladen, m. [VINE-laa-den]

wing Flügel, m. [FLEW-gel]

winter Winter, m. [VIN-te(r)]

233

wire Draht, m. *[draht]*
wish Wunsch, m. *[voonsh]*
wish, to wünschen *[VEWN-shen]*
with mit *[mit]*
without ohne *[OH-neh]*
woman Frau, f. *[frow]*
wonderful wunderbar *[VUN-de(r)-baar]*
wood Holz, n. *[holts]*
wool Wolle, f. *[VOL-leh]*
word Wort, n. *[vort]*
work Arbeit, f. *[AHR-bite]*
work, to arbeiten *[AHR-bite-en]*
workday Arbeitstag, m. *[AHR-bites-taak]*
world Welt, f. *[vehlt]*
worry Sorge, f. *[ZOR-geh]*
worse schlechter *[SHLEHKH-te(r)]*
worthless wertlos *[VEHRT-lohs]*
would würde *[VU(R)-deh]*
would like möchten *[MU(R)KH-ten]*
wound Wunde, f. *[VUN-deh]*
wrap, to einwickeln *[INE-vi-keln]*
wrist Handgelenk, n. *[HAHNT-geh-lehnk]*
wristwatch Armbanduhr, f. *[AHRM-bahnt-oor]*
write, to schreiben *[SHRYE-ben]*
writer Schriftsteller, m. *[SHRIFT-shtehl-le(r)]*

wrong falsch *[fahlsh]*

X

X ray Röntgenaufname, f. *[RU(R)NT-gen-owf-naa-meh]*

Y

year Jahr, n. *[yaar]*
yellow gelb *[gehlp]*
yes ja *[yaa]*
yesterday gestern *[GEHS-tern]*
yet noch *[nohkh]*
yield, to (traffic) Vorfahrt gewähren *[FOR-faart geh-VAY-ren]*
you du, Sie, ihr *[doo, zee, eer]*
young jung *[yung]*
youth hostel Jugendherberge, f. *[YOO-gehnt-hehr-behr-geh]*

Z

zero null *[nul]*
zip code Postleitzahl, f. *[POST-lite-tsaal]*
zipper Reißverschluß, m. *[RICE-fehr-shlus]*
zoo Zoo, m. *[tsoh]*; Tierpark, m. *[TEER-pahrk]*

234

GERMAN/ENGLISH DICTIONARY

List of Abbreviations

m. *masculine*
f. *feminine*

n. *neuter*
pl. *plural*

A

Aal, m. *[aal]* eel

abbiegen *[AHP-bee-gen]* to turn (direction)

Abend, m. *[AA-behnt]* evening

Abendessen, n. *[AA-behnt-ehs-sen]* dinner; supper

Abendkleid, n. *[AA-behnt-klite]* evening gown

aber *[AA-be(r)]* but

abfahren *[AHP-faa-ren]* to leave (depart)

Abfahrt, f. *[AHP-faart]* departure

Abfall, m. *[AHP-fahl]* garbage; trash

Abflug, m. *[AHP-flook]* departure

Abführmittel, n. *[AHP-fewr-mit-tel]* laxative

Abgase, pl. *[AHP-gaa-zeh]* exhaust (car)

abholen *[AHP-hoh-len]* to pick up

Abkürzung, f. *[AHP-kewr-tsung]* abbreviation

ablehnen *[AHP-lay-nen]* to refuse

abnehmen *[AHP-nay-men]* to lose weight

absagen *[AHP-zaa-gen]* to cancel

Absatz, m. *[AHP-zahts]* heel

abschließen *[AHP-shlees-sen]* to lock

Absender, m. *[AHP-zehn-de(r)]* sender (mail)

Abszess, m. *[ahps-TSEHS]* abscess

Abtei, f. *[ahp-TYE]* abbey

Abteil, n. *[AHP-tile]* compartment

Abteilung, f. *[ahp-TYE-lung]* department

Abzug, m. *[AHP-tsook]* print (photo)

acht *[ahkht]* eight

achte (-r, -s) *[AHKH-teh {-te(r), -tehs}]* eighth

Achtung, f. *[AHKH-tung]* attention

achtzehn *[AHKH-tsayn]* eighteen

achtzig *[AHKH-tsikh]* eighty

Adresse, f. *[ah-DREHS-seh]* address

ähneln *[AY-neln]* to resemble

Aktentasche, f. *[AAK-ten-tahsh-eh]* briefcase

Alkohol, m. *[AHL-koh-hol]* liquor

alkoholfreies Getränk, n. *[AHL-koh-hohl-frye-ehs geh-TREHNK]* soft drink

alle *[AH-leh]* all

antworten *[AHNT-vor-ten]* to answer

Anzeige, f. *[AHN-tsye-geh]* notice

anziehen *[AHN-tsee-en]* to put on (dress)

sich anziehen *[zikh AHN-tsee-en]* to dress oneself; to get dressed

anziehend *[AHN-tsee-ent]* attractive

Anzug, m. *[AHN-tsook]* suit

anzünden *[AHN-tsewn-den]* to light

Apfel, m. *[AHP-fel]* apple

Apfelsaft, m. *[AHP-fehl-zahft]* cider

Apotheke, f. *[ah-poh-TAY-keh]* pharmacy

Aprikose, f. *[ahp-ri-KOH-zeh]* apricot

April, m. *[ah-PRIL]* April

Arbeit, f. *[AHR-bite]* work

arbeiten *[AHR-bite-en]* to work

Arbeitsstunden, pl. *[AHR-bites-shtun-den]* working hours

Arbeitstag, m. *[AHR-bites-taak]* workday

ärgern *[EHR-gern]* to annoy; to bother

Arm, m. *[ahrm]* arm

arm *[ahrm]* poor

Armband, n. *[AHRM-bahnt]* bracelet

Armbanduhr, f. *[AHRM-bahnt-oor]* wristwatch

Ärmel, m. *[EHR-mel]* sleeve

Art, f. *[ahrt]* kind (type); type (sort)

Artikel, m. *[ahr-TEE-kel]* article

Arzt, m. *[ahrtst]*; **Ärztin**, f. *[EHRTS-tin]* doctor

ärztlich *[EHRTS-likh]* medical

Aschenbecher, m. *[AHSH-en-behkh-e(r)]* ashtray

Aspirin, n. *[ahs-pi-REEN]* aspirin

Asthma, n. *[AHST-mah]* asthma

atmen *[AAT-men]* to breathe

Aubergine, f. *[o-ber-ZHEE-neh]* eggplant

auch *[owkh]* also; too (also)

auf *[owf]* on

Aufenthalt, m. *[OWF-ehnt-hahlt]* stay

Aufgabe, f. *[OWF-gaa-beh]* job (task); lesson

aufgeben *[OWF-gay-ben]* to check (luggage); to mail

aufmachen *[OWF-mahkh-en]* to open

Aufmerksamkeit, f. *[OWF-mehrk-saam-kite]* attention

Aufnahme, f. *[OWF-naa-meh]* recording

aufpassen *[OWF-pahs-sen]* to be careful; to look out; to watch out

aufstehen *[OWF-shteh-en]* to get up; to stand up

aufwachen *[OWF-vahkh-en]* to wake up

Auge, n. *[OW-geh]* eye

Augenblick, m. *[OW-gen-blik]* moment

Augenbraue, f. *[OW-gen-brow-eh]* eyebrow

Augenlid, n. *[OW-gen-leet]* eyelid

Augenwimper, f. *[OW-gen-vim-pe(r)]* eyelash

August, m. *[ow-GUST]* August

aus *[ows]* over (finished); out

Ausdruck, m. *[OWS-druk]* phrase

Ausflug, m. *[OWS-flook]* excursion

ausfüllen *[OWS-fewl-len]* to fill in

Ausgang, m. *[OWS-gahng]* exit

ausgeben *[OWS-gay-ben]* to spend (money)

ausgezeichnet *[OWS-geh-tsyekh-net]* excellent

Auskunft, f. *[OWS-kunft]* information

Ausland, n. *[im OWS-lahnt]* abroad

Ausländer (-in), m., f. *[OWS-lehn-de(r) {-deh-rin}]* foreigner

Ausrede, f. *[OWS-ray-deh]* excuse

sich ausruhen *[zikh OWS-roo-en]* to rest

Ausrüstung, f. *[OWS-rews-tung]* equipment; outfit

außerhalb *[OWS-se(r)-hahlp]* outside of

Aussicht, f. *[OWS-zikht]* view

Aussprache, f. *[OWS-shprahkh-eh]* pronunciation

aussteigen *[OWS-shtye-gen]* to get off; to get out

Ausstellung, f. *[OWS-shtehl-lung]* exhibition

Austausch, m. *[OWS-towsh]* exchange

Auster, f. *[OW-ste(r)]* oyster

Ausverkauf, m. *[OWS-fehr-kowf]* sale (low prices)

ausverkauft *[OWS-fehr-kowft]* sold out

Auswahl, f. *[OWS-vaal]* selection

auswählen *[OWS-vay-len]* to choose

Ausweis, m. *[OWS-vice]* identity card; pass (permit)

Auto, n. *[OW-toh]* car

automatisch *[ow-toh-MAH-tish]* automatic

Autopanne, f. *[OW-toh-pahn-neh]* car breakdown

Autovermietung, f. *[OW-toh-fehr-mee-tung]* car rental agency

B

Baby, n. *[BAY-bee]* baby

Babysitter, m. *[BAY-bee-sit-e(r)]* baby-sitter

backen *[BAH-ken]* to bake

Bäckerei, f. *[beh-keh-RYE]* bakery

Backpflaume, f. *[BAHK-pflow-meh]* prune

Bad, n. *[baat]* bath, bathroom

Badeanzug, m. *[BAA-deh-ahn-tsook]* bathing suit

Bademantel, m. *[BAA-deh-mahn-tel]* robe

baden *[BAA-den]* to bathe

Badewanne, f. *[BAA-deh-vah-neh]* bathtub

Bahnhof, m. *[BAAN-hohf]* train station

Bahnsteig, m. *[BAAN-shtike]* platform (station)

bald *[bahlt]* soon

Balkon, m. *[BAHL-kon]* balcony

Ball, m. *[bahl]* ball

Ballett, n. *[bah-LEHT]* ballet

Band, n. *[bahnt]* ribbon; tape

Bank, f. *[bahnk]* bank (finance)

Bargeld, n. *[BAAR-gehlt]* cash

Barscheck, m. *[BAAR-shehk]* personal check

Bart, m. *[bahrt]* beard

Batterie, f. *[bah-teh-REE]* battery

Bauernhof, m. *[BOW-ehrn-hohf]* farm

Baum, m. *[bowm]* tree

Baumwolle, f. *[BOWM-vol-leh]* cotton

bedauern *[beh-DOW-ern]* to regret

bedeuten *[beh-DOY-ten]* to mean

Bedeutung, f. *[beh-DOY-tung]* meaning

Bedienung, f. *[beh-DEE-nung]* service

beenden *[beh-EHN-den]* to end

beginnen *[beh-GIN-nen]* to start

begleiten *[beh-GLYE-ten]* to accompany

Begrenzung, f. *[beh-GREHN-tsung]* limit

behalten *[beh-HAHL-ten]* to keep

behandeln *[beh-HAHN-deln]* to treat

Behandlung, f. *[beh-HAHNT-lung]* treatment

behindert *[beh-HIN-dert]* handicapped

Behinderte, m., f. *[beh-HIN-dehr-teh]* disabled

bei *[bye]* at

beide *[BYE-deh]* both

Bein, n. *[bine]* leg

Beispiel, n. *[BYE-shpeel]* example

beißen *[BICE-sen]* to bite

bekannt *[beh-KAHNT]* well-known

Bekannte, m., f. *[beh-KAHN-teh]* acquaintance

bekommen *[beh-KOM-men]* to get (fetch); to obtain

bemerken *[beh-MEHR-ken]* to notice

benutzen *[beh-NUT-sen]* to use

Benzin, n. *[behn-TSEEN]* gasoline

beobachten *[beh-OH-bahkh-ten]* to watch

bequem *[beh-KVEHM]* comfortable

berechnen *[beh-REHKH-nen]* to charge

bereit *[beh-RITE]* ready

Berg, m. *[behrk]* mountain

Beruf, m. *[beh-ROOF]* occupation; profession

berühren *[beh-REW-ren]* to touch

beschäftigt *[beh-SHEHF-tikht]* busy

beschützen *[beh-SHEWT-sen]* to protect

Beschwerde, f. *[beh-SHVEHR-deh]* complaint

besetzt *[beh-ZEHTST]* occupied

Besichtigung, f. *[beh-ZIKH-ti-gung]* sight-seeing

Besitz, m. *[beh-ZITS]* property

besitzen *[beh-ZIT-sen]* to own

Besitzer, m. *[beh-ZIT-se(r)]* owner

besondere *[beh-ZON-deh-reh]* special

besonders *[beh-ZON-dehrs]* especially

besser *[BEHS-se(r)]* better

bestätigen *[beh-SHTAY-ti-gen]* to confirm; to verify

beste *[BEHS-teh]* best

Besteck, n. *[beh-SHTEHK]* silverware

bestellen *[beh-SHTEHL-len]* to order

Bestellung, f. *[beh-SHTEHL-lung]* order

bestimmt *[beh-SHTIMT]* certainly

Besuch, m. *[beh-ZOOKH]* visit

besuchen *[beh-ZOO-khen]* to visit

Bete, f. *[BAY-teh]* beet

Betrag, m. *[beh-TRAHK]* amount

außer Betrieb *[OWS-se(r) beh-TREEP]* out of order

betrunken *[beh-TRUN-ken]* drunk

Bett, n. *[beht]* bed

Bettlaken, n. *[BEHT-lah-ken]* sheet

238

bewölkt *[beh-VU(R)KT]* cloudy

bewundern *[beh-VOON-dern]* to admire

bewusstlos *[beh-VUST-lohs]* unconscious

bezahlen *[beh-TSAA-len]* to pay

Bezirk, m. *[beh-TSIRK]* district

BH (Büstenhalter), m. *[bay-hah, BEWS-ten-hahl-te(r)]* bra

Bibliothek, f. *[bib-lee-oh-TAYK]* library

Bier, n. *[beer]* beer

Biergarten, m. *[BEER-gahr-ten]* beer garden

Bierkrug, m. *[BEER-krook]* beer stein

Bild, n. *[bilt]* painting; picture

bildende Künste, pl. *[BIL-den-deh KEWN-steh]* fine arts

Billard, n. *[BIL-yahrt]* pool (game)

billig *[BIL-likh]* cheap

Birne, f. *[BEER-neh]* pear

bis *[bis]* until; till

bitte *[BIT-teh]* please

Wie bitte? *[vee BIT-teh]* Pardon?

bitten *[BIT-ten]* to ask; to request

bitter *[BIT-te(r)]* bitter

Blase, f. *[BLAA-zeh]* bladder

blau *[blow]* blue

bleiben *[BLYE-ben]* to stay (remain)

Bleistift, m. *[BLYE-shtift]* pencil

Blinddarmentzündung, f. *[BLINT-dahr-mehnt-tsewn-dung]* appendicitis

Blinker, m. *[BLIN-ke(r)]* turn signal

Blitz, m. *[blits]* lightning

Blitzlicht, n. *[BLITS-likht]* flash (on camera)

blond *[blont]* blond

Blume, f. *[BLOO-meh]* flower

Blumengeschäft, n. *[BLOO-men-geh-shehft]* florist

Blumenkohl, m. *[BLOO-men-kohl]* cauliflower

Bluse, f. *[BLOO-zeh]* blouse

Blut, n. *[bloot]* blood

Blutdruck, m. *[BLOOT-druk]* blood pressure

bluten *[BLOO-ten]* to bleed

blutig *[BLOO-tikh]* rare (uncooked)

Boden, m. *[BOH-den]* floor; ground

Bohne, f. *[BOH-neh]* bean

Bonbon, n. *[bong-BONG]* candy

Boot, n. *[boht]* boat

Bordkarte, f. *[BOHRT-kahr-teh]* boarding pass

borgen, *[BOR-gen]* to borrow

Börse, f. *[BU(R)-zeh]* stock exchange

böse *[BU(R)-zeh]* angry

botanischer Garten, m. *[bo-TAA-nish-e(r) GAAR-ten]* botanical garden

Botschaft, f. *[BOHT-shahft]* embassy

Brandwunde, f. *[BRAHNT-vun-deh]* burn

braten *[BRAA-ten]* to fry; to roast

brauchen *[BROW-khen]* to need

braun *[brown]* brown

breit *[brite]* wide

Bremsen, pl. *[BREHM-zen]* brakes

brennen *[BREHN-nen]* to burn

Brief, m. *[breef]* letter

Briefkasten, m. *[BREEF-kahs-ten]* letterbox; mailbox

Briefmarke, f. *[BREEF-mahr-keh]* stamp (postage)

Brieftasche, f. *[BREEF-tahsh-eh]* pocketbook; wallet

Brille, f. *[BRIL-leh]* eyeglasses

bringen *[BRIN-gen]* to bring

Brite, Britin, m., f. *[BRI-teh, BRI-tin]* British

Brosche, f. *[BRO-sheh]* brooch

Brot, n. *[broht]* bread

Brötchen, pl. *[BRU(R)T-khen]* rolls (bread)

Bruch, m. *[brukh]* fracture

Brücke, f. *[BREW-keh]* bridge

Bruder, m. *[BROO-de(r)]* brother

Brunnen, m. *[BRUN-nen]* fountain; well

Brust, f. *[broost]* breast; chest (part of body)

Buch, n. *[bookh]* book

buchen *[BOO-khehn]* to book

Buchhandlung, f. *[BOOKH-hahnd-lung]* bookstore

Büchse, f. *[BEWK-seh]* can (container)

Büchsenöffner, m. *[BEWK-sen-u(r)f-ne(r)]* can opener

buchstabieren *[bookh-shtah-BEE-ren]* to spell

Bügeleisen, n. *[BEW-gel-eye-zen]* iron (flatiron)

bügelfrei *[BEW-gel-frye]* wash-and-wear

bügeln *[BEW-geln]* to iron

Bundesrepublik Deutschland, f. *[BUN-dehs-reh-poo-bleek DOYCH-lahnt]* Federal Republic of Germany

Burg, f. *[boork]* fortress

Bürger *[BEWR-ge(r)]* citizen

bürgerlich *[BEWR-ge(r)-likh]* middle-class

Bürgersteig, m. *[BEWR-ge(r)-shtike]* sidewalk

Büro, n. *[bew-ROH]* agency; office

Bürste, f. *[BEWR-steh]* brush

bürsten *[BEWR-sten]* to brush

Bus, m. *[bus]* bus; coach

Bushaltestelle, f. *[BUS-hahl-teh-shtehl-leh]* bus stop

Butter, f. *[BUT-te(r)]* butter

C

Café, n. *[kah-FAY]* café

Campingplatz, m. *[KAHM-ping-plahts]* campsite

CD, f. *[TSEH-deh]* CD

CD-Spieler, m. *[TSEH-deh-SHPEE-lehr]* CD player

Chef, m. *[shehf]* boss

chemische Reinigung, f. *[KHAY-mish-eh RYE-ni-gung]* dry cleaning

Chirurgie, f. *[khee-roor-GEE]* surgery

Creme, f. *[kraym]* cream (cosmetic)

D

da *[daa]* there

Dach, n. *[dahkh]* roof

Dame, f. *[DAA-meh]* lady

Damenbinde, f. *[DAA-men-bin-deh]* sanitary napkin

Damentoilette, f. *[DAA-men-toy-leht-teh]* ladies' room

Dänemark, n. *[DEH-neh-mahrk]* Denmark

vielen Dank *[FEE-len dahnk]* thank you very much

danken *[DAHN-ken]* to thank

dann *[dahn]* then

Datum, n. *[DAA-tum]* date (calendar)

dauern *[DOW-ern]* to last; to take time

Dauerwelle, f. *[DOW-e(r)-vehl-leh]* permanent wave

Daumen, m. *[DOW-men]* thumb

das *[dahs]* the

dass *[dahs]* that (which)

Decke, f. *[DEH-keh]* blanket; ceiling

decken *[DEHK-en]* to cover

denken *[DEHN-ken]* to think

Denkmal, n. *[DEHNK-maal]* monument

der *[dehr]* the

desinfizieren *[dehs-in-fi-TSEE-ren]* to disinfect

Deutsch *[doych]* German

Deutschland *[DOYCH-lahnt]* Germany

Dezember, m. *[deh-TSEHM-be(r)]* December

Dia, n. *[DEE-ah]* slide (photo)

Diabetiker, m. *[dee-ah-BAY-ti-ke(r)]* diabetic

Diät, f. *[dee-AYT]* diet

dick *[dik]* fat; thick

die *[dee]* the

Dieb m. *[deep]* thief

dienen *[DEE-nen]* to serve

Dienstag, m. *[DEENS-taak]* Tuesday

diese, -r, -s *[DEE-zeh, {-ze(r), -zehs}]* this, these

Dieselöl, n. *[DEE-zel-u(r)l]* diesel fuel

Ding, n. *[ding]* thing

direkt *[dee-REHKT]* direct

Dirigent, m. *[di-ri-GEHNT]* conductor (orchestra)

Dokument, n. *[do-koo-MEHNT]* document

Dollar, m. *[DOL-lahr]* dollar

Dom, m. *[dohm]* cathedral

Donner, m. *[DON-ne(r)]* thunder

Donnerstag, m. *[DON-nehrs-taak]* Thursday

Doppelbett, n. *[DOP-pehl-beht]* double bed

Doppelzimmer, n. *[DOP-pehl-tsim-me(r)]* double room

Dorf, n. *[dorf]* village

dort *[dort]* there

Dose, f. *[DOH-seh]* can (container)

Draht, m. *[draht]* wire

Drama, n. *[DRAA-mah]* drama

draußen *[DROWS-sen]* outdoors

drehen *[DREH-en]* to turn

drei *[drye]* three

dreißig *[DRYES-sikh]* thirty

dreizehn *[DRYE-tsayn]* thirteen

dringend *[DRING-ent]* urgent

drinnen *[DRIN-nen]* inside

dritte, -r, -s *[DRIT-teh, {-te(r), -tehs}]* third

Drogerie, f. *[dro-geh-REE]* drugstore

Druck, m. *[druk]* pressure

drucken *[DRUK-en]* to print

drücken *[DREWK-en]* to press; to push (a button)

du *[doo]* you

dunkel *[DUN-kel]* dark

dünn *[dewn]* thin

durch *[durkh]* across (movement); by; through

Durchfall, m. *[DURKH-fahl]* diarrhea

durchgebraten *[durkh-geh-BRAA-ten]* well-done (meat)

durchschnittlich *[DURKH-shnit-likh]* average

Durst haben *[durst HAA-ben]* to be thirsty

Dusche, f. *[DOO-sheh]* shower

Dutzend, n. *[DUT-sehnt]* dozen

DVD-Spieler, m. *[deh-fow-DEH SHPEE-lehr]* DVD player

E

Ebbe, f. *[EHB-eh]* low tide

Ebene, f. *[AY-beh-neh]* level

echt *[ehkht]* genuine; real

Ecke, f. *[EH-keh]* corner

Ehefrau, f. *[AY-eh-frow]* wife

Ehemann, m. *[AY-eh-mahn]* husband

Eier, pl. *[EYE-e(r)]* eggs

241

eigentlich *[EYE-gehnt-likh]* actually

eilen *[EYE-len]* to hurry

es eilig haben *[ehs EYE-likh HAA-ben]* to be in a hurry

ein(-e) *[ine, INE-eh]* a, an

Einbahnstraße, f. *[INE-baan-shtrahs-seh]* one-way street

Entfernung, f. *[ehnt-FEHR-nung]* distance

entscheiden *[ehnt-SHYE-den]* to decide

sich entschuldigen *[zikh ehnt-SHOOL-di-gen]* to apologize; to excuse

Entschuldigung, f. *[ehnt-SHOOL-di-gung]* apology

enttäuscht *[ehnt-TOYSHT]* disappointed

entwickeln *[ehnt-VIK-eln]* to develop

er *[ehr]* he

sich erbrechen *[zikh ehr-BREHKH-en]* to vomit

Erbse, f. *[EHRP-seh]* pea

Erdbeere, f. *[EHRT-bay-reh]* strawberry

Erdgeschoss, n. *[EHRT-geh-shos]* ground floor

Erfahrung, f. *[ehr-FAA-rung]* experience

Erfolg, m. *[ehr-FOLK]* success

erfrischend *[ehr-FRISH-ent]* refreshing

Ergebnis, n. *[ehr-GAYP-nis]* result

erhalten *[ehr-HAHL-ten]* to receive

erhöhen *[ehr-HU(R)-en]* to increase

sich erholen *[zikh ehr-HOH-len]* to recover

sich erinnern *[zikh eh-RIN-ern]* to remember

erkältet *[ehr-KEHL-tet]* cold (sick)

erklären *[ehr-KLEHR-en]* to explain

erlauben *[ehr-LOW-ben]* to permit

erlaubt *[ehr-LOWPT]* allowed

erledigen *[ehr-LAY-di-gen]* to finish

Ermäßigung, f. *[ehr-MAYS-si-gung]* reduction (price)

ernst *[ehrnst]* serious

Ersatzreifen, m. *[ehr-ZAHTS-rife-en]* spare tire

Ersatzteile, pl. *[ehr-ZAHTS-tile-eh]* spare parts

erschöpft *[ehr-SHU(R)PFT]* exhausted

ersetzen *[ehr-ZEHT-sen]* to replace

erstaunlich *[ehr-SHTOWN-likh]* amazing

erste (-r, -s) *[EHR-steh {-ste(r), -stehs}]* first

Erwachsene, pl. *[ehr-VAHK-seh-neh]* adults

erwähnen *[ehr-VAY-nen]* to mention

erwarten *[ehr-VAAR-ten]* to expect

erzählen *[ehr-TSAY-len]* to tell

Erzählung, f. *[ehr-TSAY-lung]* story (tale)

es tut mir leid *[ehs toot meer lite]* I am sorry

Essen, n. *[EHS-sen]* food

essen *[EHS-sen]* to eat

Essig, m. *[EHS-sikh]* vinegar

Esslöffel, m. *[EHS-lu(r)-fel]* tablespoon

Esszimmer, n. *[EHS-tsim-me(r)]* dining room

Etage, f. *[eh-TAH-zheh]* story (floor)

Etikett, n. *[eh-ti-KEHT]* label

etwas *[EHT-vahs]* any; some; something

Europa, n. *[oy-ROH-pah]* Europe

evangelisch *[ay-fahn-GAY-lish]* Protestant

extra *[EHK-strah]* extra

F

Fabrik, f. *[fah-BREEK]* factory

Faden, m. *[FAA-den]* thread

Fähre, f. *[FEH-reh]* ferry

fahren *[FAA-ren]* to drive; to ride

Fahrer, m. *[FAA-re(r)]* driver

Fahrgast, m. *[FAAR-gahst]* passenger

einfache Fahrkarte, f. *[INE-fahkh-eh FAAR-kahr-teh]* one-way ticket

Fahrplan, m. *[FAAR-plaan]* timetable

Fahrpreis, m. *[FAAR-price]* fare (fee)

Fahrrad, n. *[FAAR-raat]* bicycle

Fahrt, f. *[faart]* journey; ride

fallen *[FAHL-len]* to fall

falsch *[fahlsh]* false; wrong

Familie, f. *[fah-MEEL-yeh]* family

fangen *[FAHN-gen]* to catch

Farbe, f. *[FAHR-beh]* color

Farbfilm, m. *[FAHRP-film]* color film

Farbstoff, m. *[FAHRP-shtof]* dye

fast *[fahst]* almost; nearly

Februar, m. *[FAY-broo-aar]* February

Feder, f. *[FAY-de(r)]* spring (mechanical)

Fehler, m. *[FAY-le(r)]* error

Feiertag, m. *[FYE-e(r)-taak]* holiday

Feige, f. *[FYE-geh]* fig

Feile, f. *[FYE-leh]* file

fein *[fine]* fine (quality)

Feinkostgeschäft, n. *[FINE-kost-geh-shehft]* delicatessen

Feinschmecker, m. *[FINE-shmehk-e(r)]* gourmet

Feld, n. *[fehlt]* field

Felsen, m. *[FEHL-zen]* cliff

Fenster, n. *[FEHN-ste(r)]* window

Fensterladen, m. *[FEHN-ste(r)-laa-den]* shutter

Ferien, pl. *[FEHR-yen]* holidays; vacation

Ferienort, m. *[FEHR-yen-ort]* resort (place)

Ferngespräch, n. *[FEHRN-geh-spraykh]* long-distance call

Fernglas, n. *[FEHRN-glaas]* binoculars

Fernseher, m. *[FEHRN-zay-e(r)]* television (set)

Ferse, f. *[FEHR-zeh]* heel

fertig sein *[FEHR-tikh]* to be ready

Fest, n. *[fehst]* festival

Festung, f. *[FEHS-tung]* fortress

Fett, n. *[feht]* fat

feucht *[foykht]* damp

Feuer, n. *[FOY-e(r)]* fire

Feuerwehr, f. *[FOY-e(r)-vehr]* fire department

Feuerzeug, n. *[FOY-e(r)-tsoyk]* (cigarette) lighter

Fieber, n. *[FEE-be(r)]* fever

Filet, n. *[fee-LAY]* fillet

Film, m. *[film]* film; movie

Filmrolle, f. *[FILM-rol-leh]* roll (film)

Filz, m. *[filts]* felt (cloth)

finden *[FIN-den]* to find

Finger, m. *[FIN-ge(r)]* finger

Fisch, m. *[fish]* fish

flach *[flahkh]* flat

Flasche, f. *[FLAHSH-eh]* bottle

Fleck, m. *[flehk]* stain

Fleisch, n. *[flyshe]* meat

Fleischer, m. *[FLYE-she(r)]* butcher

Fleischerei, f. *[flye-sheh-RYE]* butcher shop

flicken *[FLIK-en]* to mend

fließen *[FLEES-sen]* flow

fliegen *[FLEE-gen]* to fly

Flohmarkt, m. *[FLOH-mahrkt]* flea market

Flug, m. *[flook]* flight

Flügel, m. *[FLEW-gel]* wing

Fluggesellschaft, f. *[FLOOK-geh-zehl-shahft]* airline

Flughafen, m. *[FLOOK-haa-fen]* airport

Flugzeug, n. *[FLOOK-tsoyk]* airplane

Fluss, m. *[floos]* river

Flüssigkeit, f. *[FLEWS-sikh-kite]* fluid

Flut, f. *[floot]* high tide

folgen *[FOL-gen]* to follow

Forelle, f. *[fo-REHL-leh]* trout

Format, n. *[for-MAAT]* format

Formular, n. *[for-moo-LAHR]* form

fortsetzen *[FORT-zeht-sen]* to continue

Foto machen *[FOH-toh MAHKH-en]* to take a photo

Foto, n. *[FOH-toh]* photograph

Fotoapparat, m. *[FOH-toh-ah-pah-raat]* camera

fotografieren *[fot-toh-grah-FEE-ren]* to photograph

Fotokopie, f. *[fot-toh-koh-PEE]* photocopy

Frage, f. *[FRAA-geh]* question

fragen *[FRAA-gen]* to ask

Frankreich, n. *[FRAHNK-ryekh]* France

Frau, f. *[frow]* wife; woman; Mrs., Ms

Fräulein, n. *[FROY-line]* Miss

frei *[frye]* clear (not blocked); free; vacant

Freitag, m. *[FRYE-taak]* Friday

fremd *[frehmt]* foreign

Fremdenverkehrsbüro, n. *[FREHM-den-fehr-kehrs-bew-roh]* tourist office

Freude, f. *[FROY-deh]* joy

Freund, (-in), m., f. *[FROYNT, FROYN-din]* friend

freundlich *[FROYNT-likh]* friendly

Friedhof, m. *[FREET-hohf]* cemetery

frieren *[FREE-ren]* to freeze

frisch *[frish]* fresh

Friseur, m. *[fri-ZUR]* barber; hairdresser

Frisur, f. *[fri-ZOOR]* haircut

froh *[froh]* glad

fröhlich *[FRU(R)-likh]* merry

Frosch, m. *[frohsh]* frog

Frost, m. *[frost]* frost

früh *[frew]* early

Frühling, m. *[FREW-ling]* spring (season)

Frühstück, n. *[FREW-shtewk]* breakfast

Fuchs, m. *[fooks]* fox

sich fühlen *[zikh FEW-len]* to feel

führen *[FEW-ren]* to lead

Führerschein, m. *[FEWR-e(r)-shine]* driver's license

Führung, f. *[FEW-rung]* guided tour

Füllfederhalter, m. *[FEWL-fay-de(r)-hahl-te(r)]* fountain pen

Fundbüro, n. *[FUNT-bew-roh]* lost and found

fünf *[fewnf]* five

fünfzehn *[FEWNF-tsayn]* fifteen

fünfzig *[FEWNF-tsikh]* fifty

für *[fewr]* for

Fuß, m. *[foos]* foot

zu Fuß *[tsoo foos]* on foot

Fußball, m. *[FOOS-bahl]* soccer

Fußgänger, m. *[FOOS-gehng-e(r)]* pedestrian

Fußgängerzone, f. *[FOOS-gehng-e(r)-tsoh-neh]* pedestrian zone

Fußpuder, m. *[FOOS-poo-de(r)]* foot powder

Fußweg, m. *[FOOS-vehk]*
footpath

G

Gabel, f. *[GAA-bel]* fork

Galerie, f. *[gah-leh-REE]*
gallery

Gang, m. *[gahng]* course
(meal); gear (car)

Gans, f. *[gahns]* goose

ganz *[gahnts]* whole

gar nicht *[gaar nikht]* not at
all

Garage, f. *[gah-RAH-zheh]*
garage

Garderobe, f. *[gar-deh-ROH-
beh]* checkroom (theater)

Garnele, f. *[gahr-NAY-leh]*
shrimp

Garten, m. *[GAAR-ten]* garden

Gas, n. *[gahs]* gas

Gaspedal, n. *[GAHS-peh-daal]*
accelerator

Gastfreundschaft, f. *[GAHST-
froynt-shahft]* hospitality

Gastgeber, m. *[GAHST-gay-
be(r)]* host

Gasthaus, n. *[GAHST-hows]*
inn

Gatte, m. *[GAHT-teh]* spouse

Gattin, f. *[GAHT-tin]* spouse

Gebäck, n. *[geh-BEHK]* pastry

gebacken *[geh-BAH-ken]*
baked

Gebäude, n. *[geh-BOY-deh]*
building

geben *[GAY-ben]* to give

Gebiet, n. *[geh-BEET]* area

Gebiss, n. *[geh-BIS]* denture

es gibt *[ehs gipt]* there are
(is)

geboren *[geh-BOR-en]* born

gebraten *[geh-BRAA-ten]*
fried; roasted

zu stark gebraten *[tsoo
shtahrk geh-BRAA-ten]* overdone

gebraucht *[geh-BROWKHT]*
used

gebrochen *[geh-BROKH-en]*
broken

Gebühr, f. *[geh-BEWR]* commission; charge; toll

Geburtstag, m. *[geh-BURTS-
taak]* birthday

Gefahr, f. *[geh-FAAR]* danger

gefährlich *[geh-FEHR-likh]*
dangerous

Gefallen, m. *[geh-FAHL-len]*
favor

gefallen *[geh-FAHL-len]* to like

Geflügel, n. *[geh-FLEW-gel]*
fowl

gefroren *[geh-FROH-ren]*
frozen

gegen *[GAY-gen]* against; to-
ward(s)

Gegend, f. *[GAY-gehnt]* area

Gegenstand, m. *[GAY-gen-
shtahnt]* object

Gegenteil, n. *[GAY-gen-tile]*
opposite

gegenüber *[gay-gen-EW-be(r)]*
across; opposite (across
from)

gegrillt *[geh-GRILT]* grilled

gehen *[GAY-en]* to go; to
walk

Gehirn, n. *[geh-HEERN]* brain

gehören *[geh-HU(R)-en]* to belong

Geist, m. *[gyest]* mind

gekocht *[geh-KOKHT]* boiled;
cooked

gelb *[gehlp]* yellow

Geld, n. *[gehlt]* money

Geldstrafe, f. *[GEHLT-shtrah-
feh]* fine (penalty)

Gelegenheit, f. *[geh-LAY-gen-
hite]* opportunity

Gelenk, n. *[geh-LEHNK]* joint

Gemälde, n. *[geh-MEHL-deh]* painting

gemalt *[geh-MAALT]* painted

Gemüse, n. *[geh-MEW-zeh]* vegetable

Genehmigung, f. *[geh-NAY-mi-gung]* permit (pass)

genießen *[geh-NEES-sen]* enjoy

genug *[geh-NOOK]* enough

Gepäck, n. *[geh-PEHK]* baggage; luggage

Gepäckaufbewahrung, f. *[geh-PEHK-owf-beh-vaa-rung]* baggage checkroom; checkroom

Gepäckausgabe, f. *[geh-PEHK-ows-gaa-beh]* baggage claim

Gepäckkontrolle, f. *[geh-PEHK-kon-trol-leh]* baggage check

Gepäckträger, m. *[geh-PEHK-tray-ge(r)]* porter

Gepäckwagen, m. *[geh-PEHK-vaa-gen]* baggage car

gerade *[geh-RAA-deh]* straight

Gerät, n. *[geh-RAYT]* appliance

geräuchert *[geh-ROY-khert]* smoked

Gericht, n. *[geh-RIKHT]* court; dish (food)

gern *[gehrn]* gladly

gern haben *[gehrn HAA-ben]* to like

Geschäft, n. *[geh-SHEHFT]* business; store

Geschäftsführer, m. *[geh-SHEHFTS-few-re(r)]* manager

Geschäftsreise, f. *[geh-SHEHFTS-rye-zeh]* business trip

Geschenk, n. *[geh-SHEHNK]* present (gift)

Geschichte, f. *[geh-SHIKH-teh]* history

geschieden *[geh-SHEE-den]* divorced

geschlossen *[geh-SHLOS-sen]* closed

Geschmack, n. *[geh-SHMAHK]* flavor

Geschwindigkeit, f. *[geh-SHVIN-dikh-kite]* speed

Geschwindigkeitsbegrenzung, f. *[geh-SHVIN-dikh-kites-beh-GREHN-tsung]* speed limit

Geschwür, n. *[geh-SHVEWR]* ulcer

Gesellschaft, f. *[geh-ZEHL-shahft]* company

Gesicht, n. *[ge-ZIKHT]* face

Gesichtscreme, f. *[geh-ZIKHTS-kraym]* face cream

gespannt *[geh-SHPAHNT]* tense

Gespräch, n. *[geh-SHPRAYKH]* conversation

Gespräch mit Voranmeldung *[geh-SHPRAYKH mit FOHR-ahn-mehl-dung* *[person-to-person call*

gestern *[GEHS-tern]* yesterday

Gesundheit, f. *[geh-ZUNT-hite]* health

Getränk, n. *[geh-TREHNK]* beverage; drink

Getriebe, n. *[geh-TREE-beh]* transmission

getrocknet *[geh-TROK-net]* dried

Gewicht, n. *[geh-VIKHT]* weight

gewinnen *[geh-VIN-nen]* to win

gewiss *[geh-VIS]* certain

Gewohnheit, f. *[geh-VOHN-hite]* habit

gewöhnlich *[geh-VU(R)N-likh]* ordinary; usual

Gewürz, n. *[geh-VEWRTS]* spice

Gift, n. *[gift]* poison

Gin, m. *[jin]* gin (drink)

Gipfel, m. *[GIP-fel]* peak

Glas, n. *[glaas]* glass; jar

glatt *[glaht]* smooth

glauben *[GLOW-ben]* to believe; to think (believe)

gleich *[glyekh]* equal; right away

gleiche *[GLYE-kheh]* same

Gleis, n. *[glice]* track (train)

Glück, n. *[glewk]* luck

viel Glück *[feel glewk]* good luck

glücklich *[GLEWK-likh]* happy

Glühbirne, f. *[GLEW-beer-neh]* electric bulb

Gold, n. *[golt]* gold

Golfplatz, m. *[GOLF-plahts]* golf course

Gott, m. *[got]* god

Gottesdienst, m. *[GOT-tehs-deenst]* religious service

Grab, n. *[grahp]* grave; tomb

Gramm, n. *[graam]* gram

Grammatik, f. *[grah-MAH-tik]* grammar

Gras, n. *[grahs]* grass

grau *[grow]* gray

Grenze, f. *[GREHN-tseh]* border

grillen *[GRIL-len]* to broil

Grippe, f. *[GRIP-peh]* flu

groß *[grohs]* big; great; large; tall

Größe, f. *[GRU(R)S-eh]* size

Großeltern, pl. *[GROHS-ehl-tern]* grandparents

großzügig, *[GROHS-tsew-gikh]* generous

grün *[grewn]* green

Grund, m. *[grunt]* reason

Grundstück, n. *[GRUNT-shtewk]* property

Gruß, m. *[groos]* greeting

Grüße, pl. *[GREWS-eh]* regards

mit freundlichen Grüßen *[mit FROYNT-likh-en GREWS-en]* sincerely (yours)

gültig *[GEWL-tikh]* valid

Gummi, m. *[GOOM-mee]* rubber

Gummiband, n. *[GOOM-mee-bahnt]* rubber band

Gurke, f. *[GOOR-keh]* cucumber

Gürtel, m. *[GEWR-tel]* belt

gut *[goot]* good; well

H

Haar, n. *[haar]* hair

Haarbürste, f. *[HAAR-bewr-steh]* hairbrush

Haarnadel, f. *[HAAR-naa-dehl]* hairpin

Haartrockner, m. *[HAAR-trok-ne(r)]* hair dryer

Haarwaschmittel, n. *[HAAR-vahsh-mit-tel]* shampoo

haben *[HAA-ben]* to have

Hafen, m. *[HAA-fen]* harbor; port

Hafenanlage, f. *[HAA-fen-ahn-laa-geh]* dock

halb *[hahlp]* half

Hälfte, f. *[HEHLF-teh]* half

Halle, f. *[HAHL-leh]* hall

Hallo! *[HAH-loh]* hello! (phone)

Hals, m. *[hahls]* neck; throat

Halskette, f. *[HAHLS-keh-teh]* necklace

Halsschmerzen, pl. *[HAHLS-shmehr-tsen]* sore troat

halten *[HAHL-ten]* to hold

Hammer, m. *[HAHM-me(r)]* hammer

Hand, f. *[hahnt]* hand

handgearbeitet *[HAHNT-geh-ahr-bite-et]* handmade

Handgelenk, n. *[HAHNT-geh-lehnk]* wrist

Handgepäck, n. *[HAHNT-geh-pehk]* carry-on luggage

Handschuh, m. *[HAHNT-shoo]* glove

Handtasche, f. *[HAHNT-tahsh-eh]* handbag; purse

Handtuch, n. *[HAHNT-tookh]* towel

hart, *[hahrt]* hard (tough)

Hase, m. *[HAA-zeh]* rabbit

hässlich *[HEHS-likh]* ugly

häufig *[HOY-fikh]* frequent

Hauptrolle, f. *[HOWPT-rol-leh]* lead (stage)

Hauptstadt, f. *[HOWPT-shtaht]* capital

Haus, *[hows]* home; house

nach Hause gehen *[nahkh HOW-zeh GAY-en]* to go home

zu Hause *[tsoo HOW-zeh]* (at) home

Hausschuhe, pl. *[HOWS-shoo-eh]* slippers

Haut, f. *[howt]* skin

heben *[HAY-ben]* to lift

Heftpflaster, n. *[HEHFT-pflahs-te(r)]* adhesive tape

heilig *[HYE-likh]* holy

Heilmittel, n. *[HILE-mit-tel]* remedy

Heim, n. *[hime]* home

Heimatadresse, f. *[HYE-maat-ah-drehs-seh]* home address

heiß *[hice]* hot

heißen *[HICE-sen]* to be named

heißlaufen *[HICE-low-fen]* to overheat (motor)

Heizgerät, n. *[HITES-geh-rayt]* heater

Heizkörper, m. *[HITES-ku(r)-pe(r)]* radiator

helfen *[HEHL-fen]* to help

hellbraun *[HEHL-brown]* tan

Hemd, n. *[hehmt]* shirt

Herbst, m. *[hehrpst]* autumn

Herr, m. *[hehr]* gentleman; Mr.

Herrentoilette, f. *[HEHR-ren-toy-leht-teh]* men's room

herum *[heh-RUM]* around

Herz, n. *[hehrts]* heart

Herzkrankheit, f. *[HEHRTS-krahnk-hite]* heart trouble

Heuschnupfen, m. *[HOY-shnup-fen]* hay fever

heute *[HOY-teh]* today

heute abend *[HOY-teh AA-behnt]* tonight

hier *[heer]* here

hiesig *[HEE-zikh]* local

Hilfe, f. *[HIL-feh]* help

Himbeere, f. *[HIM-bay-reh]* raspberry

Himmel, m. *[HIM-mel]* heaven; sky

hinauf *[hin-OWF]* up

sich hinlegen *[zikh HIN-lay-gen]* to lie (down)

hinten *[HIN-ten]* behind; rear

Hinterhof, m. *[HIN-te(r)-hohf]* courtyard

hinunter *[hin-UN-te(r)]* down

Hitze, f. *[HIT-seh]* heat

hoch *[hohkh]* high

Hochzeit, f. *[HOKH-tsite]* wedding

Hoffnung, f. *[HOF-nung]* hope

höflich *[HU(R)F-likh]* polite

Höhe, f. *[HU(R)-eh]* height

Höhle, f. *[HU(R)-leh]* cave

holen *[HOH-len]* to get (obtain)

Hölle, f. *[HU(R)-leh]* hell

Holz, n. *[holts]* wood (material)

Honig, m. *[HOH-nikh]* honey

hören *[HU(R)-en]* to hear; to listen

Hörer, m. *[HU(R)-e(r)]* receiver (phone)

Hose, f. *[HOH-zeh]* pants; trousers

Hotel, n. *[ho-TEL]* hotel

Hoteljunge, m. *[ho-TEL-yun-geh]* bellboy, bellhop
hübsch *[hewpsh]* pretty
Hüfte, f. *[HEWF-teh]* hip
Hügel, m. *[HEW-gel]* hill
Huhn, n. *[hoon]* chicken
Hühnerauge, n. *[HEW-ne(r)-ow-geh]* corn (foot)
Hummer, m. *[HUM-me(r)]* lobster
Hund, m. *[hunt]* dog
hundert *[HUN-dert]* hundred
Hunger haben *[HUN-ge(r) HAA-ben]* to be hungry
Hunger, m. *[HUN-ge(r)]* hunger
Hupe, f. *[HOO-peh]* horn (car)
Husten, m. *[HOOS-ten]* cough
husten *[HOOS-ten]* to cough
Hut, m. *[hoot]* hat
Hütte, f. *[HEW-teh]* hut

I

ihr *[eer]* you
immer *[IM-me(r)]* always
in *[in]* in
inbegriffen *[IN-beh-grif-fen]* included
Infektion, f. *[in-fehk-TSYOHN]* infection
Inflation, f. *[in-flah-TSYOHN]* inflation
Ingwer, m. *[ING-vehr]* ginger
Inhalt, m. *[IN-hahlt]* contents
Insektenschutz, m. *[in-ZEHK-ten-shuts]* insect repellent
Insel, f. *[IN-zel]* island
interessant *[in-teh-reh-SAHNT]* interesting
Interesse, n. *[in-teh-REHS-seh]* interest
sich interessieren für *[zikh in-teh-rehs-SEE-ren fewr]* to be interested in
irgendetwas *[IR-gehnt EHT-vahs]* anything

irgendjemand *[IR-gehnt YAY-mahnt]* anybody, anyone
irgendwo *[IR-gehnt-voh]* somewhere
Irrtum, m. *[EER-toom]* mistake

J

ja *[yaa]* yes
Jacke, f. *[YAH-keh]* jacket
Jahr, n. *[yaar]* year
Jahreszeit, f. *[YAA-rehs-tsite]* season
Jahrhundert, n. *[YAAR-hun-dert]* century
Jahrzehnt, n. *[YAAR-tsehnt]* decade
Januar, m. *[YAH-noo-aar]* January
Japan, n. *[YAH-pahn]* Japan
jede (-r, -s) *[YAY-deh {-e(r), -ehs}]* each; every
jedenfalls *[YAY-den-fahls]* anyway
jemals *[YAY-maals]* ever
jemand *[YAY-mahnt]* someone
jene (-r, -s) *[YEH-neh, {-ne(r), -nehs}]* that
jenseits *[YEHN-zites]* beyond
jetzt *[yehtst]* now
Jod, n. *[yoht]* iodine
jüdisch *[YEW-dish]* Jewish
Jugendherberge, f. *[YOO-gehnt-hehr-behr-geh]* youth hostel
Juli, m. *[YOO-lee]* July
jung *[yung]* young
Junge, m. *[YUN-geh]* boy
Juni, m. *[YOO-nee]* June
Juwelier, m. *[yoo-veh-LEER]* jeweler

K

Kaffee, m. *[KAH-feh]* coffee
Kalbfleisch, n. *[KAHLP-flyshe]* veal

kalt *[kahlt]* cold

Kamm, m. *[kahm]* comb

Kaninchen, n. *[kah-NEEN-khen]* rabbit

kann *[kahn]* to be able; can (1st and 3rd person singular only)

Kapelle, f. *[kah-PEHL-leh]* chapel

Kappe, f. *[KAHP-peh]* cap

kaputt *[kah-PUT]* broken

Karotte, f. *[kah-ROT-teh]* carrot

Karte, f. *[KAHR-teh]* map; ticket

Kartoffel, f. *[kahr-TOF-Fel]* potato

Käse, m. *[KAY-zeh]* cheese

Kasse, f. *[KAHS-seh]* box office; cash desk

Kassettenrecorder, m. *[kah-SET-ehn-reh-kohr-dehr]* cassette player

Kassierer, (-in) m., f. *[kah-SEE-re(r), {-reh-rin}]* teller (bank)

Kastanie, f. *[kah-STAHN-yeh]* chestnut

Kater, m. *[KAA-te(r)]* hangover

Kathedrale, f. *[kah-teh-DRAAL-eh]* cathedral

katholisch *[kah-TOH-lish]* Catholic

Katze, f. *[KAHT-seh]* cat

kaufen *[KOW-fen]* to buy

Kaufhaus, n. *[KOWF-hows]* department store

Kaugummi, m. *[KOW-goom-mee]* chewing gum

kein *[kine]* none

Kekse, pl. *[KAYK-seh]* cookies

Kellner, (-in), m., f. *[KEHL-ner, KEHL-neh-rin]* waiter, waitress

kennen *[KEHN-nen]* to know; to be familiar with

Keramik, f. *[keh-RAH-mik]* pottery

Kerze, f. *[KEHRT-seh]* candle

Kette, f. *[KEHT-teh]* chain

Kiefer, m. *[KEE-fe(r)]* jaw

Kilo(gramm), n. *[KEE-loh {GRAAM}]* kilogram

Kilometer, m. *[kee-loh-MAY-te(r)]* kilometer

Kind, n. *[kint]* child

Kinderarzt, m. *[KIN-de(r)-ahrtst]* pediatrician

Kinn, n. *[kin]* chin

Kino, n. *[KEE-noh]* cinema; movie theater

Kirche, f. *[KIR-kheh]* church

Kirsche, f. *[KIR-sheh]* cherry

Klappstuhl, m. *[KLAHP-sthool]* folding chair

klar *[klahr]* clear

Klasse, f. *[KLAHS-seh]* class

klassisch, *[KLAHS-sish]* classic

Klavier, n. *[klah-VEER]* piano

Kleid, n. *[klite]* dress

Kleider, pl. *[KLYE-de(r)]* clothes

Kleiderbügel, m. *[KLYE-de(r)-bew-gel]* hanger (clothes)

klein *[kline]* little; small

Kleingeld, n. *[KLINE-gehlt]* change (money)

Klimaanlage, f. *[KLEE-mah-ahn-laa-geh]* air conditioner

klimatisiert *[klee-mah-ti-ZEERT]* air-conditioned

Klinge, f. *[KLING-eh]* blade (razor)

Klingel, f. *[KLING-el]* bell (door)

klingeln *[KLING-eln]* to ring

klopfen *[KLOP-fen]* to knock

Kloster, n. *[KLOH-ste(r)]* convent; monastery

Klub, m. *[kloop]* club

Knie, n. *[knee]* knee

Knoblauch, m. *[KNOH-blowkh]* garlic

Knöchel, m. *[KNU(R)-khel]* ankle

Knochen, m. *[KNOKH-en]* bone

Knopf, m. *[knopf]* button, knob

knusprig *[KNOOS-prikh]* crisp

kochen *[KOKH-en]* to cook

koffeinfrei *[kof-feh-EEN-frye]* decaffeinated

Koffer, m. *[KOF-fe(r)]* suitcase

Kofferraum, m. *[KOF-fe(r)-rowm]* trunk (car)

Kohl, m. *[kohl]* cabbage

Kolleg(e), (-in) m., f. *[kol-LAY-geh; -gin]* colleague

komisch *[KOH-mish]* funny

kommen *[KOM-men]* to come

Komödie, f. *[ko-MU(R)-dyeh]* comedy

Konditorei, f. *[kon-dee-to-RYE]* pastry shop

können *[KU(R)-nen]* to be able; can

könnte *[KU(R)N-teh]* could (1st and 3rd person singular only)

Konsulat, n. *[kon-zu-LAHT]* consulate

Kontaktlinsen, pl. *[kon-TAHKT-lin-zen]* contact lens

Konto, n. *[KON-toh]* account

Konzert, n. *[kon-TSEHRT]* concert

Kopf, m. *[kopf]* head

Kopfkissen, n. *[KOPF-kis-sen]* pillow

Kopfkissenbezug, m. *[KOPF-kis-sen-beh-tsook]* pillowcase

Kopfsalat, m. *[KOPF-zah-laat]* lettuce

Kopfschmerzen, pl. *[KOPF-shmehr-tsen]* headache

Korb, m. *[korp]* basket

Kordsamt, m. *[KORT-zahmt]* corduroy

Korkenzieher, m. *[KOR-ken-tsee-e(r)]* corkscrew

Körper, m. *[KU(R)R-pe(r)]* body

koscher *[KOH-she(r)]* kosher

Kosten, pl. *[KOS-ten]* costs

kosten *[KOS-ten]* to cost

köstlich *[KU(R)ST-likh]* delicious

Kotelett, n. *[kot-LEHT]* cutlet; chop

Kotflügel, m. *[KOHT-flew-gel]* fender

kräftig *[KREHF-tikh]* powerful

Kragen, m. *[KRAA-gen]* collar

Krampf, m. *[krahmpf]* cramp

krank, *[krahnk]* ill

Krankenhaus, n. *[KRAHN-ken-hows]* hospital

Krankenkasse, f. *[KRAHN-ken-kahs-seh]* health insurance

Krankenschwester, f. *[KRAHN-ken-shvehs-te(r)]* nurse

Krankenwagen, m. *[KRAHN-ken-vaa-gen]* ambulance

Krankheit, f. *[KRAHNK-hite]* disease; sickness

Kräuter, pl. *[KROY-te(r)]* herbs

Krawatte, f. *[krah-VAHT-teh]* necktie; tie

Kreditkarte, f. *[kray-DEET-kahr-teh]* credit card

Kreuz, n. *[kroyts]* cross

Kreuzung, f. *[KROY-tsung]* crossroads; intersection

Krieg, m. *[kreek]* war

Krug, m. *[krook]* pitcher

Kruste, f. *[KROOS-teh]* crust

Küche, f. *[KEW-kheh]* cuisine; kitchen

Kuchen, m. *[KOO-khen]* cake

Kugelschreiber, m. *[KOO-gel-shrye-be(r)]* pen (ball point)

kühl *[kewl]* cool

kühlen *[KEW-len]* to chill

Kühler, m. *[KEW-le(r)]* radiator (car)

Kund(e), (-in), m., f. *[KUN-deh; KUN-din]* client; customer

Kunst, f. *[kunst]* art

Künstler, m. *[KEWNST-le(r)]* artist

künstlich *[KEWNST-likh]* artificial

Kupfer, n. *[KUP-fe(r)]* copper

Kupplung, f. *[KUP-lung]* clutch (car)

Kurort, m. *[KOOR-ort]* spa

Kurve, f. *[KOOR-veh]* curve; turn

kurz *[koorts]* short

kürzlich *[KEWRTS-likh]* recently

Kusine, f. *[koo-ZEE-neh]* cousin

Kuss, m. *[kus]* kiss

küssen *[KEWS-sen]* to kiss

Küste, f. *[KEWS-teh]* coast

L

lächeln *[LEHKH-eln]* to smile

lachen *[LAHKH-en]* to laugh

Laden, m. *[LAA-den]* shop

Lammfleisch, n. *[LAHM-flyshe]* lamb

Lampe, f. *[LAHM-peh]* lamp

Land, n. *[lahnt]* country; land

landen, *[LAHN-den]* to land

Landschaft, f. *[LAHNT-shahft]* countryside

landschaftlich schöne Straße *[LAHNT-shahft-likh SHU(R)-neh SHTRAHS-eh]* scenic route

Landstraße, f. *[LAHNT-shtrahs-seh]* highway

lang *[lahng]* long

Länge, f. *[LEHNG-eh]* length

Langlaufski fahren *[LAHNG-lowf-shee-faa-ren]* cross-country skiing

langsam *[LAHNG-zahm]* slow(ly)

langsam fahren *[LAHNG-zahm FAA-ren]* to slow down

Lärm, m. *[lehrm]* noise

lassen *[LAHS-sen]* to leave (behind); to let

Lastwagen, m. *[LAHST-vaa-gen]* truck

laufen *[LOW-fen]* to run

laut *[lowt]* aloud; noisy

Lautsprecher, m. *[LOWT-sprehkh-e(r)]* speaker (stereo)

Leben, n. *[LAY-ben]* life

leben *[LAY-ben]* to live

Lebensmittelgeschäft, n. *[LAY-bens-mit-tel-geh-shehft]* grocery store

Leber, f. *[LAY-be(r)]* liver

lecken *[LEHK-en]* to leak

lecker *[LEHK-e(r)]* delicious

Leder, n. *[LAY-de(r)]* leather

ledig *[LAY-dikh]* single (unmarried)

leer *[lehr]* empty

lehren *[LEHR-en]* to teach

leicht *[lyekht]* easy; light (weight)

leider *[LYE-de(r)]* unfortunately

leihen *[LYE-en]* to lend

Leinen, n. *[LINE-en]* linen

Leiter, f. *[LYE-te(r)]* ladder

Lenkrad, n. *[LEHNK-raat]* steering wheel

lernen *[LEHR-nen]* to learn

lesen *[LAY-zen]* to read

letzte(-r, -s) *[LEHTS-teh]* last

Leute, pl. *[LOY-teh]* people

Licht, n. *[likht]* light

lieb *[leep]* dear

Liebe, f. *[LEE-beh]* love

lieben *[LEE-ben]* to love

lieber *[LEE-be(r)]* rather

Lied, n. *[leet]* song

liefern *[LEE-fern]* to deliver

Lieferung, f. *[LEE-feh-rung]* delivery

Lift, m. *[lift]* elevator

Likör, m. *[li-KUR]* liqueur

Limonade, f. *[lee-moh-NAA-deh]* lemonade

Limone, f. *[li-MOH-neh]* lime

Lineal, n. *[lee-nay-AAL]* ruler

Linie, f. *[LEEN-yeh]* line

links *[links]* left

Lippe, f. *[LIP-eh]* lip

Lippenstift, m. *[LIP-pen-shtift]* lipstick

Liste, f. *[LIS-teh]* list

Liter, m. *[LEE-te(r)]* liter

Loch, n. *[lohkh]* hole

Locke, f. *[LOK-eh]* curl

Lockenwickler, m. *[LOK-en-vik-le(r)]* curler

Löffel, m. *[LU(R)F-el]* spoon

Lotion, f. *[loh-TSYOHN]* lotion

Luft, f. *[luft]* air

Luftmatraze, f. *[LUFT-mah-trah-tseh]* air mattress

Luftpost, f. *[LUFT-post]* airmail

Lunge, f. *[LUNG-eh]* lung

Luxus, m. *[LUKS-us]* luxury

M

machen *[MAHKH-en]* to make

macht nichts *[mahkht nikhts]* never mind

Mädchen, n. *[MAYT-khen]* girl

Magen, m. *[MAA-gen]* stomach

Magenschmerzen, pl. *[MAA-gen-shmehr-tsen]* stomachache

Magenverstimmung, f. *[MAA-gen-fehr-shtim-ung]* indigestion; upset stomach

Mahlzeit, f. *[MAAL-tsite]* meal

Mai, m. *[mye]* May

Mais, m. *[mice]* corn

Mal, n. *[maal]* time

Maler, m. *[MAA-le(r)]* painter

manchmal *[MAHNCH-maal]* sometimes

Mandarine, f. *[mahn-dah-REE-neh]* tangerine

Mandel, f. *[MAHN-del]* almond

Maniküre, f. *[mah-ni-KEW-reh]* manicure

Mann, m. *[mahn]* husband; man

Mannschaft, f. *[MAHN-shahft]* team

Mantel, m. *[MAHN-tel]* coat; overcoat

Markt, m. *[mahrkt]* market

Marmelade, f. *[mahr-meh-LAA-deh]* jam

März, m. *[mehrts]* March

Maschine, f. *[mah-SHEE-neh]* machine

Massage, f. *[mah-SAA-zheh]* massage

massiv *[mah-SEEF]* solid

Matraze, f. *[mah-TRAH-tseh]* mattress

Mauer, f. *[MOW-e(r)]* wall (exterior)

Mechaniker, n. *[meh-KHAH-ni-ke(r)]* mechanic

Medikament, n. *[meh-di-kah-MEHNT]* drug; medicine

Meer, n. *[mayr]* sea

Meeresfrüchte, pl. *[MAY-rehs-frewkh-teh]* seafood

Mehl, n. *[mayl]* flour

mehr *[mehr]* more

mehrere *[MEH-reh-reh]* several

Mehrwertsteuer, f. *[MEHR-vehrt-shtoy-e(r)]* value-added tax

Melone, f. *[meh-LOH-neh]* melon

Menge, f. *[MEHNG-eh]* quantity

eine Menge *[INE-eh MEHNG-eh]* a lot

Menstruationsbeschwerden, pl. *[mehn-stru-ah-TSYOHNZ-beh-shvehr-den]* menstrual pains

Messe, f. *[MEHS-seh]* mass (church)

messen *[MEHS-sen]* to measure

Messer, n. *[MEHS-se(r)]* knife

Meter, m. *[MAY-te(r)]* meter (length)

Metzger, m. *[MEHTS-ge(r)]* butcher

Metzgerei, f. *[mehts-geh-RYE]* butcher shop

Miete, f. *[MEE-teh]* rent

mieten *[MEE-ten]* to hire (rent)

Milch, f. *[milkh]* milk

mild *[milt]* mild

Milliarde, f. *[mil-YAAR-deh]* billion

Million, f. *[mil-YOHN]* million

mindestens *[MIN-dehs-tens]* at least

Mineralwasser, n. *[mi-neh-RAAL-vahs-se(r)]* mineral water

Minute, f. *[mi-NOO-teh]* minute

Minze, f. *[MIN-tseh]* mint

mit *[mit]* with

Mittag, m. *[MIT-taak]* noon

Mittagessen, n. *[MIT-taak-ehs-en]* lunch

Mitte, f. *[MIT-teh]* middle

Mittel, n. *[MIT-tel]* means

Mitternacht, f. *[MIT-te(r)-nahkht]* midnight

Mittwoch, m. *[MIT-vokh]* Wednesday

Möbel, pl. *[MU(R)-bel]* furniture

möchten *[MU(R)KH-ten]* would like

Mode, f. *[MOH-deh]* fashion

modern *[mo-DEHRN]* modern

mögen *[MU(R)-gen]* to like

möglich *[MU(R)-glikh]* possible

Molkerei, f. *[mohl-keh-RYE]* dairy

Monat, m. *[MOH-naat]* month

Mond, m. *[mohnt]* moon

Montag, m. *[MOHN-taak]* Monday

Morgen, m. *[MOR-gen]* morning

morgen, *[MOR-gen]* tomorrow

Morgenrock, m. *[MOR-gen-rok]* dressing gown

Moschee, f. *[mo-SHAY]* mosque

Motor, m. *[moh-TOHR]* engine; motor

Motorrad, n. *[moh-TOHR-raat]* motorcycle

müde *[MEW-deh]* tired

Mund, m. *[munt]* mouth

Mundwasser, n. *[MUNT-vahs-se(r)]* mouthwash

Münze, f. *[MEWN-tseh]* coin

Muscheln, pl. *[MOO-shehln]* mussels

Museum, n. *[moo-ZAY-um]* museum

Musik, f. *[moo-ZEEK]* music

Musikkapelle, f. *[moo-ZEEK-kah-pehl-leh]* band

Muskel, m. *[MUS-kel]* muscle

müssen *[MEWS-sen]* must

Mutter, f. *[MUT-te(r)]* mother

Mütze, f. *[MEWT-seh]* cap

N

nass *[nahs]* wet

nach *[nahkh]* after; to

Nachbar, m. *[NAHKH-baar]* neighbor

Nachbarschaft, f. *[NAHKH-baar-shahft]* neighborhood

nachher *[NAHKH-hehr]* afterward

Nachmittag, m. *[NAHKH-mit-taak]* afternoon

Nachricht, f. *[NAKHK-rikht]* message

nächst *[naykhst]* next

Nacht, f. *[nahkht]* night

Nachthemd, n. *[NAHKHT-hehmt]* nightgown

Nachtisch, m. *[NAHKH-tish]* dessert

Nachtlokal, n. *[NAHKHT-loh-kaal]* nightclub

nackt *[nahkt]* naked

Nadel, f. *[NAA-del]* needle

Nagel, m. *[NAA-gel]* nail (finger)

Nagellack, m. *[NAA-gel-lahk]* nail polish

nah *[naa]* near

nahe *[NAA-eh]* close (near)

in der Nähe *[in dehr NAY-eh]* nearby

nähen *[NAY-en]* to sew

Nahverkehrszug, m. *[NAA-fehr-kehrs-tsook]* local train

Name, m. *[NAA-meh]* name

Nase, f. *[NAA-zeh]* nose

Natur, f. *[nah-TOOR]* nature

natürlich *[nah-TEWR-likh]* of course

Nebel, m. *[NAY-bel]* fog

neben *[NAY-ben]* beside

nehmen *[NAY-men]* to take

nein *[nine]* no

Nerv, m. *[nehrf]* nerve

nett *[neht]* nice; kind

Netz, n. *[nehts]* net

neu *[noy]* new

Neujahr, n. *[NOY-yaar]* New Year

neun *[noyn]* nine

neunte *[NOYN-teh]* ninth

neunzehn *[NOYN-tsayn]* nineteen

neunzig *[NOYN-tsikh]* ninety

nicht *[nikht]* not

Nichtraucher, m. *[NIKHT-row-khe(r)]* nonsmoker

nichts *[nikhts]* nothing

nie *[nee]* never

niedrig *[NEE-drikh]* low

niemand *[NEE-mahnt]* no one

Niere, f. *[NEE-reh]* kidney

noch *[nohkh]* still; yet

noch ein(-e) *[nohkh ine/INE-eh]* another

noch einmal *[nohkh INE-maal]* again

Norden, m. *[NOR-den]* north

nördlich *[NU(R)RT-likh]* north

normal *[nor-MAAL]* regular

Notausgang, m. *[NOHT-ows-gahng]* emergency exit

Notfall, m. *[NOHT-fahl]* emergency

nötig *[NU(R)-tikh]* necessary

Notizheft, n. *[no-TEETS-hehft]* notebook

November, m. *[no-VEHM-be(r)]* November

nüchtern *[NEWKH-tern]* sober

Nudeln, pl. *[NOO-deln]* noodles

null *[nul]* zero

Nummer, f. *[NUM-me(r)]* number

nur *[noor]* just (only); only

Nuss, f. *[noos]* nut

nützlich *[NEWTS-likh]* useful

O

ob *[op]* if

oben *[OH-ben]* above; up

obere *[OH-beh-reh]* upper

Oberkellner, m. *[OH-be(r)-kehl-ne(r)]* headwaiter

Oberschule, f. *[OH-be(r)-shoo-leh]* high school

Objektiv, n. *[op-yehk-TEEF]* camera lens

Obst, n. *[opst]* fruit

oder *[OH-de(r)]* or

Ofen m. *[OH-fen]* oven

offen *[OF-fen]* open

255

öffentlich *[U(R)F-ehnt-likh]* public

öffnen *[U(R)F-nen]* to open

oft *[oft]* often

ohne *[OH-neh]* without

Ohr, n. *[ohr]* ear

Ohrenschmerzen, pl. *[OH-ren-shmehr-tsen]* earache

Ohrring, m. *[OHR-ring]* earring

okay, *[o-kay]* okay

Oktober, m. *[ok-TOH-be(r)]* October

Öl, n. *[u(r)l]* oil

Olive, f. *[o-LEE-veh]* olive

Omelett, n. *[om-LEHT]* omelet

Onkel, m. *[OHN-kel]* uncle

Oper, f. *[OH-pe(r)]* opera

Operation, f. *[o-peh-rah-TSYOHN]* operation

Optiker, m. *[OP-tik-e(r)]* optician

Orange, f. *[oh-RAHN-zheh]* orange

Orangensaft, m. *[oh-RAHN-zhen-sahft]* orange juice

Orchester, n. *[or-KEHS-te(r)]* orchestra

Ordnung, f. *[ORT-nung]* order

Ort, m. *[ort]* place

Ortsgespräch, n. *[ORTS-geh-spraykh]* local phone call

Osten, m. *[OS-ten]* east

Ostern, pl. *[OS-tern]* Easter

Österreich, n. *[U(R)S-teh-ryekh]* Austria

Österreicher(-in), m. (f.) *[U(R)S-teh-ryekh-e(r)/eh-rin]* Austrian

österreichisch *[U(R)S-teh-rye-khish]* Austrian

Ozean, m. *[OH-tsay-ahn]* ocean

P

Paar, n. *[paar]* pair

packen *[PAH-ken]* to pack

Paket, n. *[pah-KAYT]* package; parcel

Palast, m. *[pah-LAHST]* palace

Pampelmuse, f. *[pahm-pehl-MOO-zeh]* grapefruit

Panne, f. *[PAHN-neh]* breakdown

Papier, n. *[pah-PEER]* paper

Papiertuch, n. *[pah-PEER-tookh]* tissue

Parfüm, n. *[pahr-FEWM]* perfume

Park, m. *[pahrk]* park

Parken verboten *[PAHR-ken fehr-BOH-ten]* parking prohibited

parken *[PAHR-ken]* to park

Parkplatz, m. *[PAHRK-plahts]* parking lot

Parkscheibe, f. *[PAHRK-shye-beh]* parking disk

Parkuhr, f. *[PAHRK-oor]* parking meter

Party, f. *[PAHR-tee]* party (celebration)

Pass, m. *[pahs]* mountain pass

passen *[PAHS-sen]* to fit

Pelze, pl. *[PEHL-tseh]* furs

Pension, f. *[pehn-ZYOHN]* boardinghouse

perfekt *[pehr-FEHKT]* perfect

Periode, f. *[peh-ree-OH-deh]* period (menstrual)

Person, f. *[pehr-ZOHN]* person

persönlich *[pehr-ZU(R)N-likh]* personal

Petersilie, f. *[pay-te(r)-ZEEL-yeh]* parsley

Pfad, m. *[pfaat]* path

Pfannkuchen, m. *[PFAHN-koo-khen]* pancake

Pfarrer, m. *[PFAHR-e(r)]* minister (clergyman)

Pfeffer, m. *[PFEHF-fe(r)]* pepper

Pfeife, f. *[PFIFE-eh]* pipe

Pfeifentabak, m. *[PFIFE-en-tah-bahk]* pipe tobacco

Pferd, n. *[pfehrt]* horse

Pfirsich, m. *[PFIR-zikh]* peach

Pflaume, f. *[PFLOW-meh]* plum

Picknick, n. *[PIK-nik]* picnic

Pier, m. *[peer]* pier

Pille, f. *[PIL-eh]* pill

Pilot, m. *[pee-LOHT]* pilot

Pilz, m. *[pilts]* mushroom

Piste, f. *[PIS-teh]* runway (plane)

Plan, m. *[plaan]* map; plan

planen, *[PLAA-nen]* to plan

Planetarium, n. *[plah-neh-TAH-ree-oom]* planetarium

Platz, m. *[plahts]* place; seat; square (town)

Plombe, f. *[PLOM-beh]* filling (tooth)

plötzlich *[PLU(R)TS-likh]* suddenly

Polen, n. *[POH-len]* Poland

polieren *[po-LEE-ren]* to shine (shoes); to polish

Polizei, f. *[po-lee-TSYE]* police

Polizeiwache, f. *[po-lee-TSYE-vahkh-eh]* police station

Polizist, m. *[po-lee-TSIST]* policeman

Portier, m. *[por-TYAY]* doorman

Portion, f. *[por-TSYOHN]* portion

Porto, n. *[POR-toh]* postage

Post, f. *[post]* mail

Postamt, n. *[POST-ahmt]* post office

Postanweisung, f. *[POST-ahn-vye-zung]* money order

Postfach, n. *[POST-fahkh]* post office box

Postkarte, f. *[POST-kahr-teh]* postcard

postlagernd *[POST-laa-gehrnt]* general delivery

Postleitzahl, f. *[POST-lite-tsaal]* zip code

praktisch *[PRAHK-tish]* practical

Preis, m. *[price]* price

Preiselbeere, f. *[PRICE-ehl-bay-reh]* cranberry

Preisskala, f. *[PRICE-skah-lah]* price range

preiswert *[PRICE-vehrt]* inexpensive

Presse, f. *[PREHS-seh]* press (media)

Priester, m. *[PREES-te(r)]* priest

privat *[pri-VAAT]* private

Privatunterricht, m. *[pri-VAAT-un-teh-rikht]* private lessons

probieren *[pro-BEER-en]* to try

Programm, n. *[proh-GRAAM]* program

provisorisch *[pro-vee-ZOH-rish]* temporary

Puder, m. *[POO-de(r)]* powder

Pullover, m. *[pul-LOH-ve(r)]* sweater

Pulver, n. *[PUL-ve(r)]* powder

Pumpe, f. *[PUM-peh]* pump

pünktlich *[PEWNK-likh]* on time

Puppe, f. *[PUP-peh]* doll

putzen *[PUT-sen]* to shine

Pyjama, m. *[pi-JAA-maa]* pajamas

Q

Quadrat, n. *[kvah-DRAHT]* square (geometric)

Qualität, f. *[kvah-li-TAYT]* quality

Quelle, f. *[KVEHL-leh]* spring (of water)

Quetschung, f. *[KVEHT-khung]* bruise

Quiche, f. *[keesh]* quiche

Quittung, f. *[KVIT-tung]* receipt

R

R-Gespräch, n. *[EHR-geh-shpraykh]* collect call

Rabatt, m. *[raa-BAHT]* discount

Rabbiner, m. *[rah-BEE-ne(r)]* rabbi

Rad, n. *[raat]* wheel

Rad fahren, n. *[RAAT-faa-ren]* cycling

Radiergummi, m. *[rah-DEER-goom-mee]* rubber eraser

Radieschen, n. *[raa-DEES-khen]* radish

Radio, n. *[RAA-dee-oh]* radio

Rahmen, m. *[RAA-men]* frame

Rasen, m. *[RAA-zen]* lawn

Rasierapparat, m. *[rah-ZEER-ah-pah-raat]* shaver

Rasiercreme, f. *[rah-ZEER-kraym]* shaving cream

rasieren *[rah-ZEE-ren]* to shave

Rasierklinge, f. *[rah-ZEER-kling-eh]* razor blade

Rasierwasser, n. *[rah-ZEER-vahs-se(r)]* aftershave lotion

Rathaus, n. *[RAAT-hows]* city hall; town hall

Raub, m. *[rowp]* robbery

rauchen *[ROWKH-en]* to smoke

Raucherabteil *[ROWKH-e(r)-ahp-tile]* smoking section

Rechnung, f. *[REHKH-nung]* bill (restaurant); check

Recht haben *[rehkht HAA-ben]* to be right

rechts *[rehkhts]* right (direction)

Rechtsanwalt, m. *[REHKHTS-ahn-vahlt]* attorney; lawyer

rechtshändig *[REHKHTS-hehn-dikh]* right-handed

reden *[RAY-den]* to talk

Reformhaus, n. *[reh-FORM-hows]* health food store

Regal, n. *[ray-GAAL]* shelf

Regel, f. *[RAY-gel]* rule

regelmäßig *[RAY-gel-mays-ikh]* regular

Regen, m. *[RAY-gen]* rain

Regenmantel, m. *[RAY-gen-mahn-tel]* raincoat

Regenschirm, m. *[RAY-gen-shirm]* umbrella

reich *[ryekh]* rich

Reifen, m. *[RYE-fen]* tire (car)

Reifenpanne, f. *[RYE-fen-pahn-neh]* flat tire; puncture

Reihe, f. *[RYE-eh]* row (theater)

reinigen *[RYE-ni-gen]* to clean

Reinigung, f. *[RYE-ni-gung]* dry cleaner

Reis, m. *[rice]* rice

Reise, f. *[RYE-zeh]* trip

Reisebüro, n. *[RYE-zeh-bew-roh]* travel agency

Reiseführer, m. *[RYE-zeh-few-re(r)]* guidebook

Reisekrankheit, f. *[RYE-zeh-krahnk-hite]* motion sickness

reisen *[RYE-zen]* to travel

(Reise-)Pass, m. *[{RYE-zeh-}pahs]* passport

Reisescheck, m. *[RYE-zeh-shehk]* traveler's check

reißen *[RICE-sen]* to tear

Reißverschluss, m. *[RICE-fehr-shlus]* zipper

reiten *[RYE-ten]* to ride (a horse)

Reklamation, f. *[reh-klah-mah-TSIOHN]* complaint

Religion, f. *[ray-li-GYOHN]* religion

Rennbahn, f. *[REHN-baan]* racetrack

Reparatur, f. *[reh-pah-rah-TOOR]* repair

reparieren, *[reh-pah-REE-ren]* to fix; to repair

reservieren lassen *[reh-zehr-VEER-en LAHS-sen]* to book; to reserve

Reservierung, f. *[reh-zehr-VEE-rung]* reservation

Restaurant, n. *[rehs-to-RAHNT]* restaurant

retten *[REHT-ten]* to save (person)

Rettungsschwimmer, m. *[REH-tungs-shvim-me(r)]* lifeguard

Rezept, n. *[reh-TZEHPT]* prescription

richtig *[RIKH-tikh]* right (correct)

Richtung, f. *[RIKH-tung]* direction

Riemen, m. *[REE-men]* strap

Rindfleisch, n. *[RINT-flyshe]* beef

Ring, m. *[ring]* ring

Rippe, f. *[RIP-peh]* rib

Risiko, n. *[REE-zee-koh]* risk

Rock, m. *[rok]* skirt

Roggenbrot, n. *[ROG-gen-broht]* rye bread

roh *[roh]* raw

Rolle, f. *[ROL-leh]* role (stage)

rollen, *[ROL-len]* to roll

Rolltreppe, f. *[ROL-trehp-peh]* escalator

Roman, m. *[roh-MAAN]* novel

Röntgenaufname, f. *[RU(R)NT-gen-owf-naa-meh]* X ray

rosa *[ROH-zah]* pink

Rose, f. *[ROH-zeh]* rose

Rosé, m. *[roh-ZAY]* rosé wine

Rosinen, pl. *[roh-ZEE-nen]* raisins

rot *[roht]* red

Rouge, n. *[roozh]* rouge

Rücken, m. *[REWK-en]* back (body part)

Rückenschmerzen, pl. *[REWK-en-shmehr-tsen]* backache

Rückerstattung, f. *[REWK-ehr-shtah-tung]* refund

Rückfahrkarte, f. *[REWK-faar-kahr-teh]* round-trip ticket

Ruderboot, n. *[ROO-de(r)-boht]* rowboat

Ruhe, f. *[ROO-eh]* rest

Ruhestand, m. *[ROO-eh-shtahnt]* retirement

ruhig *[ROO-ikh]* calm; quiet

Rühreier, pl. *[REW-eye-e(r)]* scrambled eggs

Ruinen, pl. *[roo-EE-nen]* ruins

rund *[runt]* round

Rundfahrt, f. *[RUNT-faart]* (bus) tour

rutschig *[RUT-shikh]* slippery

S

Sache, f. *[ZAHKH-eh]* thing

Sackgasse, f. *[ZAHK-gaas-seh]* dead end

Saft, m. *[zahft]* juice

sagen *[ZAA-gen]* to say

Sahne, f. *[ZAA-neh]* cream

Salat, m. *[zah-LAAT]* salad

Salz, n. *[zahlts]* salt

salzig *[ZAHL-tsikh]* salty

sammeln *[ZAHM-eln]* to collect

Samstag, m. *[ZAHMS-taak]* Saturday

Samt, m. *[zahmt]* velvet

Sand, m. *[zahnt]* sand

Sandwich, n. *[SAHNT-vitch]* sandwich

Satz, m. *[zahts]* sentence (grammar)

sauber *[ZOW-be(r)]* clean

sauer *[ZOW-e(r)]* sour

Säuglingsnahrung, f. *[SOYK-lings-naa-rung]* baby food

Säure, f. *[ZOY-reh]* acid

Schachtel, f. *[SHAHKH-tel]* box

schade! *[SHAA-deh]* too bad!

wie Schade! *[vee SHAA-deh]* what a pity!

schädlich *[SHAYT-likh]* harmful

Schaf, n. *[shahf]* sheep

Schal, m. *[shahl]* scarf

Schale, f. *[SHAH-leh]* shell

Schalter, m. *[SHAHL-te(r)]* switch

Schatten, m. *[SHAHT-ten]* shade, shadow

Schatz, m. *[shahts]* treasure

schätzen *[SHEHTS-en]* to estimate

Schaufenster, n. *[SHOW-fehn-ste(r)]* show window

Schaumwein, m. *[SHOWM-vine]* sparkling wine

Scheck, m. *[shehk]* check

Scheckbuch, n. *[SHEHK-bookh]* checkbook

Scheibe, f. *[SHYE-beh]* slice

Schein, m. *[shine]* banknote

scheinen *[SHINE-en]* to seem

Scheinwerfer, m. *[SHINE-vehr-fe(r)]* headlight

Schenkel, m. *[SHEHN-kel]* thigh

Schere, f. *[SHAY-reh]* scissors

scheußlich *[SHOYS-likh]* awful

schicken *[SHIK-en]* to send

schieben *[SHEE-ben]* to push (a car)

Schiff, n. *[shif]* ship

Schild, n. *[shilt]* sign

Schinken, m. *[SHIN-ken]* ham

schlafen *[SHLAH-fen]* to sleep

Schlafsack, m. *[SHLAHF-zahk]* sleeping bag

Schlafwagen, m. *[SHLAHF-vaa-gen]* sleeping car

Schlafzimmer, n. *[SHLAHF-tsim-me(r)]* bedroom

schlagen *[SHLAA-gen]* to hit

Schlange, f. *[SHLAHNG-eh]* line (of people); snake

Schlange stehen *[SHLAHNG-eh shtay-en]* to stand in line

schlecht *[shlehkht]* bad

schlechter *[SHLEHKH-te(r)]* worse

schließen *[SHLEES-sen]* to close; to shut

Schließfach, n. *[SHLEES-fahkh]* baggage locker

Schloss, n. *[shlos]* castle; palace

schlucken *[SHLUK-en]* swallow

Schlüpfer, m. *[SHLEWP-fer]* panties

Schlüssel, m. *[SHLEWS-sel]* key

schmackhaft *[SHMAHK-hahft]* tasty

schmecken *[SHMEHK-en]* to taste

Schmerz, m. *[shmehrts]* ache; pain

schmerzen *[SHMEHR-tsen]* to hurt

Schmuck, m. *[shmuk]* jewelry

schmutzig *[SHMUT-tsikh]* dirty

Schnalle, f. *[SHNAHL-leh]* buckle

Schnecke, f. *[SHNEH-keh]* snail

Schnee, m. *[shnay]* snow

schneiden *[SHNYE-den]* to cut

Schneider, m. *[SHNYE-de(r)]* tailor

schneien *[SHNYE-en]* to snow

schnell *[shnehl]* fast; quick(ly)

Schnellimbiss, m. *[SHNEHL-im-bis]* snack bar

Schnellzug, m. *[SHNEHL-tsook]* express train

Schnittwunde, f. *[SHNIT-vun-deh]* cut (wound)

Schnur, f. *[shnoor]* string

Schnurrbart, m. *[SHNOOR-bahrt]* mustache

Schnürsenkel, pl. *[SHNEWR-zehn-kel]* shoelaces

Schokolade, f. *[sho-ko-LAA-deh]* chocolate

schon *[shon]* already

schön *[shu(r)n]* attractive; beautiful

Schönheitssalon, m. *[SHU(R)N-hite-zah-lohng]* beauty salon

Schrank, m. *[shrahnk]* closet

Schraubenzieher, m. *[SHROW-ben-tsee-e(r)]* screwdriver

schrecklich *[SHREHK-likh]* awful

schreiben *[SHRYE-ben]* to write

Schreibmaschine, f. *[SHRIPE-mah-shee-neh]* typewriter

Schreibtisch, m. *[SHRIPE-tish]* desk

Schreibwaren, pl. *[SHRIPE-vaa-ren]* stationery

Schriftsteller, m. *[SHRIFT-shtehl-le(r)]* writer

Schublade, f. *[SHOOP-laa-deh]* drawer

Schuh, m. *[shoo]* shoe

Schuld, f. *[shoolt]* debt

schulden *[SHOOL-den]* to owe

Schule, f. *[SHOO-leh]* school

Schulter, f. *[SHOOL-te(r)]* shoulder

schwach *[shvahkh]* weak

Schwager, m. *[SHVAA-ge(r)]* brother-in-law

Schwägerin, f. *[SHVAY-geh-rin]* sister-in-law

Schwamm, m. *[shvahm]* sponge

schwanger *[SHVAHNG-e(r)]* pregnant

schwarz *[shvahrts]* black

Schwein, n. *[shvine]* pig

Schweinefleisch, n. *[SHVINE-eh-flyshe]* pork

Schweiz, f. *[dee shvites]* Switzerland

schweizerisch *[SHVYE-tseh-rish]* Swiss

schwer *[shvehr]* difficult; hard (difficult); heavy

Schwester, f. *[SHVEHS-te(r)]* sister

Schwiegermutter, f. *[SHVEE-ge(r)-MUT-te(r)]* mother-in-law

Schwiegervater, m. *[SHVEE-ge(r)-faa-te(r)]* father-in-law

Schwierigkeit, f. *[SHVEE-rikh-kite]* difficulty

Schwimmbad, n. *[SHVIM-baat]* swimming pool

schwimmen *[SHVIM-men]* to swim

schwindlig *[SHVINT-likh]* dizzy

sechs *[zehks]* six

sechzehn *[ZEHKH-tsayn]* sixteen

sechzig *[ZEHKH-tsikh]* sixty

See, m. *[zay]* lake

seekrank *[ZAY-krahnk]* seasick

sehen *[ZAY-en]* to see

Sehenswürdigkeit, f. *[ZAY-ens-vewr-dikh-kite]* attraction (sightseeing)

sehr *[zehr]* very

Seide, f. *[ZYE-deh]* silk

Seife, f. *[ZYE-feh]* soap

Seil, n. *[zile]* rope

sein *[zine]* to be

seit *[zite]* since

Seite, f. *[ZITE-eh]* side; page

Sekretär(in), m., f. *[zeh-kreh-TAYR {-in}]* secretary

Sekunde, f. *[zeh-KOON-deh]* second (time)

selbe *[ZEHL-beh]* same

selbst *[zehlpst]* even; myself

Sellerie, m. *[ZEHL-eh-ree]* celery

selten *[ZEHL-ten]* rare

seltsam *[ZEHLT-zahm]* strange

senden *[ZEHN-den]* to send

Senf, m. *[zehnf]* mustard

Seniorenpass, m. *[zehn-YOR-en-pahs]* senior citizen's pass

senkrecht *[ZEHNK-rehkht]* vertical

September, m. *[zehp-TEHM-be(r)]* September

servieren *[zehr-VEE-ren]* to serve

Serviette, f. *[sehr-VYEHT-teh]* napkin

Sessel, m. *[ZEHS-sel]* armchair

sich setzen *[zikh ZEHT-sen]* to sit down

Shampoo, n. *[shahm-POO]* shampoo

sicher *[ZIKH-e(r)]* certain; certainly; safe; sure

Sicherheitsnadel, f. *[ZIKH-e(r)-hites-naa-del]* safety pin

Sicherheitsgurt, m. *[ZIKH-e(r)-hites-gurt]* seat belt

Sie *[zee]* you

sie *[zee]* she; they

sieben *[ZEE-ben]* seven

siebte *[ZEEP-teh]* seventh

siebzehn *[ZEEP-tsayn]* seventeen

siebzig *[ZEEP-tsikh]* seventy

Silber, n. *[ZIL-be(r)]* silver

singen *[ZING-en]* to sing

Sirup, m. *[ZEE-rup]* syrup (cough)

Ski, m. *[shee]* ski

Skiausrüstung, f. *[SHEE-ows-rews-tung]* ski equipment

Ski fahren *[SHEE faa-ren]* skiing

Skilift, m. *[SHEE-lift]* ski lift

Skulptur, f. *[skulp-TOOR]* sculpture

Slowakei, f. *[sloh-vah-KYE]* Slovakia

Smoking, m. *[SMOH-king]* tuxedo

Socken, pl. *[ZOK-en]* socks

Sofa, n. *[ZOH-fah]* sofa

sofort *[zoh-FORT]* at once; immediately

Sohle, f. *[ZOH-leh]* sole (shoe)

Sohn, m. *[zohn]* son

Sommer, m. *[ZOM-me(r)]* summer

Sonderangebot, n. *[ZON-de(r)-ahn-geh-boht]* bargain

Sonnabend, m. *[ZON-aa-behnt]* Saturday

Sonne, f. *[ZON-neh]* sun

Sonnenbrille, f. *[ZON-nen-bril-leh]* sunglasses

Sonnenöl, n. *[ZON-nen-u(r)]* suntan lotion

sonnig *[ZON-ikh]* sunny

Sonntag, m. *[ZON-taak]* Sunday

sonst *[zonst]* otherwise

Sorge, f. *[ZOR-geh]* worry

sorgfältig *[ZORK-fehl-tikh]* careful

Sorte, f. *[ZOR-teh]* type (sort)

Soße, f. *[ZOH-zeh]* sauce

sparen *[SHPAA-ren]* to save (money)

Spargel, m. *[SHPAHR-gel]* asparagus

Spaß haben *[shpahs HAA-ben]* to have fun

spät *[shpayt]* late

Spaziergang, m. *[shpah-TSEER-gahng]* walk

Speck, m. *[shpehk]* bacon

Speisekarte, f. *[SHPYE-zeh-kahr-teh]* menu

Speisesaal, m. *[SHPYE-zeh-zaal]* dining room

Speisewagen, m. *[SHPYE-zeh-vaa-gen]* dining car

Spesen, pl. *[SHPAY-zen]* expenses

Spezialität, f. *[shpeh-tsee-ah-lee-TAYT]* specialty

Spiegel, m. *[SHPEE-gel]* mirror

Spiel, n. *[shpeel]* game

spielen *[SHPEE-len]* to gamble; to play

Spielkarten, pl. *[SHPEEL-kahr-ten]* playing cards

Spielplatz, m. *[SHPEEL-plahts]* playground

Spielwarenladen, m. *[SHPEEL-vaa-ren-laa-den]* toy shop

Spielzeug, n. *[SHPEEL-tsoyk]* toy

Spinat, m. *[shpi-NAAT]* spinach

Spitze, f. *[SHPIT-seh]* lace; top

Sprache, f. *[SHPRAHKH-eh]* language

sprechen *[SHPREHKH-en]* to speak

Spritze, f. *[SHPRIT-seh]* injection

spülen *[SHPEW-len]* to rinse

Staat, m. *[shtaat]* state

Staatsangehörigkeit, f. *[SHTAATS-ahn-geh-hu(r)-rikh-kite]* nationality

Stadion, n. *[SHTAA-dyohn]* stadium

Stadt, f. *[shtaht]* city; town

Stahl, m. *[shtahl]* steel

stark *[shtahrk]* strong

Stärke, f. *[SHTEHR-keh]* starch (laundry)

statt *[shtaht]* instead of

Statue, f. *[SHTAH-too-eh]* statue

Stau, m. *[shtow]* traffic jam

Staub, m. *[shtowp]* dust

Steak, n. *[shtayk]* steak

Steckdose, f. *[SHTEHK-doh-zeh]* electrical outlet

Stecknadel, f. *[SHTEHK-naa-del]* pin

stehen *[SHTAY-en]* to stand

stehenbleiben *[SHTAY-en-blye-ben]* to stop

stehlen *[SHTEH-len]* to steal

steigen *[SHTYE-gen]* climb

Stein, m. *[shtine]* stone

Stelle, f. *[SHTEHL-leh]* job (employment); site

stellen *[SHTEHL-len]* to place; to put

Stern, m. *[shtehrn]* star

steuerfrei *[SHTOY-e(r)-frye]* tax-free

Stewardess, f. *[SHTOO-ahr-dehs]* stewardess flight attendant

Stiefel, pl. *[SHTEE-fel]* boots

Stil, m. *[shteel]* style (fashion)

Stimme, f. *[SHTIM-meh]* voice

Stirn, f. *[shtirn]* forehead

Stock, m. *[shtok]* floor; stick (pole)

Stoff, m. *[shtof]* cloth; material

stören *[SHTU(R)-en]* to disturb

stoßen *[SHTOHS-en]* to bump

Stoßstange, f. *[SHTOHS-shtahng-eh]* bumper (car)

Stoßzeit, f. *[SHTOHS-tsite]* rush hour

Strand, m. *[shtrahnt]* beach

Straße, f. *[SHTRAHS-seh]* street

Straßenbahn, f. *[SHTRAHS-sen-baan]* streetcar

Straßenkarte, f. *[SHTRAHS-sen-kahr-teh]* road map

Streichholz, n. *[SHTRYEKH-hohlts]* match

Streifen, m. *[SHTRIFE-en]* stripe

Stroh, n. *[shtroh]* straw

Stromspannung, f. *[SHTROHM-shpahn-nung]* voltage

Strumpf, m. *[shtrumpf]* stocking

Strumpfhose, f. *[SHTRUMPF-hoh-zeh]* panty hose; tights

Stück, n. *[shtewk]* piece; play (stage)

Student, m. *[shtoo-DEHNT]* student

studieren *[shtoo-DEE-ren]* to study

Stuhl, m. *[shtool]* chair

Stunde, f. *[SHTUN-deh]* hour

Sturm, m. *[shtoorm]* storm

suchen *[ZOO-khen]* to look for

Süden, m. *[ZEW-den]* south

Summe, f. *[ZOOM-meh]* sum

Supermarkt, m. *[ZOO-pe(r)-mahrkt]* supermarket

Suppe, f. *[ZOOP-peh]* soup

süß *[zews]* sweet

Symptom, n. *[zewmp-TOHM]* symptom

Synagoge, f. *[zew-nah-GOH-geh]* synagogue

System, n. *[zews-TAYM]* system

T

Tabak, m. *[TAH-bahk]* tobacco

Tabakladen, m. *[tah-BAHK-laa-den]* tobacco shop

Tag, m. *[taak]* day

Tageszeitung, f. *[TAA-gehs-tsite-ung]* daily newspaper

täglich *[TAYG-likh]* daily

Tal, n. *[taal]* valley

Tankstelle, f. *[TAHNK-shteh-leh]* gas station

Tante, f. *[TAHN-teh]* aunt

Tanz, m. *[tahnts]* dance

tanzen *[TAHN-tsen]* to dance

Tarif, m. *[tah-REEF]* rate

Tasche, f. *[TAHSH-eh]* bag; pocket

Taschenlampe, f. *[TAHSH-en-lahm-peh]* flashlight

Taschenmesser, n. *[TAHSH-en-mehs-se(r)]* penknife

Taschentuch, n. *[TAHSH-en-took]* handkerchief

Tasse, f. *[TAHS-seh]* cup

taub *[towp]* deaf

Taube, f. *[TOW-beh]* pigeon

tausend *[TOW-zehnt]* thousand

Taxi, n. *[TAHK-see]* cab; taxi

Tee, m. *[tay]* tea

Teelöffel, m. *[TAY-lu(r)-fel]* teaspoon

Teich, m. *[tyekh]* pond

Teigwaren, pl. *[TIKE-vaa-ren]* pasta

Teil, m. *[tile]* part

teilen *[TILE-en]* to share

Telefon, n. *[tay-lay-FON]* telephone

Telefonbuch, n. *[tay-lay-FON-bookh]* telephone directory

Telefonzelle, f. *[tay-lay-FON-tsehl-leh]* telephone booth

Telegramm, n. *[tay-lay-GRAAM]* cable; telegram

Telex schicken *[TAY-lehks SHIK-en]* to telex

Teller, m. *[TEHL-le(r)]* plate

Tempel, m. *[TEHM-pel]* temple

Teppich, m. *[TEHP-pikh]* carpet; rug

teuer *[TOY-e(r)]* expensive

Teufel, m. *[TOY-fel]* devil

Theater, n. *[tay-AA-te(r)]* theater

Thermometer, n. *[tehr-mo-MAY-te(r)]* thermometer

tief *[teef]* deep

Tier, n. *[teer]* animal

Tierarzt, m. *[TEER-ahrtst]* veterinarian

Tierpark, m. *[TEER-pahrk]* zoo

Tinte, f. *[TIN-teh]* ink

Tisch, m. *[tish]* table

Tischdecke, f. *[TISH-deh-keh]* tablecloth

Toast, m. *[tohst]* toast

Tochter, f. *[TOKH-te(r)]* daughter

Tod, m. *[toht]* death

Toilette, f. *[toy-LEHT-teh]* rest room; toilet

Toilettenpapier, n. *[toy-LEHT-ten-pah-peer]* toilet paper

Tollwut, f. *[TOL-voot]* rabies

Tomate, f. *[toh-MAH-teh]* tomato

Torte, f. *[TOR-teh]* pie

tot *[toht]* dead

Tourismus, m. *[too-RIS-moos]* tourism

Tourist, m. *[too-RIST]* tourist

tragen *[TRAA-gen]* to carry; to wear

traurig *[TROW-rikh]* sad

treffen *[TREHF-fen]* to meet

trennen *[TREHN-nen]* to part (separate)

Treppe, f. *[TREHP-peh]* stairs

Treppenhaus, n. *[TREHP-pen-hows]* staircase

trinken *[TRIN-ken]* to drink

Trinkgeld, n. *[TRINK-gehlt]* tip

Trinkwasser, n. *[TRINK-vahs-se(r)]* drinking water

trocken *[TROK-en]* dry

Tropfen, pl. *[TROP-fen]* drops

trotz *[trots]* despite

Truthahn, m. *[TROOT-haan]* turkey

Tschechische Republik, f. *[CHEH-kheesheh ree-poo-BLEEK]* Czech Republic

Tube, f. *[TOO-beh]* tube

Tuch, n. *[tookh]* shawl

tun *[toon]* to do

Tür, f. *[tewr]* door

Turm, m. *[toorm]* tower

Tüte, f. *[TEW-teh]* bag

typisch *[TEW-pish]* typical

U

U-bahnstation, f. *[OO-baan-shtah-tsyohn]* subway station

Übelkeit, f. *[EW-bel-kite]* nausea

üben *[EW-ben]* to practice

über *[EW-be(r)]* across (movement); over (above); via

überall *[EW-be(r)-ahl]* everywhere

Überdosis, f. *[EW-be(r)-doh-zis]* overdose

übergeben *[ew-be(r)-GAY-ben]* to present

überholen *[EW-be(r)-hoh-len]* to pass (car)

überlaufen *[ew-be(r)-LOW-fen]* overrun

übermorgen *[EW-be(r)-mor-gen]* day after tomorrow

übernachten *[EW-be(r)-nahkh-ten]* to stay (lodge)

Übernachtung mit Frühstück *[ew-be(r)-NAHKH-tung mit FREW-shtewk]* bed-and-breakfast

überprüfen *[EW-be(r)-PREW-fen]* to check

überqueren *[ew-be(r)-KVAY-ren]* to cross

übersetzen *[ew-be(r)-ZEHT-sen]* to translate

Überstunden, pl. *[EW-be(r)-shtun-den]* overtime

überweisen *[ew-be(r)-VYE-zen]* to transfer

überzeugen *[ew-be(r)-TSOY-gen]* to persuade

Uhr, f. *[oor]* clock; watch

Uhrmacher, m. *[OOR-mahkh-e(r)]* watchmaker

um *[um]* around

umgekehrt *[OOM-geh-kehrt]* vice versa

Umleitung, f. *[OOM-lite-ung]* detour (traffic)

Umschlag, m. *[OOM-shlahk]* envelope

umsteigen *[OOM-shtye-gen]* to change (bus, train)

Umwelt, f. *[OOM-vehlt]* environment

umziehen *[OOM-tsee-en]* move (to change residence)

unbedingt *[UN-beh-dinkt]* absolutely

unbequem *[UN-beh-kvaym]* uncomfortable

und *[unt]* and

Unfall, m. *[UN-fahl]* accident

Ungarn, n. *[UN-gahrn]* Hungary

ungefähr *[UN-geh-fayr]* about; approximately

ungerade *[UN-geh-raa-deh]* odd (number)

unglücklich *[UN-glewk-likh]* unhappy

Universität, f. *[oo-nee-vehr-zi-TAYT]* university

unmöglich *[un-MU(R)-glikh]* impossible

Unordnung, f. *[UN-ort-nung]* mess

unten *[UN-ten]* below

unter *[UN-te(r)]* among; under

Untergeschoß, n. *[UN-te(r)-geh-shos]* basement

Untergrundbahn, f. *[UN-te(r)-grunt-baan]* subway

unterhalten *[un-te(r)-HAHL-ten]* to amuse

Unterhemd, n. *[UN-te(r)-hehmt]* undershirt

Unterhose, f. *[UN-te(r)-hoh-zeh]* underpants

Unterkunft, f. *[UN-te(r)-kunft]* accommodation

Unterrock, m. *[UN-te(r)-rok]* slip

unterschreiben *[un-te(r)-SHRYE-ben]* to sign

Untertasse, f. *[UN-te(r)-tahs-seh]* saucer

Unterwäsche, f. *[UN-te(r)-veh-sheh]* underwear

unzufrieden *[UN-tsoo-free-den]* dissatisfied

Urlaub, m. *[OOR-lowp]* vacation

V

Vater, m. *[FAA-te(r)]* father

vegetarisch *[veh-geh-TAH-rish]* vegetarian

Ventilator, m. *[vehn-ti-LAA-tor]* fan

Verabredung, f. *[fehr-AHP-ray-dung]* appointment

Verantwortung, f. *[fehr-AHNT-vor-tung]* responsibility

Verband, m. *[fehr-BAHNT]* bandage

Verbandkasten, m. *[fehr-BAHNT-kahs-ten]* first aid kit

verbieten *[fehr-BEE-ten]* to prohibit

verboten *[fehr-BOH-ten]* forbidden

Verbrechen, n. *[fehr-BREHKH-en]* crime

verbringen *[fehr-BRIN-gen]* to spend (time)

verdienen *[fehr-DEE-nen]* to earn

Vereinigte Königreich, n. *[fehr-EYE-nikh-teh KU(R)-nikh-ryekh]* United Kingdom

Vereinigten Staaten (von Amerika), f. *[fehr-EYE-nikh-ten SHTAA-ten {fon ah-MEH-ri-kah}]* United States

Vergangenheit, f. *[fehr-GAHNG-en-hite]* past

Vergaser, m. *[fehr-GAA-ze(r)]* carburetor

vergessen *[fehr-GEHS-sen]* to forget

vergleichen *[vehr-GLYE-khen]* to compare

Vergnügen, n. *[fehrk-NEW-gen]* pleasure

vergnügen *[fehrk-NEW-gen]* to amuse

Vergrößerung, f. *[fehr-GRU(R)S-eh-rung]* enlargement

verhaften *[fehr-HAHF-ten]* to arrest

verheiratet *[fehr-HYE-raa-tet]* married

Verkauf, m. *[fehr-KOWF]* sale

verkaufen *[fehr-KOW-fen]* to sell

Verkäufer, m. *[fehr-KOY-fe(r)]* salesman

Verkäuferin, f. *[fehr-KOY-feh-rin]* saleswoman

Verkehr, m. *[fehr-KEHR]* traffic

verkehrt herum *[vehr-KEHRT hehr-ROOM]* upside down

verlangen *[fehr-LAHNG-en]* to demand; to require

verletzen *[fehr-LEHT-sen]* to injure

sich verletzen *[zikh fehr-LEHT-sen]* to hurt oneself

verlieren *[fehr-LEER-en]* to lose

verlobt *[fehr-LOHPT]* engaged (betrothed)

verloren *[fehr-LOR-en]* lost

Verlust, m. *[fehr-LOOST]* loss

vermeiden *[fehr-MYE-den]* to avoid

vermieten *[fehr-MEE-ten]* to rent

Vermittlung, f. *[fehr-MIT-lung]* operator (phone)

Vermögen, n. *[fehr-MU(R)-gen]* fortune

vernünftig *[fehr-NEWNF-tikh]* reasonable

verrückt *[fehr-REWKT]* crazy

Versammlung, f. *[fehr-ZAHM-lung]* meeting

versäumen *[fehr-ZOY-men]* to miss

verschieden *[fehr-SHEE-den]* different

verschiffen *[fehr-SHIF-fen]* to ship

Verschluss, m. *[fehr-SHLUS]* shutter (camera)

verschwunden *[fehr-SHVUN-den]* to be missing

Versicherung, f. *[fehr-ZIKH-eh-rung]* insurance

Verspätung, f. *[fehr-SHPAY-tung]* delay

versprechen *[fehr-SHPREH-khen]* to promise

verstauchen *[fehr-SHTOW-khen]* to sprain

verstehen *[fehr-SHTAY-en]* to understand

versuchen *[fehr-ZOO-khen]* to try

vertraut sein mit *[fehr-TROWT zine mit]* to be familiar with

vertreten *[fehr-TRAY-ten]* to represent

Verwandte, m., f. *[fehr-VAHN-teh]* relative

Verwendung, f. *[fehr-VEHN-dung]* use (purpose)

verwirrt *[fehr-VIRT]* confused

Verzeihung, f. *[fehr-TSYE-ung]* pardon

verzollen *[fehr-TSOL-len]* to declare (custom)

Vetter, m. *[FEHT-te(r)]* cousin

viel *[feel]* much

viele *[FEE-leh]* many

vielleicht *[fee-LYEKHT]* maybe; perhaps

vier *[feer]* four

vierte (-r, -s) *[FEER-teh {-te(r), -tehs}]* fourth

Viertel, n. *[FEER-tel]* quarter

vierzehn *[FEER-tsayn]* fourteen

vierzig *[FEER-tsikh]* forty

violett *[vee-oh-LEHT]* purple

Visum, n. *[VEE-zoom]* visa

Vogel, m. *[FOH-gel]* bird

Volksmusik, f. *[FOLKS-moo-zeek]* folk music

voll *[fol]* full

volltanken *[FOL-tahn-ken]* to fill up

von *[fon]* by; from; of

vor *[for]* ago; before

vorbereiten *[FOR-beh-rite-en]* to prepare

vorbestellt *[FOR-beh-shtehlt]* reserved

Vorfahrt gewähren *[FOR-faart geh-VAY-ren]* to yield (traffic)

vorgestern *[FOR-gehs-tern]* day before yesterday

Vorhang, m. *[FOR-hahng]* curtain

vormittags *[FOR-mit-tahks]* A.M.

vorne *[FOR-neh]* front

Vorort, m. *[FOR-ort]* suburb

Vorsicht, f. *[FOR-zikht]* caution

Vorsicht! *[FOR-zikht]* careful!

Vorspeise, f. *[FOR-shpye-zeh]* appetizer

vorstellen *[FOR-shtehl-len]* to introduce

Vorstellung, f. *[for-SHTEHL-lung]* performance

Vorwahlnummer, f. *[FOR-vaal-num-me(r)]* area code

vorwärts *[FOR-vehrts]* forward

vorziehen *[FOR-tsee-en]* to prefer

W

Wagen, m. *[VAA-gen]* car

Wagenheber, m. *[VAA-gen-hay-be(r)]* jack (car)

Wahl, f. *[vaal]* choice

wählen *[VAY-len]* to dial

wahr *[vaar]* true

während *[VAY-rehnt]* during

Währung, f. *[VAY-rung]* currency

Wald, m. *[vahlt]* forest

Wand, f. *[vahnt]* wall (interior)

Wanderung, f. *[VAHN-deh-rung]* hike

Wange, f. *[VAHN-geh]* cheek

wann *[vahn]* when

warm *[vahrm]* warm

warten *[VAAR-ten]* to wait

Wartesaal, m. *[VAAR-teh-zaal]* waiting room

warum *[vah-ROOM]* why

was *[vahs]* what

Waschbecken, n. *[VAHSH-beh-ken]* sink; washbasin

waschen *[VAHSH-en]* to wash

Wäscherei, f. *[veh-sheh-RYE]* laundry

Waschsalon, m. *[VAHSCH-zaa-long]* laundromat

Wasser, n. *[VAHS-se(r)]* water

fließendes Wasser, n. *[FLEES-en-dehs VAHS-se(r)]* running water

wasserdicht *[VAHS-se(r)-dikht]* waterproof

Wasserfall, m. *[VAHS-se(r)-fahl]* waterfall

Wasserhahn, m. *[VAHS-se(r)-haan]* faucet; tap

Watte, f. *[VAHT-teh]* cotton wool

Wechselkurs, m. *[VEHK-sel-koors]* exchange rate

wechseln *[VEHK-seln]* to change; to exchange

Wechselstube, f. *[VEHK-sehl-shtoo-beh]* currency exchange office

wecken *[VEHK-en]* to wake

Wecker, m. *[VEH-ke(r)]* alarm clock

Weg, m. *[vehk]* way

weg *[vehk]* away

weggehen *[VEHK-gay-en]* to go away

weh tun *[vay toon]* to hurt

weich *[vyekh]* soft

Weihnachten, pl. *[VYE-nahkh-ten]* Christmas

weil *[vile]* because

Wein, m. *[vine]* wine

Weinberg, m. *[VINE-behrk]* vineyard

weinen *[VINE-en]* to cry

Weinkarte, f. *[VINE-kahr-teh]* wine list

Weinladen, m. *[VINE-laa-den]* wine shop

Weintraube, f. *[VINE-trow-beh]* grape

weiß *[vice]* white

weit *[vite]* far; wide

welche (-r, -s) *[VEHL-kheh, (-khe(r), -khehs]* which

Welle, f. *[VEHL-leh]* wave

Welt, f. *[vehlt]* world

wenige *[VEH-ni-geh]* few

weniger *[VAY-neh-ge(r)]* less

wenigstens *[VAY-nikh-stens]* at least

wenn *[vehn]* if; when

wer *[vehr]* who

Werbung, f. *[VEHR-bung]* advertising

Werkzeug, n. *[VEHRK-tsoyk]* tool

Wert, m. *[vehrt]* value

wertlos *[VEHRT-lohs]* worthless

wertvoll *[VEHRT-fol]* valuable

West(en), m. *[VEHST (-en]]* west

Weste, f. *[VEHS-teh]* vest

wetten *[VEHT-ten]* to bet

Wetter, n. *[VEH-te(r)]* weather

Wetterbericht, m. *[VEHT-te(r)-beh-rikht]* weather forecast

wichtig *[VIKH-tikh]* important

wie *[vee]* as; how; like (as)

wieder *[VEE-de(r)]* again

wiederholen *[vee-de(r)-HOH-len]* to repeat

auf Wiedersehen *[owf VEE-de(r)-zay-en]* good-bye

wiegen *[VEE-gen]* to weigh

Wien, n. *[veen]* Vienna

wieviel *[VEE-feel]* how much

wild *[vilt]* wild

Wildleder, n. *[VILT-lay-de(r)]* suede

Wind, m. *[vint]* wind

Windel, f. *[VIN-del]* diaper

Windschutzscheibe, f. *[WINT-shuts-shye-beh]* windshield

Winter, m. *[VIN-te(r)]* winter

wir *[veer]* we

wirklich *[VIRK-likh]* really

wissen *[VIS-sen]* to know

Witwe, f. *[VIT-veh]*, **Witwer,** m. *[VIT-ve(r)]* widow, widower

Witz, m. *[vits]* joke

wo *[voh]* where

Woche, f. *[VOKH-eh]* week

Wochenende, n. *[VOKH-en-ehn-deh]* weekend

wohl *[vohl]* well

Wohnung, f. *[VOH-nung]* apartment

Wohnwagen, m. *[VOHN-vaa-gen]* trailer

Wohnzimmer, n. *[VOHN-tsim-me(r)]* living room

Wolke, f. *[VOL-keh]* cloud

Wolle, f. *[VOL-leh]* wool

wollen *[VOL-len]* to want

Wort, n. *[vort]* word

Wörterbuch, n. *[VU(R)-te(r)-bookh]* dictionary

Wunde, f. *[VUN-deh]* wound

wunderbar *[VUN-de(r)-baar]* wonderful

Wunsch, m. *[voonsh]* desire; wish

wünschen *[VEWN-shen]* to wish

würde *[VU(R)-deh]* would

Wurst, f. *[voorst]* sausage

Würze, pl. *[VEWR-tseh]* seasoning

Wurzel, f. *[VUR-tsel]* root

wütend *[VEW-tehnt]* angry

Z

zäh *[tsay]* tough

zählen *[TSAY-len]* to count

Zahn, m. *[tsaan]* tooth

Zahnarzt, m. *[TSAAN-ahrtst]* dentist

Zahnbürste, f. *[TSAAN-bewr-steh]* toothbrush

Zahnpasta, f. *[TSAAN-pahs-tah]* toothpaste

Zahnschmerzen, pl. *[TSAAN-shmehrt-sen]* toothache

Zange, f. *[TSAHNG-eh]* pliers

Zäpfchen, n. *[TSEHPF-khen]* suppository

zart *[tsahrt]* tender

Zebrastreifen, m. *[TSAY-brah-shtrife-en]* crosswalk

Zehe, f. *[TSEH-eh]* toe

zehn *[tsayn]* ten

zehnte *[TSAYN-teh]* tenth

Zeichenpapier, n. *[TSYE-khen-pah-peer]* drawing paper

zeigen *[TSYE-gen]* to show

Zeit, f. *[tsite]* time

Zeitschrift, f. *[TSITE-shrift]* magazine

Zeitung, f. *[TSYE-tung]* newspaper

Zeitungsstand, m. *[TSYE-tungs-shtahnt]* newsstand

Zeitverschwendung, f. *[TSITE-vehr-shvehn-dung]* waste of time

Zelle, f. *[TSEHL-leh]* cell

Zelt, n. *[tsehlt]* tent

zelten, *[TSEHL-ten]* to camp

Zentrum, n. *[TSEHN-trum]* center; downtown

zerbrechen *[tsehr-BREH-khen]* to break

Zeugnis, n. *[TSOYK-nis]* certificate

ziehen *[TSEE-en]* to pull

ziemlich *[TSEEM-likh]* quite; rather (quite)

Zigarette, f. *[tsi-gaa-REHT-teh]* cigarette

Zigarre, f. *[tsi-GAA-reh]* cigar

Zimmer, n. *[TSIM-me(r)]* room

Zimmerbedienung, f. *[TSIM-me(r)-beh-dee-nung]* room service

Zimmermädchen, n. *[TSIM-me(r)-mayt-khen]* maid

Zitrone, f. *[tsi-TROH-neh]* lemon

Zoll, m. *[tsol]* customs; duty (customs)

zollfrei *[TSOL-frye]* duty-free

Zoo, m. *[tsoh]* zoo

zu *[tsoo]* to

Zucker, m. *[TSUK-e(r)]* sugar

Zuckerkrankheit, f. *[TSUK-e(r)-krahnk-hite]* diabetes

Zug, m. *[tsook]* train

zuhören *[TSOO-hur-en]* to listen

Zukunft, f. *[TSOO-kunft]* future

Zündkerze, f. *[TSEWNT-kehr-tseh]* spark plug

Zündung, f. *[TSEWN-dung]* ignition

zunehmen *[TSOO-nay-men]* to gain weight

Zunge, f. *[TSUN-geh]* tongue

zurück *[tsoo-REWK]* back (direction)

zurück sein *[tsoo-REWK zine]* to be back; to get back

zurückgeben *[tsoo-REWK-gay-ben]* to return (something)

zurückkommen *[tsoo-REWK-kom-men]* to return (come back)

zusammen *[tsoo-ZAHM-men]* together

zusätzlich *[TSOO-zehts-likh]* extra

Zutritt, m. *[TSOO-trit]* admission

zwanzig *[TSVAHN-tsikh]* twenty

zwei *[tsvye]* two

zweimal *[TSVYE-maal]* twice

zweite *[TSVYE-teh]* second

Zwiebel, f. *[TSVEE-bel]* onion

zwischen *[TSVISH-en]* among; between

zwölf *[tsvu(r)lf]* twelve